# Wi-Fi Toys
# 15 Cool Wireless Projects for Home, Office, and Entertainment

**Mike Outmesguine**

WILEY

Wiley Publishing, Inc.

**Wi-Fi Toys: 15 Cool Wireless Projects for Home, Office, and Entertainment**

Published by
**Wiley Publishing, Inc.**
10475 Crosspoint Boulevard
Indianapolis, IN 46256
www.wiley.com

ISBN: 0-7645-5894-3

Manufactured in the United States of America

10 9 8 7 6 5 4

For general information on our other products and services or to obtain technical support, please contact our Customer Care Department within the United States at (800) 762-2974, outside the United States at (317) 572-3993, or fax (317) 572-4002.

Wiley also publishes its books in a variety of electronic formats. Some content that appears in print may not be available in electronic books.

**Library of Congress Cataloging-in-Publication Data is available**

# Credits

**Senior Acquisitions Editor**
Sharon Cox

**Executive Editor**
Chris Webb

**Development Editors**
Scott Amerman
Brian MacDonald

**Production Editor**
Gabrielle Nabi

**Copy Editor**
TechBooks

**Editorial Manager**
Kathryn A. Malm

**Vice President and Executive Group Publisher**
Richard Swadley

**Vice President and Executive Publisher**
Bob Ipsen

**Vice President and Publisher**
Joseph B. Wikert

**Executive Editorial Director**
Mary Bednarek

**Project Coordinator**
Erin Smith

**Proofreading and Indexing**
TechBooks Production Services

# Acknowledgments

First and foremost, I wish to thank my wife for her endless patience while writing this book and for her ceaseless trust in me as a husband and provider. Without her encouragement and devotion, I would be lucky to have a job sitting in a cube farm complaining about printer errors like "PC Load Letter." I'd like to thank my offspring, Michael, who was the perfect kid during Daddy's long days and nights away writing. And thank you to our newest bundle, Julia, for being a peaceful baby whose only gripe was "feed me!" And thanks to my family, Nana and Papa, Aunties Lori, Alysia, Diana and Jennifer, Granddude, and the Grandmas Great and Small for letting us stop by unexpectedly. And thanks to our friends from the Lang Ranch Mom's Club for being there for my family when we needed you.

I'd also like to thank my cousin Creighton and pals Brett, Sam, and Sean for helping get me out of a tight spot here and there.

The contributors of this book get special appreciation for helping to put out a great product in a timely manner. They individually pushed the envelope on the projects outlined here and their efforts made this book into more than the sum of its parts.

I'm very grateful for the help and encouragement from my editors: Scott Amerman, who kept me on my toes, Chris Webb, who believed in the book in the first place, Brian MacDonald, who helped make the book a delight to read, and everyone else at Wiley Publishing who helped make this book a reality. Thanks, everybody. I hope we can still be friends!

Special thanks to the members of the user group community in Southern California: SOCALWUG, OCCALWUG, SBWUG, and SDWUG; and the communities of BAWUG, Netstumbler.com, Nocat, NZWireless, Seattle Wireless, and SoCalFreeNet. These loose-knit groups of like-minded individuals are shaping the future world of wireless. Their feedback, suggestions, and onsite help made many of the projects in this book possible.

And thanks to you, dear reader. By picking up this book, you have delved into that interesting world of wireless and Wi-Fi Toys!

# About the Author

**Mike Outmesguine** is president and founder of TransStellar, Inc., a successful technology services company with an emphasis on wireless mobility and energy information systems. As president, Mike has directed TransStellar, online at www.transstellar.com, through his vision of "wireless anywhere" to become a leader in the emerging wireless mobility market while adopting many of these techniques for the energy information market.

Mike is the co-founder of the Southern California Wireless Users Group (SOCALWUG), a nonprofit user community with a focus on introducing wireless technology to the end-user and business community. The SOCALWUG has been holding monthly meetings for over two years and archives all of the past meetings online in streaming media format. Thousands of wireless enthusiasts from around the world look forward to the monthly meetings and videos hosted on the Web at www.socalwug.org.

Mike served in the U.S. Air Force as an electronic countermeasures specialist on B-52 aircraft and in the California Air National Guard in support of C-130 aircraft. Mike served for over 10 years and is a veteran of the Gulf War.

Additionally, Mike has been featured in several speaking engagements, newspaper, and online resources commenting on wireless technology, wireless security, and the impact on businesses and government using these technologies. Mike is FCC-licensed under the call sign KG6NHH.

His passion for technology goes back as far as he can remember. His first personal computer was a Sinclair ZX-81. (As a video-game addict, he couldn't afford the coveted Apple ][e that had just been released!) Since those early years, Mike has spent countless hours immersed in the technology fields of computers, electronics, networking, the Internet, and most recently, mobile and wireless.

Mike enjoys long wardrives on the beach.

Mike Outmesguine can be reached at:

TransStellar, Inc.
P.O. Box 1111
Agoura Hills, CA 91301
USA
Tel: 818-889-9445
Fax: 818-337-7420
E-mail: mo@transstellar.com

# Contributors

**James Burgess**—James is a student at the University of Southern California who has been conducting research in wireless communications since the late 90s. He is the co-founder of Flexilis, a disruptive technologies research and development firm, where he is currently exploring new wireless implementations and protocols. He takes particular interest in open source wireless developments, contributing much of his findings to the community. In his free time he writes for DailyWireless.com, a wireless industry news site. He resides in Los Angeles, California.

**John Chirillo**—John is a Senior Internetworking Engineer for a technology management company specializing in security. He holds an impressive number of professional certifications, including Cisco certifications and the CISSP. John has authored several books. His latest include *Storage Security* and *Implementing Biometric Security*.

**John Hering**—After only three years of study at the University of Southern California in Los Angeles, California, John Hering has already made his mark in the ever-advancing field of wireless technologies. Using past experience in entrepreneurial business, advertising, and technology, John co-founded Flexilis (www.flexilis.com), a wireless technologies research and development firm, which has been responsible for the creation of DailyWireless (www.DailyWireless.com), the Internet's premier Wireless news portal. John has played a critical role in the advancement of emerging disruptive technologies, such as wireless networking and security, while constantly exploring the use of *open source*-based solutions, and will continue to help make way for the future of wireless technologies.

**Michael Hurwicz**—Michael Hurwicz is a freelance writer, developer, designer, animator, and musician living in Eastsound, WA. He is the Flash and 3-D Guy at Late Night Design. He has been writing about technical topics for the computer trade press since 1985. Michael is the president of Irthlingz, a nonprofit organization dedicated to environmental education and entertainment. You can e-mail Michael at michael@hurwicz.com, as well as visit his Web sites at www.latenightdesign.com, www.hurwicz.com, www.flashoop.com, and www.irthlingz.org.

**David Karlins**—David Karlins (www.davidkarlins.com) writes and lectures on technology and graphic and Web design. His books include *Build Your Own Web Site*.

**Frank Keeney**—Frank is a computer security and network consultant. He works for Pasadena Networks, LLC, www.pasadena.net, on wireless projects for retail, educational, financial, and other industries. He got his start in wireless when it became clear that security was a need in wireless networks. He is the co-founder of the Southern California Wireless User Group, www.socalwug.org.

**Trevor Marshall**—Trevor is an engineering management consultant, with interests ranging from RF and hardware design to Linux internals, Internet infrastructure, Digital Video, and Biomedicine. He can be contacted at www.trevormarshall.com

**Michael Mee**—Michael started building his own computers after discovering the TRS-80 at Radio Shack years ago. He went on to work for a software startup, before dot-coms made it fashionable. Then he had several great years at Microsoft, back when "the evil empire" meant

IBM. There he worked on database products like Access and Foxpro for Windows. Returning to his hacking roots, he's now helping build high-speed community wireless for dial-up users everywhere, especially through `SoCalFreeNet.org`.

**Brett Schumacher**—After working as Systems Administrator for a Prime Missile Systems Group, Mr. Schumacher went on to lead the technology group for a private utility based in Woodland Hills, CA. While in this position, he was responsible for evaluating and deploying "Best of Breed" energy systems, hybrid systems that comprise multiple technologies, including solar, micro turbines, and internal combustion engines. Stretching from California to New York, these technologies are completely managed and controlled from Mr. Schumacher's Woodland Hills Control Center. Each of these sites is installed and acting as the primary power system for their host facility.

Each site is seamlessly integrated and has become the most unique centrally managed portfolio of assets of its kind. Each will serve as the model for others that follow. Mr. Schumacher was awarded a U.S. patent for this network design.

Mr. Schumacher is also currently working with a consortium of experts to bring communication standardization to this new and very exciting industry.

**Jack Unger**—Jack is an "old timer" in the wireless ISP industry. He's been in it and helping create it since 1993. He built one of the first-ever public WISPs and put it on the air in 1995. Jack created the first wireless ISP deployment training workshop in the world and has been presenting this workshop around the country since 2001. He wrote the first wireless ISP deployment handbook (*Deploying License-Free Wireless WANs*). This vendor-neutral book is published by Cisco Press. Jack enjoys traveling around the U.S. doing WISP training, site surveys, network designs, network troubleshooting, and WISP consulting.

**Barry Shilmover** also contributed to *Wi-Fi Toys*.

# Contents at a Glance

# Contents

## Part II: War Driving—Wireless Network Discovery and Visualization    101

# Preface

**W**ireless networking is permeating every facet of our modern society. Kids are using wireless cell phones and text messaging to keep in touch in ways never imagined a few years ago. Adults are using wireless networking to work from home, or away on vacation. Wireless Web and data works from the very depths of a Disneyland ride to cruise ship excursions and cross-country airline flights. Enthusiasts like yourself are breaking beyond packaged products to enter new realms of connectivity and mobility.

This book is a testament to the hobbyists, hackers, tweakers, and rule-benders who are constantly pushing the envelope of accepted use of technology. Wireless is especially ripe for experimentation by you rule-benders.

New social and personal dynamics are being created every day because of wireless. This book attempts to examine the practical exploitation of wireless networking. The projects here will help you get an understanding of the driving force behind the revolution. With the background and step-by-step nature of project creation, you will be able to move beyond the scope of this book and develop your own creations, to your own ends.

*Wi-Fi Toys* is an introduction to breaking down the boundaries set by manufacturers and product vendors. Seize your moment and create something astounding.

# Introduction

Internet without wires. Think about that for a minute. All of the entertainment, utility, and performance of the Internet yours, without being tied to a desk. Without even being tied to the home or office. Internet without wires...anywhere! Wireless is a growing revolution changing the way people communicate and share ideas. From cell phones to PDAs to mobile computers, wireless access puts you instantly in touch with millions of other people around the planet. Wi-Fi, in particular, is changing how people access the Internet from laptops and PDAs. It's emerging as an alternative for cellular service, and it may even replace regular telephone lines as voice conversations begin to be re-routed over Wi-Fi networks in larger numbers.

Wi-Fi is that subset of wireless communications designed for high-speed Internet access. Sometimes simply referred to as "wireless," or known by its many-lettered specification IEEE 802.11b, a, g, and so on, Wi-Fi allows compatible devices to connect without cables or physical connections.

With speeds far in excess of most cable modem, DSL, and even T1 service, Wi-Fi is rapidly becoming the standard for Internet access. The store shelves are flooded with Wi-Fi access points, clients, music players, network hubs, and printers, and myriad other consumer devices sport Wi-Fi access. Take the Xbox, Playstation 2, and TiVo—these all have Wi-Fi ability now.

Remember when people were saying how everything in the house will eventually be wired? How anything from a toaster or refrigerator to a stereo system or television would have Internet access? Well, it's been some time coming, but with wireless in the home, these are now possibilities. Refrigerators are being sold with Wi-Fi connections, and several products will now connect your digital media from your computer to your television over Wi-Fi. I wonder when my toaster will send me a wireless e-mail when the toast pops?

Wireless is awesome, but it is also somewhat limited. The hardware you can buy in the store is mass-marketed and mass-produced. So it doesn't have that extra edge that power users are looking for. Extra edges like longer range, sharing with friends, saying no to power lines, and finding every access point on your street can be yours with the projects in this book.

Wi-Fi Toys was written to help you take wireless to the next level. Go beyond the user manual and build your own projects using this book as your guide.

Few things are more liberating than a Wi-Fi connection.

## Who This Book Is For

This book is for you if you are interested in spending a little extra time with your Wi-Fi access points and computer. The primary focus is the technical enthusiasts with a few extra hours on the weekend. A small degree of technical know-how is helpful in understanding the concepts and putting together some of the more involved projects. The hardest physical skill you will encounter is drilling and soldering.

Many of the projects in this book can be accomplished with an assembly of off-the-shelf, easily purchased products, so hobbyists of all skill levels will find something in this book.

As this book is broken down into four main parts, you may wish to jump straight to the section that interests you. For example, in Part II, Chapter 5 introduces you to the art of war driving to find wireless networks in your neighborhood. In Part I, Chapter 4 shows you how to add an antenna to a wireless access point to increase usable range. And in Part IV, you can learn what it takes to get your TiVo onto your Wi-Fi network at home.

The book tries to introduce new concepts early in the book and build on them later as the book progresses. If you jump around and miss something, just go back and read the concept.

# What This Book Covers

The projects in this book are based on the Wi-Fi, IEEE 802.11b standard. This standard is commonly understood to support a theoretical transfer rate of 11 megabits per second (Mbps). In practice it can be as "low" as 3 Mbps. But that's still way faster than most Internet connections.

Wi-Fi 802.11b was chosen because of the extremely widespread adoption of the technology. It is the de facto standard throughout the world. Almost every product that supports another wireless standard also supports 802.11b. For example, wireless cards can come in tri-mode flavors which support 802.11b/a/g on the same card. Also, 802.11b is the cheapest of the three popular standards. If it's good enough for 20,000 public hotspots, it's good enough for us!

Several new and promising wireless technologies are being developed and tested all the time. These emerging wireless technologies may vary greatly in cost, speed, and function. The projects in this book are meant to be adopted to new technologies as they become popular in the marketplace.

# How This Book Is Structured

This book was designed for the novice wireless user. We expect you to know what a wireless access point is and how to plug it into your network at home. Where wireless gets really interesting is when you start to go beyond the plug-and-play nature of Wi-Fi-enabled devices.

This book is divided into four parts. Each part separates a general concept and builds upon that concept. You can jump around to the different projects in each part. But it should be noted that earlier parts introduce earlier concepts.

## Part I: Building Antennas

This section of the book introduces you to the concept of an antenna as a transmission line. All wireless signals travel into and out of a network through the antenna. By understanding what the antenna does, you can take a wireless radio signal and cow it to your will by choosing the right antenna. You will be shown how to make and find cables, build antennas, and finally add one to your wireless access point.

## Part II: War Driving—Wireless Network Discovery and Visualization

Some of you will jump straight to this section and that's fine. War driving is one of the coolest things about Wi-Fi. In fact, it's one of the reasons I co-founded SOCALWUG. It can be argued that war driving has increased the popularity of wireless. It certainly got Wi-Fi its day in the news more than once. Hardly a week goes by without some newspaper somewhere mentioning war driving. This section shows you how to war drive and how to use the most popular program, NetStumbler. It also introduces many techniques for mapping your results.

## Part III: Playing with Access Points

This section can be very interesting. Wireless access points are the gateway between the wired and unwired world. By exploiting this ability to create connections between the physical and ethereal world of wireless, access points become a tool for your Wi-Fi endeavors. In this section, you will see how to build a weatherproof access point and create a free hotspot to share your wired connection with neighbors. Also, you will build a solar-powered repeater, connecting users to the Internet with no wires at all! And finally, we coined the term "AP games" to help describe the growing trend of using wireless access points for sport.

## Part IV: Just for Fun

Well, perhaps not all fun and games, this section presents some very cool projects as well as one or two that you may not be able to live without. Learn how to add Wi-Fi to your TiVo and create a wireless digital picture frame. Add Wi-Fi to a roadtrip and perform car-to-car video-conferencing. And ultimately, bring a computer more than 20 miles away onto your local wireless network by creating a long-distance Wi-Fi link.

# What You Need to Use This Book

Some of the projects in this book can be performed using stand-alone wireless networks, especially if you are experimenting or just "playing around." At a minimum, you should have a computer with wireless capability. Ideally, this computer is a laptop. Laptops with 300 MHz processors can now be found used for just a few hundred dollars on eBay.

If you will be sharing Internet access or setting up an in-home network, a high-speed connection is practically a must. On the other hand, if you just want to build an in-home network, all you need is two computers.

About the only strong requirement for this book is the desire to obtain wireless equipment. Each chapter will describe which components you will be working with.

You will also need tools. Tools are mentioned at the beginning of each chapter. You can expect to use common tools such as screwdrivers, wire cutters and strippers, crimping tools, and soldering irons.

Wi-Fi security is an ever-present concern. As you will see in Chapter 5, "Gearing Up for War Driving," finding a wireless network is not difficult. If you do not secure your network, anyone within range can eavesdrop on your network and possibly gain access to your files. It's like letting them in the front door. Basic steps to secure your network are to enable the built-in encryption capabilities of your wireless devices, using WEP. If you plan to share your connection with others, make sure you install a personal firewall on your computer.

# Building Antennas

part

I

# Building Your Own Wi-Fi Antenna Cable

Think back to the olden days, say three or four years ago, when computers were tied to the desk with a phone line or network cord. Surfing the Web, reading e-mail, or checking your *PetCam* meant plugging in, jacking in, or getting wired. Now just about any device can be "unwired" to use a wireless network. You still need electricity though, so batteries or power cords are still in the picture. At least for a little while.

Ironically, wireless seems to use twice as many cables as wired connections. This wireless paradox arrives in the form of extra power cords, antenna cables, pigtail jumper cables, and Ethernet patch cables.

One critical component to a successful wireless project is the antenna cable, used to extend the reach of the radio to the antenna. This chapter will show how to build an antenna cable for use with many of the projects in this book. You can purchase this type of cable in pre-defined lengths from online sources. However, building your own antenna cable is easy and can take less than 5 minutes.

**Note** The instructions in this chapter apply to a Wi-Fi coaxial antenna cable (also called *coax*). The steps in this chapter can be adjusted to apply to any type of coaxial cable, like that used in cable televisions.

You will need the following items:

➤ Wi-Fi network device with an external connector (client adapter or access point)

➤ Wi-Fi pigtail cable, if using a wireless client adapter

➤ Coaxial cable, preferably Times Microwave LMR-400

➤ Coaxial cable cutters

➤ Crimp tool, ratcheting style

➤ Crimp tool "die" with hex sizes .429, .128, and .100

➤ Long-nosed pliers

➤ Small wire cutters

➤ Single-sided razor blade

➤ Scissors

➤ Type-N connectors, reverse-polarity male

➤ Digital multimeter or electrical continuity tester

➤ Known-good coax cable for comparison testing

Some of these items are specific to building an antenna cable (crimp tools, connectors, and so on). Don't worry if they are unfamiliar to you. All will become clear as the chapter progresses.

# About Wi-Fi

If you want to understand what is going on with a wireless network, you first need to know some of the basics of wireless communication and radio transmission.

Wireless networking is accomplished by sending a signal from one computer to another over radio waves. The most common form of wireless computing today uses the IEEE 802.11b standard. This popular standard, also called *Wi-Fi* or *Wireless Fidelity*, is now supported directly by newer laptops and PDAs, and most computer accessory manufacturers. It's so popular that "big box" electronics chain stores carry widely used wireless hardware and networking products.

**Note** Wi-Fi is the root of a logo and branding program created by the Wi-Fi Alliance. A product that uses the Wi-Fi logo has been certified by the Wi-Fi Alliance to fulfill certain guidelines for inter-operability. Logo certification programs like this one are created and promoted to assure users that products will work together in the marketplace. So, if you buy a Proxim wireless client adapter with the Wi-Fi logo branding, and a Linksys access point with the same logo on the product, they should work together.

The IEEE 802.11b Wi-Fi standard supports a maximum speed of 11 megabits per second (Mbps). The true throughput is actually something more like 6 Mbps, and can drop to less than 3 Mbps with encryption enabled. Newer standards like 802.11a and the increasingly popular 802.11g support higher speeds up to 54 Mbps. So why is 802.11b so popular? Because it was first and it was cheap. Even 3 Mbps is still much faster than you normally need to use the Internet.

**Note** A *megabit* is one million binary digits (*bits*) of data. Network speed is almost always measured in bits per second (bps). It takes 8 bits to make a *byte*. Bytes are used mostly to measure file size (as in files on a hard disk). A *megabyte* is about 8 million bits of data. Don't confuse the term *megabyte* for *megabit* or you will come out 8 million bits ahead.

The 802.11a standard, which operates in the 5 GHz frequency band, is much faster than 802.11b, but never caught on, partly because of the high cost initially and partly because of the actual throughput in the real-world conditions of a deployed wireless network.

The fast and inexpensive 802.11g standard (which uses the same 2.4 GHz band as 802.11b) is rapidly moving to unseat 802.11b from the top of the heap. The very cool thing about "g" is the built-in backwards compatibility with 802.11b. That means any "b" product can connect to a "g" access point. This compatibility makes 802.11g an easy upgrade without tossing out your old client hardware.

Because of the compatibility with 802.11b and 802.11g, there is no great hurry to push the myriad of funky wireless products to the new "g" standard. Most manufacturers have support for basic wireless infrastructure using 802.11b and 802.11g with access points and client adapter.

Wi-Fi 802.11b really shines when you look at the host of wireless products available. Not only are there the basic wireless networking devices, like adapters, base stations, and bridges, there are also new products that were unthinkable a few years ago. Wireless disk drive arrays, presentation gateways, audiovisual media adapters, printer adapters, Wi-Fi cameras, hotspot controllers, and wireless broadband and video phones dominate the consumer arena. And the enterprise market is not far behind.

We've been tossing out the terms *wireless*, *gigahertz* (GHz), and *frequency*. Next, we'll discuss how Wi-Fi uses wireless radio waves, also called RF, to communicate amongst the devices in a wireless network.

## About RF

Entire books, libraries, and people's careers are devoted to understanding more about radio frequencies (RF) and electromagnetism. The basics are covered here to help make your projects a success.

Wi-Fi wireless products use microwave radio frequencies for over-the-air transmissions. Microwave RF is very similar to the radio used in your car, only at much higher frequencies.

**Tip**     For a downloadable PDF of the spectrum assignments in the United States, visit www.ntia.doc.gov and look under "Publications" for the "Spectrum Wall Chart." The chart is a few years old, but most of the information is accurate. And it's suitable for framing.

For frequency spectrum assignments covering most of Europe, check out the European Radiocommunications Office at www.ero.dk and look under the CEPT National Frequency Tables. The ERO "Report 25" document also covers much of this information in a single report file. To find this deeply buried document, search the Web for *ERO Report 25*.

Visualizing the radio frequency signals helps to understand the behavior of the electromagnetic (EM) spectrum. Imagine dropping a rock in a pond. Waves are created in concentric circles coming from the point where the rock was dropped. These waves are just like radio waves, except at a very low frequency of perhaps 10 waves per second, which are called *cycles per second* or *hertz*.

Now imagine a cross-section of those waves. Perhaps the rock was dropped in a fish tank and the waves are visible from the side. The wave would look similar to that shown in Figure 1-1.

The electromagnetic spectrum spans frequencies from subaudible sound of 1 hertz all the way through radio and visible light to beyond X-rays and cosmic rays at a frequency of 10 followed by

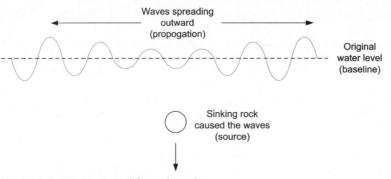

FIGURE 1-1: Waves viewed from the side.

24 zeros. The frequency of an FM car radio operates at about 100 million hertz, or 1 megahertz (MHz). For example, 103.1 MHz FM is a radio station in Los Angeles. Wi-Fi operates at about 2,400 MHz or 2.4 GHz. Table 1-1 shows a frequency chart to help you understand the scale.

Microwave ovens also operate at 2.4 GHz, but at *much* higher power than Wi-Fi gear. One-tenth of a watt (0.1 W) is typical for a Wi-Fi device, versus 1,000 watt for a microwave oven. That's a difference of over 10,000 times the power! Still, to be safe, always observe caution and minimize unnecessary exposure when working with RF.

## Frequency versus Wavelength

Frequency and wavelength are inseparably related to each other. As frequency increases, wavelength decreases and vice versa.

- *Frequency*: The rate at which a radio signal oscillates from positive to negative.
- *Wavelength*: The length of a complete cycle of the radio signal oscillation.

### Table 1-1    Frequency Ranges

| Range | Abbreviation | Cycles Per Second | Application |
|-------|--------------|-------------------|-------------|
| Hertz | Hz | 1 | Ripples in a pond, ocean waves |
| Kilohertz | kHz | 1,000 | AM radio, CB radio |
| Megahertz | MHz | 1,000,000 | FM radio, television, cordless phones, 2-way radios, older cell phones |
| Gigahertz | GHz | 1,000,000,000 | Wi-Fi, satellite, microwave ovens, cordless phones, newer cell phones, GPS |

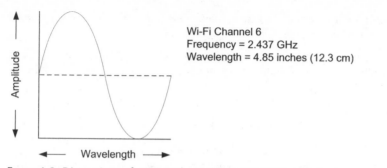

Wi-Fi Channel 6
Frequency = 2.437 GHz
Wavelength = 4.85 inches (12.3 cm)

FIGURE 1-2: Dimensions of a Wi-Fi channel 6 (2.437 GHz) radio wave.

Wavelength is, of course, a length measurement, usually represented in metric (meters, centimeters, and so on). And frequency is a count of the number of waves occurring during a set time, usually per second. Cycles per second is represented as *Hertz* (Hz).

Figure 1-2 shows a Wi-Fi radio wave for channel 6 (2.437 GHz). The dimensions are important to note, because the physical properties of the wave define antenna, cable, and power requirements. Wavelength is critical for antenna design and selection as we will cover in the next chapter.

Wi-Fi signals operating at a frequency of 2.4 GHz have an average wavelength of about 12 cm. Since the wavelength is so short, antennas can be physically very small. A common design for antennas is to make them 1/4 of a wavelength or less in length, which is barely more than an inch long. That's why Wi-Fi antennas can perform so well even though they are physically very small. As a comparison, a car radio antenna is much longer to get a decent signal because FM radio signals are an average of 10 feet long.

Wavelength and antenna length go together. To oversimplify, the longer the antenna, the more of the signal it can grab out of the air. Also, antenna length should be in whole, halves, quarters, eighths, and so on of the intended wavelength for best signal reception. The highest reception qualities come from a full wavelength antenna.

**Tip**  Perform this simple math formula to find wavelength: 300 / frequency in megahertz. The answer will be the wavelength in meters. So, 300 / 2437 = 0.12 meters or 12 cm.

## Unlicensed 2.4 GHz Wi-Fi

Wi-Fi makes use of the internationally recognized unlicensed frequency band at about 2.4 GHz. The IEEE standards body created 802.11b and defined the "channels" and frequencies for use by manufacturers worldwide. Different countries accepted the standard and allowed the use of devices in this frequency range with few restrictions. The word *unlicensed* as it applies to Wi-Fi specifically means that products can be installed and used without prior approval from the local governing body. That's the Federal Communications Commission (FCC) for users in the United States. Radio systems that operate in "licensed" bands require an application and permission procedure before turning on or using a radio system. For example, FM radio stations require permission from the FCC before broadcasting.

Certain other unlicensed products have been in use for some time: CB radios, walkie-talkies or consumer two-way radios, cordless phones, and many other radio products operate in unlicensed bands.

Unlicensed is not equivalent to unregulated, though. There are still rules that need to be followed to stay legal, especially regarding power output. This is covered in Chapter 2.

**Note** In the United States, 802.11b usage is regulated by the FCC. The FCC laws define maximum power output, among other more specific regulations. In addition, the FCC approves products for use in the U.S. market. Manufacturers must submit their product for testing and authorization. The FCC then grants an "FCC ID" for the product. Anyone can look up an FCC ID from the Web site at www.fcc.gov (look under Search, for "FCC ID Number" searches). This can help you track down the true manufacturer of a Wi-Fi radio product, despite the label or brand.

## Wi-Fi Channels

As defined in 802.11b, Wi-Fi consists of 14 channels worldwide. Only channels 1 to 11 are available in North America. Channels in other countries vary. Table 1-2 shows each channel and frequency, and the countries with approval to use that channel. (The lucky ones in Japan can use all 14!)

What is not easily shown in Table 1-2 is *channel separation*. To make the channel numbering scheme work with different radio technologies, the IEEE community defined these 802.11b channels with significant overlap. For example, channel 6 is centered on 2.437 GHz, but it extends in both directions by 11 MHz (0.011 GHz). That means channel 6 uses 2.426 GHz

**Table 1-2   802.11b Specified Channels**

| Channel | Center Frequency (GHz) | Countries |
|---------|------------------------|-----------|
| 1 | 2.412 | USA, Europe, Japan |
| 2 | 2.417 | USA, Europe, Japan |
| 3 | 2.422 | USA, Europe, Japan |
| 4 | 2.427 | USA, Europe, Japan |
| 5 | 2.432 | USA, Europe, Japan |
| 6 | 2.437 | USA, Europe, Japan |
| 7 | 2.442 | USA, Europe, Japan |
| 8 | 2.447 | USA, Europe, Japan |
| 9 | 2.452 | USA, Europe, Japan |

| Channel | Center Frequency (GHz) | Countries |
|---------|------------------------|-----------|
| 10 | 2.457 | USA, Europe, Japan, France, Spain |
| 11 | 2.462 | USA, Europe, Japan, France, Spain |
| 12 | 2.467 | Europe, Japan, France |
| 13 | 2.472 | Europe, Japan, France |
| 14 | 2.484 | Japan |

to 2.448 GHz, which, as shown in Table 1-2, means it uses frequencies already assigned to channels 4, 5, 6, 7, and 8. Clearly, Wi-Fi devices using channels 6 and 7 would not operate together in harmony because of the interference.

To ensure trouble-free operation, with little interference from any other Wi-Fi devices, the channels need to be separated.

In the United States, channels 1, 6, and 11 are the sweet-spots for maximum usage with the least interference. In Europe, the recommended channels are 1, 7, and 13, and in Japan, the channels are 1, 7, and 14. For this very reason, most products come with one of these channels as the default setting, and most Wi-Fi hotspots are set to one of these three channels.

**Note**  Recently, users have been squeezing these nonoverlapping channels down to minimal-overlapping channels 1, 4, 8, and 11. This opens up significantly more options for Wi-Fi device and access point placement. There are possible downsides due to the increased interference, but it's worth testing if your setup needs a lot of devices in a small space.

Now you would have a basic understanding of how Wi-Fi works in a physical and logical sense. There's lots more to Wi-Fi technology and specifications, but that's all you need to know about the theory for now. Next, we'll get down to the specifics about building your own Wi-Fi projects.

# Parts of a Wi-Fi Project

Every Wi-Fi project contains specific primary components to make the system work properly. These are broken down into five simple components:

- Data signal (Ethernet, computer interface, USB, and so on)
- Data to RF converter
- Radio transceiver
- Transmission line
- Antenna system

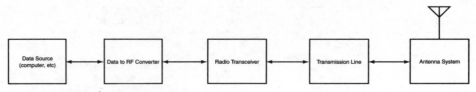

FIGURE 1-3: Parts of a Wi-Fi project.

Figure 1-3 shows the breakdown. The data to RF converter and radio transceiver are nearly always in the same appliance, and even on the same circuit board as on a PC card.

## Data Signaling

The data signal is the digital signal with which every Wi-Fi access point or client project will interface. In some cases, the data will come from a computer via PC card slot or USB cable. In others it may be an Ethernet camera or the network itself.

The data signal is usually based on the Internet protocol, TCP/IP. TCP/IP is a protocol used to transmit data between computers on normal, wired networks. Wi-Fi is meant to convert TCP/IP traffic into radio waves and back.

## Wi-Fi Devices

The category of Wi-Fi devices consists of the digital data to RF converter and the radio transceiver. Most often, these two items are in the same product. In this book, projects will not break down these two components; we're describing them separately here for clarity. For example, cable and antenna modifications to a wireless access point are covered in several chapters throughout the book. Wi-Fi devices have two jobs: convert the data from the computer into a radio signal, and transmit and receive radio signals to and from the data converter. They come in several forms that can be broken down into the following four major groups:

- *Wireless Access Point*: Attached to an Ethernet network, an access point provides a wired network gateway to wireless clients. An access point is the essential component for setting up a typical wireless network.

- *Wireless Client Adapter*: Connected or installed in a computer, a client adapter provides wireless connectivity to a wireless access point and then to a wired network. This can be inserted into a desktop computer, a laptop, a USB adapter, or any other computer interface.

- *Wireless-to-Ethernet Bridge*: Provides a direct connection between a wireless and wired (Ethernet) network without the need of a computer interface. It usually acts as a client connecting to an access point.

- *Specialized Components*: These include dedicated wireless networking devices, audiovisual devices, music streaming devices, digital picture frames, wireless scanners, wireless printers, and many more to come.

**Note** A radio transceiver is merely a transmitter and receiver in one unit. Your car radio is a receiver. An AM or FM radio station uses a transmitter. A CB radio is a transceiver. Wi-Fi devices are transceivers constantly sending and receiving radio signals when in use.

## Transmission Lines

When you work with Wi-Fi products, you will find that the transmission line is nearly always a *coaxial cable*. Internal transmission lines may be of very small diameter, high loss cable. But usually the cable run is less than a few inches, so line loss is not much of a factor. See Figure 1-4 for an internal view of a transmission line for the Linksys WAP11, a popular 802.11b wireless access point.

An RF transmission line transfers RF energy from the transmitter to the antenna while both losing and radiating as little as possible. Radiation should be left to the antenna system. It also transfers RF energy from the antenna to the receiver in the same fashion.

## Antenna System

The antenna system is where the rubber hits the road, so to speak. The antenna emits the electromagnetic radio frequency signal out of the Wi-Fi device. Antenna systems will be covered in Chapter 2 while building a simple antenna for a laptop PC card.

FIGURE 1-4: Internal RF transmission line on a Linksys WAP11.

At this point, what you need to know is that the antenna is where you want to send as much signal as possible. The transmission line should be designed to be as short as possible with the least line loss to pass power to the antenna.

Once the RF signal leaves the antenna, it immediately begins to lose power. (Really, as soon as it leaves the transceiver it begins to lose power.) The design of the antenna can redirect the amount of power available to shape the beam pattern as needed, much like a flashlight reflecting a tiny light bulb into a bright light.

Now that you know more about Wi-Fi projects in general, we can start to focus on the project for this chapter: building an antenna cable. Before you pick up your tools, though, you need to understand how coaxial cable works, which is the subject of the next section.

# Understanding Coaxial Cables

Coaxial cables (commonly called *coax*) are used as the transmission line in a Wi-Fi system. There are probably instances of Wi-Fi systems using a different transmission line, but the most common is coax.

A coax cable is built in layers of the following materials (see Figure 1-5):

- *Core*: A center of electrically conducting material like copper (solid or stranded)
- *Dielectric*: A nonconducting material surrounding the core
- *Shield*: An outer layer of conducting material like steel (solid and/or stranded)
- *Jacket*: A nonconducting protective surface like rubber or plastic

The RF signal is created or received and then placed (or *injected*) onto the core of the cable. In theory, the signal is meant to travel along the core of the cable, while the shield prevents the signal from emanating outside the cable. In reality, some signal is radiated outside the cable, while electrical resistance in the cable reduces the signal within the cable.

Coax cables come in two flavors when used with Wi-Fi:

- Coax jumper
- Coax pigtail

A *coax jumper* is a larger diameter cable with low loss, meant for runs between larger diameter connectors. A common use of a jumper would be from a wireless access point antenna jack directly to an antenna.

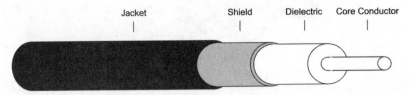

FIGURE 1-5: Diagram of the layers of a coaxial cable.

A *coax pigtail* is used as an interface between larger diameter cables and the very small connectors commonly used on PC cards. A common use of a pigtail would be to connect a PC card to a coax jumper to an antenna.

Constructing pigtails takes much skill and patience in soldering the tiny connectors to the small diameter cable necessary for PC card connectors. For best results, purchasing a pre-configured pigtail is the way to go. Selecting a pigtail is covered in detail later in the chapter.

## What Sizes of Coax Are Available

Cables come in many forms from different manufacturers. We have found the optimum cable for ease-of-use and low-loss performance is the LMR-400 cable from Times Microwave. This cable has become the popular choice in building wireless networks.

Table 1-3 shows various cable sizes from Time Microwave. These represent the most commonly available cables for use with 2.4 GHz Wi-Fi gear. The larger diameter cables are harder to work with than the smaller cable because of their rigidity and bulkiness. However, the larger cables have lower signal loss. It's a trade-off between ease of use, performance, and cost. LMR-400 is a good balance and costs about half the price of LMR-600.

## Keep It Short!

As shown in Table 1-3, cable loss is measured by distance. Therefore, to keep the strongest signal and the lowest loss, you should keep the cable as short as possible. For most of the projects in this book, you will need cables of less than 10 feet in length. For larger projects, such as creating a free wireless hotspot, you would need a longer cable.

Also, the cable type is very important at high frequencies. For example, using 10 feet of LMR-100 cable induces a loss of 3.9 dB, while the same length of LMR-400 induces a tiny loss of 0.7 dB.

Because of the high loss factor of LMR-100, an access point should have no more than 3 feet of LMR-100 cable between it and the antenna. On the other hand, an access point using the more efficient LMR-400 cable could have a 20 foot–long cable and work just as well.

 **Note**    Manufacturers list cable line loss as measured in 100 feet of cable. This does not mean you should, or even can, use 100 feet in your cable runs. You usually want as strong a signal as possible coming out of the other end of the cable, so either keep it short or use a larger diameter cable.

### Table 1-3    Cable Sizes Commonly Used for 2.4 GHz

| TM Part Number | Diameter | Line Loss at 2.4 GHz (Per 100 Feet) |
| --- | --- | --- |
| LMR-100 | 1/10" | –38.9 dB |
| LMR-240 | 3/16" | –12.7 dB |
| LMR-400 | 3/8" | –6.6 dB |
| LMR-600 | 1/2" | –4.4 dB |

Many radio enthusiasts and some manufacturers host line loss or attenuation calculators on the Web. Search the Web for *coax line loss* to find some of these simple-to-use calculators.

## Measuring Line Loss in Decibels

The concept of *decibel* measurement, or dB, is covered more in Chapter 2. But for now, it's easy to think of it as the higher the number, the stronger the signal. Remember that negative numbers descend as they get higher (−80 is less than −30). Transmission line loss is represented as negative dB.

Wi-Fi radio transceiver effectiveness is described as a measurement of power output and receive sensitivity. Generally, these two measurements are expressed as power in *milliwatts* (expressed as mW, meaning 1/1000 of a watt) or as "dBm" (decibels related to 1 mW).

Decibel measurement can be confusing. But there are two key concepts to make this easy to understand:

- Decibels are relationship-oriented
- Decibels double by threes

Relationship-oriented means that there is no set value for a dB. The trailing letter in a dB measurement defines the relationship. For example, dBm means decibels related to 1 mW of power. 1 dBm equals 1 mW. When you know the value of the relationship, decibels are easy to calculate.

Doubling by threes is due to the logarithmic nature of RF energy. When comparing a signal of 1 dBm (1 mW) to a signal of 3 dBm (2 mW) you see that it's double the power.

This doubling nature of power measurement or line loss makes it easy to see how a cable can quickly reduce the RF signal to almost nothing.

## Calculating Line Loss

Continuing the last example (LMR-100 versus LMR-400), let's start with a signal of 100 mW (+20 dBm) and send it out along the 100 foot–cable, as shown in Table 1-3.

Start with the transmit power, +20 dBm or 100 mW, subtract the negative dB of line loss, and the result is the power at the other end of the cable:

1. LMR-100 (38.9 dB loss): +20 dBm − 38.9 dB = −18.9 dBm (about 0.001 mW)

2. LMR-400 (6.6 dB loss): +20 dBm − 6.6 dB = +13.4 dBm (about 20 mW)

In each case, it's a large drop. But look at the difference! LMR-100 drops power to a tiny fraction of the original signal. LMR-400, on the other hand, while inefficient, still has a usable signal. With either cable, once the signal gets to the antenna and out into the air, there will be even more signal loss. (See Chapter 13 for more on airspace loss and link budget.)

The significant loss in the cable makes repetition important: keep it short!

Cable usually comes in bulk on reels of 500 feet. Bulk cable vendors will happily cut a length of cable for your order. When ordering bulk cable, select a length of cable that is several feet longer than required. Although it adds a few extra dollars to the order, the extra cable makes it easy to repair construction mistakes or connector problems.

## Types of Coax Connectors

Connectors, obviously, are used to connect RF components together. In Wi-Fi there are only a few common connectors for large diameter coax. Unfortunately, the connector styles are not commonly used outside of the Wi-Fi arena. So, picking up a connector at your local consumer electronics store is generally out of the question. Hopefully in the future, more specialized retail establishments will carry this type of equipment. But for now, expect to buy online or purchase directly from distributors.

### Male versus Female Coax Style

Connectors are designated as male and female, which is another way of describing them as plug and socket. A male coax connector has a solid center pin or plug with an outer casing that enshrouds the female connector (see Figure 1-6). A female coax connector has an open center socket which accepts the male center pin.

In Wi-Fi coax cables there are often other components to the cable connectors, such as the inner ring on a Male N-type connector. The male/female designation is defined by the center conductor (plug or socket).

### Reverse Polarity

*Reverse polarity* is another way of saying that a connector has gone from plug to socket or socket to plug, reversing its polarity. This adds confusion to the entire male/female designation. When using reverse polarity connectors, male and female is reversed, where a male connector is the same design except that its center conductor is a socket. Female reverse polarity connectors use a plug for the center conductor.

The outer casing is generally the same for normal and reverse polarity. The RP style only changes the center conductor. So a male RP connector still enshrouds the female connector. See Figure 1-7 for a diagram of reverse polarity connectors. Hopefully that will make it a bit less confusing.

Standard Polarity RF Connectors

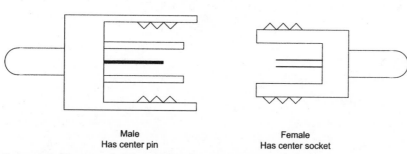

Male
Has center pin

Female
Has center socket

**FIGURE 1-6: Diagram of male and female coax connectors.**

Reverse Polarity RF Connectors

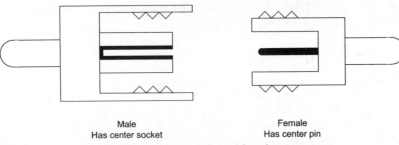

Male
Has center socket

Female
Has center pin

FIGURE 1-7: Diagram of reverse polarity male and female connectors.

Reverse polarity is a commonly used connector type in Wi-Fi devices. The style is not commonly used in other coax applications. The general understanding regarding reverse polarity connectors is that it fulfills government requirements to make it more difficult for the average consumer to modify Wi-Fi devices. Now that you know the secret, you're not an average consumer.

# Building a Coaxial Cable

That's enough theory! Now it's time to get your hands dirty and get started on this chapter's project, which is building a coax antenna cable.

Cable construction opens new freedom to creating wireless projects. With this skill, you can order the components you need and custom-build a cable that fits your application perfectly. And the cost of the components is usually lower than buying a pre-built cable.

N-Male is the most commonly used connector for Wi-Fi cabling, because most antennas have N-Female connectors. And, as you know, N-Male mates to N-Female. So, these steps will assume you have chosen LMR-400 cable with the standard N-Male connector. Please adapt the steps to your application where needed. Figure 1-8 shows the necessary dimensions for a Times Microwave N-Male connector.

Table 1-4 shows a list of connectors for use with LMR-400 cable. These connectors are solderless and each requires only two crimps. The connector types listed here are for hand-tightening. A myriad of other connector types are also available.

With the right set of tools, building a cable is a step-by-step process:

1. Prepare the cable

2. Slide the crimp ring onto the cable

3. Strip off the outer jacket

4. Pull back the inner shield

5. Strip the dielectric foam core

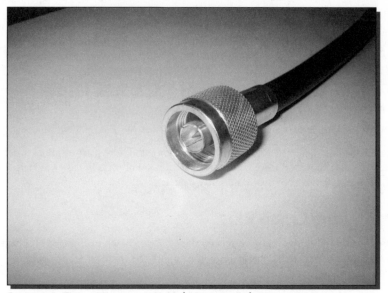

FIGURE 1-8: Times Microwave N-Male Reverse Polarity connector.

**6.** Remove any shorting material on the foam core

**7.** Cut the center conductor to correct size

**8.** Place the center pin onto the center conductor

**9.** Crimp the center pin

**10.** Place the connecter body onto the cable

**11.** Replace shield over the connector body

**12.** Place the crimp ring over the shield and connector body

**13.** Crimp the crimp ring

**14.** Inspect your finished product

### Table 1-4    Common Connector Types for LMR-400 Cable

| Connector Type | Application | Times Microwave Part Number |
| --- | --- | --- |
| N-Male | Cable jumper ends | EZ-400-NMK |
| N-Female | Antenna termination | EZ-400-NF |
| TNC Male | Cable jumper ends | EZ-400-TM |
| TNC Female | Antenna or pigtail termination | EZ-400-TM-RP |

There are a lot of steps, but it's actually very simple. Each step is discussed in detail in the paragraphs that follow.

## Step 1: Preparing the Cable

The cable is treated as a bulk item until ready to assemble the end connectors. So the ends are often cut into an irregular shape.

Use the cable cutters to square off the end of the cable, as shown in Figure 1-9.

After cutting the cable, the dielectric foam will become elongated. Use a set of pliers to reform the foam into a rounded shape, as shown in Figure 1-10. This will make it easier to strip later. Don't worry about the shape of the shield and outer jacket.

## Step 2: Placing the Crimp Ring

Before going any further, place the crimp ring onto the cable as shown in Figure 1-11. Slide it out of the way down the length of the cable. Later, you'll pull the crimp ring into place on the back of the connector shell.

FIGURE 1-9: Cutting the end of the cable to make it square.

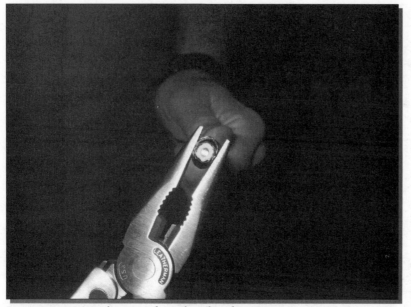

FIGURE 1-10: Using pliers to reform the white foam core.

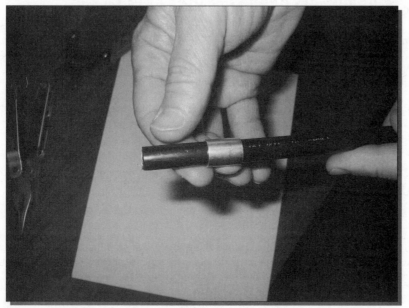

FIGURE 1-11: Placing the crimp ring before any other work.

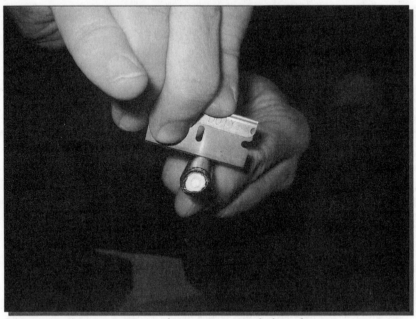

FIGURE **1-12: Stripping using a rocking motion. Watch those fingers!**

## Step 3: Stripping and Removing the Outer Jacket

There are special tools for stripping all types of cables, but a razor blade works well, costs less, and is more versatile. If you are very good at handling sharp objects, a pocket knife works too. Check the instructions that came with the connector for exact dimensions needed. Strip off about 1/2 inch more than necessary to leave room for trimming.

**Tip**

When stripping a cable with a razor blade or sharp knife, try not to nick the underlying elements of the cable. By rocking the razor blade, you will score through the jacket without harming the shield underneath.

Figure 1-12 shows a cut taking place around the entire circumference of the cable. It's a little unclear at this angle, but my fingers are being kept well out of the way!

Cut through the outer jacket just enough to be able to pull away the jacket without harming the shield.

After stripping around the cable, make a groove along the length of the cable. Make three or four cuts with just enough force to cut a little deeper each time, as shown in Figure 1-13. The goal is to come as close to the shield as possible without cutting all the way through the cable.

Now grab the end of the outer jacket with a set of long-nosed pliers and pull away the jacket. Tear along the grooves scored into the jacket and peel off the jacket with your fingers to reveal the shield mesh underneath, as shown in Figure 1-14.

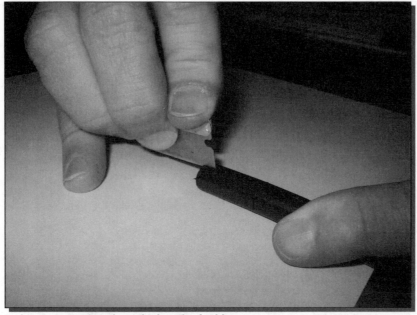

FIGURE 1-13: Scoring along the length of cable.

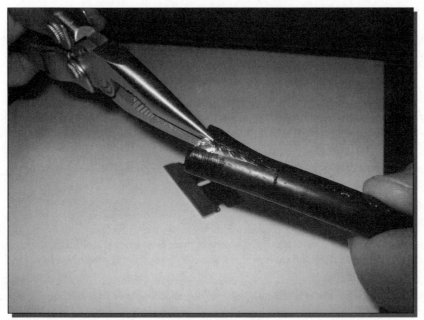

FIGURE 1-14: Peeling off the outer jacket of the cable.

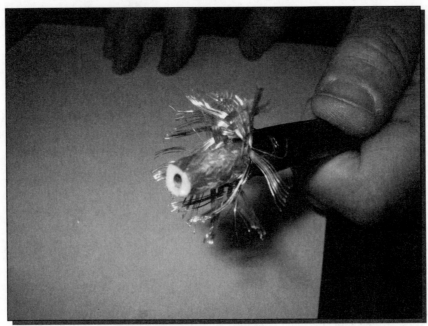

FIGURE 1-15: Fanning out and pulling back the shield.

## Step 4: Pulling Back the Inner Shield

To get the next cut ready, use your fingers to carefully fan out and pull back the shield mesh layer, as shown in Figure 1-15.

## Step 5: Stripping the Dielectric

Now strip off the foam dielectric core along with the solid aluminum wrapping. This requires much less force than the cable jacket. Be sure to apply light pressure and try not to nick the center conductor. (See Figure 1-16.)

To remove the foam core from the center conductor, just twist and pull.

## Step 6: Checking for Shorts

At this stage, you need to inspect the cable for shorts along the dielectric. Remember that the dielectric material is a nonconductor of electricity. If there is an electrical short from the center conductor to the outer shield, the cable will not perform well, i.e. if it works at all.

The easiest way to accomplish this is with a visual inspection. Check for any stray shielding strands or aluminum foil material. See Figure 1-17 for an example of foil shorting the center pin.

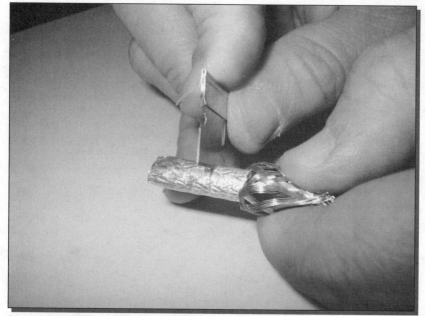

FIGURE 1-16: Make gentle cuts to remove the dielectric and foil.

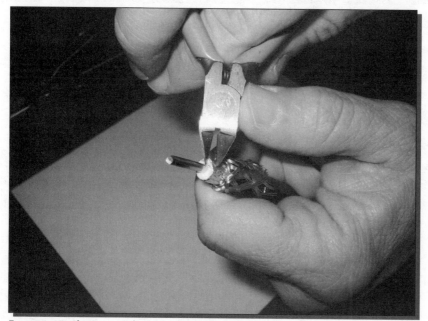

FIGURE 1-17: Shorts must be removed at this stage.

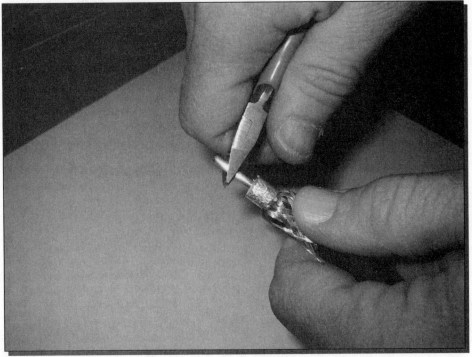

FIGURE 1-18: Clipping the core conductor.

To remove a foil short, use small wire cutters to scrape away and cut the foam at an angle. You can also use a fingernail for any smaller, more elusive bits. The corrected foam should be white all the way around.

## Step 7: Clipping the Core

Clip off the center core to the proper length for the connector being used. The connector packaging or data sheet should have this specific measurement. In the case of this connector, we clipped it to 3/16 of an inch. If the center conductor is too short or too long, the connector shell will not seat correctly. Figure 1-18 shows the relative length for an N-Male connector.

After trimming back the core, remove any ridges or burrs around the cut edge. This will allow the pin to seat properly.

## Step 8: Inserting the Center Pin

Place the center pin onto the conductor as shown in Figure 1-19. Ensure the center conductor bottoms out at the first stop of the pin. Also, ensure the pin rests within 1–2 mm of the foam dielectric.

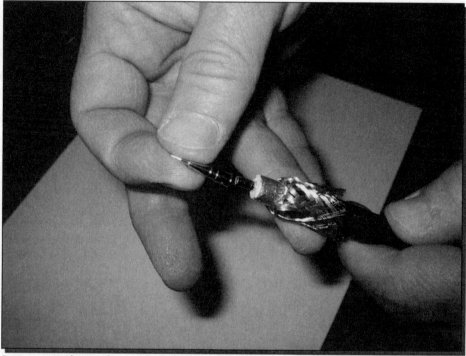

FIGURE 1-19: Placing the center pin onto the conductor.

## Step 9. Crimping the Core

This is the first of two crimps for the connector. Ensure your crimp tool has the correct die for the type of cable and connector being used. For LMR-400, the crimp tool should have a die with hex sizes of 0.429 for the outer ring, and 0.128 and 0.100 for the center pins.

The center pin for an N-Male connector is crimped using size 0.128.

**Tip**

When you crimp coax cables, press all the way down once only. The hex design of the crimp tool die ensures the pin will grip the core properly in six places. If another crimp is applied to "make it tighter," it could misshape the pin.

Place the pin into the crimp tool as shown in Figure 1-20. The bottom edge of the pin usually will have a small ridge to help line it up and keep the pin seated on the core.

Crimp down with even, strong pressure. If your crimp tool has the ratcheting feature, it will apply only the necessary amount of pressure before releasing.

FIGURE 1-20: About to crimp the center pin onto the center conductor.

Figure 1-21 shows a properly crimped center pin. Notice the marking around the edges where the crimp actually clamped the pin to the center conductor.

## Step 10: Placing the Connector Body

It's time to place the connector body over the pin. Figure 1-21 shows the connector about to slide onto the pin.

Before continuing, be very sure that the crimp ring from Step 2 is still waiting for you down the cable behind the splayed out shield before you place the connector body onto the cable.

Ensure the crimp ring is on the cable before snapping the connector shell into place. Once the shell is snapped into place, it will be difficult to remove. Also, removing and replacing the shell would degrade the cable performance. If the ring is not in place, you'll need to cut the connector off and rebuild the cable with a new connector.

Line up the connector, and begin to slide the connector over the pin, over the dielectric foam, and butt it up against the shield strands. If all goes well, there may be an audible click when the

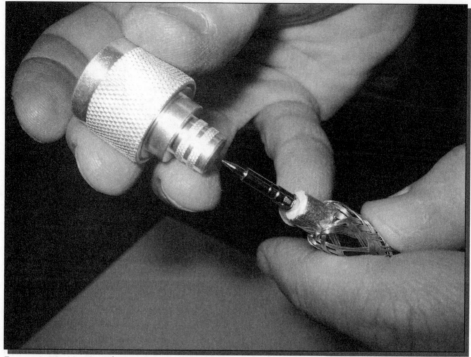

**FIGURE 1-21:** Moving the connector into position.

connector mates with the pin. This mating is meant to hold the connector on the pin until the last crimp.

Tug lightly at the connector like you are going to pull it back off. It should stay in place under light pressure. If forced or yanked, it may come off, so be gentle.

Figure 1-22 shows the connector fully inserted with the shield still pulled back. Notice that the center pin does not extend past the inner ring of the connector.

## Step 11: Shields Up!

Fan out the shield strands and trim down with scissors, as shown in Figure 1-23. To help cleanup, hold the cable over a wastebasket. The goal is to trim down the shield but still have enough to fit under the crimp ring. Trim the shield down to about a quarter of an inch.

Shield strands are made of steel. The thin wires can pierce the skin like a needle in some circumstances. Make sure to handle the waste strands with care, and clean up the area to minimize the chance of accidents.

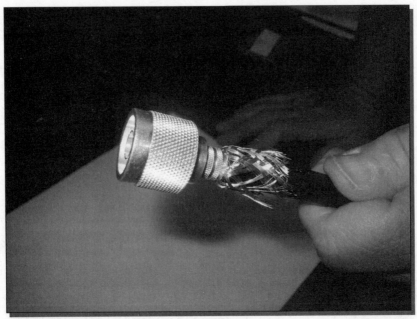

FIGURE 1-22: Connector and pin are in position.

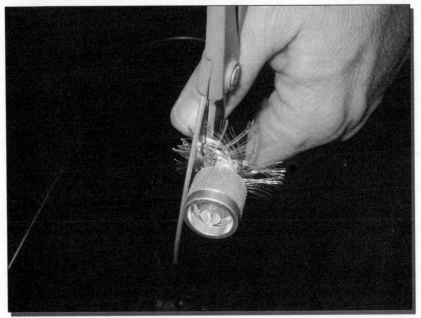

FIGURE 1-23: Trimming the shield with scissors.

FIGURE 1-24: The shield splayed out under the crimp ring.

## Step 12: Placing the Crimp Ring

Now pull up the crimp ring you placed in Step 2. The shield will slip under the crimp ring and should be splayed out evenly around the connector body, as shown in Figure 1-24.

If the shield is still too long, move the crimp ring out of the way and trim a little more of the shield with the scissors. Try to get just enough shield under the crimp ring, but not sticking out past the ring.

## Step 13: Crimping the Ring

Finally, it's time to crimp the crimp ring onto the cable. This is the second of the two crimps needed to make the cable. As in Step 9, use the crimping tool. But this time crimp with the larger diameter hex size of 0.429.

Place the tool at the upper edge of the crimp ring, butted against the connector body as shown in Figure 1-25. Crimp with strong, even pressure, and only crimp once, just like in Step 9.

FIGURE 1-25: Crimping the crimp ring onto the cable.

## Step 14: Inspecting the Finished Product

Now that the cable is complete, it's time for a visual inspection. Check the back of the connector at the seam of the crimp ring. If there are any shield strands sticking out, cut them off with the razor blade, as shown in Figure 1-26.

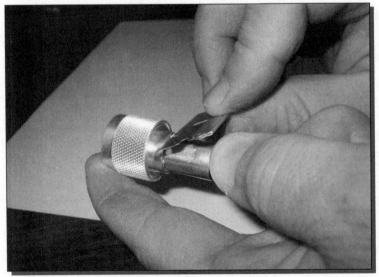

FIGURE 1-26: Cutting off the pokey bits.

**Caution** Clipping off the loose strands at the back of the connector reduces the chance of injury when you're screwing on the cable. Loose strands are like splinters that may pierce the skin of unwary fingers.

Visually check the front of the connector for any loose bits of metal that may have dropped into the connector during construction. If you find any, remove them to prevent shorts.

That's it! Now repeat steps 1 to 12 for the other end of the cable. After doing a few of these, it will become second nature. With practice, building a cable connector can take just a few minutes.

# Choosing a Wi-Fi Pigtail

A *pigtail* acts as a converter between large diameter cables and small connecters commonly used on Wi-Fi cards.

Because of the very small connector sizes, pigtails are difficult to build and require highly skilled soldering techniques. We recommend that you purchase pigtails for use in your projects. Several online stores sell pre-built pigtails in specific lengths.

To purchase a pigtail, the vendor will need to know a few things:

- *Length of pigtail*: should be less than 2 feet to keep signal loss low
- *Cable connector*: the type of connector to plug into the larger cable (usually male)
- *Device connector*: the type of connector to plug into the Wi-Fi device (usually female)

The device connector is specific to the type of Wi-Fi card or access point being used.

**Table 1-5    Connector Types for Common Wi-Fi Products**

| Connector | Type of Product | Wi-Fi Product |
|---|---|---|
| MMCX | PCMCIA Card | Cisco, Engenius, Proxim, Senao, Symbol |
| MC-Card | PCMCIA Card | Apple Airport, Avaya, Orinoco |
| RP-SMA | Access Point, PCI Card, Wi-Fi Camera, Wireless Media Adapter | Belkin, D-Link, Linksys, Netgear, SMC, U. S. Robotics |
| RP-TNC | Access point, Bridge, Wireless Booster | Linksys |
| MCX | Base Station, Adapter Card | Apple Airport Extreme |
| Note: RP in the connector designation refers to "Reverse Polarity." | | |

FIGURE 1-27: Various Wi-Fi connector types.

## Connector Types for Wi-Fi Cards

There are almost as many connector types as there are Wi-Fi device manufacturers. Table 1-5 lists some of the most popular connectors.

The MMCX, MC-Card, RP-SMA, and RP-TNC male connectors and some of the female devices to which they attach are shown in Figure 1-27.

## Finding Pigtails

Pigtails are not available in stores. They must be purchased from vendors that construct them on a regular basis. Sometimes you can find them locally at swap meets or user group meetings. Usually it's easier to buy them online. Here are some popular sites:

- www.ecwest.com
- www.fab-corp.com
- www.hyperlinktech.com
- www.wlanparts.com
- www.ydi.com

These stores generally sell antennas, wireless devices, and cables as well as pigtails.

# Cheap Cable Testing

When a transmission problem arises in a Wi-Fi system, the first place to look is at the cables and connectors. Connectors generally take the most physical stress in a system, and also can be the first piece to break down while operating in poor conditions. The middle of the cable or the inside of an antenna is less likely to sustain damage if stressed when compared to the cable ends and connectors.

This is where simple cable testing can be of great value to troubleshoot a system. To check for continuity and for shorts, use the ohm-meter function on a multimeter. Test the entire length of the cable through each connector.

1. Check for continuity from center pin to center pin. This should be a short or zero ohms.

2. Check from connector body to connector body. This should be a short or zero ohms.

3. Check from center pin to connector body. This should be open or infinite ohms.

**Tip**

Often when you're testing a cable, it's already installed on-site, which limits access to the cable ends. To get around this, disconnect both ends of the cable and short the center pin to the connector body on one end only. Then measure resistance of the pin to the body on the other end. The resistance should still be zero ohms (or very close).

For the unlimited budget, products like a time domain reflectometer (TDR), spectrum analyzer, RF Power meter, and network analyzer can be used to test entire transmission systems, including the cable. These usually cost several thousand dollars to buy and hundreds to rent.

If the connector is presumed bad, replacing it is often much less costly than extensive testing. And very often, the only way to fix a bad connector is to replace it and start over.

# Summary

Wi-Fi is radio at microwave frequencies. Transmission lines at 2.4 GHz are more prone to signal loss and must therefore be considered an important part of the entire Wi-Fi system.

A low-loss, large diameter cable and a pigtail adapter makes it easy to position the antenna for the best radiation pattern and signal strength.

Building connectors on-the-fly opens up a new realm of independence. By obtaining the cable in bulk, and the various types of connectors, it becomes a simple process to build your own custom cables tailored to each application. And the cable will be exactly as long as necessary.

Read on to the next chapter to explore antennas: how antennas are defined, antenna radiation patterns, choosing an antenna, and pros and cons of high-gain antennas. You'll even see how to build a simple omni antenna that will boost your range by up to 200 feet.

# Building a Classic Paperclip Antenna

**H**ave you ever had this survivor fantasy? You're stranded on a desert island (with your laptop of course!) and desperately need to connect to the outside world. You empty your pockets on the ground, and find nothing but commonplace objects. But then... in a frenzy of creative brilliance you whip all the ordinary pocket-objects together to come up with a jerry-rigged wireless antenna. Within minutes you are e-mailing potential rescuers from the beach, and surfing your favorite sites to kill time.

Of course, that is only a fantasy. But, this chapter offers you a project which comes pretty close to the fantasy in both results and ingenuity.

This chapter will show you how to put together the ultimate "homebrew" antenna—a working Yagi antenna for 2.4 GHz Wi-Fi out of little more than paperclips stuck together. This model is commonly called the *Frisko antenna*, after the French Frisko brand of ice cream cups whose wooden spoons were used in the first prototypes. Figure 2-1 shows a completed paperclip antenna.

The current designs of most external Wi-Fi cards put the antenna in a flawed position, with the antenna very close to the computer. This means that the pattern of emissions is often blocked by the computer itself. Not only that, the small packaging of wireless cards prevents an optimal design for the internal antenna to pick up wireless network devices more than a couple of 100 feet away.

This is one of the reasons that attaching even a small external antenna like the one in this chapter can greatly improve signal strength, especially if it is oriented properly.

## Recognizing Different Antennas

If you do any research on antennas, you will notice that there are several different types of antennas around. Two common types are directional and omnidirectional. The difference between these two types of antenna is a simple but important one. A *directional antenna* transmits its information in a single direction, while an *omni antenna* transmits the information in all horizontal directions.

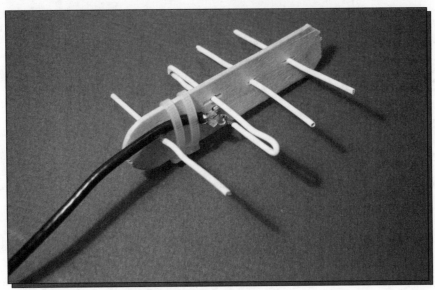

FIGURE 2-1: A finished paperclip antenna.

In addition, you need to understand how antenna efficiency, or gain, works as related to other antennas. Antenna gain is measured in *decibels, isotropic* (dBi), defined as the strength of an antenna as related to a theoretical sphere around an imaginary antenna. dBi is a logarithmic measurement, so every 3 dBi is a doubling of gain. What you need to know is the higher the dBi, the more sensitive and focused the antenna.

**Tip**    An omni antenna sends and receives signals equally in front, behind, to the left, or to the right of the antenna. However, when you go above or below the antenna, signal strength drops off significantly. The trade-off you make when choosing a high-gain antenna is this focusing, or thinning, of the above and below energy. The low-gain omni works better vertically than a high-gain omni, but it won't extend as far horizontally.

Figure 2-2 shows a diagram of two antennas viewed from the top. The directional antenna is most sensitive in one direction, meaning signals being sent and received by the antenna will be strongest in the direction the antenna is pointing. The omnidirectional antenna sends and receives signals in all directions equally. This is a generalization, but it's mostly accurate. Later chapters will delve further into the specifics of antenna operation.

Since directional antennas direct their information at a specific target (or at least in the direction of the target), they require less power to transmit, but more precision in their placement. Omnidirectional antennas need little precision in their placement, but require more power to send and receive signals.

You are probably familiar with these different types of antennas, because you see them almost every day. A satellite dish would be considered highly directional, looking up into space, while

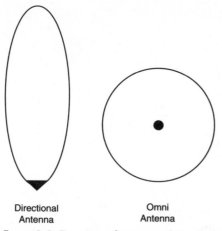

Directional
Antenna

Omni
Antenna

FIGURE 2-2: Top view of coverage for a directional and an omni antenna.

the antenna on your car is omnidirectional, listening to radio no matter which direction your car is facing. Let's take a closer look at these different types of antennas.

## Omni Antennas

The omnidirectional antenna is probably the most common Wi-Fi antenna available. Just about every Wi-Fi device you can buy comes with an omni antenna. This is because the omni is so easy to set up, and generally works in consumer environments without much planning. There are a few different types of omni antennas. Omni signals spread out sideways, but not vertically (see Figure 2-3).

**Note**  Even though an omni antenna does not work very well above and below, it is not considered a directional antenna. Wi-Fi antennas are generally rated in two-dimensional space that assumes it is mounted parallel to the Earth's surface. Knowing how the beam is shaped, and that an antenna is not truly omnidirectional will help you choose the right antenna for your Wi-Fi toys.

### Dipole Antenna

The *dipole antenna* is just about the simplest antenna there is. The dipole is a half-wave antenna that consists of two opposing radiating elements. It's made up of two quarter-wavelength poles

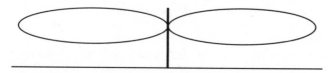

FIGURE 2-3: Side-view of an omnidirectional antenna signal.

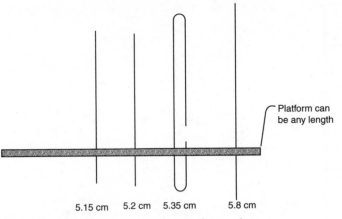

Platform can
be any length

5.15 cm    5.2 cm    5.35 cm    5.8 cm

FIGURE 2-4: A dipole antenna made out of paperclips.

that are not connected to each other and fed in the middle by the transmission line. A standard dipole is open on each end, but it can also be folded over on itself. The dipole you will build in this chapter is a folded dipole.

Figure 2-4 shows a simple dipole made from steel paperclips. Each *arm* of the dipole is 31 mm in length, or 1/4 of a wavelength for Wi-Fi channel 6. The center conductor is soldered to the right arm, while the shield is soldered to the left arm. It doesn't matter to which side you solder.

The dipole antenna is unique in that it can be mounted vertically or horizontally. When standing vertically, the dipole antenna is omnidirectional. When horizontal, this antenna will radiate outward in two directions off the sides (and slightly upwards), like turning a donut on its edge.

## Coaxial Antenna

A coaxial is another common antenna used in Wi-Fi. It's used on most wireless access points you can buy. If the access point has a stubby little antenna on it, chances are it's a *coaxial antenna*. The coaxial antenna works in much the same way as a dipole antenna. The construction is slightly different though. The antenna feed comes up through the bottom with a metal casing around the shield-connected arm. Coaxial antennas are usually a total of half a wavelength with each arm being one quarter wavelength of the frequency.

The antenna in Figure 2-5 is from a common access point with two antennas. The plastic on one of the antennas is removed to show you the actual antenna element. You can see that the cable runs through the base of the antenna. The center conductor extends to the top while the shield is soldered to the metal cylinder that becomes the base radiator.

**Note**  Antennas are not really affected by plastic, rubber, and other nonconductors of electricity. When determining antenna shape, you can sometimes get an idea from the outer covering. However, you will need to check the antenna specifications to be sure of the design. Or build it yourself!

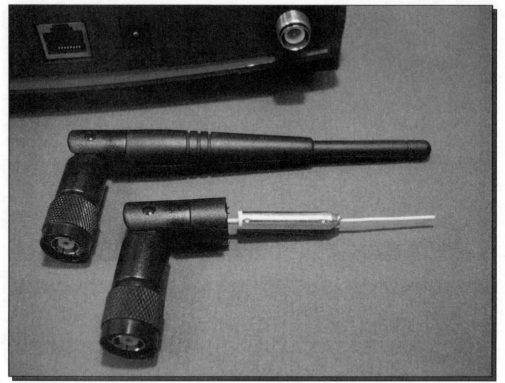

**FIGURE 2-5: A cut-away interior of a popular coaxial antenna.**

## Vertical Driven Array Antenna

The *driven array antenna* is often used for mobile applications. This is a vertical antenna with gain created by multiple segments of half-wavelength elements arranged vertically end-to-end to achieve gain. An array is simply more than one element working together.

The driven array means that each element has an electrical connection with the one next to it. The signal is driven into each radiating element via an antenna coil that maximizes the transfer of energy between adjacent elements.

Figure 2-6 shows a magnetically mounted driven array antenna with one quarter-wavelength element on the bottom and one half-wavelenegth element on top separated by a coil. The coil is used to match the antenna elements to each other. If an antenna has a coil on it's structure, it is most likely separating antenna elements.

**Note**

A driven array connects elements directly and electrically. A parasitic array connects passively without a direct electrical connection to the driven element.

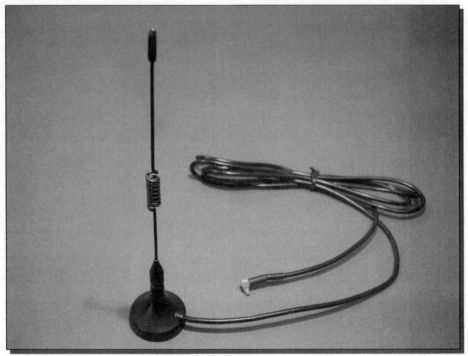

FIGURE 2-6: Magnetic-mount driven array antenna.

## Directional Antennas

You will build a directional antenna in this chapter. A directional antenna increases gain in one direction. By becoming sensitive in a single direction, the directional antenna is a good choice for setting up links between distant objects with a known location. Directional antennas are well suited for the corner of a room, side of a building, or in a hand-held mobile environment.

Directional antennas generally only work well in one direction. The design of the antenna determines the field of view, or beam pattern, for the antenna. Antenna beam width is measured in degrees of a circle, as viewed from the top or the side. The top view is measured as vertical beam width. The side view is measured as horizontal beam elevation. Figure 2-7 shows these measurements for a directional antenna.

**Note**   Directional antennas are very helpful in pinpointing a signal location, or for establishing a long-distance link. The antenna you build in this chapter and in Chapter 3 will help you later in the book.

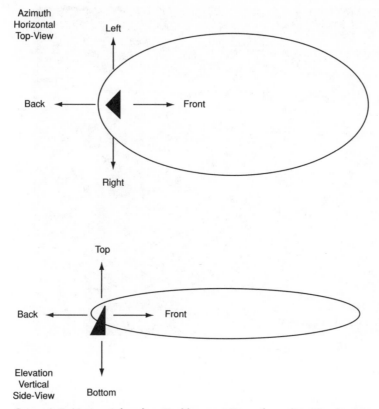

FIGURE 2-7: Horizontal and vertical beam patterns for a directional antenna.

## Yagi Antenna

A *Yagi antenna* is a highly directional parasitic array antenna. The shaping elements are not electrically connected to the driven element. The Yagi basically consists of a driven element, a reflector, and two or more directional elements. Figure 2-8 shows a common Yagi antenna with 14 directional elements and one reflector.

In a very basic sense, the radiating element of the Yagi is the only part that actually receives a signal. The other components bend and shape the pattern of RF energy for that single element. It works something like this: A transmitted signal comes up the cable and leaves the driven element. It hits the reflector and bounces toward the front of the antenna. Each directional element then carries that signal further while making it stronger. When the signal leaves the last element of the antenna, it's focused in a single direction. The reverse is true for signals being received by the antenna.

The antenna you will build in this chapter is a Yagi antenna. There is a driven element, a reflector, and two directional elements. While the Yagi in Figure 2-8 uses aluminum and fiberglass, you will construct yours of steel and wood.

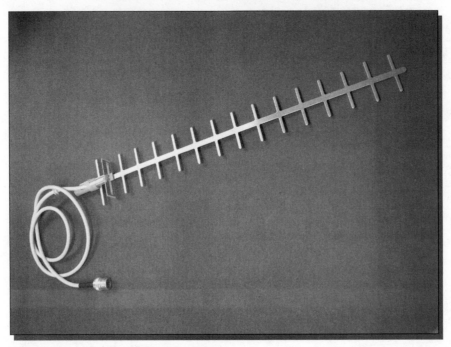

FIGURE 2-8: A high-gain Wi-Fi Yagi antenna.

## Parabolic Antenna

A parabolic antenna is very intuitive when you see one, like the one shown in Figure 2-9. The rear portion of the antenna is a curved reflector that bounces incoming signals into the focal point of the curve. A small antenna is placed at the focal point and becomes the *antenna feed point*. The feed point usually has a half-wave dipole or other basic antenna. For transmitted signals, the reverse is true as signals bounce off the reflector out into the distance.

Parabolic antennas have very high gain and are very directional. They are most often used for direct links from one station to another. When deploying a parabolic antenna you need precise physical aim.

## Panel Antenna

A *panel antenna* is an array of rectangular flattened dipole antennas arranged in a pattern on a panel. These flattened dipole antennas are sometimes called *patch antennas*. Because the patches are laid out in an array, the shape of the radiation pattern is aligned and focused in one direction. The more patches in the array, the more focused the antennna and the higher the gain. Figure 2-10 shows the inside array of a very high-gain panel antenna.

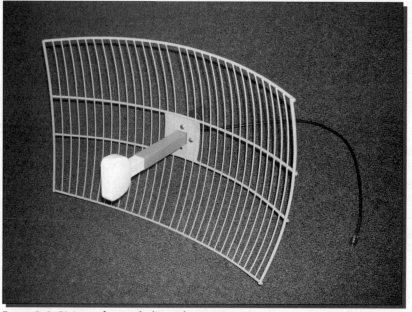

FIGURE 2-9: Picture of a parabolic grid antenna.

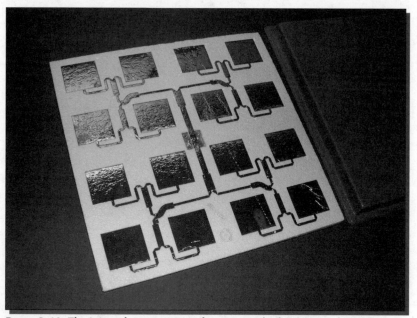

FIGURE 2-10: The internal components of a common high-gain panel antenna.

Panel antennas work well in one direction off the face of the antenna. The metal backing surface is employed as a reflector and mounting point for the panel antenna. The face of the antenna is often covered in nonconducting plastic for weather proofing and to help prevent damage.

## Waveguide Antenna

A *waveguide antenna* is very strange indeed. This type of antenna is actually formed by the space and the surface surrounding an electrically conductive enclosure.

The size and shape of the waveguide determines the frequency at which the waveguide will operate best. A small driven element in a precise location near the rear of the waveguide creates the signal that is shaped by the metal surface of the enclosure. The shape of the enclosure directs the beam pattern outward, away from the opening. Figure 2-11 shows a basic home-made waveguide antenna made from a tin can.

Waveguide antennas are often built from aluminum. However, a tin can is a very good conductor, and it's the perfect size and shape for the waveguide antenna you will build in Chapter 3.

FIGURE 2-11: A waveguide antenna you can build.

## Understanding Antenna Polarization

Antenna polarization stems from how an antenna radiates energy. The design of an antenna forces certain physical and electrical characteristics. As radio frequency (RF) energy is shaped and radiated by the antenna, the antenna changes the shape and beam pattern of the RF.

Antennas are usually designated with vertical or horizontal polarization. At this point, the important thing for you to know is that polarizations like each other. For example, a vertically polarized antenna will work best receiving signals from another vertically polarized antenna (vertical-to-vertical). In fact, the signal strength can be 100 times less if you use mismatched polarization (vertical-to-horizontal).

You can use mismatched polarization to your advantage when working with closely placed antennas. The solar-powered repeater you will buld in Chapter 9 uses two antennas mounted on the same pole. To help keep them from interefering with one another, they are placed in opposing polarizations (horizontal and vertical).

The end-result of all this polarization talk is that you will want to hold your antenna vertically upright (vertically polarized) to pick up a typical store-bought access point (which is also verti-cally polarized). When we say "vertical" we mean that the paperclips are sticking straight up and down. "Horizontal" is when it is flat as compared to the ground.

# Before You Start

Before you start this journey, you should understand one thing: You don't end up with a power-ful, durable antenna for long-term use. For that you want to build, or buy, a more rugged, com-mercial-grade unit. In Chapter 3, we will show you how to make the famous coffee can waveguide antenna, which can be made quite a bit more powerful and sturdy than this lightweight paperclip model.

But, with that cautionary note, this paperclip antenna will work. It will extend the range of the antenna built into your wireless Network Interface Cards (NICs), and can produce a gain of up to 9 dBi. And you will be able to point to it with pride as your entry in that unofficial scavenger contest to push more and more bits for less and less cost.

There are more efficient and probably more effective ways to build a Wi-Fi antenna than using a paperclip. But are there any more fun? What could be better than using the humble paper clip as the central ingredient for your next antenna?

For many reasons, the paperclip appears over and over as the ultimate MacGyver tool. It is dirt cheap, found anywhere and easily hidden in the palm of the hero's hand even while his captors pat him down. How many times have you seen the paperclip open handcuffs and locks in the movies?

**Caution**

As with many of the projects in this book, local laws may regulate the usage of such an antenna. You should familiarize yourself with the local rules and regulations before you dive in.

# What You Need

Use the following list to collect and prepare the items you'll need to build your antenna. I've listed dimensions in both metric and foot/inches units where possible.

I've included eye protection in the list of items you need to have before you start. Don't skip this, or other safety precautions—please!

Here's what you need:

- Four large paperclips (the largest has to be at least 11.49 cm (4.52 inches) when straightened)

- A flat wooden spoon, the kind that comes with ice cream cups—or some other suitable platform for supporting your antenna prongs (perhaps a floppy disk)

- Wi-Fi pigtail cable connected to your laptop NIC (wireless PCMCIA card with an external connector).

- Solder iron and solder. An iron in the 15 W to 30 W range will work fine. Thin rosin core solder (0.75 mm is a good size) is preferred for electronic work because acid core solder will corrode components.

- Small bottle or tube of craft glue (virtually any kind will do)

- Small wire cutters

- Needle-nosed pliers

- A ruler that marks tenths of an inch (such as a drafting ruler from a craft store) or a metric ruler with markings for millimeters

- A pen for marking hole locations

- Eye protection for cutting wires and soldering

- A pair of vise grips or (even better) a small tabletop vise (the kind used for making fishing flies) for holding your antenna securely while working on it

- A drill with a bit slightly smaller than the diameter of the paperclips or else a thin wire brad and a light hammer for tapping it through the wood.

You can get more background information on this antenna design at the following Web sites:

- www.xaviervl.com/Antenne/Frisko/

- www.seattlewireless.net/index.cgi/MicroTVAerial

- www.wifi-montauban.net/communaute/index.php/DisquettAntenna

The pioneers of the paperclip antenna speak French, and their Web sites are in the French language, but they include translation links for English (and other) readers.

**Tip**

Some popular Web search engines provide translation tools for dozens of languages. Visit the language section at `www.altavista.com` or `www.google.com` and use the Language Translation links to view the sites in other languages. Sometimes the translated text is a little choppy, but the meaning comes through.

# Choosing a Wireless Card

You will have more success in your paperclip antenna project if you are working with a good wireless card. Wireless cards can come with or without built-in external connectors.

The cheaper cards without such connectors are mainly bought by corporations that assume their employees will only be connecting to the nearby access points in the workplace environment.

It is possible to access the internal connectors of wireless cards (NICs) that don't have such external jacks—but doing that is its own separate bit of technical wizardry that involves "cracking the case" of the NIC to get at its connectors.

**Tip**

Close-up photos of this feat are online at `www.ivor.it/wireless/pigtail.htm`.

However, 802.11b cards are now much cheaper than they were in the past, and it generally just makes more sense to buy a new card that comes with built-in external connectors you can attach the coaxial pigtail to (see Figure 2-12). These come in several varieties ("MC-Card,"

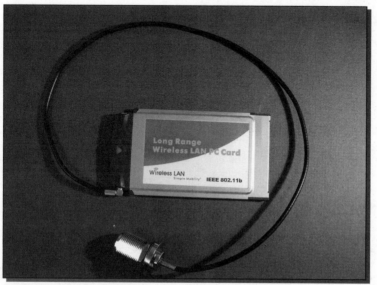

FIGURE 2-12: Card and pigtail.

"MMCX," and others) so make sure that your pigtail connector matches the kind you have on your wireless card. Increasingly, the cards seem to have standardized on using female MMCX connectors—for which the pigtail then needs a male MMCX connector.

# Choosing Platform Materials

This antenna was first made using a wooden spoon from a French ice cream cup called "Frisko" (hence its name). It is just large enough to accommodate the four prongs, and just thick enough to allow them to stand up well.

However, the mind boggles at all the many possible materials that can be used. These antennas have been made with medical tongue depressors, floppy diskettes, and small cardboard tubes. We used a jumbo-sized craft stick, also known as a popsicle stick.

Credit cards don't work well, because they are too thin. They don't support the prongs well (without mounds of glue) and so the prongs tend to flop over and even touch.

You can glue a wooden clothespin to the platform you select, so that the antenna can be easily clipped on a stable mount, like the side of your laptop screen.

# Building the Paperclip Antenna

Building the antenna is a seven-step process, as follows:

1. Prepare the antenna elements

2. Get the mounting platform ready

3. Create the driving element or *dipole*

4. Prepare the pigtail

5. Attach the pigtail to your new antenna

6. Secure the pigtail

7. Insert the last few elements into the antenna

Figure 2-13 shows the basic components and how they come together. Note that the rounded paperclip (piece 3) is the actual driven element of the antenna. That is, it's the wire getting the radio signal from the wireless card. The other paperclips (pieces 1, 2, and 4) shape the beam to make it more directional.

## Step 1: Preparing Your Wire Prongs

Each radio frequency has a specific wavelength. To function as an antenna, the dipole loop has to be half the length of that wavelength.

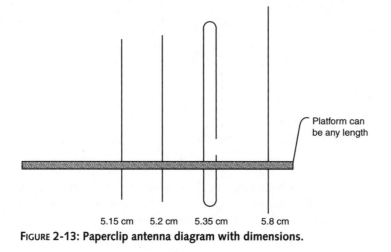

FIGURE 2-13: Paperclip antenna diagram with dimensions.

Take your needle-nosed pliers and carefully straighten four large paper clips. Cut them to the lengths indicated in Table 2-1.

## Step 2: Preparing Your Antenna Platform

Carefully mark on the wooden platform the five places where the wires of your antenna will be passing through. See Figure 2-14 for hole spacing for the paperclips.

**Note** This design is optimally tuned for reception on Wi-Fi Channel 6 (the approximate middle of the frequency band). It will also work on the other Wi-Fi channels. But if you really want to get peak frequencies, paperclip length and distance apart from each other will differ for each channel. See the section *How Are Dipole Dimensions Calculated* later in this chapter.

Using your hand drill, drill the five holes using a drill bit slightly smaller than the paperclip wires.

| Table 2-1    Paperclip Lengths in Inches and Centimeters | | |
|---|---|---|
| Element | Inches | Centimeters |
| Piece 1 | 2.03 | 5.15 |
| Piece 2 | 2.05 | 5.2 |
| Wire that will be bent into your dipole | 4.52 | 11.49 |
| Piece 4 | 2.28 | 5.8 |

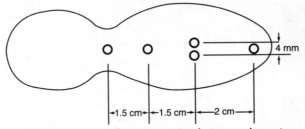

FIGURE 2-14: Diagram showing spacing between elements.

As an alternative, you can punch the holes by laying the platform flat on a table surface, and gently tapping a thin wire brad through the wood with a hammer. However, you can easily split the wood this way (especially on platform materials like an ice cream spoon or a popsicle stick).

**Tip** Patience is a virtue when mounting the paperclips. Work the paperclip into the material slowly with a gentle twisting and pressing force and everything should be fine.

## Step 3: Creating Your Dipole

Take the longest wire (the one that is 4.52 inches long) and form it to match the template in Figure 2-15. This template is printed to scale. After bending the paperclip as described here, lay it on top of this diagram to ensure the correct dimensions

Take your needle-nosed pliers and make a line on the nose at the point where it is 0.16 inches (4 mm) thick. Clamp the largest wire with the pliers and make a bend that starts 1.3 inches from one end,. Slowly wrap the paper clip wire around the needle nose, creating a fishhook that is 0.16 inches wide (4 mm).

Carefully press the longest end of the fishhook through the first appropriate hole on your platform. Work the wire into the hole, until the second end comes up to its appropriate hole. Ease that second wire through so that its end just pokes through on the other side of the platform.

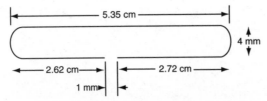

FIGURE 2-15: Radiating dipole paperclip dimensions—note that figure is not drawn to scale.

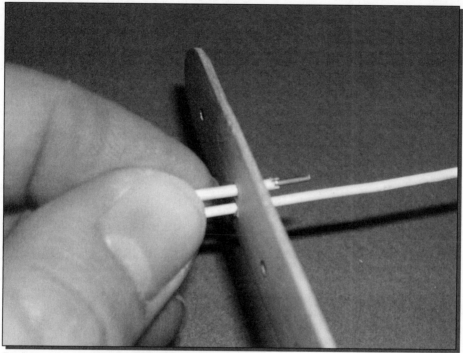

FIGURE 2-16: Inserting the driven element/paperclip.

Take the long protruding end of the wire and carefully create the second bent end, bringing the two ends extremely close together (about 1 mm or 0.04 inches), and create your radiating dipole. (See Figure 2-16.)

## Step 4: Preparing the Pigtail for Attachment

Take your wire cutter and simply snip off the large standard N connector on the end of the pigtail. This is where a factory-built antenna would be connected to the pigtail or jumper cable (as described in Chapter 1). Since we are soldering the antenna directly to the pigtail, the connector is not needed.

**Caution**

Be careful not to snip off the smaller end of the pigtail, which needs to be attached to your laptop wireless card.

Strip off about three-fourths of the outer insulating jacket and the inner dielectric insulation surrounding the core conductor.

You will need about 1/4 inch of the central core free, to create a soldered connection to one end of the dipole. And you will twist about 3/4 inch of the outer shield into a tight coil in order to solder it to the other end of the dipole. (See Figure 2-17.)

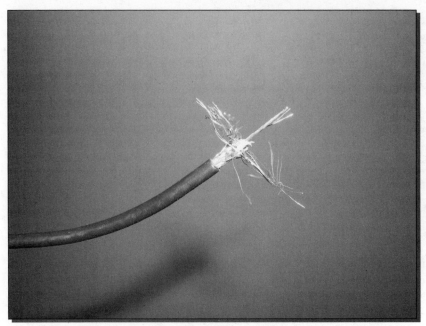

FIGURE 2-17: Pigtail cable ready for soldering.

## Step 5: Soldering the Pigtail to the Dipole

Put the bent paperclip dipole in a stable grip, either in a small tabletop vice, or in a pair of vise grips.

**Caution**

Don't touch the paperclip or the solder iron while you work on this, both will be very hot. Be sure to wear eye protection because splattering solder can cause serious eye damage. Also, the solder resin causes some fumes that can damage your lungs, so make sure your workspace is ventilated to avoid any unhealthy buildup of vapors.

Carefully solder the core conductor and the shield to either end of the bent dipole radiator (as shown in Figures 2-18 and 2-19).

**Note**

Both sides of the paperclip need to be soldered to the pigtail, but they must not touch each other or the antenna will be useless. When you choose a mounting platform, plan ahead to prevent the ends from touching.

## Step 6: Securing the Pigtail

Run the pigtail cable alongside the wooden platform (as shown in Figure 2-20). Use small drops of glue or some tape to fix the first inch of insulation firmly to the wooden platform. Zip ties or plastic bundle-ties also work great. Just don't use anything made of metal or antenna characteristics could change.

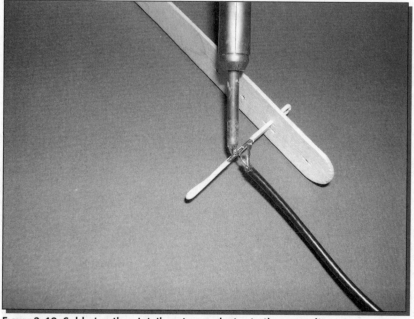

FIGURE 2-18: Soldering the pigtail center conductor to the paperclip.

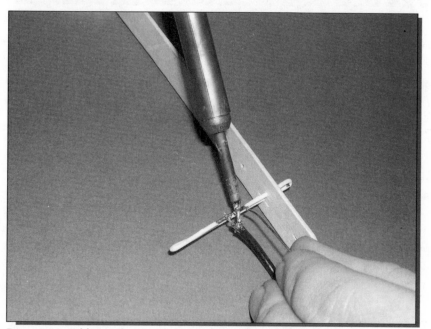

FIGURE 2-19: Soldering the pigtail shield to the other side of the paperclip.

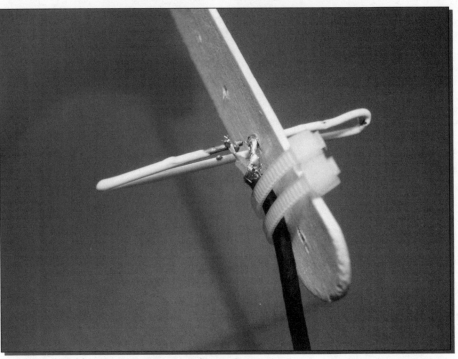

FIGURE 2-20: Cable management on your tiny antenna.

**Caution** Do not use metal twist-ties to secure the pigtail. Twist-ties are often used to bundle cables together in consumer electronics, especially with wireless networking gear. The metal inside the twist-tie may adversely affect the antenna properties. Use a nonconducting plastic or glue for best results.

This will guarantee that the fragile soldered connections do not need to bear the weight of the antenna, and will help prevent breakage when the antenna is moved relative to the laptop.

## Step 7: Inserting the Antenna Elements

Insert the remaining three wires in their appropriate locations as "elements." The prongs don't need to be centered on the platform, but it is best to center them in relationship to each other. (See Figure 2-21.)

Touch each wire with a drop of glue where it passes through the platform, just to hold the wires in place. (See Figure 2-22.)

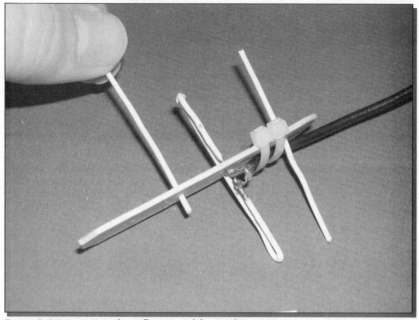

FIGURE 2-21: Inserting the reflector and focus elements.

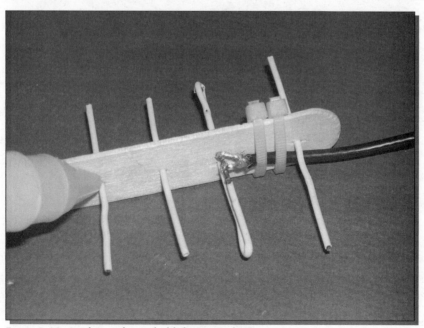

FIGURE 2-22: Applying glue to hold things in place.

# Mounting and Testing Your Paperclip Antenna

Now let's take this baby out for a spin!

1. After you have soldered the pigtail to the antenna and secured it with tape, connect the pigtail to your wireless card.

2. Mount the antenna and try it out.

3. If you have glued a clothespin or clamp to the wooden platform, you can clip it to various objects, so that the antenna itself is either vertically or horizontally polarized.

4. Position and aim the antenna in search of the strongest signal.

5. Observe (and learn about) the link quality differences with the antenna in each position.

Wireless networking software should come with some program or component used to measure signal strength on your computer. In Windows XP, the Wireless Network Connection Status dialog displays a Signal Strength bar graph. The more green bars that light up in the display, the stronger the signal.

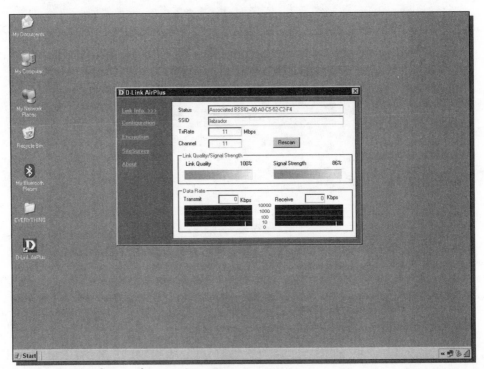

FIGURE 2-23: Signal strength survey in progress.

You can also use the software that came with the wireless adapter. This software will have some form of signal strength meter. Figure 2-23 shows the signal strength meter for an Engenius Wi-Fi adapter.

Use your "signal strength meter" to see what happens to the signal strength as you vary where the antenna is positioned and how it is oriented. You can adjust and re-orient the antenna for the best connection.

**Tip**   Other software can be used to measure signal strength. See Chapter 6 for details on using NetStumbler as a signal measurement tool.

# Hitting the Road with Your Paperclip Antenna

Paperclip antennas are the ultimate cheap tool for connecting to Wi-Fi signals. They're not the most efficient, but they might be the most fun.

Your new, lightweight, budget-conscious paperclip antenna will expand the receptivity of the antenna that comes with your wireless network adapter. As noted in the beginning of this chapter, you can expect a gain of up to 9 dBi, which is probably two to three times better than your laptop card.

With this type of antenna, your laptop should work better in fringe coverage areas. You can probably use your laptop an additional 100 to 200 feet from the wireless access point.

Experiment with this new range by taking your laptop to a part of your network that doesn't usually have good signal quality. Attach your new paperclip Yagi and see how the signal strength changes. By pointing away from the access point, it should go down. Also, you can hold the antenna sideways or upright to change antenna polarization. This simple act can change your signal strength by 20 percent or more.

# Summary

You now have a nice little gadget that will boost your Wi-Fi signal when the wimpy internal antenna just won't bring in the signal. By walking around with your new antenna, you should be starting to understand how radio waves move through the air. You saw that just by rotating the antenna from horizontal to vertical and pointing it in different directions drastically affects the signal strength.

By creating this simple antenna, you have entered the realm of microwave RF engineering. The device you built in this chapter would have been unthinkable a short time ago when these microwave radio frequencies were reserved for military and scientific use.

Read on to the next chapter. We expand on the concept of homebrew by introducing the waveguide antenna—a very powerful, highly focused antenna that can be built using an empty coffee can and some ingenuity. (Plus knowing where to drill!)

# Building a Directional Tin Can Antenna

In Chapter 1, you learned how to make a Wi-Fi antenna cable that can be used to connect an external antenna to your Wi-Fi card or access point. It is now time to build an antenna and put the cable from Chapter 1 to good use. While there are many commercial antennas available on the market today, they can be expensive. And hey, let's face it, attaching a commercial antenna to your Wi-Fi network will not turn heads like making your own will.

There are several different types of antennas that you can build. The most famous Wi-Fi antennas are made from either a coffee can or a Pringles potato chip can. In this chapter, you will learn how to build your own antenna from a regular, metal coffee can. You will be able to build it quickly and cheaply. As an added bonus, you will have lots of coffee, which will come in handy in staying awake for the other projects in this book.

Here are the items you will need for this chapter's project:

➤ The coaxial cable you built in Chapter 1

➤ Metal can about 4 inches in diameter and 5½ inches long (100 mm–135 mm)

➤ Type N-Connector

➤ Long-nosed pliers

➤ Small wire cutters

➤ Single-sided razor blade

➤ Scissors

➤ Hammer

➤ Drill

➤ Soldering iron and solder

➤ Copper embossing material (optional)

# Types of Can Antennas

There are two popular types of homebrew Wi-Fi can antennas, the Pringles can antenna and the tin can antenna. They both have the same means to an end—increase signal strength in one direction—but they differ radically in operation and construction.

The Pringles can antenna is actually a Yagi antenna with a Pringles can covering used to mount the antenna components. You may recall from Chapter 2 that a Yagi antenna uses a single element as a radiator, with additional metallic elements. A single reflector element and multiple director elements help to shape the beam into a directional pattern.

In fact, the Pringles can isn't really a can, it's just a cylindrical cardboard container. Figure 3-1 shows the internal components of the Pringles can antenna. The primary components are the radiator and the beam-shaping elements. All other components serve to hold the antenna together in the correct position for best efficiency.

While the Pringles can is merely a shell, the tin can is the actual antenna on a tin can antenna. This is because the tin can antenna is a "waveguide" antenna (see Figure 3-2). That is, the size, shape, and electrical conductivity of the tin can act upon the radio frequency signals. When you place a small radiator in the right location, the dimensions of the can itself will shape the beam and light up the sky.

FIGURE 3-1: The popular Pringles can Yagi antenna and the insides.

FIGURE 3-2: The tin can waveguide antenna.

**Note** A *waveguide* is a type of radio frequency (RF) transmission path. Where low-frequency systems can use copper wires, like that used in your car radio, high-frequency RF will sometimes use waveguides to route high-power, high-frequency signals. Military radar systems often use waveguide transmission lines.

## Understanding Waveguides

A waveguide is a type of transmission line, like coaxial cable (see Figure 3-3). But, unlike coaxial cables, waveguides can carry microwave frequencies with almost no loss. RF energy as high as 60 GHz or higher travel easily through a waveguide conduit. A waveguide is constructed from metal in a very specific size and shape, usually rectangular. It is also very costly to manufacture, install, and can be difficult to maintain. Because it's made from metal, and must be of exact dimensions, waveguide transmission lines are very rigid.

Waveguides exploit a very interesting aspect of electromagnetic RF energy: The duality of electromagnetism. Electromagnetic energy is composed of an electric field and a magnetic field (hence the name). In a coaxial wire, these fields are present along the center conductor and reflected from the outer shield. In a waveguide, these two fields travel along the waveguide

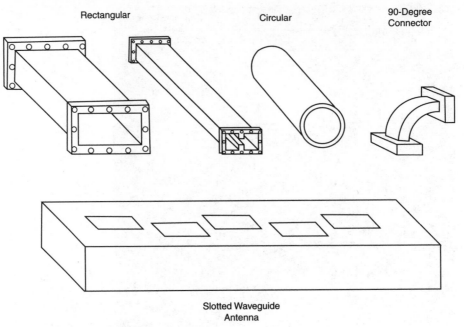

Rectangular          Circular          90-Degree Connector

Slotted Waveguide
Antenna

**FIGURE 3-3: Examples of various waveguides.**

without the need for a center conductor. The inner surface of the waveguide essentially directs the signal through the empty space of the interior itself.

Waveguide theory breaks apart all of the elements of radio frequency transmission. The details are quite complicated and can fill volumes. For this book, the important thing to note about waveguides is that size and shape of the waveguide itself is important, and placement of the radiator inside the waveguide is important.

Constructing a waveguide transmission line is difficult. To use a waveguide antenna, however, is a snap. You only need a short portion of the waveguide path to make an antenna. And Wi-Fi frequencies dictate a size and shape that is easily available at any grocery store.

## Sizing a Waveguide Antenna

As you know, a waveguide needs to be of specific dimensions. The waveguide antenna, therefore, must be the correct size for the frequency you are working with. In this case, you are working with Wi-Fi operating in the 2.4 GHz band.

Let's size this antenna for the middle of the band at channel 6, which has a frequency of 2.437 GHz (see the frequencies in Table 1-2 in Chapter 1). With proper construction, this antenna should operate well across all Wi-Fi frequencies from channels 1 to 14.

To ensure a can that's sized well, it should follow the dimensions shown in Figure 3-4.

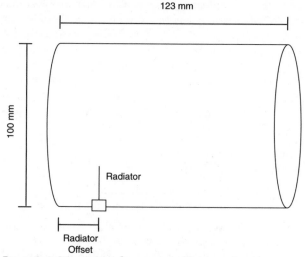

**FIGURE 3-4: Dimensions for a waveguide can antenna.**

The dimensions for the can antenna built in this chapter are:

- Diameter: ideally 100 mm plus or minus 10 percent (90–110 mm)
- Length: about 123 mm or a full wavelength, plus or minus 10 percent
- Wedge-shaped radiating element: 24 mm (about 1/5 of a wavelength)
- Radiator offset: 27 mm (about 7/32 of a wavelength)

**Tip** To calculate wavelength, use the formula wavelength in millimeters = 300 divided by the frequency in gigahertz. So, the wavelength for channel 6 is 300 / 2.437 = 123 mm.

# Finding the Right Can

For this project, you can use just about any smallish coffee can. There are a couple of things you have to keep in mind: it has to be a metal can and it should be close to the dimensions noted in the previous section. Remarkably, Maxwell House and Folgers Coffee cans are the exact dimensions needed for this project. The ounces (or grams) measurements vary somewhat from 11.5 oz. (368 g) to 13 oz. (326 g) because they are measuring weight. But the can dimensions are identical for these two brands and probably many more.

To find the right can, go to your local grocery store with a measuring tape or ruler and measure the cans on the shelf. The store personnel might look at you funny. Just tell them you are buying some coffee to make your Internet access go further.

In choosing your coffee, remember that one can make many cups of coffee to drink. You really have two choices; you can dump the coffee or keep a pot of coffee ready at all times for the other projects in this book. For this chapter, we used an 11.5 oz. Maxwell House coffee can.

# Preparing the Can

It's time to get the can ready to be converted into a directional antenna. You can do this in two steps: preparation and cleaning.

## Step 1: Preparing the Can Opening

The coffee can you purchased probably has a plastic cover on the top and a metal cover protecting the coffee freshness. Remove the plastic lid and put it aside; you will use it later.

You will also want to make sure that the can itself is intact with no indentations. Most cans will have ridges around the circumference of the can which are okay; you just want to make sure that it has not been dropped or mishandled. These indentations or dents can affect the efficiency of the can.

The coffee can will be sealed in one of two ways. With many of the older coffee cans, you needed to open the can with a can opener and discard the removed lid. If this is the coffee can you have, make sure that you grind down or file the inside edge of the can so that it is smooth.

FIGURE 3-5: The empty coffee can.

If it's a newer can, it will have a thick tin foil covering with a ring to pull the cover off. Simply remove the cover and discard it.

## Step 2: Cleaning the Can

While having coffee grounds in the antenna will not affect its operation much, it sure can make a mess of things, so make sure that you clean the can out well. Also make sure that you clean the opening of any foreign objects, such as glue, pieces of the original tin or tin foil cover. The coffee can should now look similar to that shown in Figure 3-5.

# Where to Drill

We will be using a copper wedge as the driven element or radiator. The location and length of this element is extremely important. Although we will not be going too deep into the math here, it's important to understand where this driven element is to be installed.

The rule of thumb is that the driven element should be at one quarter of the "closed-space wavelength" from the inside edge of the can when the connector is installed. The difficulty here is that the closed-space wavelength will vary based on can and radiator dimensions.

Table 3-1 shows some of these dimensions for channels 1, 6, and 11 using two different types of radiators. A narrow-band pole, and wideband wedge. The wideband wedge needs to be built only for channel 6 because it operates well across the entire Wi-Fi range of frequencies.

On our can, with an inner diameter of 100 mm, this offset was slightly more than 1 inch or 27 mm. Once you have this measurement, it is time to prepare the hole in the can where the N-Connector is to be installed.

Remember to measure this carefully, because a mistake means you need to buy and use more coffee.

**Table 3-1    Radiator Offset: Distances From Back of Can to Drill-Point**

| Radiator Type | Channel | Frequency (Hz) | Offset for Can Diameter 90 mm | Offset for Can Diameter 100 mm | Offset for Can Diameter 110 mm |
|---|---|---|---|---|---|
| Round pole or wire | 1 | 2.412 | 53 mm | 45 mm | 42 mm |
| Round pole or wire | 6 | 2.437 | 51 mm | 44 mm | 41 mm |
| Round pole or wire | 11 | 2.462 | 50 mm | 44 mm | 40 mm |
| Wedge | 6 | 2.437 | 29 mm | 27 mm | 26 mm |

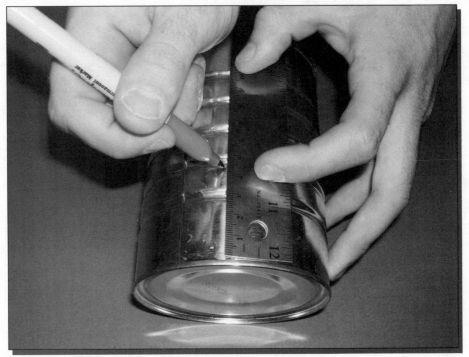

FIGURE 3-6: Marking the correct location for the N-Connector.

## Step 1: Measuring the Distance to the Opening

As mentioned earlier, measuring the distance to the opening is critical to the operation and efficiency of the antenna. The old saying "measure twice and cut once" is also true here. But instead, remember to "measure twice and drill once."

Measure the correct distance from the top of the ridge at the bottom of the can, as shown in Figure 3-6.

When you measure this distance, disregard the bottom lip of the can. This crimped edge of the can has no influence on the interior workings of the waveguide. You are only interested in the bottom material of the can, which becomes the back of your can antenna.

## Step 2: Starting Small

There are several ways to get the hole for the N-Connector the right size. The method you use is up to you. The final hole should be the diameter of the N-Connector stem.

In one method you can drill a small hole and work your way up to the desired hole size. Another method, which is more time-consuming, is to use a nail to make the initial hole and

FIGURE 3-7: Drilling a hole in the can.

use a file or cutter to enlarge the hole. If you use this method, make sure you don't dent the side of the can. The can should stay completely round.

We drilled the hole using a 3/4 inch drill bit, as shown in Figure 3-7.

## Step 3: Preparing for the Connector

There are different types of N-Connectors that you can use for this project. The type does not really matter. As you can see from Figure 3-8, our connector had four screw holes (one at each corner). The best way to ensure that the connector is installed properly is to insert it into the opening you created in Step 2, line it up, and mark out the holes for the four mounting screws. Once this is done, you can drill them with a drill of the same diameter as the mounting screws.

## Step 4: Finishing the Hole

The final step in preparing the N-Connector hole is cleaning it. Using a small file, make sure that there are no edges or burrs around the openings. This will ensure a tight fit when the connector is inserted and connected to the coffee can.

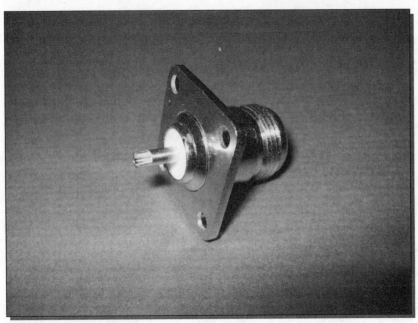

FIGURE 3-8: The N-Connector.

# Fitting the Radiating Element

One of the most important parts of the antenna is the radiating element. While different shapes will change the way the antenna works, its signal strength, and its efficiency, it is not super critical if you do not get it bang on.

The radiating element can be of three shapes (see Figure 3-9):

- Round
- Wedge
- Cone

FIGURE 3-9: Three shapes for the radiating element.

## Table 3-2    Length of Radiator Elements

| Radiator Type | Channel | Frequency (Hz) | Wavelength of Frequency (mm) | Length of Radiator (mm) |
|---|---|---|---|---|
| Round pole or wire | 1 | 2.412 | 124 | 31.0 |
| Round pole or wire | 6 | 2.437 | 123 | 30.7 |
| Round pole or wire | 11 | 2.462 | 122 | 30.5 |
| Wedge or cone | 6 | 2.437 | 123 | 24 |

While the cone shape is the most efficient, it is also the hardest one to make. So, we will only go into detail for the round element and wedge element. The round element is very simple to make since it is simply the core copper conductor from an LMR-400 coaxial cable (used extensively in Chapter 1). The round element also has the most narrow frequency band. If you create an antenna using the round element, effective power will drop considerably across all of the channels.

The wedge element is a bit more complex to make, but it has great coverage of the Wi-Fi channels. It's a little less efficient than the cone, but not significantly. The wedge is worth the extra time and effort, and it's what we use when playing with the can antenna toy.

**Tip** The cone element follows closely with the wedge shape in dimensions. If you want to try to make one, use the same dimensions and spacing as the wedge (6 mm diameter at the top, 1 mm diameter at the bottom).

The length of the radiating element is important. Table 3-2 shows specific lengths for your radiating element. Note that can dimensions do not factor into the element size.

With our wedge antenna, we needed the radiating element to be 24 mm in length. Figure 3-10 shows how to measure the radiating element.

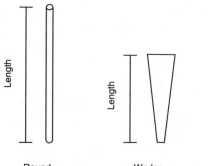

Round          Wedge

FIGURE 3-10: Measurements of a radiating element.

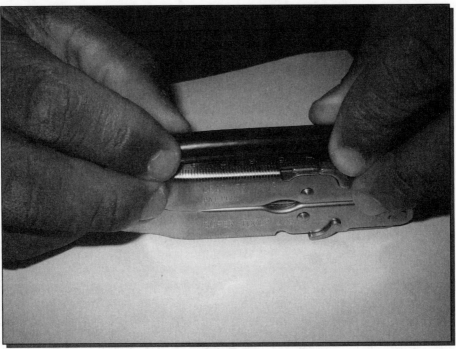

FIGURE 3-11: Starting with a piece of coaxial cable.

Radiator element length is measured from the end of the connector jack, not the length of the piece of copper alone. Wait to make the final cut until after soldering the connector in place and measuring the connector and element together.

## A Round Radiating Element

Making the round radiating element is extremely simple because it is the core copper conductor from a coaxial cable. To make the round radiating element, follow these steps:

### Step 1: Cut Too Much

Once you know the length of the radiating element, you will need to make sure you have the correct length. Having said that, make sure that you don't trim the coaxial cable to the exact length of the element. Instead, cut extra. Starting with a piece of coaxial cable that is twice the final length is a good starting point, as shown in Figure 3-11.

### Step 2: Strip the Insulation

Using a single-sided razor blade, strip the outer jacket, inner shield, and dielectric core as described in Chapter 1. As Figure 3-12 illustrates, you will be left with just the core copper

FIGURE 3-12: The core copper conductor.

conductor. Make sure that you add a little bit to the length of the connector with respect to the length determined in Table 3-2, to make sure that the radiating element can be inserted and soldered into the N-Connector.

### Step 3: Cut to Length

Now that you have the core conductor to work with, start by trimming one side as square with the edge as possible. Then measure the desired distance from that trimmed edge and cut the final length. Ensure that you take into account the portion of the conductor that will fit into the N-Connector body.

If you are not sure about the length, wait until after you solder the conductor into the body before making any final length adjustments.

## A Wedge Radiating Element

Making a wedge radiating element is not a complex process but it does take some talent to solder it to the connector.

To cover the Wi-Fi spectrum, the wedge radiating element needs to be 1 mm wide at the base (where it connects to the N-Connector) and 6 mm at the tip. Figure 3-13 shows the wedge.

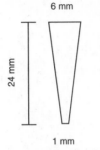

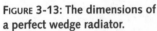

**FIGURE 3-13: The dimensions of a perfect wedge radiator.**

One way to make this wedge is to start with a copper embossing sheet (this is available in most arts and crafts stores). Simply trace out the desired wedge shape of the radiating element and cut to size with either a knife or strong scissors. We created the wedge in Figure 3-14 using the one foot-square copper embossing sheet.

A second way to make this wedge shape is to use a hammer to hammer out the shape. As you can imagine, this process is more work-intensive, but requires less precision on your part. The object in Figure 3-15 is a cross between the wedge and round element. The forgiving nature of this antenna design allows for a good bit of fudging.

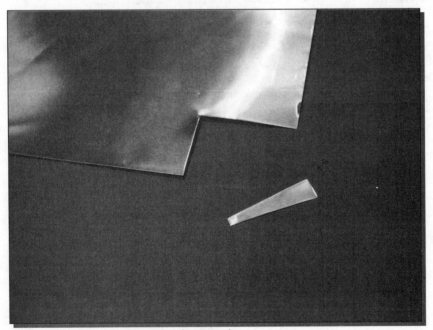

**FIGURE 3-14: Copper wedge and embossing sheet.**

FIGURE 3-15: A bashed-out round connector with a wedge end.

This process produces a semi-wedge-shaped element that is not as efficient as the "true" wedge radiating element, but is better than the round radiating element.

# Final Construction and Weatherizing

This is the final stage of the coffee can antenna project. Time to put it all together!

## Step 1: Building the N-Connector

Putting this together is fairly straightforward. The radiating element should fit inside the opening of the N-Connector. This might be a snug fit, but that's okay. If you find that the radiating element will not fit properly, sand one end of the connector using some sandpaper until the element fits.

When the fit is snug, solder the radiating element to the connector to make a permanent and electrically strong connection. Soldering even a small amount will make the difference between a great antenna and a lousy one.

Once this is done, you should have a completed Connector/Element assembly similar to the one shown in Figure 3-16.

FIGURE 3-16: The completed Connector/Element assembly.

## Step 2: Mounting the N-Connector

You can now insert the completed assembly into the hole you drilled in the side of the coffee can. As we mentioned, your N-Connector might be different than the one we used. Ours had four mounting holes. Mount the connector assembly to the coffee can using the screws provided. Make sure that the screws are just the right length or only slightly longer. If they are too long and protrude into the can more than a few millimeters, the signal will be adversely affected. Figure 3-17 shows the connector mounted to the can.

Also ensure that the wedge's flat edge is parallel to the bottom base of the can (see Figure 3-18). This isn't critical, but it looks better!

## Step 3: Weatherizing the Antenna

Weatherizing the antenna is easy. If you plan on using the antenna outdoors, you may want to spray paint the exterior of the antenna with a rust proof paint. To protect the interior of the antenna, simply cover the opening with the original plastic cover that came with the can (you may want to glue this cover on).

FIGURE 3-17: The connector mounted in the can.

FIGURE 3-18: The mounted N-Connector assembly.

FIGURE 3-19: The completed can antenna hooked up to a laptop.

**Caution**

Some plastics block microwave energy. To test if the lid to your can is microwave safe and will keep your antenna working great, try the following: Using a standard microwave oven, place the lid on the floor of the microwave at least 2 inches from a cup of water. Start the microwave and run it until the water starts to boil. Carefully check the lid to see if it's hot or not. If it's cool to the touch, microwave energy does not affect the plastic and the lid is a good covering.

**Note**

The cover of an antenna that keeps weather out but does not interfere with the antenna operation or signal is called a *radome*. In a sense, the plastic lid on your can antenna is the radome. Neat!

Your can antenna is now done! Now put the antenna to use by attaching it to the cable and pigtail you built in Chapter 1 (see Figure 3-19).

# Extra: Antenna Simulation and Patterns

There is some free antenna simulation software available on the Web called 4NEC2. The basis of the simulation is the "Numerical Electromagnetic Code," hence NEC. This software can be used to simulate thousands of different antennas. One such antenna is our sweet little waveguide

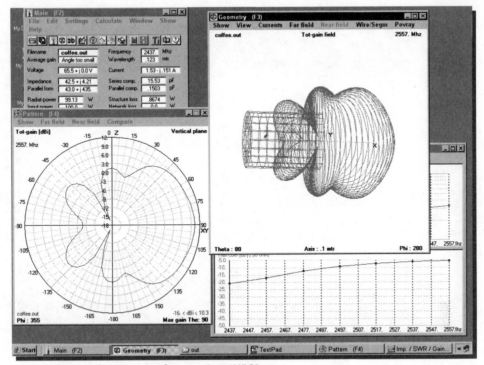

FIGURE 3-20: Can antenna simulation using 4NEC2.

antenna. The screenshot in Figure 3-20 shows the simulation for the can antenna we built in this chapter. You can obtain a recent copy of NEC2 from the "links" section at www.nec2.org and download the coffee can antenna simulation model from www.nec2.org/coffee.txt.

Antenna radiation patterns are created to show the strength and direction for antennas. There are two types of antenna radiation patterns: vertical plane (or E-plane) and horizontal plane (or H-plane). Antenna manufacturers use both of these pattern diagrams to show how an antenna works.

The antenna radiation patterns in Figure 3-21 are for a common dipole omnidirectional antenna. This type of antenna simulation makes distinction between the vertical versus horizontal. An omni antenna radiation pattern looks a lot like a flattened donut.

The diagram in Figure 3-22 shows the relationship between the two pattern diagrams. Notice the vertical plane is perpendicular to the Earth's surface, while the horizontal plane is parallel to the Earth's surface. Each plane is like a two-dimensional slice or circle with the center of the slice at the center of the antenna.

Moreover, 4NEC2 has a neat 3-D engine to show you what the antenna would look like if you could see RF radiation. See the screenshot in Figure 3-23 for a 3-D simulation of the can antenna from this chapter.

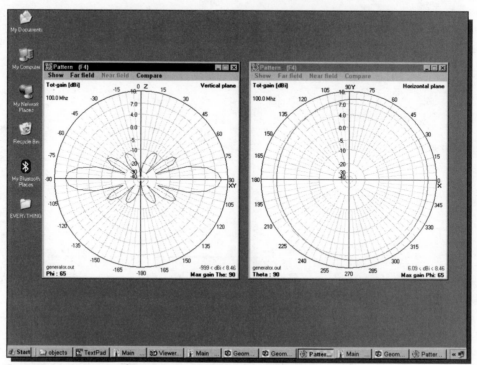

FIGURE 3-21: Antenna radiation patterns for an omni antenna.

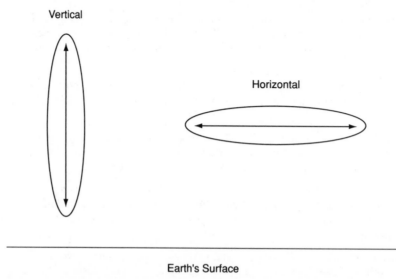

FIGURE 3-22: Relationship of a vertical (E) plane and a horizontal (H) plane.

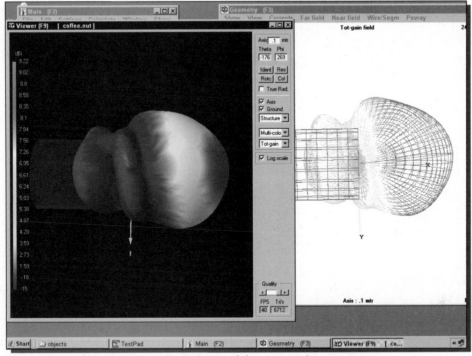

FIGURE 3-23: A three-dimensional simulation of the waveguide can antenna.

This antenna works great in one general direction. Also, it has about the same gain vertically as it does horizontally.

# Summary

In this chapter, you learned about waveguides and the types of can antennas you can build on your own. The waveguide antenna is very easy to build, but you need to know where to drill. You also learned about antenna simulation and what antenna radiation patterns are and how to read them.

With the knowledge from this chapter, you can go on to build and experiment with many different types of antennas. And understanding antenna radiation patterns puts you in the driver's seat when choosing what antenna would work best for any situation.

Next up, let's add a high-gain antenna to your wireless access point. You'll learn how to choose the antenna type: omni versus directional. And you'll find out how to stay within the spirit of the law when it comes to RF power. Read on to get the maximum range out of your wireless network.

# Modifying Your Access Point with a High-Gain Antenna

You buy a wireless access point and a laptop card with visions of working or surfing the net in the kitchen, in the bedroom, on the deck, or in a hammock in the backyard. No longer will you be chained to a desk or a table! Only one problem: No matter where you place the access point in your house, there are significant areas where your laptop can't maintain a consistent connection and downloads take forever when you do have a connection. In other words, in technical terms, "coverage stinks."

What do you do? One likely answer is to use a high-gain antenna for the access point. A high-gain antenna multiplies the access point's range for both transmission and reception. That is, it boosts both receiver sensitivity and transmitter output. Increased signal strength means faster transmissions, too, since most access points are configured to drop back to a lower data rate when the quality of the connection deteriorates. Although an indoor high-gain antenna may cost about as much as the access point itself, (an outdoor model would cost even more), it will be worth it if it makes the difference between a pokey, limited, unreliable network and one that is fast, far-reaching, and robust. A sample setup is shown in Figure 4-1.

The mechanics of attaching the antenna can be really easy, especially if you have a Linksys access point. You do have to make sure that you get (or build) the right pigtail cable for connecting the access point to the antenna cable. You should also choose an antenna that will cover the intended area while minimizing interference. Positioning and aiming the antenna for best results can take a bit of experimentation, too.

You should be aware that it is possible to make your Wi-Fi network *too* powerful. As wireless networks extend their reach, they are more likely to "jostle" one another. Your neighbors could start picking up your signals, or you might start picking up theirs. The FCC has rules to keep such interference to reasonable levels. There are also FCC safety rules about how much RF energy human beings should be exposed to over how long a period of time. By keeping interference and safety guidelines in mind when you design your system, you'll protect yourself and others, and you'll have the added comfort of knowing that you're legal.

## in this chapter

- ☑ Selecting the right antenna
- ☑ Following government regulations
- ☑ Surveying the site
- ☑ Attaching an antenna to your access point
- ☑ Using an amplifier

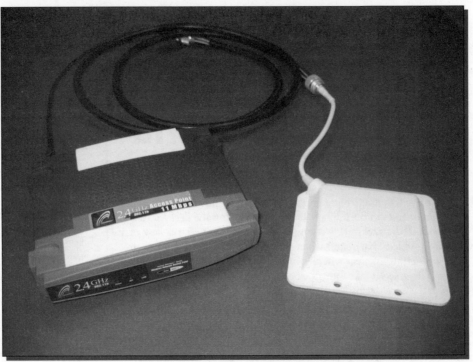

FIGURE 4-1: System using a Linksys WAP11 with a high-gain external antenna.

**Note** The chances of getting busted for going over the limit for an indoor network are about the same as for removing one of those little "do not remove on pain of death" tags on a mattress. Basically, someone has to complain before the FCC does anything. However, if you are counting on this system, say for your business, it's best to stay within the rules.

If you get decent performance when the access point and the client are close, but things get flakier the farther away you get, a high-gain antenna on the access point could be just the thing to pump up your signal.

Here's what you will need for this project:

1. Wireless access point with an external antenna connector and detachable antenna

2. High-gain antenna

3. Pigtail cable

4. Antenna cable

5. Hardware and tools (such as screws and screwdriver) for mounting the antenna

6. Opposable thumbs

See Chapter 1 for instructions on building the antenna cable. In fact, even if you don't want to make your own antenna cable, Chapter 1 has good background information for many of the topics in this chapter.

**Note** Although the 2.4 GHz technology is relatively uniform worldwide, the rules about who can use it and how it can be used vary from country to country. If you are located outside the United States, manufacturers and governmental agencies may be good sources of information on what is allowed in your region.

# Choosing an Antenna

There are two kinds of high-gain antennas: *omni* and *directional*. An omni antenna transmits and receives in all directions, though usually more horizontally than vertically: Its radiation pattern looks like a doughnut, with the antenna at the doughnut hole.

A directional antenna transmits and receives in a narrow beam, usually within a 30 to 60 degree "slice" of a full circle (see Figure 4-2.). You can envision its radiation pattern as a spot-light. A directional antenna with a fairly broad beam, such as 120 degrees, is called a "sector" antenna.

Chapter 5 has a section on *Picking the Right Antenna* that provides some more information on this topic.

The focused beam of a directional antenna provides three advantages: First, by focusing your beam, you get a more powerful signal for the same transmission power. Second, you're less likely to cause or experience interference problems, because you can aim your transmission beam and focus your receptivity. Third, directional antennas, due to their reduced potential for interference, typically can have higher gain than omnis. You should use a directional antenna if possible. If you need broader coverage than a highly directional antenna can provide, you may be able to compromise on a sector antenna, and put it in one corner of the desired coverage area. (See Figure 4-3.)

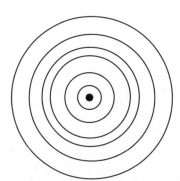

FIGURE 4-2: Omni antenna (left) and directional antenna (right).

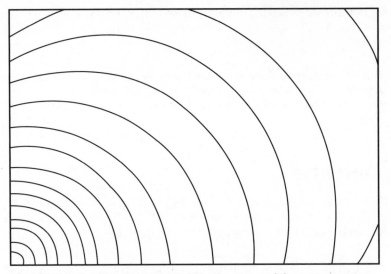

FIGURE 4-3: A directional antenna (left) in the corner of the coverage area.

With both omni and directional antennas, there is an inverse relationship between gain and coverage. For an omni antenna, the higher the gain, the flatter its radiation pattern. So if you want one access point to cover two floors of your house, for example, you may be better off with a medium-gain omni than a high-gain one. Similarly, higher gain directional antennas usually have more focused beams.

If you need both broad coverage and high gain, you may need to get two antennas and "aim" them in different directions. For example, you could set up two 120 degree sector antennas for 240 degree coverage. The usual approach for this kind of setup, however, is to attach the antennas to two different access points and run the access points on two different channels to minimize any possible interference.

# Staying Legal

FCC regulations specify three things:

- Maximum permitted transmitter power output (TPO) of the radio in the access point, before the signal reaches the antenna
- Maximum permitted antenna gain without requiring a reduction in TPO
- Required reduction in TPO for every decibel (dB) of antenna gain above that maximum

For an introduction to decibels, see *Measuring Line Loss in Decibels* in Chapter 1. We will introduce just one unit of measurement here that wasn't mentioned in Chapter 1: dBi, decibels referenced to an *isotropic* radiator.

**Note** An isotropic radiator transmits equally in all directions. The radiation pattern of a perfect isotropic antenna would look like a beach ball, with the antenna in the center of the ball. The term "isotropic" basically refers to an ideal omni antenna.

For instance, since each 3 dB represents a doubling of power, 6 dBi describes an omni antenna that doubles power twice—that is, one that multiplies power by a factor of four.

The FCC regulations do not talk in terms of omni and directional antennas. Instead, they talk about "point-to-multipoint" and "point-to-point" networks. Strictly speaking, every network in which an access point is accessed by clients is point-to-multipoint in its design. However, the apparent intention of the regulations is to permit more gain for more focused transmissions, because they are less likely to cause interference. It is this intention which is followed in common practice. Thus, omni antennas are treated as point-to-multipoint, while directional antennas are treated as point-to-point. Figure 4-4 shows a point-to-point versus multipoint network.

In addition, the regulations state that each specific antenna model must be certified with each specific access point model, before they can legally be used together. However, we are not aware of any effort to enforce this at the end user level, and common practice seems to be: to stay within certification guidelines, as opposed to actually certifying in every case.

**Caution** We are not attorneys. Our interpretation of FCC regulations and practices is not authoritative. In fact, much of this is under review by the FCC and industry. Regulations or legal definitions may change any time.

## FCC Point-to-Multipoint Rules

Here's a summary of the FCC rules for point-to-multipoint transmissions:

- The radio in the access point can have up to 30 dBm TPO.

- You can have a 6 dBi antenna without reducing TPO. Assuming 30 dBm TPO, that's a 36 dBm signal from the antenna.

- The TPO needs to be reduced 1 dB for every dB of antenna gain over 6 dBi. (In other words, for every step forward, you have to take one step backward.)

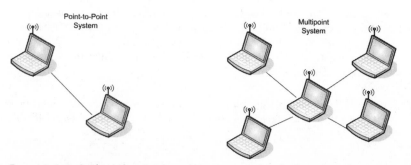

FIGURE 4-4: A single path point-to-point system and multiple path multipoint system.

30 dBm means you take 1 mW and double it ten times (because 30 is 10–3, and 3 dB is a doubling). This works out to a number that is so close to 1 W (1.024 W, to be exact) that everyone just calls it 1 W. Because each 3 dB represents a doubling of wattage, 6 dBi means the maximum permissible transmitted signal from the antenna is 4 W Equivalent Isotropically Radiated Power (EIRP). (1 W × 2 × 2)

The bottom line: If you're using an omni antenna, design your system so that it doesn't radiate more than 4 W EIRP.

The radio in the Linksys BEFW11S4 access point, for instance, puts out 68–78 mW, depending on the channel. Even assuming 100 mW TPO, a 9 dBi antenna would bring that up to just 800 mW EIRP. You'd have to go over 15 dBi before you might be in danger of exceeding the 4 W EIRP limit ($100 \times 2^{(15/3)} = 3200$). With a 78 mW TPO, a 17 dBi antenna is still under the limit (though just barely). ($78 \times 2^{(17/3)} = 3962$)

**Note** You can look up the maximum output of your access point radio on the FCC Web site, if you have the FCC ID of the radio, which should be provided on the access point. For instance, on our Linksys BEFW11S4, the FCC ID of the radio is MXF-C901114. You can go to www.fcc.gov/oet/fccid/ and search on the FCC ID. One place that TPO information should be listed is under RF Exposure Info.

The omni antennas that come with access points are generally 3 dBi or so. Therefore, anything much less than 6 dBi would be only marginally better than the manufacturer's antenna.

Most of the add-on omni antennas on the market are in the 6 to 15 dBi range, which is the sweet spot for equipment like Linksys access points—safely legal yet definitely worthwhile.

## FCC Point-to-Point Rules

Point-to-point rules are the same as point-to-multipoint rules, except that you need to reduce TPO 1 dB for every 3 dBi of antenna gain over 6 dBi. In other words, three steps forward, one step backwards: A big improvement over the corresponding point-to-multipoint rule!

For example, a 24 dBi antenna is 18 dB over a 6 dBi antenna. So, to use a 24 dBi antenna, you would have to lower a 1 W (30 dBm) radio 18/3 or 6 dB to 24 dBm or 1/4 W. (18 steps forward, 6 steps back.)

In practice, many access points don't allow you to adjust the TPO. However, you can take into account the fact that the existing TPO of the access point is less than 1 W. For instance, 125 mW is 9 dB less than 1 W. Therefore, we would be very safe in using the 24 dBi antenna in the previous example with our Linksys BEFW11S4, because its radio comes "pre-lowered" more than the required 6 dBm.

**Note** Some wireless devices let you reduce TPO, allowing you to use a more powerful antenna without increasing EIRP. The main advantage of doing this is the increased receive sensitivity of the more powerful antenna.

In fact, the rated Linksys TPO of 78 mW is actually about 11 dBm below 1 W. Therefore, if you wanted to push the limits, you could use a 39 dBi antenna—33 dB above 6 dBi—because 33 dB divided by three is 11. (33 steps forward, 11 steps back.)

In practice, most of the available directional antennas for Linksys access points are in the 12 to 27 dBi range, keeping them within the intention of the FCC regulations.

## FCC Safety Rules

The 2.4 GHz frequency band is used in microwave ovens, because RF in this band tends to generate a lot of heat when it hits something. This heat can be dangerous to the human body. For this reason, the FCC has specified Maximum Permissible Exposure (MPE) limits for 2.4 GHz signals.

The FCC has also issued a bulletin, OET Bulletin 65, "Evaluating Compliance with FCC-Specified Guidelines for Human Exposure to Radio Frequency Radiation" that spells out the guidelines. (It's at http://ftp.fcc.gov/oet/info/documents/bulletins/#65.)

These guidelines deal with how much radiation hits people, not how much the antenna puts out. As with a microwave oven, the size of the heated body is also important. Specifically, the FCC guideline states that potentially hazardous exposures may occur at levels over 4 watts per kilogram (4 W/kg) averaged over the entire body. Even continuous exposure to 4 W/kg or less should be okay.

We're not going to get into the mathematics of calculating exposure levels. Also, we are not doctors, nor are we dispensing medical advice. But we will note that the exposure is inversely proportional to the square of the distance (double the distance, one fourth the exposure). Therefore, the easy way to minimize health hazards is to avoid spending extended periods of time near high-gain antennas. Figure 4-5 shows the relative exposure from someone standing 3 feet and 6 feet from the antenna. We would not stay within two feet of an ordinary Linksys access point with 3 dBi antennas for more than five minutes on a regular basis. And we'd double the distance for each 6 dBi of added antenna gain.

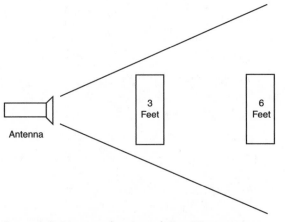

**FIGURE 4-5: Diagram showing relative RF exposure.**

# The Site Survey

To help you pick the right antenna for the job, first survey the site to get an idea what coverage pattern you want, and what degree of signal loss you are currently encountering. Start by mapping out the site on a piece of graph paper, noting possible locations for the high-gain antenna. Then place the access point (with the existing antenna) in a possible location, and walk around with your laptop to the areas you want to cover. If you have NetStumbler on your laptop, you may be able to use it to measure the signal-to-noise ratio (SNR) in each desired coverage location. The higher the SNR, the better. Lacking that, just note whether the laptop can connect to the network, and if it can, how long it takes to perform some common tasks, such as transferring files. See the basic site survey document in Figure 4-6.

If nothing else, this will give you a point of comparison, to determine how much boost you get from your high-gain antenna. In addition, you'll probably get a better idea what kinds of transmission losses you're experiencing. Typically, you may see three kinds of losses: propagation losses, multipath losses (signal fading), and interference.

## Propagation Losses

Propagation loss represents the "resistance" of whatever the RF has to pass through. Every medium, including air, has a particular loss at a given frequency. The loss is proportional to

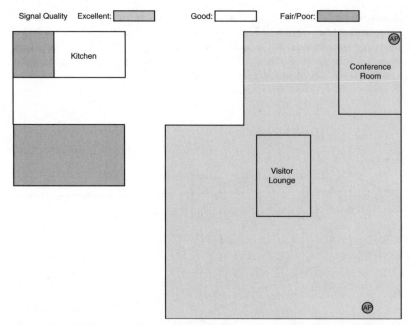

FIGURE 4-6: A site survey document created from a hand-drawing on graph paper.

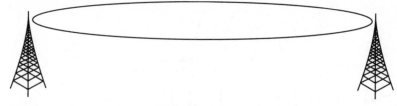

**FIGURE 4-7: The Fresnel Zone is like a football.**

the distance that the signal has to travel through the medium. For example, the signal will probably lose about 6 dB going through a wall with 2-by-4 wood studs and sheetrock on both sides.

Beyond about 20 feet from the access point, propagation losses can increase at up to 30 dB per 100 feet, depending on building construction and layout. You'll get losses not only from walls, ceilings and floors, but even from furniture and people.

Visualize the signal as half a football, with the antenna at the point. Beyond 20 feet or so from the access point, anything that pokes into that area (called the *Fresnel Zone*) will degrade the signal. See Figure 4-7 for an example.

Fresnel Zone incursions are a secondary factor when it comes to interference. The most critical factor is objects that are in the direct line-of-sight (LOS) between the access point antenna and clients. However, objects below the LOS but in the Fresnel Zone can have a significant effect, as well. That's why, in long-distance outdoor installations, antennas are usually positioned higher than is necessary just for LOS. Outdoors, it's standard practice to calculate the size of the Fresnel Zone and use that to determine how high the antenna should be. Indoors, antennas may be installed in the attic or on the ceiling, in order to avoid Fresnel Zone incursions. If that's not possible, you just have to get a more powerful antenna, in order to overcome the losses.

Whether you can clear the obstacles, or whether you just have to compensate for them, it's good to know what your Fresnel Zone Clearance is. There are simple calculators available on the Web that will allow you to calculate this very quickly. (For instance, www.thirdheight. com/support/downloads/wireless/SOM_calcs.xls.)

This calculator will help you not only with Fresnel Zones, but with your overall "link budget," a calculation to determine whether the signal transmitted from your antenna is powerful enough to reach the intended receivers. A link budget calculation takes into account a variety of factors, including TPO, transmit antenna gain, losses in the transmission antenna cable, free space propagation losses, Fresnel Zone losses, losses in the receive antenna cable, receive antenna gain, and receiver sensitivity. Other factors such as connectors and lightning arresters in the cables can also be taken into account. (Figure 4-8 shows the variables involved in a typical link budget calculation.)

A common rule of thumb is that the signal should be 10 dB stronger than the minimum required for communication. This 10 dB is referred to as the *System Operating Margin (SOM)*.

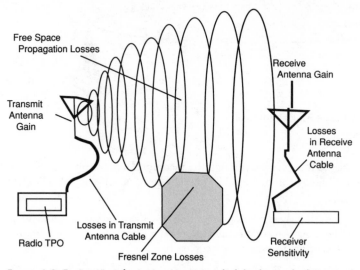

FIGURE 4-8: Factors to take into account in a link budget calculation.

## Multipath Losses and Interference

Multipath losses occur when signals take different paths to a receiver. If one path is significantly longer than the other, the peaks and troughs of the two signals will be significantly out of sync with one another ("out of phase") when they get to the receiver. Signals that are totally out of phase (180 degrees) will completely cancel one another, as the troughs of one signal cancel the peaks of the other (see Figure 4-9). In practice, the phases of the two signals will usually drift constantly, so the signal cancellation changes, resulting in a constantly fluctuating signal ("signal fade").

Having two receiving antennas usually helps substantially. Phase cancellation will be different for the two antennas, because of the differences in the length of the two paths required to reach the antennas. With properly spaced antennas, the signal at one antenna can be strong when the other is weak.

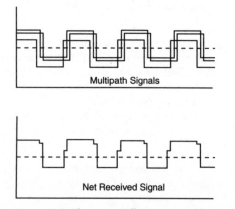

FIGURE 4-9: Phase cancellation caused by multipath interference.

When you attach a high-gain antenna to an access point, you lose the advantage of two antennas, and you tend to increase multipath losses. The high-gain antenna should more than make up for this, but you may want to take this effect into account in calculating your antenna gain requirements. If your connection seems to continuously fade in and out, suspect multipath losses.

Interference may come from any other equipment running at 2.4 GHz (including other Wi-Fi networks), particularly if they're using the same channel as you are, or equipment generating broad spectrum RF. Interference is often "bursty" in nature, as the interfering equipment is seldom operating full-out all the time. If your network experiences sudden and seemingly random attacks of deteriorating performance, look for a source of interference. You may be able to change channels or locate your network equipment and antenna to get away from the offending source. Otherwise, you'll have to up your power to overcome the interference.

# Attaching a High-Gain Antenna

To attach the high-gain antenna to the access point, you basically build a "chain" with four links in it: the access point, the pigtail, the antenna cable, and the antenna. (See Figure 4-10.)

To attach the antenna to the access point, follow these steps. Assuming the access point is already working correctly, and you have good cables with the right connectors, these three steps should take just a few minutes. (We'll talk more about the cables in a minute.)

1. Configure the access point to use only one of its two antennas (optional, but recommended if your access point supports it).

2. Attach the pigtail cable to the access point.

3. Run the antenna cable from the pigtail to the antenna.

4. Position and install the antenna.

And you're done!

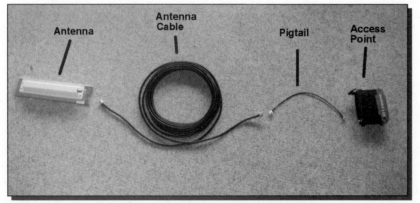

FIGURE 4-10: The chain of components in your antenna project.

**Tip** Try using the Cantenna you built in Chapter 3 to boost gain on an access point. This antenna works as well on an access point as it does on a laptop computer.

## Step 1: Configure the Access Point to Use Just One Antenna

Since you're going to all the trouble of installing a high-gain antenna, you want to make sure that the access point uses it consistently. You configure this using the access point's firmware. It takes just a minute or two. Here is a guideline for the process on a Linksys WAP11 or BEFW11S4 access point:

1. Access the access point using your browser. If you haven't changed the IP address, it's 192.168.1.1. Enter your username and password. If you haven't changed it yet, the default is a blank username, and a password of "admin".

2. When you get to the Setup screen, click the Advanced tab in the upper-right corner.

3. In the Advanced section, click on the Wireless tab.

4. Go to the Antenna Selection drop-down menu, and select either Right Spread or Left Spread, depending on which antenna output you are using. (You look at the access point while viewing the front panel when determining right and left.)

5. Click the Apply button at the bottom of the screen.

Figure 4-11 shows the Wireless tab in the Advanced section of the Linksys configuration program.

In case you're curious, the Default setting is a "diversity" setting, in which both antennas are active. Diversity Spread should automatically select the antenna with the strongest signal. However, since you know which one is always going to be the high-gain antenna, we're choosing not to depend on the automated function.

**Tip** Some access points transmit through only one antenna. Make sure you choose the correct antenna. Vendors tend to refrain from listing these engineering anomalies, so your best bet is to test the antenna after installation to make sure which transmit antenna works best.

## Step 2: Attach the Pigtail Cable to the Access Point

Connecting a pigtail to an access point can be extremely easy, if you have a pigtail with the proper connector, and if the access point manufacturer designed the antenna for easy removal. Linksys access points, for example, have easy-to-remove antennas. The difficulty of finding the proper connectors argues for buying rather than building pigtails.

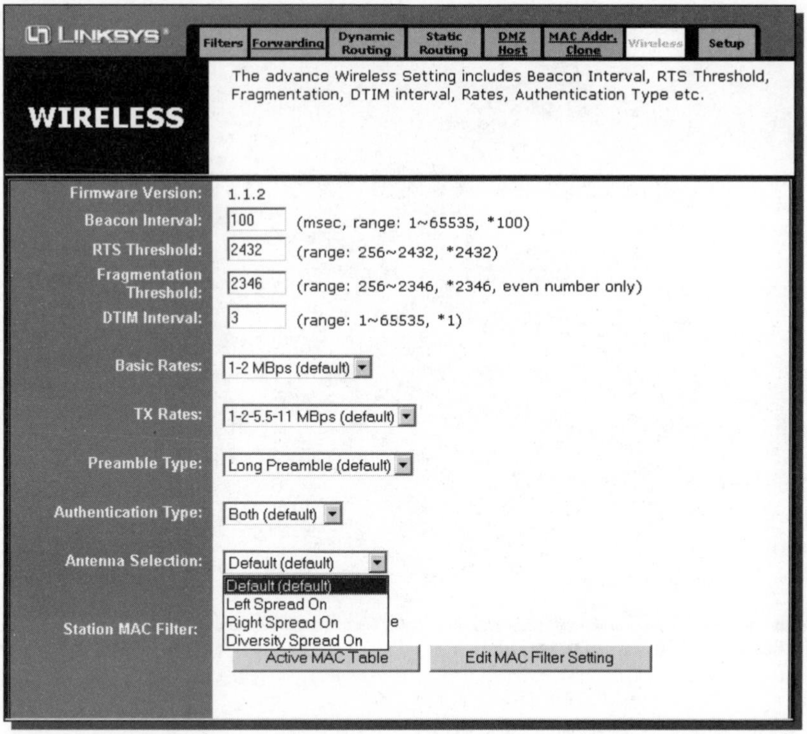

FIGURE 4-11: The Linksys configuration program: Advanced section, Wireless tab, Antenna Selection menu.

## Linksys Makes It Easy

If you have a Linksys WAP11 or BEFW11S4 access point, connecting your high-gain antenna to the access point is a snap, because these Linksys access points have detachable antennas. (Here's where your opposable thumb comes in). Just grip the antenna base firmly between thumb and forefinger and turn counter-clockwise to remove. (See Figure 4-12.)

Other access points may not be so easy. We recommend an access point with external connectors and detachable antennas, because otherwise you may have to open up the access point, disconnect the existing antenna wires, and solder a new connector onto the wires—undoubtedly voiding any warranty in the process. Figure 4-13 shows a hard-wired antenna in a Cisco access point.

## The FCC Makes It Hard

The other area where you might run into a slight hiccup is in building a pigtail to connect the access point to the antenna cable. The antenna side of the pigtail is no problem: Your antenna cable probably has standard female N-Connectors. So, to make the connection, the pigtail needs to have a standard, easy-to-find male N-Connector.

FIGURE 4-12: Removing the original antenna.

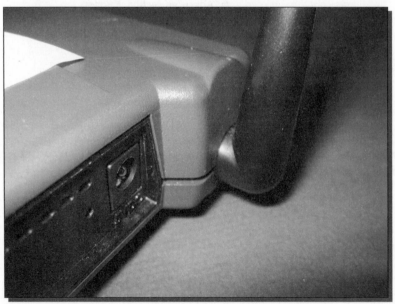

FIGURE 4-13: Cisco access point with a soldered antenna connector.

FIGURE 4-14: Standard male connector (left) and standard female connector (right).

**Note** The male connector has a pin in the middle. The female connector has a socket. In addition, male connectors have threads on the inside of the connector body, while female connectors are threaded on the outside. (See Figure 4-14.)

The problem stems from the connector on the access point. The FCC mandated weird connectors for Wi-Fi antennas, because they were afraid that hobbyists would do things like connecting high-gain antennas to access points and possibly jack-up the power of their wireless networks beyond the legal limit. (Why would anybody want to do that?) They didn't make it illegal to hook up a high-gain antenna, but they did try to ensure that you would use only antennas specifically designed for the wireless system. They did this by specifying connectors that you couldn't find in your local Radio Shack, and which are incompatible with standard antenna connectors.

Linksys, for example, satisfies the weirdness requirement with reverse polarity (RP) TNC connectors. At first glance, Reverse Polarity (also called "Reverse Gender") connectors look like normal male and female connectors. On closer inspection, however, you'll find a major difference: The male connector has a socket, and the female connector has a pin. The Linksys access points, for instance, have Reverse Polarity female connectors (female body with a pin), so the

FIGURE 4-15: Reverse Polarity TNC connectors.

pigtail has to have a Reverse Polarity male (male body with a socket). Figure 4-15 shows RP-TNC connectors.

Another common example is the reverse polarity SMA connector used on many D-Link products. Figure 4-16 shows RP-SMA connectors.

Don't confuse RP with Reverse Threading (RT), which apparently also satisfies the weirdness requirement, and which refers to male bodies threaded to turn counter-clockwise to tighten, unlike normal male bodies, which turn clockwise to tighten.

The FCC's desire to thwart users wishing to attach standard antennas to Wi-Fi equipment has been less than entirely successful. However, the weirdness requirement has created a thriving pigtail industry, which you will now be supporting with a modest purchase (assuming you follow the advice in the next paragraph).

In Chapter 1, we recommended purchasing pre-configured pigtails for wireless client adapters, because of the hassle of soldering the tiny connectors needed to fit PC card connections. Buying pigtails is the easy way to go for access points as well. There aren't any tiny PC card connectors to deal with. But you would probably have to special-order the RP connector for the pigtail anyway, so why not just go ahead and special-order the pigtail itself?

## Step 3: Run the Antenna Cable From the Pigtail to the Antenna

Ultimately, you'll probably install the antenna, and then run the cable to it. However, before you do that, we suggest that you put everything together in one room. That way, if it doesn't

FIGURE 4-16: Reverse Polarity SMA connectors.

seem to be working correctly, you'll easily be able to do tests (such as cable continuity tests) without running back and forth between the access point and the antenna.

When you do install the cable in its final position, avoid crimping and excessive bending of the cable. Also avoid possible sources of interference, which would primarily be other equipment operating in the 2.4 GHz band (like cordless phones and microwave ovens), but could include sources of broad spectrum RF such as fluorescent lights.

The shorter the cable, the better. Consider locating the access point and the antenna within a few feet of one another, as this will give you the highest power output for your antenna. In out-door installations, this may not be possible, since you may need to put the antenna in a location where power cannot easily be run. However, indoors, you should be able to get power almost anywhere fairly easily, even if it means running a long extension cord.

## Step 4: Position and Install the Antenna

Positioning the antenna may be an iterative process. If you have multiple possible locations for the antenna, you'll want to do some testing in each location before settling on the best one. Mounting the antenna higher up, like on a wall or on top of a file cabinet, is usually better. Think light bulb or flashlight. Does the room light up better when the light is near the ceiling away from obstructions or down on the floor behind a desk? Figure 4-17 shows a typical install of a high-gain antenna.

FIGURE 4-17: A wall-mounted high-gain antenna.

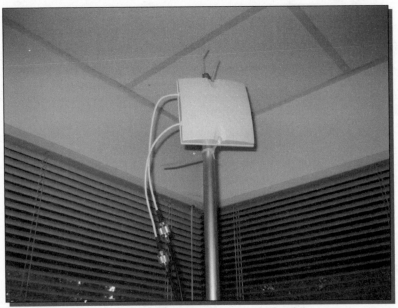

FIGURE 4-18: Antenna on a pole during a site survey test point.

Do not damage the housing of the antenna, or any metallic surfaces. Often, an antenna will use a metal backplane as a reflector to increase the gain. If you drill through that reflector, the gain will be adversely affected.

As a final step, perform another site survey as described earlier in this chapter. This time, use the new configuration with the new antenna. Figure 4-18 shows a site survey test point with a high-gain antenna.

| Tip | For maximum mobility, fill a sports bag with a 12-volt battery, a DC-to-AC inverter, and an access point. The access point is configured to transmit a beacon so the client can monitor signal strength. This setup keeps you highly mobile for hours during the survey—no power cords. |

# What About Signal Amplification?

This is an appropriate place to mention the alternative of using amplifiers, as opposed to antennas, to boost signals. For instance, Linksys sells a Wireless Signal Booster (WSB24) that amplifies both transmit and receive signals. Tests indicate that amplifiers are effective for improving connection reliability and throughput within your existing coverage area. However, a high-gain antenna is still the way to go if you need to expand your coverage (see www.smallnetbuilder.com/Reviews-38-ProdID-WSB24-1.php.).

Figure 4-19 shows a test of the Linksys WSB24 using NetStumbler in power monitor mode.

FIGURE 4-19: Linksys WSB24 adds power to a Linksys access point.

**Tip** RF signal amplifiers work in different ways. Make sure you understand the input and output requirements before investing in an antenna and configuring your access point. For example, the Linksys WSB24 requires antenna diversity to be enabled on its input. It then converts the signal to only transmit through the Right and receive only on the Left antenna jacks.

## Summary

In this chapter, you've learned the basics required to successfully install a high-gain antenna, a process that is usually not terribly difficult or expensive, and can yield highly gratifying results. Not only do you have instructions for installing the antenna, you have a game plan for doing the job right, determining your equipment needs based on a site survey, a link budget, and legal and safety restrictions.

Now that your stay-at-home network is super-charged, read on to Chapter 5, "Gearing Up for War Driving," to learn about taking wireless networking on the road—peering into the invisible world of wireless networks operating all around you.

# War Driving — Wireless Network Discovery and Visualization

part

II

# Gearing Up for War Driving

**M**ost computer enthusiasts find the idea of seeing the invisible radio waves of wireless networks somewhat thrilling. There is a sort of voyeuristic interest in seeing Wi-Fi hotspots appear on your screen. After driving a few blocks, you start to see the names others have come up with, the type of equipment, where these networks are, and so on. It's like peering into the ether and seeing a whole new world around you, unseen to those without the right tools. We find it quite compelling.

It's pretty simple to get started war driving. This chapter will show you how to gather the components needed for a war drive. We will install the system into a car, go on a drive and record what we find. You may be surprised at what's out there!

You will need the following items:

- ➤ Laptop computer—To run the war driving software and record results
- ➤ Wireless network adapter—To scan the airwaves for wireless networks
- ➤ External antenna and pigtail—To increase range
- ➤ Some form of mobility, like a car, bike, boat, stroller, or even feet
- ➤ Scanning software—The actual program doing the scanning
- ➤ GPS unit—Optional; use this to plot hotspots on a map

## Overview of the War Drive

Imagine yourself driving late at night. You have a full tank of gas, it's dark, and a faint electronic glow illuminates the right side of your face. As each house or building passes by, your laptop blips out another group of unusual words like tsunami, default, dog house, taffy, 101, spock, or who knows?

Or picture yourself driving home from work, taking the scenic route—through the commercial district. Just to see what pops up.

Perhaps on a road trip, you are passing trucks as if they are standing still. As you approach a weigh station, a blip pops up on your laptop. Hmm... a new access point. This one reveals the presence of a Wi-Fi weigh station network.

You've started to experience the allure of war driving. Invisible waves pop up on your computer screen revealing the unknown and unseen.

The act of driving a car equipped with a computer, a wireless card, and software designed to scan for wireless networks has come to be known as *war driving*. The term war driving derives from an idea from the early 1980s to dial many telephone numbers to find a computer modem: war dialing. The term itself was coined from the dialing program made popular in the 1983 movie *WarGames*.

One of the interesting aspects of war driving is that you will find wireless access points where you least expect it. From a deserted highway in the middle of nowhere to a rural truck stop to a bustling cityscape, wireless networks are exploding onto the airwaves. The phenomenon is quite remarkable.

Here are some places to visit to get you started:

- Your own neighborhood
- Industrial parks
- Downtown
- Highways and freeways
- Off the beaten path
- Take your rig on a family road trip!

Figure 5-1 shows the view during a rare daytime war drive.

The original term war driving has also spawned a host of derivatives applying to many situations in which people scan while not actually driving — for example, war walking, war strolling, war boating, and war flying. They all mean one thing: looking for wireless networks, usually while moving. We prefer to scan while driving.

**Note**  Some people have promoted the idea that the *war* in war driving is actually an acronym for "Wireless Access Reconnaissance." This is really an after-the-fact case of creating an acronym for a simple word. But it sure sounds less ominous than *war*.

War driving software has no problem scanning at freeway speeds, although range is limited. And you can start the laptop and leave it alone during normal commutes or take side trips on the way home just because you haven't scanned that area before. Regular war drivers frequently go out of their way to grab the signals along a stretch of road they haven't war driven before. If you become enamored with the results of your war driving, it becomes a numbers game where you seek the highest number of access points found.

Keep in mind that the software does most of the work during war driving. You just need to keep the laptop running. Figure 5-2 shows how all this comes together.

FIGURE 5-1: On a daytime war drive bathed in wireless.

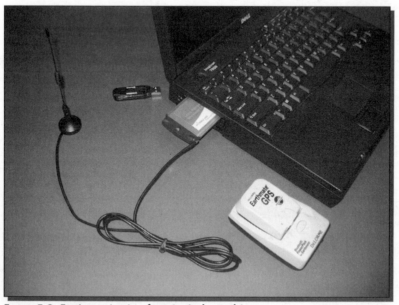

FIGURE 5-2: Equipment setup for a typical war drive.

# It All Starts with the Wireless Adapter

The essence of war driving is to use the innate capacity of a wireless network adapter to scan for networks, just as it was designed to do. The IEEE specification for 802.11b (and other 802.11 specs) specifically requires that an adapter be able to detect wireless networks in the area. The design calls for a user to bring up some sort of network selector and be able to choose the network as displayed by the SSID. War driving software in general exploits this scanning ability, with the special distinction that it records and saves the networks for later review.

**Note** Recall from setting up your wireless access point in Chapter 4 that an SSID is the identification broadcast by a wireless access point. War drivers will record the SSID along with a host of other information sent out by the access point.

You need to plug in the adapter somewhere, so it really starts with a computer. Since computers come in every form, it is important to determine the interconnections available.

## Types of Adapters

The explosion of Wi-Fi products on the market has created every form imaginable for wireless network adapters. Recent mass-market developments have begun the transition from external, after-market devices like PCMCIA cards and USB adapters to integrated wireless devices, such as laptops using Intel Centrino mobile technology and PDAs with built-in Wi-Fi adapters. See Table 5-1 for a general overview of the types of adapters available.

### Table 5-1    Types of Adapter Interfaces

| Type | Advantage | Downside |
|---|---|---|
| PC Card, PCMCIA | Most popular. Easy to find with external connector | Sits in laptop. Needs external antenna for range |
| PCI | Most have external connector | Not compatible with laptop or PDA devices |
| USB | Easy to mount remotely. USB cable can run more than 10 feet | Does not usually have external antenna connector |
| Integrated Wi-Fi | Comes built-in to computer | Does not usually have external connector. May not work with WD software |
| Compact Flash | Works in PDAs. Can work in laptop with adapter | Does not usually have external connector |

**Tip** You will have the best luck getting software to work with an after-market adapter. Most integrated devices do not have the open-development community backing the drivers and integration needed for the most popular war driving software. But don't give up. Everything is worth a try!

When choosing an adapter, look for a few key items:

- Is the adapter supported by your computer? Most war driving software requires that the Wi-Fi card be supported by your computer's operating system (such as Windows) before it is recognized by the software.

- Is the adapter supported by the war driving software? War driving software tends to work only with specific cards with each specific program. And, since most war driving software is the result of a labor of love, comprehensive lists of supported cards are not generally available. On the plus side, war driving software tends to support more cards with each new release.

- Does the adapter sport an external connector? If you're using a USB card, placing the adapter high up in the car works similar to an external antenna. When you're using a PC card, an external connection is necessary to allow attaching a mobile antenna for the best war driving results.

Some wireless cards outshine others in the war driving arena. A few PC cards are very popular with seasoned war drivers. Many of the cheapest wireless cards are not used much due to their poor performance. Results from those cheaper cards will be mixed. But if you have something laying around, go ahead and give it a try.

The Orinoco PC card in Figure 5-1 (www.orinocowireless.com) has a good balance between its internal antenna, external connection, and receive sensitivity. It is also fairly low cost and is well supported by the war driving community. This is the card of choice for most war drivers, mostly due to early support by NetStumbler. Unfortunately, this card goes by many names as the companies supporting it have been bought and sold. Some names are Proxim, Lucent, Agere, and WaveLAN.

**Note** The first few versions of NetStumbler only supported cards like the 802.11b Orinoco, which then used an internal chip set called Hermes. Old school war drivers reminisce about using Windows 98, NetStumbler version 0.20, and an Orinoco card. All the tools needed for a fun evening spent cruising around town.

A fairly recent addition to the marketplace is the Senao PC card (www.senao.com). This 200 mW card produces a lot of power for a PC card. (Most cards only transmit about 30 mW!) And it may also have a more sensitive receiver. The Senao card comes in several variations. This card is a great war driving card, but is not very well supported by the manufacturer or by the war driving community. If you have problems getting it working with your system, a Google search may end up being your best hope.

FIGURE 5-3: External connector and internal antennas on the Orinoco PC card.

## External Antenna Connectors

Wireless network adapters are designed by the manufacturer to connect to a wireless LAN. There are some exceptions to this, but in general, they are not designed for war driving and don't have the external antenna connector, you will need to add an antenna.

The antenna built in to the adapter is made to connect to a strong, local signal. When war driving, you want to pick up the weakest signal possible to increase your chances of detecting more distant wireless nodes.

The diversity antennas on a PC card are designed to be small enough to fit on the card. And they work just well enough for a local wireless network. Figure 5-3 shows the internal antennas on the popular Orinoco PC card used for war driving. Notice the small footprint of the card's internal antennas (the two L-shaped metal plates). Attaching a high-gain external antenna will add receiver sensitivity and boost the output signal beyond the capability of the card itself.

Also in Figure 5-2, you can see the connector used to add an external antenna. As discussed in Chapters 2 and 3 on building antennas, an external antenna is essential for best results. This is crucial when driving in a car. The large amount of metal around the passenger cabin acts as a giant shield, blocking many wireless signals. A rooftop external antenna will increase results at least twofold.

**Note** A Faraday Cage is a shielded enclosure used to test radio and microwave equipment without leaking signals to the outside of the cage. The passenger cabin of cars and trucks acts much like a Faraday Cage in that signals do not transmit well outside of the passenger cabin due to the surrounding steel.

When choosing a wireless adapter, consider the extra benefit you get from an external antenna. As discussed in Chapter 1, you will need to use a pigtail to connect the fat RF cabling, used with an antenna, to the smaller connectors used on Wi-Fi adapters.

# Choosing the Right Software

There are many software applications that can be used for war driving. The most popular scanning software can be downloaded from the Web for free.

You will need to pick a software package that works with your laptop or PDA. Also you should consider other factors, such as setup, support, and results output. For example, for casual, easy war driving, NetStumbler works great. For more extreme war driving and network scanning, Kismet is good choice. Also, there are several commercial (for pay) products on the market that can be used.

When choosing war driving software, interoperability becomes a major factor in your success of getting the system to work. Most of the scanning software out there requires certain types of network adapters to function properly. In fact, some software requires a very specific type of adapter before it will even detect the adapter.

Research the software you wish to use, and compare it to the wireless adapters available to you. Remember that your operating system will also factor in to what works together. We will focus mainly on Microsoft Windows XP, but software is available for just about every OS on the market, including open sources like Linux.

## NetStumbler

Made for handy, simple war driving using Windows 98, Windows 2000, and Windows XP, NetStumbler is available at www.stumbler.net. This is by far the easiest program to use to get started and produces great results. Indeed, it is used by long-time war drivers. It is also the most innocuous since it only detects networks that broadcast their existence and reply to NetStumbler requests. We prefer publishing maps made by NetStumbler because it only shows these broadcasting hotspots. See Figure 5-4 for a screen shot of a typical main screen of NetStumbler. As you can see, this screen shows a huge amount of information, but it is all automatically tracked, leaving you to the driving. NetStumbler presents the most significant info on the left and the more geeky info to the right.

## MiniStumbler

Made for war driving using a PDA running Microsoft Pocket PC 2002, the MiniStumbler is available from www.stumbler.net. This Mini version of NetStumbler is used for high portability. The screen is not as complete as the full NetStumbler, but the log files contain the same information as the full version (see Figure 5-5). Copy the log files to your computer to view in NetStumbler for Windows. You also need NetStumbler to export the files to your mapping software.

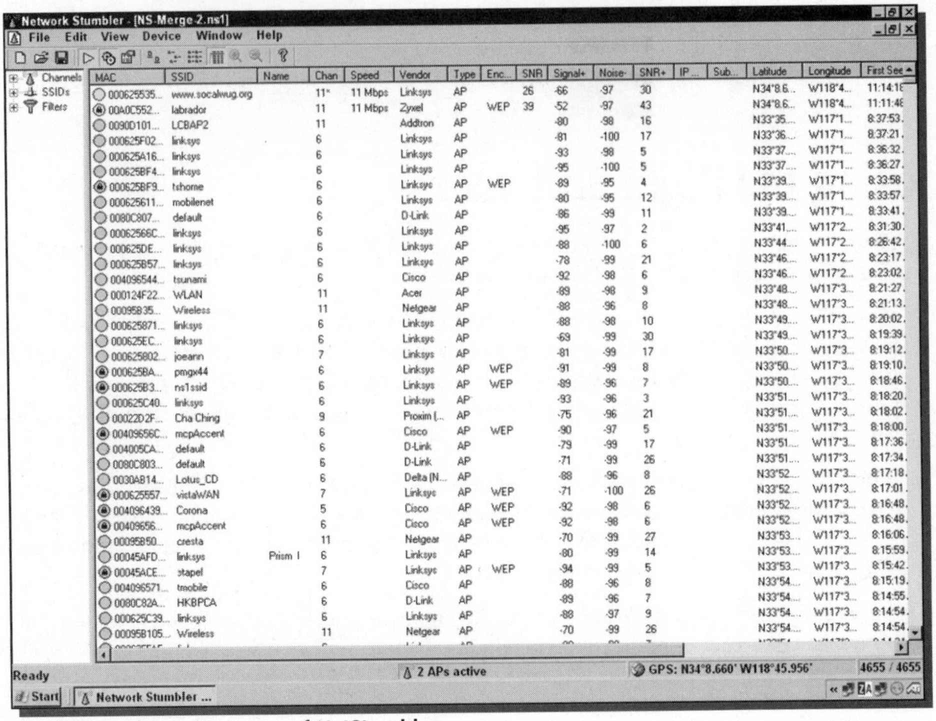

FIGURE 5-4: The main screen of NetStumbler.

## Kismet

Made for war driving using a laptop or PDA running Linux, Kismet is available from
www.kismetwireless.net. This is the most sophisticated of the free wireless scanners. It
works on laptops and PDAs running Linux. This is a powerful software, but it's also the most
complicated to get working. Kismet is a great tool for scanning networks that don't show up in
NetStumbler. It also includes features for recording the wireless traffic detected during scanning See Figure 5-6 for what the main screen in Kismet would look like. Note that Kismet has
several different screens and the display can be customized to present information in a myriad
of choices.

Kismet is a passive wireless scanner in the sense that it does not broadcast and request packets
of information from the networks being scanned. It is like a radio receiver tuned to Wi-Fi signals. Kismet features an ever-increasing list of network recording functions. For a complete list,
visit the Documentation section on the Kismet Wireless Web site. Some notable features of
Kismet include:

- The ability to detect other scanning programs like NetStumbler
- It will highlight the detected default access point configurations

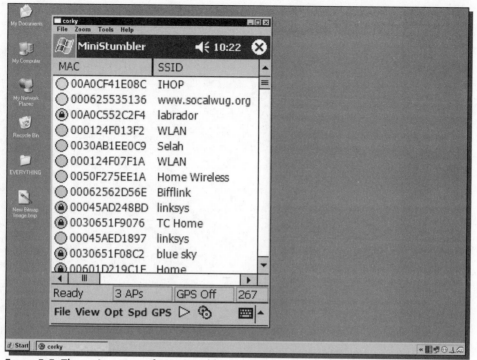

**FIGURE 5-5: The main screen of MiniStumbler, a simple version of NetStumbler that runs on a PDA.**

- The ability to reveal "hidden" SSIDs from APs with SSID broadcast disabled
- The ability to passively sniff and record wireless network data packets

**Note**  Kismet detects hidden, or cloaked, SSIDs first by detecting the generic signal from the access point. Then it watches for a wireless client to connect to the AP. When the client connects, it reveals the associated SSID.

**Tip**  Kismet can and will sniff and record all wireless traffic that passes through it. Encrypted data packets will appear as garbage and will be much harder, or impossible, to decode and view. Unencrypted data is totally vulnerable to interception. If a network is unencrypted, Kismet can watch everything happening without a second glance. Always encrypt your wireless traffic.

These are just a few of the many programs you can use to get your car ready for war driving. For now, the concern is to get the gear set up and have your car "wired for wireless."

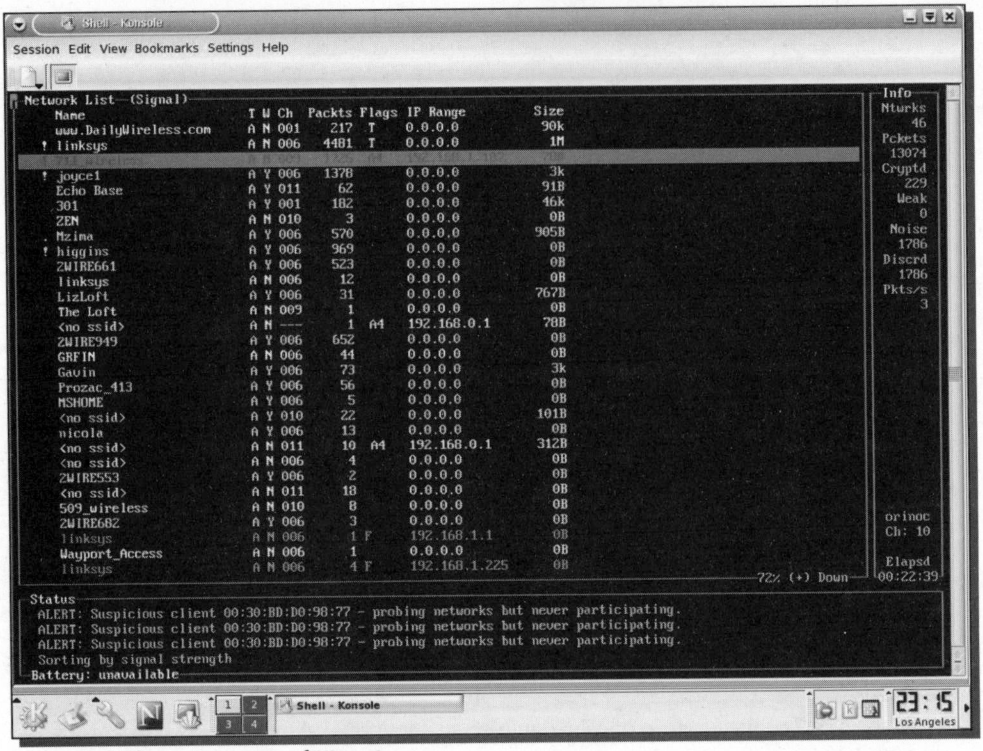

FIGURE 5-6: The main screen of Kismet.

# Using GPS on Your Laptop

One of the most interesting facets of war driving is being able to plot your discoveries on a street map. This brings a remarkable visual aspect to your efforts. The results of a war drive are instantly recognizable, and you can make these maps over time to see how Wi-Fi is growing in your area.

You will need a Global Positioning System (GPS) receiver to feed location information to the laptop. We will cover this topic in greater detail in Chapter 6, "War Driving with NetStumbler," but for now you will want to know a little bit to get your car set up to have a GPS satellite track your location.

The Global Positioning System is made up of a "constellation" of 24 satellites circling the Earth. These satellites are continuously beaming a location signal Earthward. A GPS receiver uses the exact time and location of the satellite to precisely determine your location anywhere on the globe. The accuracy of your location information is directly related to the quality of your GPS equipment. The term GPS is generally used interchangeably to refer to either satellites or receiver.

FIGURE 5-7: Handheld, dash-mounted, and dedicated GPS receivers.

## Globally Positioning Your System

As one would expect, GPS receivers come in many forms. The most common are the hand-held, dash-mounted, and dedicated receivers, which are illustrated in Figure 5-7. The most popular form for in-car use is either the handheld or dash-mounted receiver. Recently, dedicated computer-use-only receivers have become available. These dedicated receivers connect directly to your laptop or PDA and require the computer to power and display data. Although you can't take a dedicated GPS with you on the trail, they work great for war driving!

**Note** Universal serial bus (USB) connectors have come to replace the old 9-pin serial ports in most laptops these days. Dedicated GPS receivers often use USB to connect with the laptop. The GPS hardware ships with software drivers that enable the GPS and power it up when inserted into the USB port. Follow the instructions included with the GPS software to get it working with your computer.

**Note** Many newer cars come with a built-in GPS navigation system. Having this on hand is great for finding your way around town. But they generally don't have the outputs needed to interface with a laptop. Extensive hardware hacking is usually necessary to get a navigation system configured for war driving.

To feed your location to the computer, the GPS needs to send latitude and longitude information to the war driving software. When the software detects a wireless network, not only does it record the access point and signal strength info, it also adds the location information. The latitude and longitude info can be exported later to plot in one of many mapping programs available.

## Picking a GPS Interface

War driving software needs to interface with the GPS via a serial COM port on your operating system. This COM port can be a physical port, like a 9-pin connector on the back of your computer connected to COM 1. Or it can be a virtually mapped port.

Virtual port mapping is necessary when using a USB or Bluetooth GPS receiver. It's also necessary if you are using a Serial-to-USB converter as would be needed on a laptop without a 9-pin serial interface.

**Tip**    Some of the newer PDAs and GPS receivers have built-in Bluetooth connectivity. You can configure the GPS and the PDA to communicate using Bluetooth with a virtual serial port. Set the Bluetooth serial interface to emulate a COM port, such as COM 5. And set the WD software to listen on COM 5.

The driver software for the interface (for example, USB or Bluetooth) should have a setting to perform this virtual mapping. Figure 5-8 shows a USB GPS receiver port emulation screen.

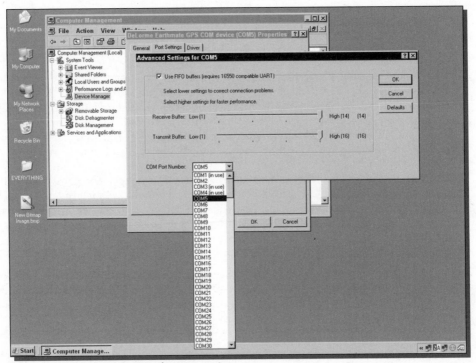

FIGURE 5-8: USB to COM virtual port mapping.

The war driving software must be configured to listen on the port to which the physical or virtual port is set. In addition, make sure your GPS and software is configured to communicate using the same GPS protocol such as the industry-standard 4,800 baud protocol, "NMEA 0183."

With so many GPS receivers in the market, you may need to fool your OS to mimic a visible serial port. The type of GPS will determine the interface available for your computer.

Finally, the GPS communication protocol needs to be compatible with the war driving software. Most GPS units have a selectable output. Just make sure it's set to the same protocol on both ends.

# Picking the Right Antenna

For best results, use an external antenna for the wireless adapter. Since the laptop is resting inside the car, signals will be very weak. An external antenna (especially a magnet mount) will pick up more access points from a further distance. Optionally, a USB adapter sitting on the dash or out on the sunroof has been known to produce good results.

A cross-section of several types of antennas are shown in Figure 5-9.

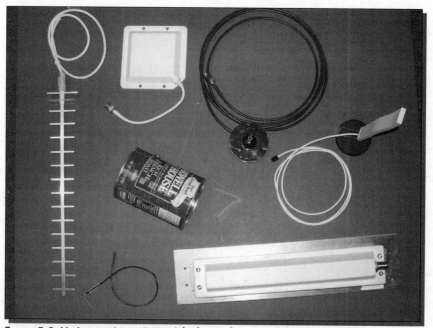

FIGURE 5-9: Various antenna types (clockwise from top-left): directional Yagi, directional panel, Magnet mount omni, desktop omni, directional sector, directional homemade can antenna, and homemade omni.

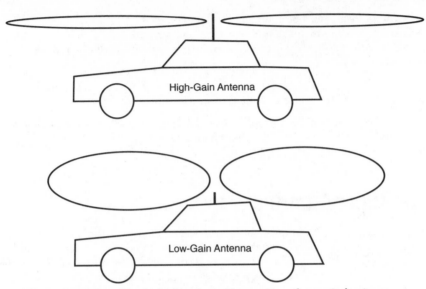

FIGURE 5-10: Vertical profile of a high-gain and low-gain roof-mounted antenna.

FIGURE 5-11: Commonly used medium-gain antenna. Magnet-mount base makes for easy rooftop mounting.

**Tip**    The antenna we built in Chapter 3 can be used to increase distance while war driving. However, since it is highly directional, a navigator will have to sit in the passenger seat to sweep "interesting" areas or buildings.

By now, you know that bigger isn't always better. A high-gain antenna becomes more directional either vertically or horizontally. Picking the ideal antenna for war driving will depend on your geography and where you plan to war drive.

For the area that you are scanning consists of very flat terrain with one- or two-story buildings, you can get away with using a high-gain antenna with a low vertical profile. On the other hand, if the terrain is mountainous, or you are driving downtown with multistory high-rises on either side of you, a lower gain antenna works best. See Figure 5-10 for a side view of antenna profiles.

A medium-gain omnidirectional antenna like that shown in Figure 5-11 is the most flexible for a variety of terrains and building heights. It's the popular choice for war drivers in mountainous Southern California.

# Powering Your Rig

Longevity requires power. If you want to run for more than a few hours, the car's energy will have to be tapped. Here are a few tools you can use to extend the uptime of your rig:

- DC Power Supply—Most laptops have accessories for the in-car cigarette lighter or airplane power port. Handheld GPS units have two-in-one power and serial cables.

- DC-to-AC Inverter—The mainstay of flexible installations. This converts DC car power to 110 VAC used by laptops, cell phone chargers, TVs, DVD players, and so on.

- Lighter power splitter—Few cars these days have more than one or two power ports available. Turn one port into three and power all of your DC devices at once.

Figure 5-12 shows all of these items working in harmony. As you can see, cable management becomes an issue. Passengers can ride in back!

When using a DC-to-AC power inverter, be sure the inverter has ample wattage for your laptop's input. Look at the power requirements of your laptop. (This is usually on a sticker on the bottom of the laptop, or on the AC power brick.) Look for DC Output.

Use the formula Power = Volts $\times$ Amperes. For example, if your laptop needs 15 V and draws 4 A, you will need an inverter capable of at least 60 W ($15 \times 4 = 60$). See Table 5-2 for actual power requirements of some popular laptops.

The downside of using a higher wattage inverter is more drain on your vehicle electrical system and fan noise. The upside is that you won't tax the inverter causing heat and possible circuit overload. We prefer inverters of at least double the power than needed.

### Table 5-2 Power Consumption on Various Models

| Model | Volts | Amperes | Power Requirements (Watts) |
|---|---|---|---|
| Dell Inspiron | 20 | 3.5 | 70 |
| Compaq Presario | 19 | 3.16 | 60.04 |
| Sony Vaio | 19.5 | 5.13 | 100.035 |

FIGURE 5-12: DC adapter, DC-to-AC inverter, three-way splitter. This rig can run forever.

# Installing the System in Your Car

Now is the time to install everything into the car. All of the above items will be gathered together and quickly installed. When the ideal configuration is achieved, more permanent mounting options can be explored. For now, let's just make it safe and easy (and flexible).

The installation is relatively quick and easy. It can be done in six simple steps:

1. Make sure that the wireless card is properly installed.

2. Position the laptop in an ideal place.

3. Attach the rooftop antenna.

4. Add the Global Positioning System.

**5.** Plug it all in.

**6.** Launch the software.

Each of these steps is discussed in detail in the paragraphs that follow.

## Step 1: Installing the Wireless Card

The laptop should have the wireless card already installed and verified to be working with the war driving software. If you have a glitch, it's better to troubleshoot it where you can reach the keyboard without straining.

**Tip** Chapter 1 covered the essential but delicate wireless pigtail. The pigtail and the connector to which it is mated are physically the most fragile components in a war driving setup. It's easier and safer to attach pigtail cables before the laptop is securely strapped down. Also, bring extra pigtails on your war drives in case of connector breakdown.

## Step 2: Placing the Laptop

The ideal position for the laptop is within arms' reach but not obstructing your view. When doing a temporary mounting option, you can ensure that the laptop doesn't slide by using the seatbelt on the passenger seat. Figure 5-13 shows this setup. Remember to treat cables nicely. Don't bend RF cables too tightly and don't put strain on the connectors.

FIGURE 5-13: Laptop placed securely on the passenger seat.

## Step 3: Attaching the Rooftop Antenna

This is where a magnet mount antenna comes in so handy. Place the antenna as close to the center of the roof as possible while staying away from any roof racks or other antenna.

Run the cable using the least damaging method to get to the interior of the car. You can leave a window down, but that's far from ideal. If the cabling is of sufficient strength, you can get away with closing it in a doorway without much loss. LMR-400 is very good and can take minor pinching without too much damage.

Figure 5-14 shows a typical magnet mount antenna placed on a roof. Notice how the antenna is placed well away from the roof rack and the cable comes down through the doorway.

 Use care in placing and removing the magnet mount antenna. To avoid damage, pull from the base, not the cable or aerial. Also, try to pull directly up to avoid scratch marks.

## Step 4: Adding the GPS

The GPS receiver needs a clear view of most of the sky. Nowadays, receivers are pretty good at obtaining a signal without seeing the entire sky. The front or rear window of the car usually has

FIGURE 5-14: Magnet mount antenna placement with cable running through doorway.

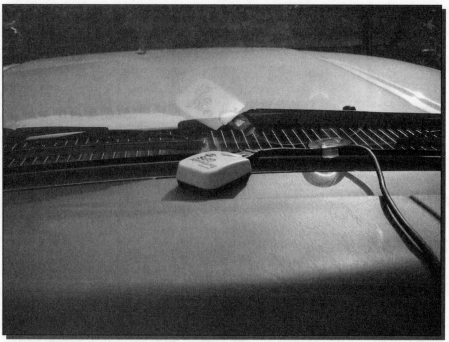

FIGURE 5-15: The dashboard makes a nice home for this USB GPS.

enough view to maintain a decent signal. If you have problems getting a location lock, try repositioning the GPS. Or try a magnet mount external GPS.

Temporary, but functional, placement of a USB GPS is shown in Figure 5-15. Note the simple suction cup cable management.

**Tip**   GPS receivers have many options. Review all of the options to ensure the GPS is configured correctly. In particular, make sure it's not set in a demo or simulation mode.

## Step 5: Plugging It All In

All these different components need unique power sources. Let's look at how to hook them all together. Figure 5-16 shows the setup all plugged in and ready.

1. The laptop uses its own AC power supply plugged in to a power inverter, which itself is plugged in to a cigarette lighter.

2. The USB GPS pulls power from the laptop. Alternatively, a DC power source is available for most GPS receivers.

3. Extra ports are available for the myriad of portable components used while driving.

FIGURE 5-16: Everything is ready to go!

Tip

If you are just experimenting, battery power is fine. Laptops and GPS units have batteries. But the radio in your wireless adapter pulls a lot of juice from your laptop. Expect shortened run-times.

## Step 6: Launching the Software

Now that your equipment is up and running, go ahead and launch the war driving software. It's best to do this near a known access point to verify that the software is working.

Ensure that your software is set to reconfigure the adapter on-the-fly. This can be a channel hopper, as used in Kismet, or a "reconfigure automatically" option, as used in NetStumbler.

Tip

War driving software has been known to glitch where it stops detecting new networks. If you have two known access points, this makes a good test before getting too far down the road.

Finally, make sure the software is receiving GPS data. If you just powered up, the status will say something like "acquiring" or "locating." When your position is acquired, the status should show your actual latitude and longitude coordinates.

# Your First War Drive!

Everything is ready. It's time to get on the road. Start small at first. Drive up and down your street to see how far away your home network is visible. Then start driving around the neighborhood.

You will be tempted to watch the screen while driving. This habit is very dangerous and definitely *not* recommended. Close the lid on your laptop to avoid distraction. Make sure the power management option is set up for Always On operation so the laptop doesn't go to sleep.

 The laptop does all of the work for you. There is no reason to avert your eyes from the road while driving. Always pay attention to the road. If something happens on the system, find a safe place and stop before trying to use the laptop. Don't let a computer crash turn into a car crash.

 Disconnect cables that may get in your way before entering and exiting the car at pit stops. Cables have a way of finding human appendages. One frantic exit at the Quick Stop can pull cables loose, never to connect again.

## Discovering the Invisible

You will be surprised where wireless networks appear. And you will be even more surprised when the names people have chosen for their network SSID comes across your screen. Be prepared for the humorous, laughable, obscene, and bizarre.

A remarkable number of access points are using the default configuration. Many people buy an AP and just plug it in. Since most APs are designed to work out of the box, people just leave them at the minimum configuration.

The results of your war driving will reveal apparent default configurations. Compare what you find with the SSIDs listed in Table 5-3. If the SSID is the default, it's a good chance the owner just plugged in the new AP and left it that way.

The message boards on Netstumbler.com have many threads on the SSIDs, war drivers have discovered. This is by far the most interesting social aspect revealed by war driving.

 While war driving, you will discover that about 30 percent of the networks recorded have WEP Encryption enabled. This 30/70 "rule" has been evident since the earliest war driving results were posted online. A default SSID that is not WEP-enabled is almost surely a default configuration.

## Where to Go? Anywhere!

There is no set rule of where to find the best locations. Since wireless networks are used everywhere, the best locations are, well, everywhere!

Here are some simple tips to help keep you on your way:

1. Set up an audio trigger that announces when new access points are detected.

2. Run the antenna cable through the trunk. Trunks open and close less often than doors.

**Table 5-3    Factory Default SSIDs**

| Manufacturer | SSID |
| --- | --- |
| Belkin | WLAN |
| Cisco | tsunami |
| D-Link | WLAN |
| Linksys | linksys |
| Microsoft | MSHOME |
| Netgear | NETGEAR |
| Orinoco | WaveLAN Network |
| SMC | WLAN |
| Symbol | 101 |

**3.** Bring extra pigtails in case of breakage.

**4.** Auto-save the log files every few minutes.

**5.** When driving at night, switch the color scheme to high-contrast black background.

**6.** Above all, drive carefully!

A huge number of networks are "wide open," meaning you could jump onto the network and surf the Web, check e-mail, or access computers on that WLAN. This tactic is ill-advised and probably illegal. Even if the "door is open," it may still be considered a crime to use a network without permission.

Be sure to get permission from the network owner before trying to use any resources on that network, including the Internet. Disable the TCP/IP interface on your computer to avoid accidentally associating with a network.

Although few laws or court cases approach the subject, war driving is generally considered lawful (by non-lawyer war drivers) since it does not intrude upon network resources or cause monetary loss. The fuzzy gray line of legality appears when resources are tapped. However, there are actions that are certainly illegal. Be a good neighbor and look but don't touch.

# Summary

This chapter has introduced the enlightening and entertaining hobby of war driving. With the basics covered here, you should be ready to choose a Wi-Fi adapter, war driving software, GPS, and antenna to install into a car and be ready to go on a war drive.

There are plenty of options available depending on the equipment you have handy, but the essence is clear. Load some software and take a drive. This is such a new phenomenon that you will be one of the few who have first-hand access to wireless usage in your neighborhood. Not only that, it's fun to go on a drive and see the invisible wireless waves.

Read on to Chapter 6, "War Driving with NetStumbler", for an in-depth look at NetStumbler in action. NetStumbler is more than a war driving software. Learn about its easy-to-use features and interface in the next chapter.

# War Driving with NetStumbler

N etStumbler is by far the most popular wireless network scanning utility around, partly because of its extreme capabilities, partly because it was one of the earliest programs available, partly because of its ease of use, but mostly because it's free.

NetStumbler was designed for war driving, so many of its basic features are well suited to network discovery and logging. NetStumbler connects to your wireless card and gathers driver-level details from the card. NetStumbler will also interface with a GPS unit to log the location information along with the *access point* (AP) details. This is the essence of war driving: scanning, discovery, logging, and eventually mapping your results.

When you go beyond the basic war driving functions, you'll find that NetStumbler is also a capable network analysis tool. It certainly lacks the power of dedicated network analysis software, but the signal graphing and multiple access point tracking makes it very functional in some environments.

NetStumbler is one of the basic tools for war driving. Your next question is most likely, why war drive? And the short answer is because it's fun! Once you start war driving, you will see and learn more about wireless networks than you thought possible. Using NetStumbler is an art in itself, and expanding into the subtleties of its operation and abilities will bring you a deeper understanding of wireless networking in general.

It's hard to determine a specific purpose of war driving, and yet, you could say that it helps one learn more about wireless in its own way. There are so many aspects to war driving that it will take some time to learn what is most interesting to you. This chapter will prepare you to go out and discover some networks with NetStumbler. Chapter 7 will show you how to plot them on a map. As you delve into this new hobby, you will find new and interesting ways to work with and visualize wireless networks.

In this chapter, you will learn how to install NetStumbler, read the data files, and use it to scan for wireless networks. You will also learn about using NetStumbler for activities other than war driving. After reading this chapter, you will be able to use NetStumbler like a professional.

## in this chapter

☑ Installing and configuring NetStumbler

☑ Coordinating NetStumbler and GPS

☑ Using the NetStumbler interface

☑ Exporting NetStumbler files

Here are the items you will need for this chapter's project:

1. Laptop computer

2. Wireless adapter compatible with NetStumbler and your version of Windows

3. NetStumbler software—free download

4. GPS receiver to save location information for mapping later (optional)

# Installing NetStumbler

Your first and foremost task is to get a copy of NetStumbler working on your computer.

There are many compatibility issues in the world of wireless, and NetStumbler is no exception. It will help to have a few different Wi-Fi adapter cards on hand. Multiple Windows versions are supported from Windows 98 on up.

The core NetStumbler executable is quite small, weighing in at less than 500K. But don't let the size fool you. Huge features are crammed into that small space.

**Note**

NetStumbler is beta software and support is limited. It may not work without some experimentation on your part. There are online user forums and FAQ lists available. Still, plan for a bit of trial and error before finding an equipment combination that works for you.

For Macintosh computers, try *Kismac* or *MacStumbler*. Both of these programs are designed for war driving. Kismac has more network scanning functions and is similar to Kismet for Linux. MacStumbler is almost a direct clone of NetStumbler. Linux computers have many options available for war driving.

## Step 1: Downloading NetStumbler

NetStumbler is a free download. To get it, surf www.netstumbler.com and click on the "Downloads" link. (You can also download it from the author's site at www.stumbler.net.)

**Note**

NetStumbler is deemed by the author as "BeggarWare." The software is supported only by donations directly to the author, Marius Milner. For license and donation details, see the Help ➪ About ➪ License dialog after you install the software.

There are two different versions of "stumbler," called *NetStumbler* and *MiniStumbler*. NetStumbler is the full application, which runs on Windows 98, ME, 2000, and XP. MiniStumbler is like NetStumbler's little cousin. MiniStumbler runs on handheld PDA platforms running Microsoft Pocket PC 2002 or 2003. Both applications can be used for war driving, but there are user interface limitations on MiniStumbler.

MiniStumbler is a very good, highly portable wireless network discovery platform. It's easy to mount in a car or backpack. If you plan to run MiniStumbler, you should also install NetStumbler on a computer to work with the files directly. MiniStumbler output files are directly compatible with NetStumbler, so import and export is not an issue.

The Downloads page will show you the most recent versions of NetStumbler and MiniStumbler. There is also a link for older versions, and third-party software. Download the latest version and try that with your system. If you find problems later, you can uninstall it and try an older version. To download the file, simply click the filename in the Download section. Save the file to your Windows Desktop.

Since you are here, you should note that the Netstumbler.com home page is a great news outlet for all that is happening in the wireless world. And the Forums section is the online hangout for NetStumbler users. The forums have been active since the first release of NetStumbler (over 2 years). So it's a wealth of information, and practically the sum total of all knowledge on NetStumbler. Before posting technical questions to the forums, forum etiquette requires that you use the search function to see if the topic has been answered before.

## Step 2: Installing

To install the newer versions of NetStumbler, launch the file that you just downloaded. The installation is automatic. Just click Next at the prompts to start the process.

The earliest versions of NetStumbler did not have an installation program. The executable was downloaded in a Zip file. For this version, you must copy the Netstumbler.exe file to a folder on your hard disk.

The setup screen for NetStumbler version 0.3.30, shown in Figure 6-1, is quick and easy. Click the installation options if you would like to change anything. For this chapter, we will assume a complete install with all options selected.

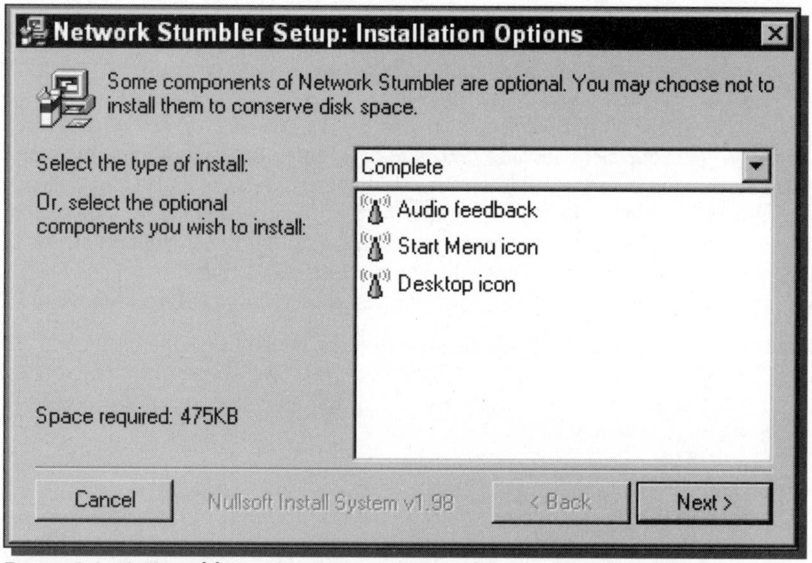

FIGURE 6-1: NetStumbler setup options. Notice the actual product title, "Network Stumbler."

**Note** NetStumbler is continuously being revised. At the time of this writing, version 0.4 has not been released. Expect similarities to previous versions with greater compatibility and user interface enhancements, including the setup program.

## Step 3: Launching for the First Time

To run NetStumbler, click on the shortcut on your desktop. The software will launch to the main screen and a few things will happen:

1. NetStumbler will create a new "document" with an automatically generated name based on the date and time

2. It will attempt to locate a suitable wireless adapter

3. If enabled, it will attempt to interface with the GPS

4. It will start scanning if it can

Check the bottom of the NetStumbler window for status on the wireless card and GPS interface. Table 6-1 shows common status messages and what they mean.

**Tip** When you're using multiple Wi-Fi adapters, select between them from the Device menu in NetStumbler. Try selecting NDIS 5.1 or Prism2 if these options are available.

Figure 6-2 shows the NetStumbler program running with multiple active access points. Notice the colored circle next to the address in the MAC address column. This circle will change colors to reflect signal strength. Green is strong, yellow is medium, and red is weak. The circle will turn gray when the AP is not active. Also, in the newer versions of NetStumbler, the circle will show a padlock for access points with WEP enabled.

**Note** WEP stands for Wired Equivalent Privacy and is a basic form of wireless network security employing data encryption over the air. It is considered the first defense against intruders on a wireless LAN. If a network is using WEP, consider it a "no tresspassing" sign. When WEP is enabled, do not expect to get on the network very easily. Although the encryption can be broken with network cracking tools, it takes some time and effort, and it might actually be unlawful. When you discover a network with WEP enabled, it's best to note its location and move on.

WEP has some serious limitations for highly secure networks, which has earned it the unflattering nickname "Weak Encryption Protocol." Yet WEP is a great way to protect a network from casual hackers. If you have serious security concerns, consult a wireless security expert to help you design a secure wireless network.

## Step 4: Testing Your Installation

As with all software, the publisher needs to play catch-up with manufacturers that change firmware and hardware with each upgrade. So, some older cards and Windows versions may work better with the older NetStumbler versions. Conversely, later versions of Windows and newer cards tend to work better with the later versions of NetStumbler.

## Table 6-1    Status Messages

| Status | Description |
| --- | --- |
| Card not present | Wi-Fi card was not detected. Make sure the card is installed and detected by Windows |
| A device attached to the system is not functioning | Problem interfacing with Wi-Fi card, try switching interface modes on the device menu |
| Not scanning | Scanning is not enabled. Click the Play button or select Enable Scan from the file menu |
| No APs active | Wi-Fi card is working, but not detecting any networks |
| 3 APs active | NetStumbler is detecting three networks right now |
| GPS: Disabled | A GPS port is not defined, Disabled is selected in the options |
| GPS: Timed out | A connection could not be made to the GPS. Try a different COM port, or perhaps the GPS is turned off |
| GPS: Port unavailable | The port is locked by another program. Close any other programs using the GPS |
| GPS: Listening | NetStumbler is attempting to interface with the GPS |
| GPS: Disconnected | The GPS was working but stopped. Check GPS power and try restarting NetStumbler |
| GPS: Acquiring | Message received from GPS device. GPS interface is active but location is being determined |
| GPS: No position fix | Move the GPS so it has a clear view of the entire sky |
| GPS: N:something W:something | GPS is working and this is your position! |
| 1/10 | Currently displaying 1 AP in the list of 10 APs total in this file. (This status may not appear unless the window is maximized to fill the entire screen.) |

Fortunately, the kind folks at Netstumbler.com have been maintaining an archive of all releases of NetStumbler. If your setup isn't working, try an older version.

If you find a problem, you can uninstall the current software and install the older version. You can get away with running them in separate directories, but it may get confusing, especially when you start creating a lot of log files.

**Caution**    NetStumbler 0.3.23 and 0.3.22 do not recognize files created with version 0.3.30. Unfortunately, the file types use the same extension (.ns1) and there is no easy way to tell file formats apart. To read the newer files, you will need the newer version.

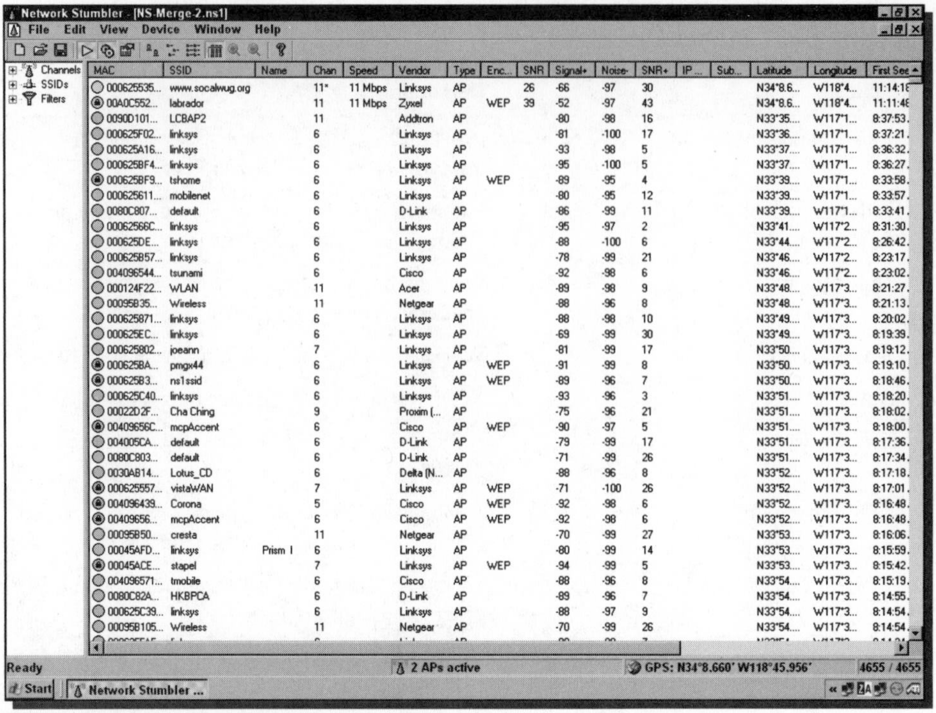

FIGURE 6-2: The NetStumbler overview screen.

There is one superior method for testing your installation: Set up two wireless access points with different SSIDs on different channels and scan the air waves. Figure 6-3 shows NetStumbler detecting and analyzing two APs simultaneously.

You will be testing that NetStumbler can:

1. Detect and interface with the wireless adapter

2. Reconfigure the card as needed to scan for a single AP

3. Reconfigure the card immediately to scan for a different AP

4. Continue analyzing these two APs while reconfiguring and scanning for more

There must be a limit to how many APs can be visible at once, but NetStumbler seems to be able to analyze a high number of APs in dense areas. Perhaps as many as 10 or more may show up as active at one time.

The key distinction to this test is for the APs to have different SSIDs (the name your Wi-Fi card looks for when associating). NetStumbler should be able to auto-reconfigure the card to switch back and forth on-the-fly between two access points.

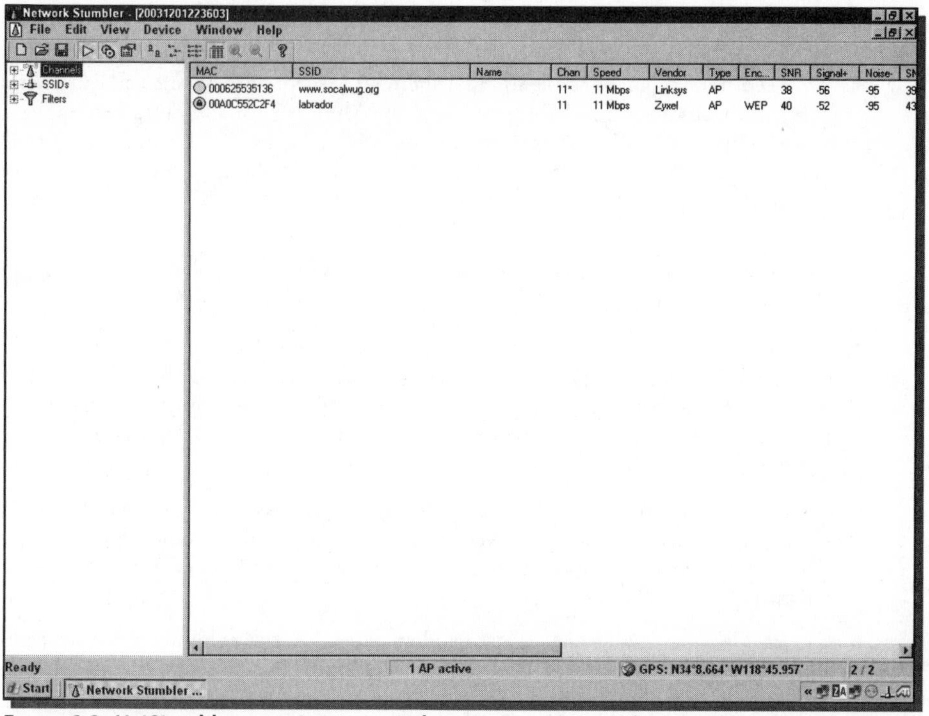

FIGURE 6-3: NetStumbler scanning two wireless access points at the same time tests that it will scan multiple targets on-the-fly.

If both APs are detected and listed as active, NetStumbler should be able to detect any number of new APs. (Lists can grow into the 100s or 1000s without a problem.)

Not everyone has two access points (or even one). To work around this, try driving in a section that you know will have wireless access points operating, for example, a coffee shop that advertises Wi-Fi service. There is no built-in way to test or simulate AP detection.

**Caution**

NetStumbler sends small messages to the wireless access point requesting its identity. If the AP does not respond with the SSID, NetStumbler will not detect it. AP vendors call this "SSID blocking" or "Disable SSID Broadcasting," among other titles. For this reason, do not count on NetStumbler to detect those APs operating in "stealth mode."

# Configuring NetStumbler

There are several ways to customize and configure NetStumbler. Some of them are visual, like fonts and zoom level. Others change scanning options. Feel free to adjust these settings to find out more.

Here is a quick overview of the menus in NetStumbler and some of the important menu items:

- *File menu*: This menu controls file management (except auto-save). You can open, close, and save files from this menu. Also, the Merge command takes two native NetStumbler files and merges them into one. Merge is helpful for making a single file with all of your findings. The file menu also contains the Export function, which is used to export data files for use in other programs like StumbVerter, Excel, and Mapping software.

- *Edit menu*: This menu contains the Delete item command, which you can use to delete access points from the list.

- *View menu*: This menu lists the common Windows commands to change the view, and also has the Fonts and Options commands. Adjusting the fonts setting will change the entire display. If you like large, easy to read fonts, this is where you should make changes. The options command opens the Options dialog with several settings. More on the options dialog in a bit.

- *Device menu*: This menu lets you manually select which wireless adapter NetStumbler will use. If you have one adapter, NetStumbler should decide automatically. Otherwise, you can force NetStumbler to attempt to use any of the recognized adapters in your computer.

- *Windows*: This menu lets you adjust window panes. Set cascading windows or stack them on top of each other. NetStumbler can run several windows at once. It may help to have different windows open with different contents in each window.

- *Help*: There is currently not a help file included with NetStumbler, so the "Help Topics" option will generate an error. The Help About will show version information. And the Help License selection will display the license agreement and extra contact information.

NetStumbler is not well-documented, so trial and error is often the best way to learn exactly what each option does, and some options are self-explanatory.

There are of course some differences in the features between the different NetStumbler versions available. The options panel directly reflects these differences. As an overview, we'll cover the basic Options panel for NetStumbler 0.3.30. Figure 6-4 shows the General Options panel.

The options are plentiful on the General tab:

- *Scan Speed* determines the rate at which data is captured and updated. Faster speeds create larger data files.

- *Auto adjust using GPS* connects the scan speed to the GPS velocity measurement. Faster vehicle speed increases Scan Speed.

- *New document starts scanning* will begin scanning when NetStumbler is started, or when a new "document" is created.

- *Reconfigure card automatically* sets the Wi-Fi card parameters for war driving. Turn this off when you want to use a network that NetStumbler found.

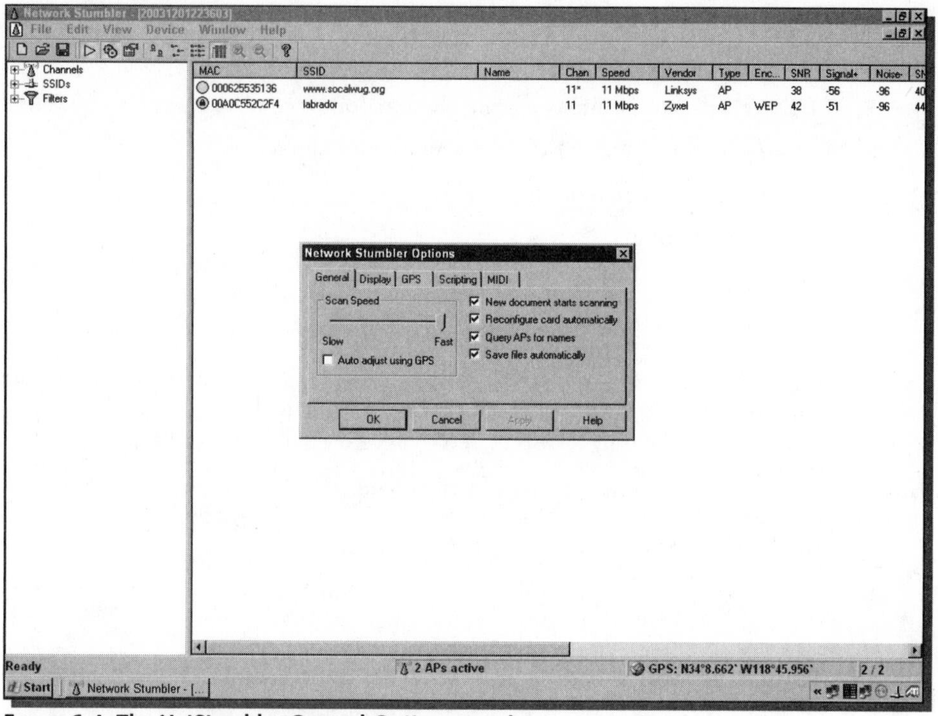

FIGURE 6-4: The NetStumbler General Options panel.

- *Query APs for names* sends additional requests to the discovered network for the "Name" field. Name is completely separate from the SSID.

- *Save files automatically* saves the log file every few minutes. NetStumbler 0.3.30 was the first version to include this option. Use with caution: it can overwrite existing files of the same name.

The GPS tab is used to configure communication options for the GPS receiver. (See the next section.) The Scripting tab is for enabling third-party Visual Basic scripts.

The MIDI tab is used in direct connection with signal strength monitoring. Enable MIDI output of SNR ties the signal-to-noise ratio to a MIDI register. A higher pitch means a higher SNR. This is a handy feature for tracking down an AP without watching the screen.

# Setting Up a GPS

NetStumbler will record GPS position with all of the other data gathered during scanning. All you need is a GPS reciever with a plug for your laptop. NetStumbler has a few requirements to use a GPS. Most off-the-shelf GPS receivers support these requirements, but it's a good idea to check the manual:

- Must have serial compatibility using a physical port or emulated through software.
- Must support one of the four GPS communications protocols:
    - NMEA 0183 (preferred)
    - Garmin Binary
    - Garmin Text
    - Tripmate

NetStumbler only recognizes serial data. Serial compatibility is common on handheld GPS receivers. But the GPS receivers with USB interfaces require special interface drivers for Windows. More on configuring a USB to Serial converter is available in Chapter 5.

In addition, NetStumbler supoprts a few different methods of communicating to the GPS receiver as shown in the list above. Make sure your GPS reciever is set to output its data in the same protocol that NetStumbler is configured to receive.

GPS settings are adjusted using the GPS tab in the NetStumbler options panel (as shown in Figure 6-5).

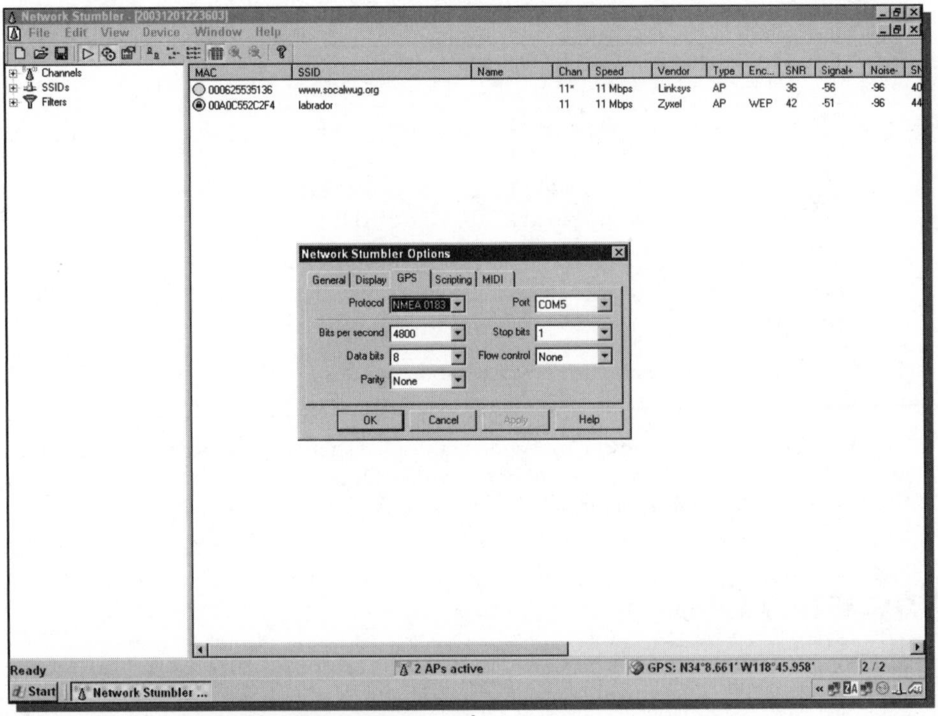

FIGURE 6-5: The NetStumbler GPS Options panel.

GPS works great using a low serial port speed; 4,800 bits per second is the NetStumbler default. This data rate works fine for almost any application. If your GPS receiver requires a different setting, make changes as necessary.

When you plug in a GPS receiver, make sure that NetStumbler is configured to listen on the same serial port in the GPS Options dialog box. NetStumbler will report GPS status in the bottom right corner of the window. See Table 6-1 earlier in this chapter for a list of common status messages.

After attaching the GPS to the laptop, and configuring NetStumbler, you may need to restart NetStumbler to refresh the GPS port. If the port is unavailable, try using a different serial port. If the port times out, check the cable connections and make sure your GPS is set up to use a serial output with the correct protocol.

If all is set properly, you should see a status message from the GPS right away. "GPS Acquiring" is the most common initial message. That means the GPS is looking for satellites and attempting to resolve its position.

When the GPS is operating correctly, NetStumbler will show the current latitude and longitude in the status message box. Now, every time NetStumbler records information about a wireless access point, it will also record the latitude and longitude reported by the GPS.

# Navigating the NetStumbler Screens

NetStumbler presents data onscreen in five modes:

- Overview
- Channels
- SSIDs
- Filters
- Signal and Noise Graph

## Overview Mode

Overview is the default view for NetStumbler. All wireless access points are displayed on the right side of the window. The left side still shows the different modes, but none of these modes are selected. (See Figure 6-6.)

To display the Overview mode, ensure that only a top category is selected on the left window. For example, click on Channels (not a channel number).

**Note** The only marker for the mode you are currently viewing is the highlighted selection on the left window. The highlighting will turn off when you click your mouse on the right window, or on another program in Windows. In Windows terms, this is called losing focus.

Use the "number of number" display on the bottom right of a maximized NetStumbler window to ensure you are seeing all APs in the list. If the number says something like "41/41," everything is being displayed. If it shows "10/41," NetStumbler is filtering some of the results.

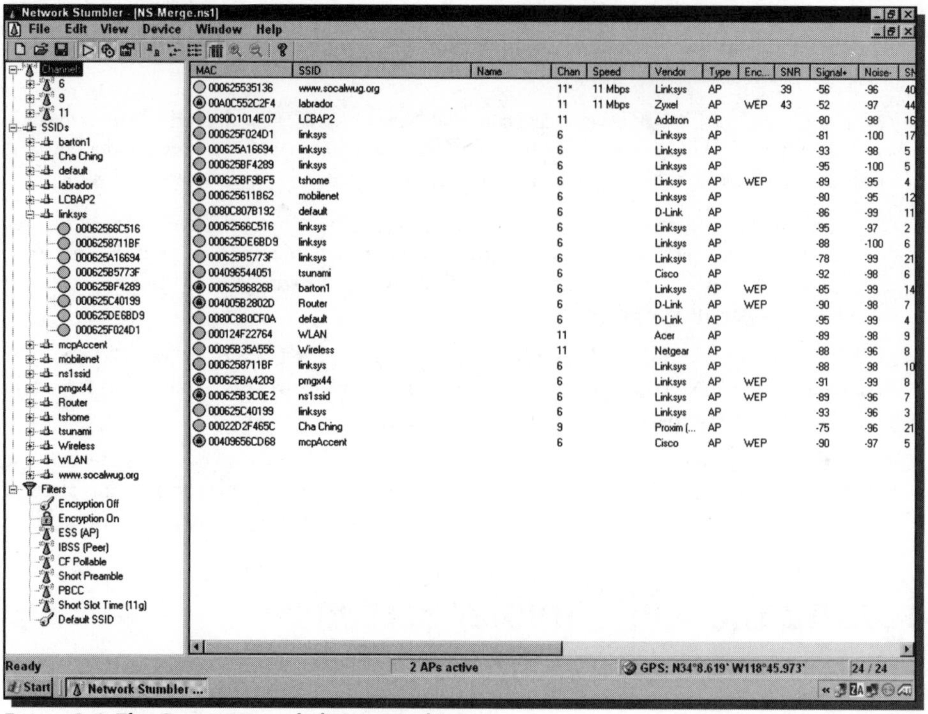

FIGURE 6-6: The Overview mode lists everything.

NetStumbler enables sorting of the results by clicking on the results headers in the right window. Default sorting is in descending order on "Last Seen." This will keep the most current results at the top of the window.

Another nice feature is the ability to rearrange the report headers. Click and drag a header title to move the column. Use the "Save Defaults" option on the View menu to save the new arrangement.

## Channels

In the United States, Wi-Fi defines 11 channels for operation of equipment. The Channels mode filters the display for devices using only that channel.

To enter this mode, expand the channels category in the left window and click on a channel. For example, channel 6 will filter the display to only show those APs broadcasting on channel 6.

## SSIDs

Expand the SSIDs category and a list of every unique SSID appears in the left window. Click on one of these SSIDs and the right window will show only those access points with a matching SSID.

When scanning a known network, this mode becomes helpful in filtering extraneous APs.

**Table 6-2    NetStumbler Filters**

| Filter | Description |
| --- | --- |
| Encryption Off | Only shows devices with WEP encryption disabled |
| Encryption On | Only shows devices with WEP encryption enabled |
| ESS (AP) | Only shows devices in Access Point mode |
| IBSS (Peer) | Only shows devices in Peer-to-Peer mode |
| CF Pollable | Only shows devices that are contention-free pollable |
| Short Preamble | Only shows devices with the short preamble setting enabled |
| Default SSID | Lists devices with the default SSID for that manufacturer |

## Filters

The Filters category has several built-in filters. Expand the Filters item to list the subcategories. See Table 6-2 for a description of the categories in NetStumbler 0.3.30.

These built-in filters are just one more way to quickly sort through the on-screen display.

### Signal and Noise Graphing

NetStumbler excels at visual representation. It's probably the most usable side-feature included in the software. Figure 6-7 shows the signal strength window. Notice the great variation from high to low in this figure. This shows the signal level dropping as the laptop moved away from the access point.

The graphical nature of the window allows you to easily determine signal strength and noise levels as reported by the Wi-Fi card. Signal and noise level is displayed on the same graph and is measured in dBm. Noise appears in red, signal appears green. Although signal-to-noise ratio is not directly shown, a high signal with a low noise level reflects a good SNR.

To display the Signal Strength window, select a MAC address listed on the left window. For example, select SSIDs, then select Linksys, then 000625123456.

If the AP is active, you will see updates occur immediately on-screen at the same rate as the scanning speed. (See the Configuration section above.)

# Working with NS1 Log Files

To really expand on the data that NetStumbler gathers, you need a good way to work with the data directly. NetStumbler saves all of its work in the NetStumbler log file format, `filename.NS1`.

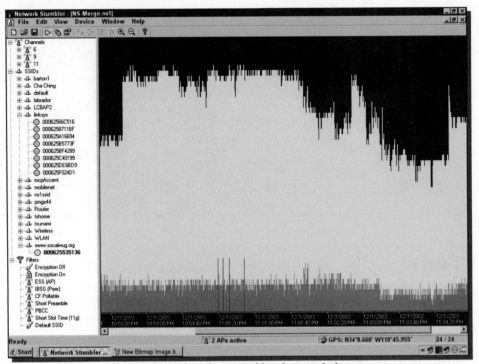

FIGURE 6-7: The Signal Strength graph makes signal levels crystal-clear.

## Merging

One of the sweetest options of NetStumbler is the Merge function. It can turn dozens of small files into one large file. The single, large file allows operations on the entire set of data instead of operating in several small steps.

Since NetStumbler automatically creates a filename and can also save it automatically, it's inevitable that a large number of these files will pile up. The best way to manage these is to merge the smaller files created each session into a single file.

Merge only works on NetStumbler native NS1 files.

**Note** Some online NetStumbler resources allow the uploading and downloading of merged NS1 files. With these files you can work on a massive amount of data at once. Some files can contain more than 10,000 access points!

To merge an NS1 file, follow these steps:

1. Create a new file, or open an existing file.

2. Click File ⇨ Merge.

3. Select the file to merge into the one already open. To select more than one file, hold down CTRL. There is a limit to the number of files you can select at once. This is probably due to the length of the filenames, not the size of the file. Try selecting five files or less at one time.

4. Click Open.

Using the Merge function will allow you to keep all of your results in one place. Then you can archive or delete older files from previous sessions.

## Exporting

The NS1 file is a binary formatted file. The NS1 file is readable by few applications directly. Stumbverter is one good example. But most applications will need to import the data in some sort of text format. NetStumbler offers three export options. These formats have unique differences. It is important to understand what may be skipped over when exporting.

The three export options are Summary, Text, and Wi-scan. Each selection uses a tab-delimited output with header information.

To export a file, first open an NS1 file from the File menu. Next, select File ➪ Export ➪ "format." The format is one of the three export types. Enter a name for the file. Remember to add a file type extension like `filename.txt` (text file) so you can open the file easily from other Windows applications.

**Note**    There are several programs or scripts available online to manipulate NetStumbler files. Most of these are available via the forums on http://www.netstumbler.com. After registering for the forums, perform a search for "scripts." The membership of the Netstumbler.com forums are constantly revising existing scripts and writing new scripts to perform a number of unique tasks, such as tracking your location, exporting to mapping software, and even making NetStumbler talk using voice synthesized speech.

The fields of export are as follows:

- Latitude: GPS latitude position
- Longitude: GPS longitude position
- SSID: The SSID for the wireless device
- Type: Type of device, Access Point, Peer, and so on
- BSSID: MAC address of the device
- Time (GMT): Greenwich Mean Time for the line item
- SNR Sig Noise: A three-part field separated by a space: Signal-to-noise ratio, Signal level, Noise level
- Name: The descriptive name for the access point if available
- Flags: Specific NetStumbler items, includes WEP state, Infrastructure mode, and so on

- Channel Bits: Field NetStumbler uses to record the Wi-Fi channel

- Beacon Interval: The time between beacon frames for the wireless device

**Note** Microsoft Excel is a great program for working with NetStumbler text files. Excel can open the file directly with the Open command. Use "Files of type: Text Files (.txt)" in the Open window. In the Text Import Wizard, select Tab delimited format so each field uses a separate column in Excel.

Export formats also include the date. Scroll down an exported file and the date will be entered on a line for each different day that data was recorded.

```
# $DateGMT: 2003-06-03
```

The date and other line items are commented using the # symbol. Scripts created to work on NetStumbler exports will often filter out these comments automatically.

## Summary Format

Summary includes only one line per device detected. This is the most common output you will use when working on the data directly. Like the Text format, summary includes every field.

The Summary format includes all of the header fields available. It chooses the entry with the highest SNR level for export. This is often the closest location to the wireless device.

Latitude and Longitude are exported in the Decimal Degrees format.

## Text Format

The Text format includes every data point recorded in the NS1 file. This format is useful when you want to work with the data in another program. Text format could be used to analyze signal strength for a given access point in another program like Excel.

Latitude and Longitude are also exported in the Decimal Degrees format.

## Wi-Scan Format

Wi-Scan is very much like Text format, except for the reduced number of fields included. This format does not include Flags, Channel Bits, or Beacon Interval in the output.

Wi-Scan is intended to be a universal war driving file format. Other stumbling programs may be able to import this format directly, and NetStumbler should be able to import other Wi-Scan files.

One problem you may encounter in using the Wi-Scan format is with the GPS coordinates essential for mapping. Latitude and Longitude are exported using the "Degrees Minutes.Minutes" formula, but are formatted using the Decimal notation.

For example, if the displayed format looks like this:

```
N 34.0827760     W 118.4277460
```

The format should look like this, in degrees and minutes:

```
N 34* 08.27760'     W 118* 42.77460'
```

When you're working with the Wi-Scan data, it may be necessary to reformat the latitude and longitude coordinates to get accurate results from your mapping application.

# Using War Driving Data

With the lessons learned in Chapter 5 and the use of NetStumbler data files, you should have a nice collection of war driving data. Now you can take a look at some ways to apply that data to look at your neighborhood through the eyes of a wireless network.

There are several different ways to look at the data from NetStumbler. You could make a simple text file, plot the data on a map (as in Chapter 7), or go crazy with Microsoft Excel to create a chart based on your data.

Here are a few ways to use this data:

- Determine how many wireless networks are in your neighborhood. By trolling the neighborhood, you will see how many of your neighbors are on the cutting edge.

- Locate public hotspots. Discover hotspots that you can use for Internet access. It's recommended you get permission before using any hotspot, though.

- Discover if other devices are interfering with your network. Troubleshoot interference issues by scanning for wireless networks competing with yours.

- Perform a site survey by tracking signal strength. Use the powerful signal strength meter to test antennas, determine range, check link status, and so much more.

- Determine the range of a wireless network. Travel around the perimeter of your wireless access and see how far the signal carries. It may go farther than you think.

- Perform informal market research on wireless vendors. The Vendor comun shows what products are the most popular. Will Linksys continue to rule the roost?

- Gain insight into user behavior. See how many networks are not secure. See how many use the default settings. For some people, it must be a challenge just plugging in the box.

Admittedly, the information you glean from war driving may not be authoritative, but it is accurate for the areas you've been scanning. When you put the data together you will see your neighborhood as a wireless adapter would see it. In a sense, you are looking through the eyes of a computer. There might not be a readily apparent use for this stuff, but it sure is neat.

# Summary

NetStumbler is a capable and comprehensive application. The features can be used in so many different ways that it will take some time to explore. Some of the features rival software costing thousands of dollars. Indeed, some functions in NetStumbler have even been integrated into these high-cost products after its popularity has grown.

It's not only a great war driving application, but is useful for wireless network troubleshooting, informal market research, finding hotspots, and much more!

Spend some time experimenting with it and it will surely become an indispensable tool in your no-cost wireless arsenal.

Next, you can plot your war driving results in a mapping program to visualize where all of these networks are in your city. You will learn how to take data from your war driving application and convert it into a format that most mapping programs can use. Make cool maps and show them to your friends. The extent of wireless networking becomes instantly recognizable when over-layed onto a map of your city.

# Mapping Your War Driving Results

Y ou've been out war driving (see Chapter 5). You've set up your car, bike, backpack, or who-knows-what to detect wireless networks and record their GPS locations. You've been war driving for hours, days, or weeks now. Now it's time to show off the results of your new-found skill to the neophytes. What better way than a high-tech visual representation of your discoveries?

Maps are universally understood and appreciated. When you get right down to it, mapping is very much to blame for the huge explosion of war driving hobbyists, and why the news likes to cover it. It's obviously a highly visual and instantly recognizable report of a war driver's activities. Figure 7-1 shows a map of West Los Angeles. The triangles represent wireless networks. While driving along boulevards and freeways, NetStumbler picked up over 300 wireless networks in that region alone. And it's clear that only a few of the main streets were "war driven."

There are many different war driving software applications and even more mapping applications. This chapter will narrow the scope to the most popular ones that are used in the war driving community. Also, most war driving applications have the ability to either save or export to a file format compatible with the tools described here.

The basics needed to map your results are as follows:

➤ Computer

➤ Mapping software, such as Microsoft MapPoint or DeLorme Street Atlas

➤ War driving software, such as NetStumbler

➤ War driving results in the form of a NetStumbler *.NS1 file

 **Note** A good retail product for war driving and mapping is the combined GPS and street mapping package, DeLorme's Earthmate USB GPS & Street Atlas USA hardware/software bundle. This is a retail product that can be purchased in a bundle at most software retail stores. (You still need to download the war driving software.)

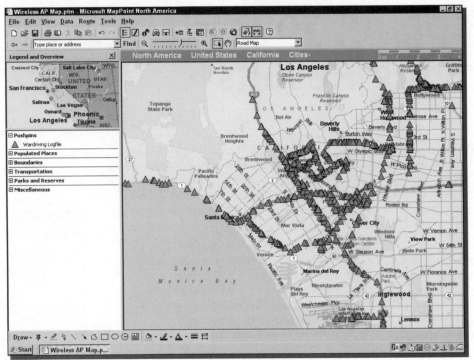

FIGURE 7-1: Map of war driving results in West Los Angeles.

Enter the world of Geographic Information Systems (GIS) and plot your newly discovered war driving data on top of a professionally researched GIS mapping software. (See Figure 7-2.)

# Mapping Overview

The essence of mapping a war drive is simple: generate a map of your area of interest and mark up the map using location coordinates.

But before we get into the step-by-step details, let's cover some basic information about mapping software, GPS technology, and data converters.

# Mapping Software

Dozens of mapping programs are available for the casual user. Programs can be purchased for as little as $40 for a simple travel package with GPS support, on up to several hundred dollars for a business-grade program with sophisticated population and demographic tools. There are also free applications, but these tend to rely on Web-based mapping sources like MapQuest for map generation, which reduces effectiveness while on the road.

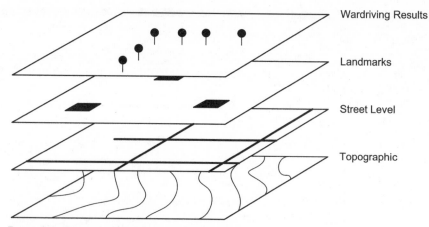

Wardriving Results

Landmarks

Street Level

Topographic

**FIGURE 7-2: Diagram of GIS layers of information.**

Table 7-1 shows some common mapping applications and some features. The applications reflect the most common products used by the war driving community. If you have a preferred package, by all means, give that a try first.

**Note** Topographic features allow mapping software to present elevation data. This can be in the form of topographic lines on the map display, 3-D imaging, or a "knife-edge" point-to-point profile. Topographic features help tremendously when you're planning a long-distance Wi-Fi link (as discussed in Chapter 13).

By far, the most popular war driving map generation program is *Microsoft MapPoint*. It's more expensive than the rest, but the features and ease-of-use make it the best choice for war drivers.

### Table 7-1   Mapping Software Applications and Features

| Developer and Title | GPS Interface | Imports "Pushpins" | Trip Navigation | Topo-graphic Features | NetStumbler Converter Available |
|---|---|---|---|---|---|
| Microsoft Streets & Trips | Yes | Yes | Yes | No | Netstumbler.com |
| Microsoft MapPoint | Yes | Extensive | Yes | No | StumbVerter, Netstumbler.com |
| DeLorme Street Atlas USA | Yes | Yes | Yes | No | WiMap |
| DeLorme XMap | Yes | Yes | No | Yes | Perl script |
| DeLorme TopoUSA | Yes | Yes | No | Yes | Perl script |

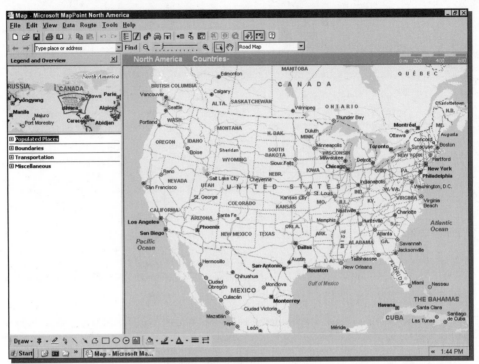

FIGURE 7-3: The Microsoft MapPoint 2004 interface.

And yet, the excellent navigation and turn-by-turn route planning features in most popular mapping programs can make those old gas-station maps obsolete.

## Microsoft MapPoint

This business-grade mapping program provides extensive "pushpin" features and Microsoft's COM programming plug-in capabilities. At a retail price of about $300, it's the most costly of the programs listed here. See Figure 7-3 for a screenshot of the MapPoint interface.

The pushpin feature is fairly common across digital mapping programs, although different names may apply. The MapPoint pushpin lets you place a marker anywhere on the map (manually or automatically) with notes and other data assigned to the object.

The COM add-in ability is especially nifty, because it allows third-party developers to run programs using the MapPoint mapping engine and data set. The most notable of these for war drive mapping is the StumbVerter program. StumbVerter is a free download, but donations are encouraged. StumbVerter takes exported NetStumbler "Summary" text files and automatically plots them on a map using the MapPoint engine and data.

MapPoint is also a powerful business tool including demographics, census data, and several geographic trend tools. Of particular note is the drive time calculator. Mark a location, select the drive time zone tool, enter the drive time, and the software will determine how far you can drive in, say, 10 minutes.

## Microsoft Streets & Trips

*Streets & Trips* is a basic travel and street-level mapping program that provides the essentials for mapping and vacation planning. It includes route planning, turn-by-turn directions, GPS support, and locates points of interest. Streets & Trips costs about $40.

Although StumbVerter does not support it, Streets & Trips will read converted war driving files formatted for Microsoft MapPoint. For example, the Netstumbler.com site has a Web form that will convert the data and display it on-screen. (More on this later in the chapter.)

## DeLorme Street Atlas USA

*Street Atlas USA* is a very popular mapping program, usable only in North America, that provides the essentials for travel and vacation planning. It compares with Microsoft Streets & Trips with one major advantage. A freeware conversion program is available that automatically formats a NetStumbler text file into the correct DeLorme format.

The WiMap Utility is a downloadable Windows program that reads NetStumbler Summary text files and creates a "latlon" file recognized by most DeLorme products, including Street Atlas USA.

Figure 7-4 shows the main interface for WiMap. The buttons on the left allow for useful selection and formatting capabilities.

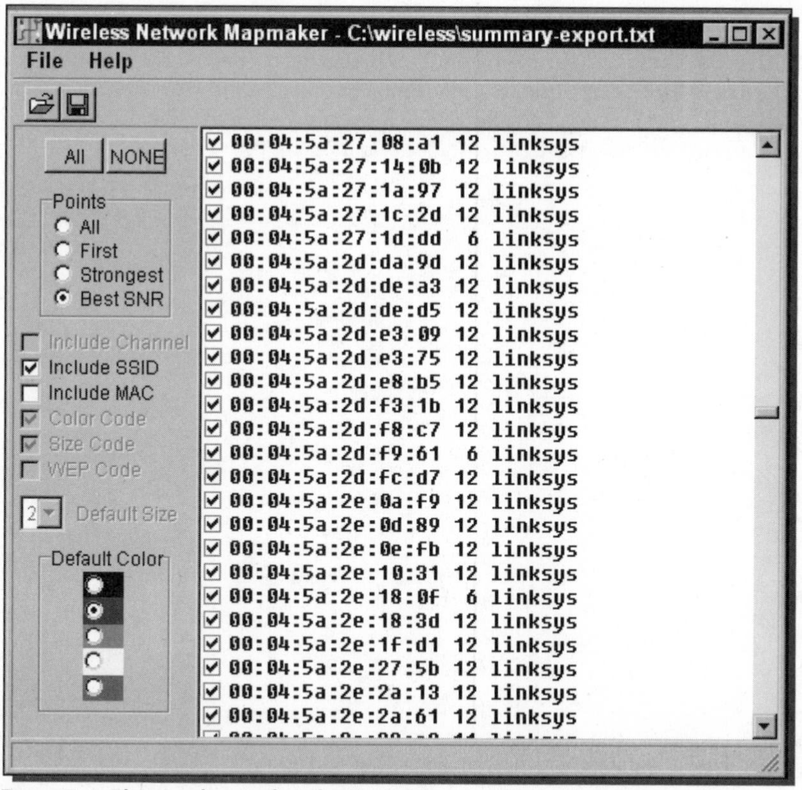

FIGURE 7-4: The simple interface for the DeLorme-compatible WiMap Utility.

# The Global Positioning System

The Global Positioning System, known as GPS, is made up of a number of satellites in orbit around the Earth. These satellites (24 active, with a few spares) maintain a precise position relative to Earth. GPS receivers continuously receive updates of the position of all 24 satellites in orbit. By computing the distance from the receiver to each visible GPS satellite, your GPS receiver triangulates its position on Earth in the form of Latitude, Longitude, and Altitude.

Consumer-grade GPS receivers are not completely accurate. High accuracy is more costly, but most consumer GPS receivers using the new Wide Area Augmentation System (WAAS) or Differential GPS (DGPS) capability can give you a position accuracy of less than 3 to 5 meters. In the case of mapping results, often the maps you are working from are not entirely precise, either. Mapping accuracy is always a game of ever-increasing accuracy and the cost of obtaining that accuracy. For our purposes, though, a $100 GPS and $40 mapping software works perfectly.

## How GPS Works

GPS works on the very basic principle of triangulation. Each satellite beams down a signal to Earth. It also beams down the time the signal was sent, and of course, which satellite the signal came from.

GPS is also about the most accurate time source available to consumers. Each satellite carries an atomic clock, and keeps your handheld unit timed to that clock. By knowing the exact time (to the nanosecond) that the signal left the satellite, the time when the signal reached the receiver, and knowing the speed of light, distance is computed. (See Figure 7-5.)

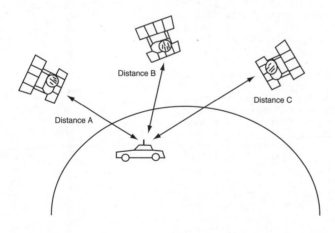

FIGURE 7-5: GPS uses triangulation to find your position on Earth.

Table 7-2    Several Formats for the Same Location

| Coordinate Type | Number Format | Location of Dodger Stadium |
|---|---|---|
| Degrees | dd.ddddd* | N34.07385* W118.23985* |
| Degrees Minutes | dd* mm.mmm' | N34* 04.431' W118* 14.391' |
| Degrees Minutes Seconds | dd* mm' ss.ss" | N34* 04' 25.86" W118* 14' 23.47" |

When at least three distances are known (from three GPS satellites) the receiver's position on Earth is known and recorded as latitude and longitude. If a fourth satellite is visible, altitude will also be computed.

## Formats for Recording Latitude and Longitude

Altitude is pretty standard, measured in meters or feet. Latitude and longitude is another matter. In its basic form, latitude and longitude is recorded as degrees, minutes, and seconds, north or south of the Earth's equator and east or west of the Prime Meridian (the line that separates the Western and Eastern hemispheres).

Table 7-2 lists three different methods for recording latitude and longitude position in a data file. Additionally, there are hundreds of different map formats or *datums* used to record latitude and longitude onto a paper or electronic map product. The most popular map datum used today is the World Geodetic System 1984 (WGS-84). Make sure your GPS is set to the same map datum as your mapping software. Most modern maps record the map datum being used somewhere with the map itself or with the software documentation. Note that North and East may also be represented as positive (+) numbers while South and West are represented as negative (−) numbers (for example, +34.07385 −118.23985).

# Creating a Map

The procedure for mapping is a basic step-by-step process:

1. Gather data by war driving.

2. Export the data into a common war driving text format.

3. Convert the data into a format readable by mapping software.

4. Import the data into the mapping software as location flags or pushpins.

5. View the results.

I'll cover each of these steps in the following sections.

## Step 1: Gathering Data

To gather the data, someone needs to go war driving. See Chapter 5 for more on war driving. If you don't have your own results, others may have posted their files. Try performing a Google search for *Netstumbler NS1*.

The minimum amount of data needed to make a map is the latitude and longitude of a single wireless access point. More information will make the map more interesting, but is not necessary.

## Step 2: Exporting Into a War Driving File Format

NetStumbler has become the de facto standard when it comes to working with war driving data. Most war driving programs have a converter available to export into NetStumbler Summary Export format, also called "wi-scan summary with extensions."

NetStumbler supports this format directly from the File menu. Click File ⇨ Export ⇨ Summary. Then enter a file name using the .txt extension to ensure that Notepad or another text editor will be able to open the file directly. In this example, use `summary.txt`.

For more about exporting file formats from NetStumbler, see Chapter 6.

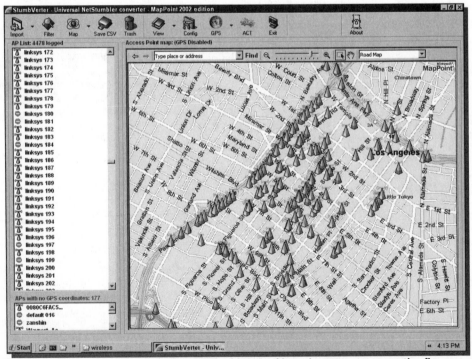

FIGURE 7-6: StumbVerter converts the NetStumbler text file and creates a map on-the-fly.

## Step 3: Converting to Mapping Format

The conversion process is the most difficult part of war drive mapping. There are so many different mapping programs and, of course, they don't all speak the same language.

This is where Microsoft MapPoint and StumbVerter make things simple. One program, StumbVerter, imports the Summary.txt file and plots the APs on a map. See Figure 7-6 for StumbVerter in action.

If you don't have the $300 MapPoint program, try searching at Netstumbler.com for a conversion tool for your mapping program. In the meantime, we'll do a conversion using one of the best data manipulation programs available, Microsoft Excel.

The NetStumbler Summary format is a tab-delimited ASCII file. To read this file into Microsoft Excel, click File ➪ Open. In the the Files of Type drop-down list, select the All Files option. This will show text files and more in the Open dialog. Select the Summary.txt file and click Open.

When Excel opens this type of file, it immediately starts the Text Import Wizard, as shown in Figure 7-7.

Choose the Delimited option and click Next. Make sure that Tab is the delimiter type. Click Next again, then click Finish. There is no need to specify data formats for each column.

Once your data is in Excel, it's just a matter of deleting fields that aren't needed, and formatting the data to work with your mapping software. See Figure 7-8 for an example of a stripped down spreadsheet.

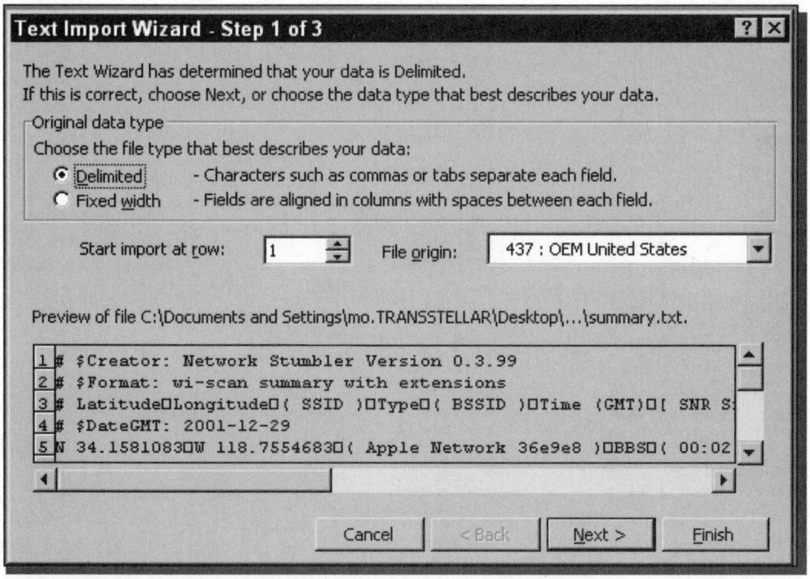

FIGURE 7-7: Microsoft Excel and the Text Import Wizard.

**Note** NetStumbler export files use the letter format (N S E W) for compass direction. Some mapping programs do not read letters, instead using positive (+) and negative (−) signs. Positive is North or East, and negative is South or West. Use the "Replace" tool in Excel to replace "N" with "+," "S" with "−," and so on. Be sure to replace the trailing space "N<space>" with the symbol "+" without a space to ensure success.

After deleting columns that aren't needed, select File ➪ Save As, and save the file with a different name in the proper text format. Some programs need comma delimited files, others may need tab delimited, and so on. The documentation or support site for your mapping program should have details on the suitable import format.

# Step 4: Importing and Displaying in a Mapping Program

Mapping programs, in general, have an import function. This is helpful to add the addresses of points of interest, and of course, access point locations. A few different programs will be covered here. Also, the manual import from Microsoft Excel will be performed using Microsoft MapPoint. (Surprise: They work really well together!)

## Microsoft MapPoint Import Procedures

In Microsoft MapPoint, the import comes in the form of a "pushpin." Extra detail on the location is stored in a text "balloon." Figure 7-9 shows an example of the standard pushpin and a

| | # Latitude | Longitude | ( SSID ) | ( BSSID ) |
|---|---|---|---|---|
| 2 | 34.1541767 | -118.756955 | ( SpaceMonkey ) | ( 00:02:b3:65:de:de ) |
| 3 | 34.1554717 | -118.765115 | ( linksys ) | ( 00:04:5a:d1:71:8d ) |
| 4 | 34.1552883 | -118.77879 | ( default ) | ( 00:05:5d:f1:0e:57 ) |
| 5 | 34.1555267 | -118.7795967 | ( linksys ) | ( 00:04:5a:2f:bf:f9 ) |
| 6 | 34.146735 | -118.7847683 | ( tsunami ) | ( 00:40:96:22:f0:50 ) |
| 7 | 34.1449267 | -118.8014067 | ( WLAN ) | ( 00:04:e2:0e:63:11 ) |
| 8 | 34.1450867 | -118.8037983 | ( default ) | ( 00:90:4b:08:5a:1b ) |
| 9 | 34.146015 | -118.805885 | ( Local ) | ( 00:02:2d:01:f6:3d ) |
| 10 | 34.14585 | -118.8053483 | ( gunn ) | ( 00:40:96:59:cd:b6 ) |
| 11 | 34.1586833 | -118.827015 | ( linksys ) | ( 00:04:5a:0e:e1:f0 ) |
| 12 | 34.1598417 | -118.837175 | ( WaveLAN Network ) | ( 00:02:2d:03:91:0c ) |
| 13 | 34.1586633 | -118.8353933 | ( mikes ) | ( 00:50:18:05:a0:16 ) |
| 14 | 34.1477883 | -118.815975 | ( linksys ) | ( 00:04:5a:e8:20:8b ) |
| 15 | 34.14484 | -118.80208 | ( linksys ) | ( 00:04:5a:26:76:a5 ) |
| 16 | 34.1535183 | -118.7518867 | ( linksys ) | ( 00:04:5a:26:e8:69 ) |
| 17 | 34.15348 | -118.75192 | ( linksys ) | ( 00:04:5a:0e:3c:2c ) |
| 18 | 34.1400033 | -118.7112633 | ( Wireless ) | ( 00:30:ab:0b:25:3d ) |
| 19 | 34.15528 | -118.6481267 | ( linksys ) | ( 00:04:5a:26:f3:2b ) |
| 20 | 34.163155 | -118.630065 | ( linksys ) | ( 00:04:5a:d0:e9:0f ) |
| 21 | 34.1697567 | -118.5995483 | ( monkey ) | ( 00:40:96:37:dc:10 ) |
| 22 | 34.1733233 | -118.5398183 | ( WLAN ) | ( 00:90:d1:00:c8:78 ) |
| 23 | 34.173165 | -118.5350633 | ( linksys ) | ( 00:04:5a:0f:21:e2 ) |
| 24 | 34.171225 | -118.5192967 | ( linksys ) | ( 00:04:5a:2e:69:3d ) |
| 25 | 34.1704817 | -118.5011167 | ( default ) | ( 00:10:e7:f5:50:ea ) |
| 26 | 34.2678017 | -118.47211 | ( Wireless ) | ( 00:30:ab:0a:85:7f ) |
| 27 | 34.1405333 | -118.7344683 | ( linksys ) | ( 00:04:5a:26:a5:23 ) |
| 28 | 34.145205 | -118.7780883 | ( linksys ) | ( 00:06:25:51:a6:c2 ) |
| 29 | 34.1604067 | -118.829235 | ( default ) | ( 00:90:4b:08:5e:c6 ) |
| 30 | 34.1767167 | -118.8649417 | ( linksys ) | ( 00:04:5a:0e:4f:86 ) |
| 31 | 34.21749 | -119.0427117 | ( linksys ) | ( 00:04:5a:27:02:87 ) |
| 32 | 34.2175083 | -119.0480117 | ( linksys ) | ( 00:04:5a:0e:68:b9 ) |
| 33 | 34.2243617 | -119.155545 | ( WaveLAN Network ) | ( 00:02:2d:22:96:58 ) |
| 34 | 34.231215 | -119.1725267 | ( aphews ) | ( 00:02:2d:0c:cf:60 ) |

FIGURE 7-8: Microsoft Excel spreadsheet after cleaning up the data.

text balloon showing details about a plotted wireless network. This concept of pushpins and balloons is followed by other applications, too.

MapPoint has some pretty sophisticated data visualization abilities. To get simple pushpins onto a map requires navigating through the maze of wizards and checkboxes. Other programs have simple import procedures (see below) but they don't have the massive ability to show data in so many ways. See the section "Visualizing Extras" later in this chapter for an example.

Here are the steps to bring in a formatted text or Excel file:

1. Open Microsoft MapPoint and click Data ⇨ Import Data Wizard.

2. Change the Files of type field to the file type being imported. Find the file you want to import, and click Open.

3. The Import Data Wizard opens at this point. If prompted, make sure that the correct separation character is selected. The data should be separated into columns. If it looks garbled or hard to read, try a different separation character.

**Note**  The tab character is the separation character (also known as a delimiter) used in NetStumbler export files.

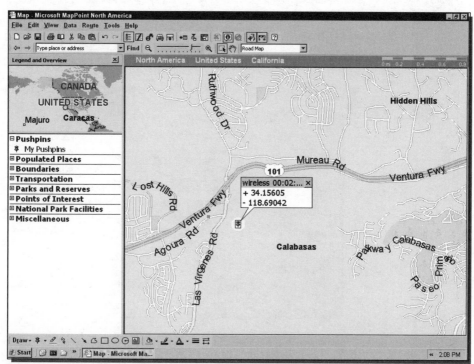

FIGURE 7-9: Microsoft MapPoint pushpin and text balloon.

**4.** The wizard will now ask for column headings and data types. Change the automatic selections at this point. For example, set the SSID data type to "Name," and change the SNR/Sig/Noise column to "<Other Data>."

**Note** If you do not want the contents of a column to be displayed in the text balloon, select "Skip Column." To have the data show up, assign it the value of Name, Name 2, or Other Data.

**5.** Click Finish to begin the import process. If there are a lot of APs, a progress bar will show the number of APs being plotted.

**6.** Next comes the Data Mapping Wizard. There is so much to this wizard, but we'll just cover pushpins at this point. Select "Pushpin" and click Next.

**7.** Change the Pushpin set name as desired. Select a Symbol that suits your taste. Choose which fields should be displayed in the text balloons.

**8.** Click Finish, and you're done.

The Data Mapping Wizard has many features and accesses some interesting stuff. Later in this chapter we will use it to plot signal strength using the Shaded Circle feature. It has nine differ-

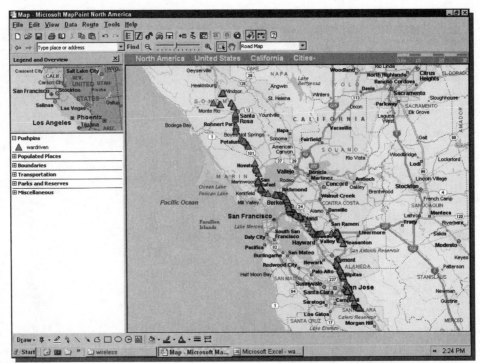

FIGURE 7-10: Microsoft MapPoint displaying APs after a war drive.

ent ways to display data: shaded area, shaded circle, multiple symbol, pie chart, sized pie chart, column chart, series column chart, and everyone's favorite, the pushpin. Also, with MapPoint's built-in demographic data, you can spend hours viewing the strange habits of your neighbors, such as "Adults who use sore throat products" as viewed by state, Zip code, or census tract.

Sometimes while war driving, the GPS will conk out, get disconnected, and so on. If that happens, you may record an AP with the latitude and longitude of N 0.0 by E 0.0. MapPoint will happily plot that and expand the map to show those APs off the coast of Africa at 0 degrees latitude by 0 degrees longitude. When plotting these sources, you can delete them, or ignore them. If you war drive the same access point at a later time, the coordinates will be updated.

See Figure 7-10 for a map created by MapPoint using a text file import.

## Microsoft MapPoint Using StumbVerter

*StumbVerter* is a free program that converts files from NetStumbler format into Microsoft MapPoint format (see Figure 7-11). The unique feature of StumbVerter is that it uses Microsoft's common object model (COM) programming interface to work directly with the MapPoint map data. The practical upshot is that you do not need to import into MapPoint. StumbVerter does it all automatically.

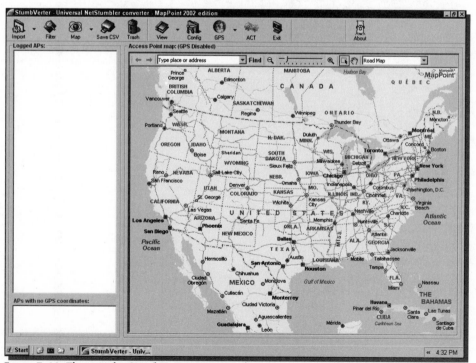

FIGURE 7-11: The popular StumbVerter program plots in its own window.

Follow these steps to begin working with StumbVerter:

1. Download StumbVerter from www.sonar-security.com and install it onto your system. (Note that you need MapPoint installed before you can use StumbVerter.)

2. Run StumbVerter and select the down arrow next to the Map button to choose "Create New North America."

3. Now click the down arrow next to the Import button to select NetStumbler Summary.

4. Open the file previously exported from NetStumbler. Progress is shown during loading and drawing the map. Be patient if there is a lot of data.

That's it! StumbVerter is practically automatic. There are also a lot of features with filtering, signal strength, and a sweet antenna comparison tool called ACT. Experiment with StumbVerter to get the most out of it.

**Note**   If you feel inclined, send donations to the programmers of StumbVerter. Much effort is expended putting the program together and making it available for free.

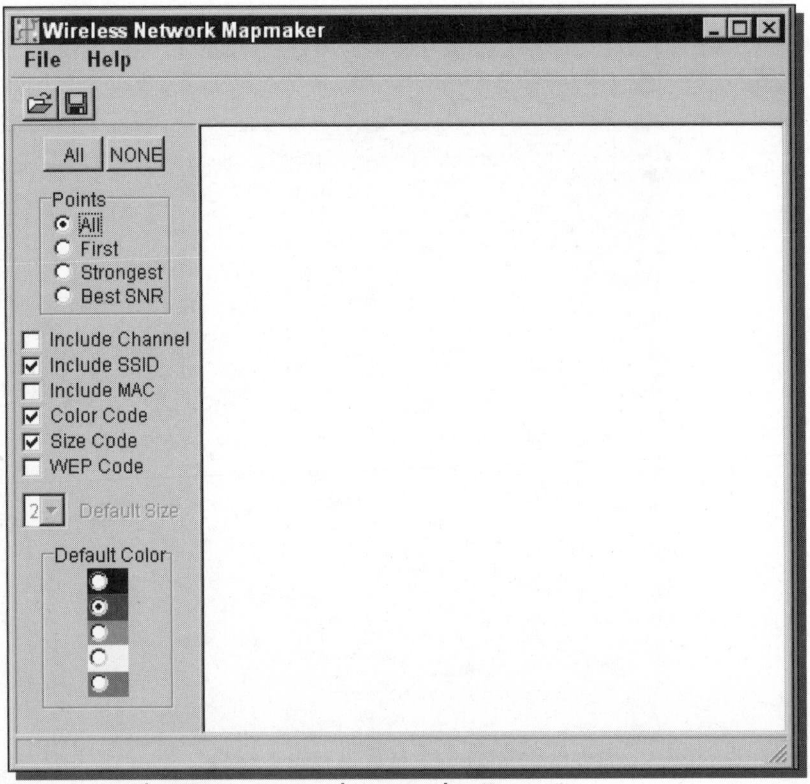

FIGURE 7-12: The WiMap program has several options.

## DeLorme Street Atlas USA Using WiMap

WiMap is another free program that automatically converts NetStumbler export files into a DeLorme-compatible "Solus Mark File" with the `.txt` file extension. See Figure 7-12. WiMap has several options for sorting, selecting, and presenting data in the map program.

You can download WiMap from `www.honet.com/WiMap`. It's a free utility created expressly for wireless mapping.

**Note**    Support the developer of WiMap by sending an e-mail to the author at `wimap@honet.com`. There's no cost or donation. Just express your gratitude! Programmers love praise almost as much as they love high-end hardware (money).

Use the following steps to convert a NetStumbler Summary export file into DeLorme Street Atlas:

1. Downloading WiMap. Then just run the program; there is no installer.

2. From the WiMap screen, click File ⇨ Open to open the previously exported NetStumbler file.

3. Select the items to display and convert over to the DeLorme map. The checkboxes next to the MAC address entry determine if the AP will be included on the map.

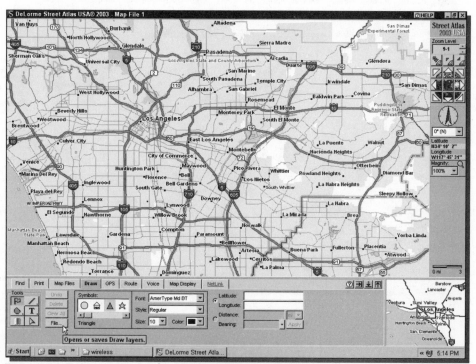

FIGURE 7-13: DeLorme Street Atlas USA preparing to import.

4. Click File ➪ Save and enter a filename, like `Summary-delorme.txt`.

5. Open Street Atlas USA and click the Draw tab.

6. Click the flag icon under Tools and select the symbol to represent the pushpins.

7. Click the File button (see Figure 7-13).

8. The File button opens the file section of the Draw tab. Click the Import button and select the file you saved in Step 4 ("`Summary-delorme.txt`").

9. Ensure that Files of type: "Solus Mark File (`*.txt`)" is selected, and click Open.

10. Click the Done button to close the draw file management window.

11. Observe your newly plotted war driving results. (See Figure 7-14.)

Another great way of converting data is to use any one of dozens of Perl scripts that massage the data for almost every mapping program available. These take more effort to get working, and require Perl be installed on your computer. It's worth the effort if the methods we've presented so far don't suit your needs, though. Search Google, and the `Netstumbler.com` forums, for "scripts" to learn more about these efficient and flexible data manipulation tools.

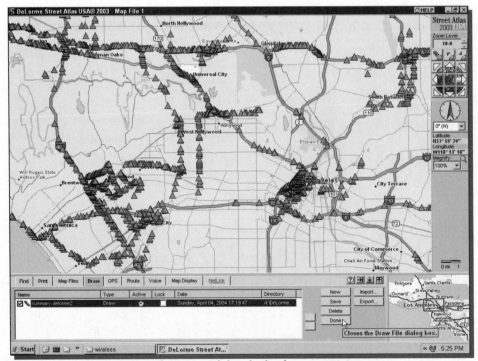

FIGURE 7-14: DeLorme Street Atlas USA with hundreds of access points.

## Step 5: Viewing the Results

The final step in importing results is showing it off! Each program has a different format for presenting data, but it's all easily understood. Sharing your maps with others makes for some great conversations.

As you can see from the maps we created in this section, much of our war driving took place on freeways around Los Angeles. In some areas, APs are so dense it's almost like leaving a trail of breadcrumbs showing your path of travel.

# Visualizing Extras

The beginner war driver will plot data onto a map and call it a day (or night). You can go a few steps further with these extras and really get noticed. The following sections cover a few interesting visualization techniques that the professionals use.

## 3-D Rendering

Some mapping applications have 3-D visualization extras. DeLorme TopoUSA* and XMap have this feature built-in. Figure 7-15 shows a 3-D topographic map overlayed with satellite

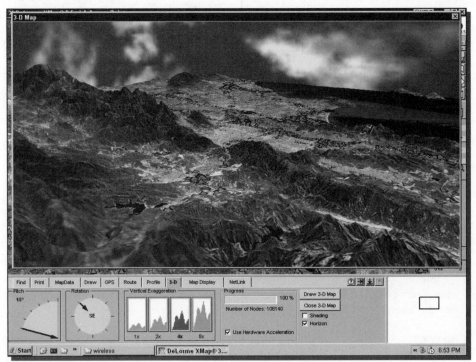

FIGURE 7-15: 3-D visualization from DeLorme TopoUSA.

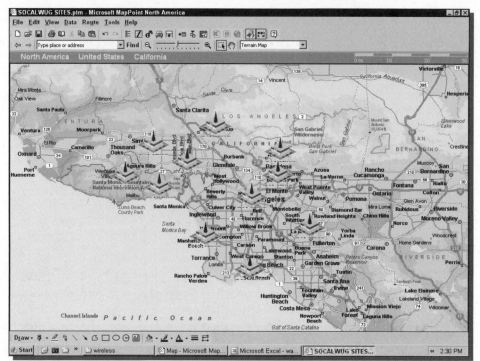

**FIGURE 7-16: A map with custom symbols representing hotspots.**

imagery and war driving access points plotted onto the image. There's a lot of visual information in this type of picture.

## Custom Symbols

Most mapping program that import pushpins (whether they are called pushpins, symbols, icons, or something else) have some method of changing, or creating your own graphic for the pushpin.

You can really spice up a map plot by using, say, a recognized logo for the Wi-Fi hotspot. For example, the map in Figure 7-16 was created using the SOCAL WUG logo and shows several real and hypothetical SOCAL WUG hotspots in the Los Angeles area.

**Note**

Filter your war driving results before importing the NetStumbler summary file into the mapping program. Microsoft Excel (again) is great for sorting entries to make it easy to delete sites you don't want to map.

Your specific software should have information available on creating your own symbols. But in case it doesn't, a little digging on Google Groups will find others that have the same question.

**Note**

Microsoft has made their MapPoint icons available as Windows .BMP (bitmap) files. Search Microsoft for "mappoint" to find the file in the download center. Use these files as a starting point to make changes.

DeLorme provides downloadable `.DIM` files (DeLorme Image Files) that can be installed in the Symbols directory to add hundreds of icons.

This list explains how to make a custom logo in Microsoft MapPoint:

1. Open a new MapPoint map without any pushpins.

2. Select View ⇨ Toolbars and make sure that the Draw toolbar is active.

3. Click the tiny upside-down triangle next to the pushpin icon on the Draw toolbar.

4. Click the button marked Import Custom Symbol.

5. Select a supported image file to import (currently Icons, BMPs, and Cursor files) and click Open.

That's it! Now you have a custom symbol that can be placed manually using the symbol button. Or you can select the symbol while importing latitude longitude data.

Make sure the file you select is smaller than 128 × 128 pixels, and note that the color white will be made transparent. 128 pixels square is pretty big on-screen. You probably want something in the 40 to 80 pixel range to really stand out.

## Satellite and Aerial Imaging

One of the more interesting mapping imagery trends in recent years is the high availability of satellite and aerial photography. Satellite images cover vast swaths of the globe. Commercial vendors have satellites in orbit with their only job being to take pictures and make them available for purchase by the commercial sector. Spy satellites for the masses!

Aerial photography is similar to satellite, but usually at a much higher resolution (you can see the color of cars in the driveway and find out who has a pool in your neighborhood). A specially equipped airplane will fly a pattern over an area while taking photographs. These photos are stitched together to create a highly accurate aerial view.

DeLorme products allow you to purchase and download overlays for your basic data sets. 10-meter-resolution satellite overlays (SAT-10) are available for every state for a reasonable cost (about a hundred dollars). If you don't need this type of aerial view, the built-in data works great, too.

There are also vast resources on the Web for creating aerial and satellite image files to play around with. Much of this data is freely available from sources like the U.S. Geological Survey, a government operation that makes much of the data free for download in small quantities. Your tax dollars at work!

Some sites to try out with satellite and aerial images:

- Space Imaging—Gallery of IKONOS and other satellite images: `www.spaceimaging.com`.

- USA PhotoMaps—Free aerial photo viewing software: `http://jdmcox.com`.

- U.S. Geological Survey—Downloads and links to images: `http//www.USGS.gov`.

■ Microsoft's original Terraserver—View images online:
`http://terraserver-usa.com`.

■ GlobeXplorer—Incredibly accurate satellite and color aerial photography online:
`www.globexplorer.com`.

 **Note** Some sites incorporate aerial and satellite images seamlessly. So when you are zoomed out the view is from a satellite photo. Zoom in and the system automatically switches to aerial photos. Neat!

## Signal Strength Mapping with MapPoint and Excel

This is the last time the chapter will mention Excel (well, maybe in the *Summary*). In this section, we will use Excel to ferret out all of the signal information from a single access point. By plotting these signals with the MapPoint "Shaded Circles" feature, the signal area can be easily plotted. Figure 7-17 shows the final results from tracking a single AP. The dark spots show the stronger signals, and that's very likely where the AP is located.

 **Note** When you are war driving, choose the type of antenna that's appropriate for the task. To locate an access point after the fact, as we're doing here, an omnidirectional antenna works best to evenly capture the Wi-Fi signal. A directional antenna would be used to see how far a signal reaches, but it would be harder to locate an AP. This stems from the signal information being

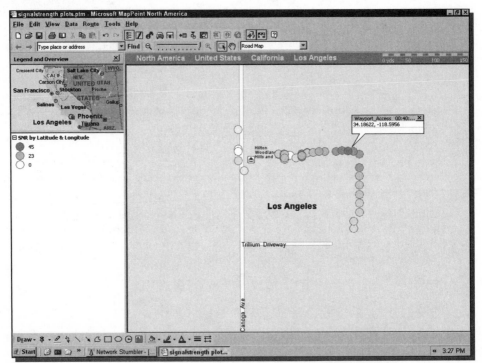

FIGURE 7-17: Plotting relative signal strength. Darker spots are stronger signals.

recorded along with the latitude and longitude of where the antenna is *located*, and not where it is pointing.

These are the steps to build a signal strength plot using NetStumbler, Excel, and MapPoint:

1. In NetStumbler, turn off the automatic save feature under Options.

2. Choose an access point to plot (it works best one at a time) and delete every other AP in the list. (Again, disable the "Save Automatically" feature before deleting, or you may erase data permanently.)

3. Export the NetStumbler file in Text format. This format saves every data point for every AP in the list.

4. Open the exported text file in Microsoft Excel.

5. Follow the prompts on the Import Text Wizard to choose a tab-delimited file.

6. Perform a Data ⇨ Sort to remove fields that begin with the "#" symbol. These are comments and can be removed. Keep the one commented row with the field headers.

7. Delete extra columns that you will not be using so you are left with the Latitude, Longitude, and the "[SNR Sig Noise]" column.

8. Now you get to use the "Text to Columns" feature in Excel to split that [SNR Sig Noise] column into usable numbers. Select the column with the [SNR Sig Noise] header (probably column C).

9. From the menu choose Data ⇨ Text to Columns. This opens a wizard.

10. In the Convert Text to Columns Wizard, choose "Delimited" in Step 1. Choose "Space" as the delimiter in step 2. You will see the numbers split up in the data preview window. Click Next, and then click Finish to close the wizard. The signal data should now be split into five columns "[", "SNR," "Sig," "Noise," and "]."

11. Now it's time to choose which signal data is going to be plotted. SNR (signal-to-noise ratio) is the most usable, but may not help you locate the AP. Sig (signal strength) does not always equate to a usable signal, but makes finding an AP easier. Delete the columns that will not be plotted. (Our example will use the Sig field, so brackets, SNR, and Noise will be deleted.)

12. Convert the Latitude and Longitude data into the +/− format required by MapPoint using the Find and Replace feature in Excel.

13. Now select Save As to save the file as an Excel Workbook (.XLS).

14. Open Microsoft MapPoint.

15. Choose Data ⇨ Import Data Wizard from the menu and choose the Excel file you just saved.

16. Make sure the "First row contains column headings" check box is selected. Click Finish if the data matches up (Latitude under Latitude, and so on).

17. Next comes the "Data Mapping Wizard - Map Type" dialog box. Usually you select push-pin to mark where an AP is located. This time select "Shaded Circle," and click Next.

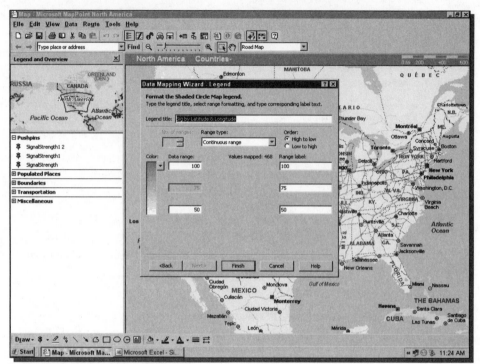

**FIGURE 7-18: The shaded circle wizard.**

**18.** The data field to map should read "Sig." Click Next.

**19.** Now comes the fun part. Adjust the data range numbers (see Figure 7-18) to choose a range that will give some meaning to the map. Something like 100 at the top and 50 at the bottom works well for plotting signal strength.

**20.** Click Finish.

Now you have a great representation of signal strength on an easy-to-use map. Use this for site surveys, finding how far your hotspot reaches, searching for elusive access points, and impressing your friends!

# Summary

Data visualization can come in many forms. The great thing about war driving is that you, yourself, can gather data quite easily. And mapping it is just one way to visualize what's truly going on in the ether. Did you ever think so many people had wireless networks? It's amazing to see them pop up on your screen when nothing is visible to the naked eye.

This truly is a way to see the invisible and get a glimpse of the popularity of wireless networking. You are performing your own research with the data being gathered and visualized.

In the next chapter, we will switch gears a little and start working directly with access points. You have plotted the location and signal strength of APs in your neighborhood. Now how about finding a way to bring Wi-Fi to poor coverage areas? Read on to Chapter 8 to build your own weather-resistant, outdoor access point.

# Playing with Access Points

part

# Build Your Own Outdoor Access Point

The neighborhood is mapped out in glorious color maps. There's an antenna on your laptop, a cantenna on your desktop in the basement, and an external antenna feeding them both. You can surf in the backyard, the front yard—but not quite from the park down the street.

Your neighbors are starting to ask what's going on. They're feeling left out. There's only one logical conclusion: Provide wireless Internet access for everyone on your street. Hey, why shouldn't they reap the benefits of your expertise? Besides it's a great way to introduce yourself: "Hi, I'm the geek on your street. Would you like free high-speed Internet access?"

Before long they'll be throwing parties in your honor and waving as you walk down the street with your laptop open—instead of looking at you strangely and shaking their heads.

Or, maybe you just want to extend your range a little further, or you just like to climb up on your roof. Read on for how to get started.

You can build an outdoor access point using several different parts (different enclosures, antennas, mounting hardware). To get started, you will need the following items:

➤ Access point

➤ Power-over-Ethernet adapter

➤ Waterproof box

➤ Mounting hardware

➤ Lightning protector and grounding wire

➤ Antenna and mounting hardware (see Chapter 4)

➤ Matching pigtail (see Chapter 1)

➤ Ethernet cable

➤ Electrical tape

➤ Waterproof sealant

# Location, Location, Location

Wi-Fi range is all about line-of-sight. That is, if you can see the antenna, you can get online. If you can't see it, all bets are off. Most of the time the antenna should be nice and high, where everyone can see it. If you added an external antenna as described in Chapter 4, then you discovered this during the site survey.

There's a Catch-22 with antenna placement. You need a longer cable to put the antenna in a better place, but the longer the cable, the more signal you lose.

The solution? Move your access point closer to the antenna—put it right on the pole. This keeps the cable nice and short and transfers all the power where you want it—into the air instead of into the cables and connectors.

## Line-of-Sight

As discussed in Chapter 4, good line-of-sight is the best predictor of a successful installation. The site in Figure 8-1 has clear line-of-sight.

Consider the following when trying to pick a good location for outdoor access:

- It's possible to get a good wireless connection through the outside walls of most buildings, but rarely through multiple walls, and especially if there are no windows.

- Big leafy trees absorb a lot of signal, especially when they're wet. Remember trees if you're choosing a location in winter, so it doesn't slowly stop working as spring arrives and the leaves grow back.

FIGURE 8-1: No problem with line-of-sight here!

- Use natural obstacles to block coverage where you don't want it to go. The side of a building is better than the rooftop if you only want coverage in one area.

- Remember, you can use an antenna to boost reception at the receiving end as shown in Chapters 2 and 4. This is handy if you've found the perfect location, except for that one place where it's unreliable.

- Prioritize within your coverage area. Sometimes there is no perfect solution, so knowing what's most important will help you make tradeoffs.

For example, if you only want coverage across the road, there's no need to mount an omni antenna on a high mast on the chimney. Instead, mount a directional antenna above your (street-facing) garage door. It's much easier to get at, and you won't waste half the signal on an area you don't need and create radio interference where it's not wanted.

## Providing Power and Data

Your outdoor access point will need a source of power and a connection to the Internet. We'll get sneaky and provide both of those in a single cable using "Power-over-Ethernet" or PoE for short. Running Ethernet cable is far easier than antenna cable. It's much cheaper, more flexible and can go up to 328 feet (100 m) without data loss.

**Note** PoE injects direct current (DC) into two of the unused wires in standard Cat-5 Ethernet cable. By combining the power and data into a single cable, only one cable is needed for the longer runs going outside to the access point.

One end of the cable will go into the outdoor box you'll build. The other end will go to your digital subscriber line (DSL) or cable connection to the Internet (or an existing router). You'll need a power outlet at that location to provide power for the access point. See Figure 8-2 for an example PoE setup.

Something else to consider is whether you want wired connections to the Internet as well as wireless. A fully wireless system may give you more flexibility. You could relocate your cable or DSL box away from your computer where it's more convenient for outside installation, such as in the attic, an upstairs room, or the garage.

## Safety

Lightning can strike almost anywhere, but it generally goes for high points, and if they're metal, then so much the better. You should take lightning protection seriously and plan for it in your installation. Don't think, "Come on. The outdoor gear is only worth $100, I'll take my chances," because that's not the issue. Even with good lightning protection, the outside gear is likely to be toast anyway. You need lightning protection to prevent a fire, and to ensure the safety of both the people and electronics inside the house.

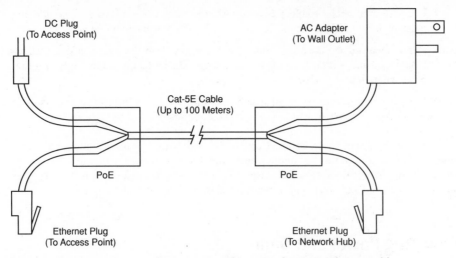

**FIGURE 8-2: Internet access and Power-over-Ethernet in the same Ethernet cable.**

You need to install lightning protection to protect against fire, and to reduce damage to people and equipment inside the building.

Lightning protection is covered in more detail later in the chapter, but think about where the copper grounding wire will go when you're planning the outdoor location. If electrical storms are common in your area, and the mounting location is high and exposed, you *must* take this very seriously indeed. See Figure 8-3 for a diagram on lightning strike protection.

Other common sources of accidents are ladders and high places. Be careful up there. No matter how good a job you do the first time, chances are you'll be up there again to fix something, so it might be worth compromising a little on the best location to provide safer and simpler access to the equipment.

## Balance the Trade-Offs

There's rarely a perfect place to put the outdoor access point and antenna. It's a balance between the following factors:

- Line-of-sight to the desired coverage area
- Physical access to the equipment for ease of installation or repair
- Suitable route for Ethernet cable from inside
- Suitable route for lightning ground cable
- Protection from the elements (sun, rain, lightning, snow)
- Aesthetic appeal: will the neighbors or landlord complain?

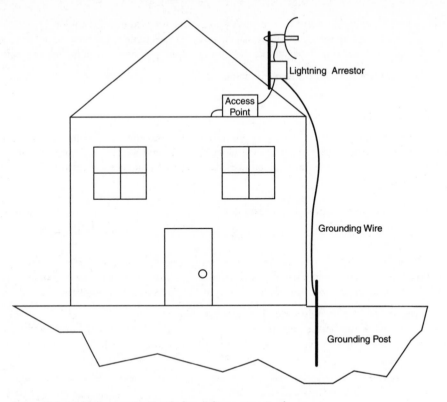

FIGURE 8-3: Lightning protection helps reduce property damage.

You can save some time, effort, and money by making an early decision about where the antenna and box will go. For example, if you choose a sheltered location tucked under an eave, you won't need a more expensive highly waterproof enclosure. If you already have a mast with a TV antenna, then half the job is over.

# Choosing the Parts

The most time-consuming part of building your outdoor AP is getting all the parts together. The actual assembly takes less than two hours once you have everything in one place.

There are no special tools required. A drill, some drill bits, a small handsaw, and a pair of pliers or wrench to tighten everything onto the pole should be enough.

You may be surprised to find that the access point is less than half the total cost. Although most parts cost about $20, there're a few of them and they add up fast. The antenna is more expensive and may cost up to $100 depending on your requirements.

Research carefully and plan ahead to save on shipping costs. For example, the antenna, pigtail, and lightning protector are all specialized items. Buying all of these online at the same time from a single vendor may be cheaper than paying the best price plus shipping from three different suppliers.

Let's take a look at each of these items in detail.

## Access Point

The most important element is the access point. It is best (and cheapest) to choose an 802.11b based device for outdoor use rather than the newer 802.11a and 802.11g equipment. The range is better and there are more equipment choices. The exact type of access point you choose isn't critical as long as:

- It has a removable antenna (many do not)

- You can find (or build) a matching PoE adapter, as discussed later in the chapter

The D-Link DWL-900AP+ is the device used in this chapter and shown in examples. However there are many manufacturers of this type of equipment. Read reviews online or ask friends for their recommendations. Figure 8-4 shows a common access point for outdoor use.

Some access points also include a four-port hub for connecting other computers via Ethernet. Since the box will be up on the pole, it will be hard to use those extra ports, but apart from the extra size, a combination router and access point will also work just fine.

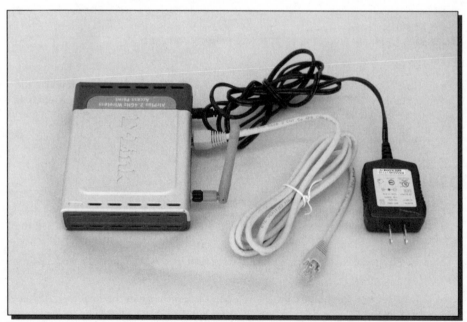

FIGURE 8-4: A wireless access point with detachable antenna and standard accessories.

Be careful not to get a wireless Ethernet bridge, because they are not a complete access point. Instead, they take a wireless signal from an access point in at one end and convert it to Ethernet at the other. This is handy for getting computers online that only have an Ethernet port (many older Macintosh computers for example) or to simplify installation.

**Tip** Some access points are more reliable than others, so be sure to search online for comments about specific models. Physically, most brands are quite reliable, but software quality varies a lot. Look for reports of slow downs, hangs, reboots or spontaneous resets. Although resetting the access point is easy enough via the PoE plug, it can be a chore to retrieve it to reconfigure it.

## Power-Over-Ethernet Adapter

You need to get power to your equipment when it's up on the pole. A good way to do this is to use "Power-over-Ethernet" or PoE. This adds power directly to unused wires in your Ethernet cable to save running a separate power cable to your access point.

Ethernet cable is four twisted pairs, but only two pairs are used for data. Manufacturers realized this years ago and started building proprietary solutions that add power to the unused pairs. This has the advantage of halving the number of cables required. However, it was years before they got together and agreed on a standard, so PoE is usually limited to high-end commercial equipment and still isn't often found on consumer gear.

Now that a standard exists (802.3af), companies are making converters that work with consumer equipment, and sometimes it's possible to build your own adapter. Some background on how it all works will help you decide on the best solution.

The challenge with sending low-voltage DC PoE cable is that voltage drops with distance. Also, the amount of current is restricted by the small gauge wire used in the Ethernet cables. Search online for "PoE calculator" and you'll find resources like www.gweep.net/~sfoskett/tech/poecalc.html that estimate the voltage drop.

The PoE standard sends a much higher 48 VDC voltage over the wire. This requires less current for the same amount of power, but the receiving equipment needs to be able to convert the 48 VDC to something usable.

Several companies now supply solutions for their consumer equipment. For example, D-Link makes the DWL-P100 PoE adapter. This comes with a 48 V plug pack that runs on AC power and is sent over the Ethernet cable to another box which converts the 48 V back into the 5 VDC needed by the access point.

The PoE adapter shown in Figure 8-5 combines Ethernet data and 48 VDC into a single Ethernet cable and then splits it back to Ethernet and converts it down to 5 V at the other end.

**Tip** If the access point operates at 12 V and it's a short Ethernet cable, the voltage drop may be small enough to work with a simple splitter you can build yourself. Web sites like www.nycwireless.net/poe/ provide detailed instructions on how to build one. Unfortunately, 5 V is generally too low for this hack to work.

With some careful research, you could use this same adapter with other brands' access points. However, you need to be sure that the output voltage matches, that the current drawn is lower

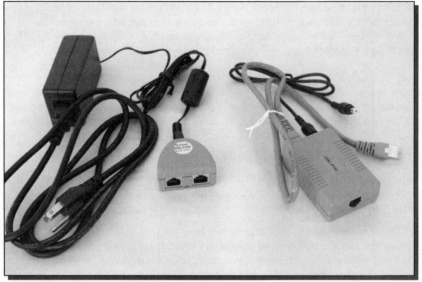

FIGURE 8-5: A Power-over-Ethernet adapter.

than the adapter rating, that the power plug is the same size, and that the plug uses the same polarity. If in doubt, buy the access point and PoE adapter from the same manufacturer for the specified equipment.

## Waterproof Box

Your access point has to stay dry and at a reasonable temperature to operate as expected. Finding and building a case can be the most challenging part of this project, especially if you don't want to spend more on the case than all the other equipment combined.

Tip    Your hardware manufacturer has already determined temperature range and humidity tolerance for your product. Check the access point's specification sheet or product manual for the exact tolerance.

Ultimately the local weather conditions will dictate the type of case used. Other factors include the ease-of-access and the expected installation lifetime.

Tip    Continuous below-freezing temperatures or snow and ice buildup can be challenging conditions that require special solutions including box heaters and antenna de-icing. These are not addressed here. More information on extreme-weather enclosures can be found online at Tessco (www.tessco.com), Talley (www.talleycom.com), ElectroCom West (www.ecwest.com), and other wireless equipment suppliers.

By far the cheapest and simplest box to work with is a plastic food container, as shown in Figure 8-6. These are readily available in lots of sizes. They're easy to drill, cut and glue, and

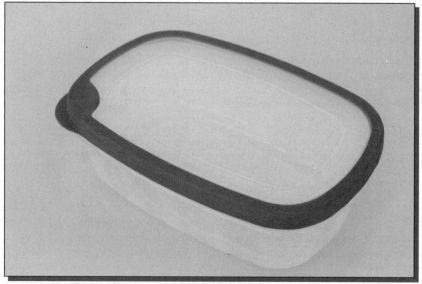

FIGURE 8-6: A cheap, effective, easy-to-modify case.

are cheap. Their main downside is they can degrade quickly if they're always in the sun. Don't put one up and expect it to last for ten years. However, in most locations you should get a year or so before it needs replacing.

The next step up is to visit a large hardware store, or better still an electrical supply store. They usually stock outdoor "rainproof" metal boxes in various sizes for under $20 (see Figure 8-7).

FIGURE 8-7: This 8 inch × 8 inch metal case was $13.

These metal cases are not completely waterproof, but they'll withstand most weather, especially if mounted in a sheltered location. The metal is harder to work with than plastic, but a metal hacksaw and sharp drill bits will solve most modification needs.

The same stores also stock molded plastic junction boxes designed for burying in the ground. These are completely waterproof, and as they're made of plastic, they're simple to modify. They cost 50 to 100 percent more than the metal cases. They're air-tight, so they may get too hot if you seal them completely. Some bottom ventilation holes may be needed for cooling.

Another source to explore is waterproof equipment carrying cases used for cameras or other electronic gear. One large manufacturer is Pelican. They have a wide range of sizes, shapes, and colors, and are completely waterproof. Prices are reasonable, though more expensive than junction boxes. The cases are plastic and fairly simple to modify, though the molded fittings and indents can complicate internal mounting.

Last but not least, there are cases made especially for mounting electronic equipment outdoors-on poles and walls. These usually have hinged doors, pole mounting points for U-bolts, rubber gaskets for weather proofing, and cable through-holes. They range in cost from $50 to $100. There's no single source for these as they tend to be custom made for specific industries. Search for "wisp outdoor enclosure" and similar to find suppliers online. (See Chapter 9 for an example usage of one of these heavy-duty exclosures.)

## Mounting Hardware

Once you've chosen your box, you'll need to figure out how to mount it to the pole or wall. A good source of pole mounting hardware is the TV antenna section of your local hardware or electronics store. An example is shown in Figure 8-8.

FIGURE 8-8: TV antenna mounting hardware like this pole and mounting bracket is widely available.

## Lightning Protector and Grounding Wire

Lightning protectors provide important safety protection for your equipment and your building. A properly installed lightning protector should prevent a fire starting if your equipment goes up in flames after a direct hit.

Lightning protectors are specialized equipment like other wireless gear such as high-gain antennas and pigtails. Some online vendors are:

```
www.fab-corp.com
www.pasadena.net/shop
www.hyperlinktech.com
www.wisp-router.com
www.ydi.com
```

Plan carefully to ensure the protector matches your cable and antenna connectors. A common version is N-Male to N-Female (see Figure 8-9). It can be put inline anywhere there is an existing N-Connector, such as your antenna.

Unless you ground the protector, though, it won't do much except slightly weaken your signal strength. You'll need 8-gauge copper wire (i.e., thick) from your local hardware store, along with appropriate fittings. For complete protection, this wire should run all the way to an eight foot copper clad steel pipe driven into the ground and connected via a special ground fitting. This isn't always possible or practical. In low-lightning areas, more often the wire is taken to the nearest copper water pipe and connected via a fitting designed for grounding. If you have a metal case, it should be grounded too.

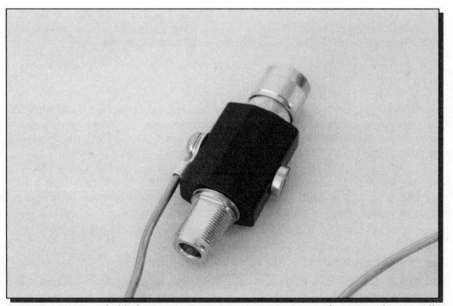

FIGURE 8-9: A grounded lightning protector is an important part of every outdoor installation.

# Configuring Your Access Point

If the existing network consists of a single computer hooked directly to a cable or DSL modem, you should add a broadband router before continuing. You'll need a router to share the connection between multiple computers, including computers connecting via the wireless access point.

The one exception to this is if *all* your computers will connect via a wireless connection and your access point supports connection sharing (usually via a combination of services called NAT and DHCP). If your access point has two or more Ethernet ports as well as wireless support, then it almost certainly supports sharing. Check the documentation to be sure.

## Preparation

You can configure your wireless access point for your network in many ways. To leave room in this book for more projects, it's assumed that you're adding this new outdoor access point to an existing network. This network already has a working broadband connection connected via a broadband router that provides facilities for sharing the connection between multiple computers. In geek speak, your network provides DHCP, NAT, and gateway services.

Now it's time to get the access point configured. The steps are:

1. Download the most recent firmware file from the manufacturer's Web site to your computer. This has the latest bug fixes and it may not be on your device already.

2. Unplug the computer from your network and plug it into your access point. Follow the access point setup directions to access the administrative interface via a Web browser.

3. Skip the suggested configuration steps and update the firmware using the file you downloaded earlier. This option is usually under a System or Tools menu. If you get stuck, see the manufacturer's Web site from where you downloaded the firmware.

4. Again connect to the administrative interface via a browser. Now you can start the configuration.

The configuration steps that follow require a few settings and decisions. Of course you can change anything you want later on, but after people start using the system some things are easier to change than others. See Figure 8-10 for an example of upgrading the firmware on an access point.

 **Caution** Always perform the firmware upgrade through the Ethernet port on the access point, not through the wireless connection. A mis-applied firmware upgrade could result in damage to the access point and a warranty replacement through the manufacturer.

## Access Point Password

It goes almost without saying that you should always set a new password for your access point so people can't change the configuration and even disable or hijack it. Make sure that you

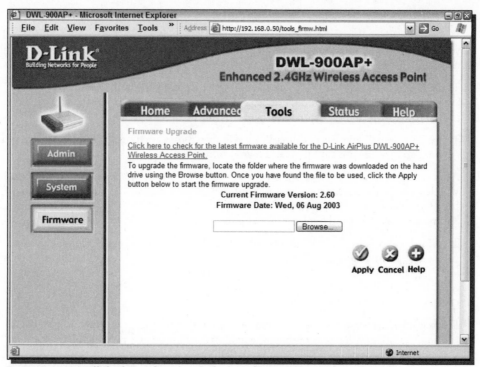

FIGURE 8-10: Install the latest firmware before configuring the access point.

change the password for the administrative user ("admin" in most cases) and the user-level passwords, if applicable.

## SSID

Choose a unique SSID instead of the default that comes with your access point. This reduces confusion for people trying to use your system and allows you to easily identify your system from other wireless signals you may find nearby.

It's considered good form to provide an SSID that allows someone to contact you if necessary. This is useful if your new access point starts interfering with their signal. You could use a Web site name or even an e-mail address. Or you might use your house or apartment number with or without your street name depending on your expected coverage area. Most systems support SSIDs that are case-sensitive, are 2 to 32 characters long and include most common punctuation characters.

Some examples of SSIDs you could use are: house922, www.socalfreenet.org, myname@fastmail.fm, janewireless. Avoid mixing upper- and lowercase letters to prevent configuration problems.

The SSID is essentially the personal address of your access point. This is what people will see when setting up their computer to get on your wireless network.

## WEP

Wired Equivalent Privacy (WEP) was designed to provide security for wireless networks. If you want to start a debate amongst a group of wireless experts, ask them whether you should use WEP on your wireless network.

Those against will say that WEP can be cracked easily and will cite the seminal paper www.isaac.cs.berkeley.edu/isaac/wep-faq.html in their support and point to one of several readily available programs that automate breaking a WEP key.

Those in favor will say that enabling WEP will stop most casual people from accessing your network and you should turn it on as a matter of routine.

As is so often true, both sides are correct and the right answer for your network is "it depends." Wireless security is a large topic that fills entire books: *How Secure is Your Wireless Network?* by Lee Barken is a good starting place. *Wireless Security End-to-End* by Brian Carter and Russell Shumway is another good book on the subject.

The short answer is to leave WEP off unless you have access to all the computers that will use your access point. If you turn WEP on at your access point, you'll need to configure each wireless computer individually to use it. And no one else will be able to use your network until their computer is similarly configured—except the patient hacker running the cracking tools of course.

For example, if you want to have an open access point that others can share, leave WEP off. If you want to share with a select group of neighbors, turn it on and then configure each of their computers—and be prepared to reconfigure them when they mess up the settings.

If you do use WEP, also enable Media Access Control (MAC) filtering on your access point (most of them support it). It will require you to gather the unique MAC address of every computer that will use your access point, but you can do this when you're setting up WEP on each of them. See your access point manual for details.

---

### Wireless LAN Security

Use good security practices whether you use WEP or not. Here are some steps that will keep your data safe from prying antennas:

- Install a firewall on each wireless computer. Free firewalls are available from

  www.agnitum.com/

  www.zonelabs.com/

- You may need to hunt around a little to avoid the paid versions, though. This stops the spread of worms within your wireless LAN and limits the damage if one does get loose.

- Install anti-virus software and keep it updated. In addition to the standard off-the-shelf products, consider smaller companies like www.nod32.com that provide competitive bulk licensing and yearly renewals if you call them directly. Then as you help people get onto your wireless LAN, you can offer them virus protection too. A comprehensive list of products is available at

`http://directory.google.com/Top/Computers/Security/Anti_Virus/Products/`

- Secure your e-mail. Well-known Web mail services like yahoo.com and hotmail.com provide an optional secure logon, but they don't secure the messages. Consider switching to a provider like fastmail.fm that provides secure Web pages for all your messages, just as your online bank does. If you use an e-mail program, be sure to set the Advanced settings to "This server requires a secure connection (Secure Socket Layer or 'SSL')" (or similar) for both outgoing and incoming mail. If your e-mail provider doesn't support SSL for e-mail, switch to one that does (for example, `fastmail.fm` again).

- When you use Web sites with sensitive personal data, double-check that they are in 'secure mode'. Most Web browsers indicate this with a lock icon of some sort, and the URL will generally begin with `https://` instead of the usual `http://`.

- Surf completely anonymously, if you care, by using a third-party-paid service like

`www.freedom.net`

`www.anonymizer.com`

A good overview of these services is found at

`www.webveil.com/matrix.html`

and a general directory is available at

`http://directory.google.com/Top/Computers/Internet/Proxies/`

Wireless or not, continue to use good security practices like choosing good passwords (a mix of characters and symbols), not reusing the same password in multiple places, and changing your passwords regularly. A good password helper program like `www.roboform.com` can make this much easier to manage.

### Channel

Your access point can operate on any of the 11 channels (plus a few more in some countries). However, each channel actually overlaps with two or three channels on either side. Thus only three distinct channels are actually available: 1, 6, and 11. However, recent research suggests that a scheme of 1, 4, 8, and 11 is a reasonable alternative.

Do a mini-war drive in the region your outdoor access point will cover, as described in Chapter 6. Pay particular attention to the channels used by any access points you discover. Choose the least occupied channel for your access point.

When the access point is installed, you may need to adjust the channel based on real-world usage. Fortunately, any client computers using your SSID will automatically adjust, so this is not as critical as, say, the SSID you choose or the WEP key you set (if you enable WEP).

## LAN Settings

When you first configure your access point, it will be on a private LAN consisting of just your computer and the access point, so the settings used don't matter as long as they're compatible. However, when you add the access point to your main LAN, it will need to have compatible settings so it is accessible and doesn't cause conflicts with other devices on the network. The settings needed are:

- IP address: A unique address for the access point. Choose a number that's easy to remember and doesn't conflict with other devices. For example, many routers use the range from 192.168.0.1 to 192.168.0.254, and often reserve the first number, 192.168.0.1, or last number, 192.168.0.254, for their own address. So you might choose 192.168.0.2 as the address for the access point.

- Subnet mask: On most home networks, this will be set to 255.255.255.0.

- Gateway: Usually the router acts as the gateway and the address commonly ends in .1. Thus, 192.168.0.1 is a common setting.

- DNS server: This value is supplied by your Internet Service Provider (ISP) so refer to their setup instructions. Sometimes the router will forward or cache DNS requests so it may be the same as the gateway value.

One way to determine these settings is to find the same settings on a computer on your network. Usually the router supplies these settings automatically via Dynamic Host Configuration Protocol (DHCP). On a Microsoft Windows machine, you can find the value from a command prompt as follows:

```
C:\>ipconfig /all
Windows IP Configuration
        Host Name . . . . . . . . . . . . : mike
        Primary Dns Suffix  . . . . . . . :
        Node Type . . . . . . . . . . . . : Unknown
        IP Routing Enabled. . . . . . . . : No
        WINS Proxy Enabled. . . . . . . . : No

Ethernet adapter Local Area Connection:
        Connection-specific DNS Suffix  . : local
        Description . . . . . . . . . . . : Intel(R) PRO/100 S Desktop Adapter
        Physical Address. . . . . . . . . : 00-02-B3-B7-xx-xx
        Dhcp Enabled. . . . . . . . . . . : Yes
        Autoconfiguration Enabled . . . . : Yes
        IP Address. . . . . . . . . . . . : 192.168.1.199
        Subnet Mask . . . . . . . . . . . : 255.255.255.0
        Default Gateway . . . . . . . . . : 192.168.1.1
        DHCP Server . . . . . . . . . . . : 192.168.1.1
        DNS Servers . . . . . . . . . . . : 192.168.1.1, 66.80.131.5
        Lease Obtained. . . . . . . . . . : Monday, March 22, 2004 9:53:47 AM
        Lease Expires . . . . . . . . . . : Monday, March 22, 2004 10:53:47 AM
```

Here you can deduce that Internet Protocol (IP) addresses range from 192.168.1.1 to 192.168.1.254 with a subnet mask of 255.255.255.0. The gateway is 192.168.1.1, and the DNS servers are both the gateway and an alternate of 66.80.131.5.

## Configuration Example

The DWL-900AP+ has a configuration wizard that guides you through the installation. It is useful to skip the wizard and configure the settings screen-by-screen to see some of the useful choices that the wizard doesn't offer and to see how to use them. We'll walk through these selections in this section.

### Basic Wireless and LAN Settings

If the access point has several operating modes, set it to "access point" (also called "infrastructure access point"). Other modes are used in other wireless applications, such as a wireless relay (see Chapter 9), or to connect to another access point.

Find the page in your access point to set the SSID, channel, and often a name for the device (see Figure 8-11). The name is sometimes visible to client software, but is mostly useful for maintaining multiple access points as it sometimes gets confusing which one you're editing when you have several.

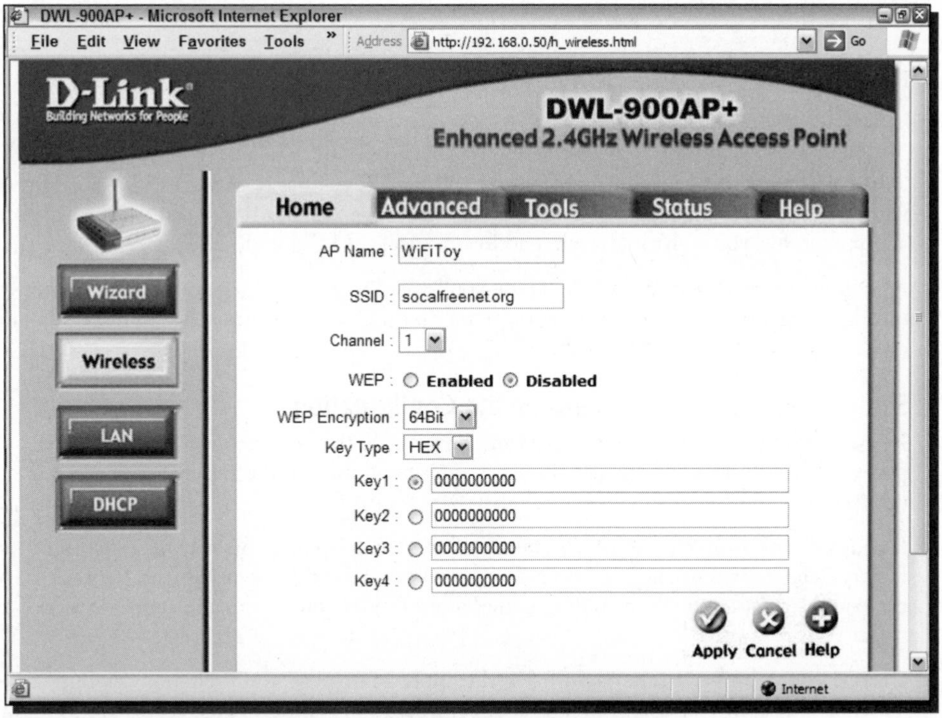

FIGURE 8-11: Set the SSID, channel, and name for your access point.

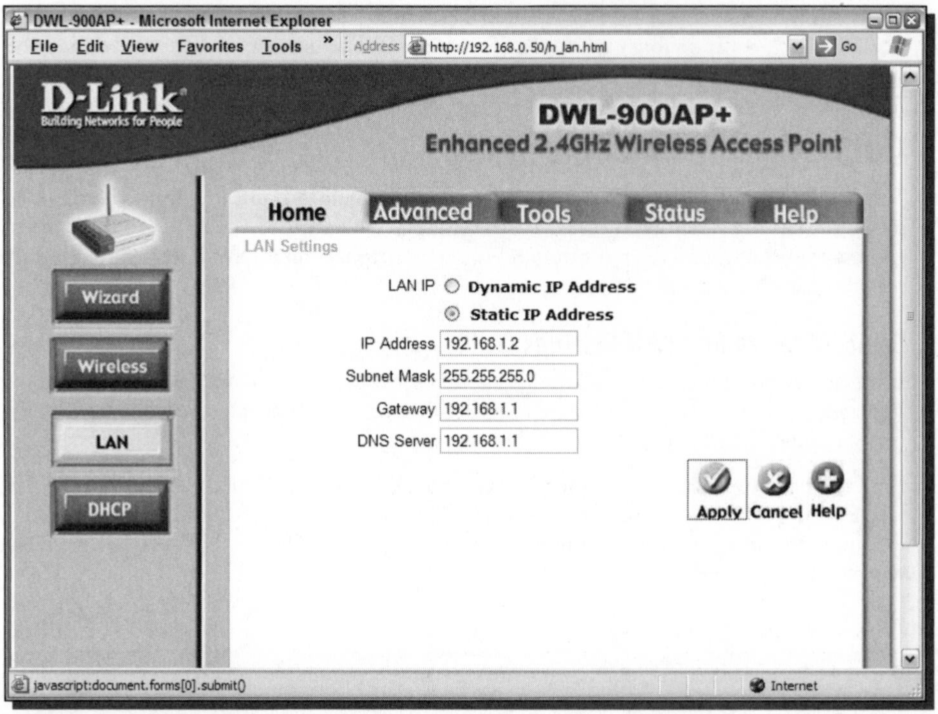

FIGURE 8-12: Set the LAN settings for your network.

Be sure to save the wireless settings, and then find the page to set the LAN settings you calculated.

Select the "Static IP Address" setting. If you choose "Dynamic IP Address," the access point will work when it's plugged into your network, but it will be hard to find it via the browser to administer it as you won't know what address to use! (See Figure 8-12.)

After you enter and save the LAN values, you'll need to either adjust your computer network settings to match, or plug both your computer and the access point back into the LAN and continue the configuration from there.

## Setting Your Password and Saving the Configuration

Be aware that your access point is live from here on, so the next step is to change your password. The browser address of the access point will now be the static IP you entered (for example, http://192.168.1.2).

If you can't get back into the configuration of your access point, you may need to reset it to the factory default settings and start over. The instructions for this are usually on the CD that came with the access point or on the manufacturer's Web site. The same steps are used if you forget your password.

Change your administration password at the appropriate page and then log back in to continue. At this point, it's useful to save your configuration settings. Most access points allow you

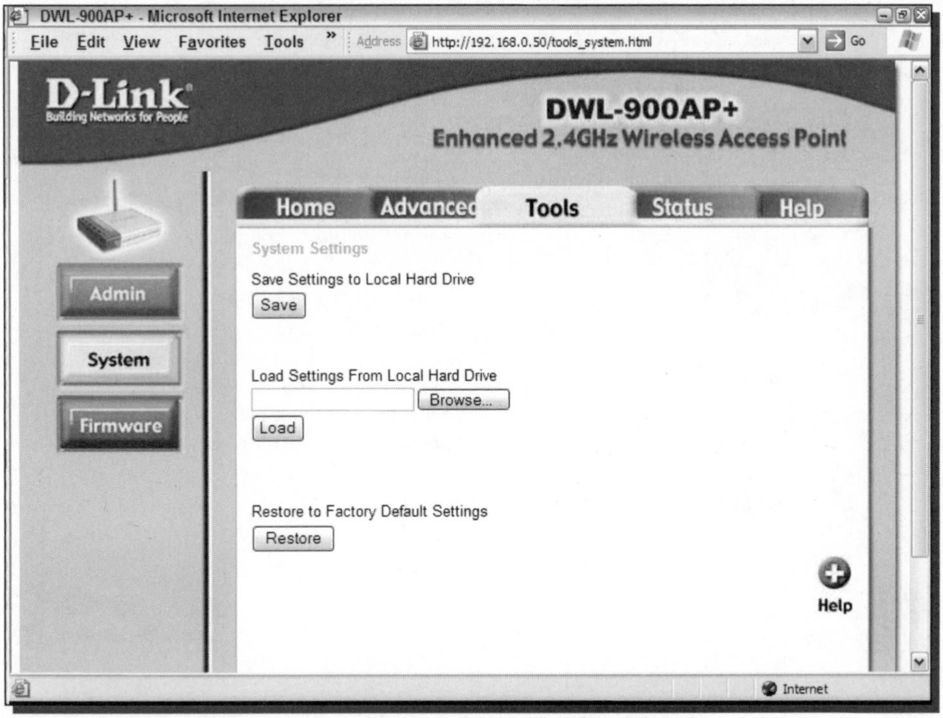

DWL-900AP+ - Microsoft Internet Explorer

File  Edit  View  Favorites  Tools  »    Address  http://192.168.0.50/tools_system.html    Go

**D-Link**
Building Networks for People

**DWL-900AP+**
**Enhanced 2.4GHz Wireless Access Point**

Home    Advanced    **Tools**    Status    Help

System Settings

Save Settings to Local Hard Drive
[ Save ]

Load Settings From Local Hard Drive
[_____]  [ Browse... ]
[ Load ]

Restore to Factory Default Settings
[ Restore ]

Admin

System

Firmware

⊕
Help

Internet

FIGURE 8-13: Frequently save your configuration to a file (if supported).

to download the settings to a file on your computer so you can easily restore them later. As you now have the access point basically configured and accessible from your network, it's a good time to save the settings. As you continue changing other settings, you can save again (and again) to ensure you don't miss anything. Figure 8-13 shows the save-to-file setup page.

**Tip**

Saving your settings becomes even more important if you turn on WEP and start using MAC filtering to protect your network. It's tedious to re-enter MAC addresses and key values (and be sure to keep a backup copy).

## Advanced Settings

Your access point will have a page of advanced wireless settings somewhere that contains items like those shown in Figure 8-14. Some are more useful than others:

- *Antenna selector*: It's important to set this if your access point has two antennas, because you'll only be using one. It isn't always clear whether left and right are while facing the front or back of the access point, but the manual or manufacturer's Web site should clarify.

- *Speed (Tx/Basic Rate)*: You can increase the range of your network by decreasing the maximum allowed speed. In theory, it shouldn't make any difference because Wi-Fi should automatically downgrade to a lower speed if the connection is poor. In practice, it's useful

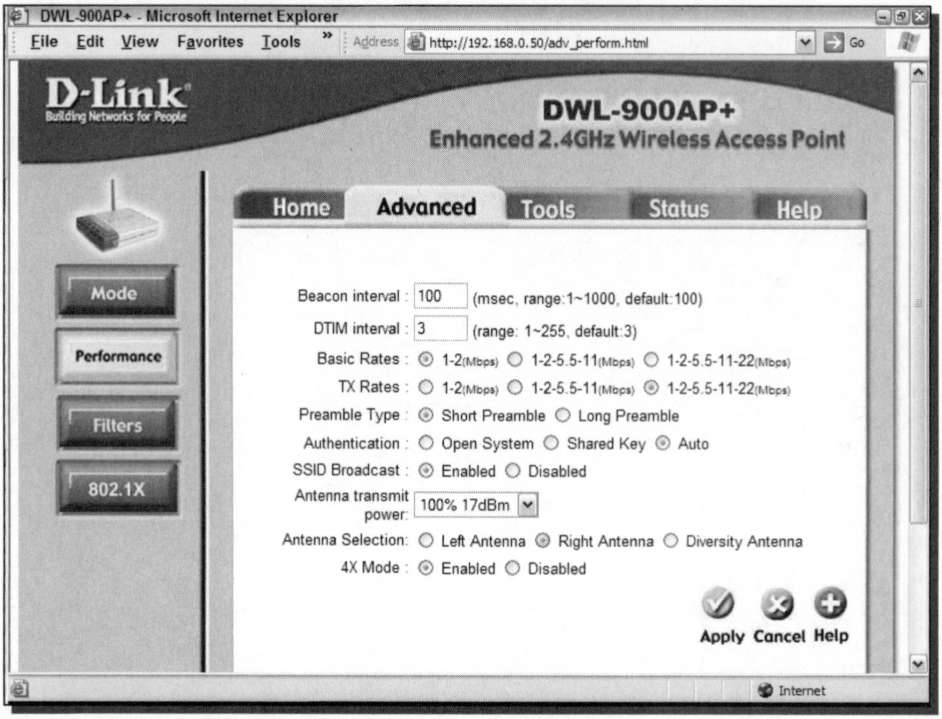

FIGURE 8-14: There are many useful advanced wireless settings.

to force everyone to a lower speed and save the overhead of all the hunting around for the best speed. Note, though, that you can significantly lower the maximum speed of your network and reduce sharing among users, because now all transmissions will take longer and everyone has to wait until each transmission completes before getting a turn.

■ *Authentication and SSID Broadcast*: If you use WEP, you can change these two settings to Shared Key and Disabled, respectively. These hide your system more effectively from hackers. Sometimes disabling the SSID Broadcast can cause problems with some client adapters, so test this first.

■ *Power*: If there are a lot of access points in your area, it's good form to turn down the power if all the computers connecting to you are close by. This reduces interference to other users. This is also a good security practice as it makes your access point less visible and your network harder to access from further away. Experiment to find a reliable value.

If you're in doubt about what the settings do, change and test them one at a time. Be sure to save your configuration changes so you can revert to a previous version if something stops working.

Don't be afraid to explore other settings. If the supplied documentation doesn't explain the settings adequately, a Web search will quickly find more information.

When you're all done, save the settings to disk, power everything off, take a break, and then come back and do one final test. If possible, find a computer that hasn't had wireless installed before, then add an adapter and ensure that you can configure it to work with your access point. If you're using WEP and advanced security measures, this is especially important, as some of the details are hard to get just right.

It's much easier to work out what's wrong with all the pieces of the puzzle right in front of you, than when half the gear is up a pole in the rain.

# Assembling the Box

Now that the access point is configured and all of the hardware is available, it's time to get everything together, test it, place the access point into an enclosure, and set it up on the roof.

## Testing

When you have all the parts together, plug everything in and make sure it all works and fits together. Although you just tested the access point *settings*, you didn't test the PoE adapter and the *actual* cables you'll be using. This is a great time to find the bad connection on that old Cat-5 cable you got from a friend's garage. Use as much of the final equipment as possible, including the high-gain antenna and any pigtails. Figure 8-15 shows an example of this test.

FIGURE 8-15: Testing all of the parts before deployment.

A laptop is connected to the access point via a PoE adapter, while the long Ethernet cable connects much of the equipment that will go inside the case.

If it doesn't work the first time, start removing equipment to simplify things, or start with what used to work and gradually change things. For example, first use the original power supply and a standard Ethernet cable, and add the external antenna.

If possible, connect the AP to the Internet in its final software configuration. Then try to surf via a wireless connection. When you're done testing, you can be confident that the hardware and software setup all work before you start cutting metal and climbing on rooftops.

## Measure Twice, Cut Once

Place the access point and PoE adapter into the case and arrange them for best ventilation and fit. Then add the internal cables and confirm that it still fits. It may be better to replace a supplied cable with a shorter version, especially for stiff Ethernet cables. As shown in Figure 8-16, lay out all the parts before modifying the case to ensure everything fits. All cables should exit the case at the bottom to help stop water from entering.

Next, add the pigtail and outside Ethernet cable. The pigtail may be thick and stiff, so anticipate carefully where it will run. It is important to have all cables exit from the bottom of the case. This stops water from running down the cable and into the case.

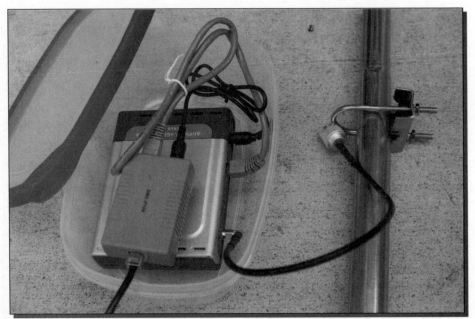

FIGURE 8-16: Finding the optimal device layout and cable management.

When everything is in place and connected, then you can plan where the holes will go.

If the fit is snug enough for everything in the plastic food container, leave the access point and PoE adapter loose in the enclosure. This will eliminate the need for extra holes and mounting hardware.

**Tip**  You can remove the access point electronics from its plastic case to reduce the space needed and enhance cooling. However, this may void the warranty, and you have to be extremely careful that no metal touches the electronics.

Be sure to plan for the case mounting to the pole or wall as well. If bolts will protrude into the case, as shown previously in Figure 8-9, make sure the equipment will still fit.

When everything is in place, mark the case carefully to show where holes and mounting points are located. Then you're ready to start drilling and cutting.

## Modifying the Case

The plastic case is easy to modify using simple tools like a drill and small handsaw.

First drill holes in the case where the cables will pass through (see Figure 8-17). Make sure your drill bit matches the cable thickness. The cable should be snug, but not pinched. Any extra gap can be filled with sealant.

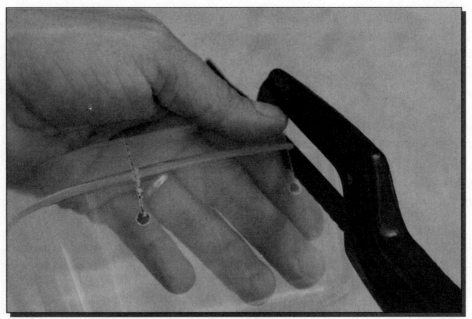

FIGURE 8-17: Drill the case first, then cut down to the holes.

With a plastic case, you can cheat a bit and cut a line down to the holes. The plastic is flexible enough to bend and allow the cables to pass down to the hole via the cut.

If you're using a metal or thick molded plastic case, you have a few options:

- Make much larger holes to pass the connector through. You can use sealant to fill in the gaps afterwards.

- If you have an Ethernet cable crimper and plugs you can thread the bare cable through the hole and add your own connector afterwards. This would be more difficult for the pigtail, but fortunately, pigtail connectors are usually smaller anyway.

- Saw a channel down to the hole using two cuts instead of the one shown in Figure 8-17. You can put the holes closer to the lid to minimize cutting and sealing.

A thin metal file like a rattail file is useful for smoothing out holes or even cutting channels.

When using plastic, bend the plastic to thread the cables through the cut. The cable should be snugged but not pinched in the hole. (See Figure 8-18.)

If the enclosure is larger than the plastic box shown here, you may need to mount the equipment directly inside the box. The plastic box shown is already snug and there's no exposed electronics, so no mounting is needed.

Condensation can form on the inside of a metal case during changing temperatures, so mount equipment away from the walls to avoid water running onto the electronics. Another reason to

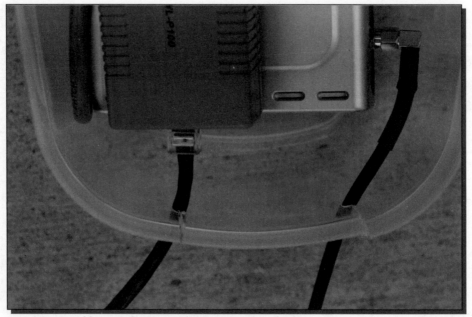

FIGURE 8-18: Cables exit the case without strain or pinching.

mount equipment inside the box is to avoid movement and damage in high winds or even during installation. Also, connectors may develop poor connections over time if they're continually moved or strained.

Make a final check to ensure that everything fits as you expect and that nothing is touching or rubbing where it shouldn't be.

## Mounting the Case and Antenna

The case is now ready to be mounted on a pole or wall. The steps are:

1. Mount the case on the pole
2. Mount the antenna on the pole
3. Connect the lightning arrestor, antenna, and pigtail
4. Make the connectors watertight
5. Zip tie the cables, leaving drip loops (drip loops give water a place from which to fall)

Mount the case on the pole and then mount the antenna using the instructions that came with your antenna and its mounting hardware. Add the lightning protector between the antenna and pigtail and attach the bare copper grounding wire. (See Figure 8-19.)

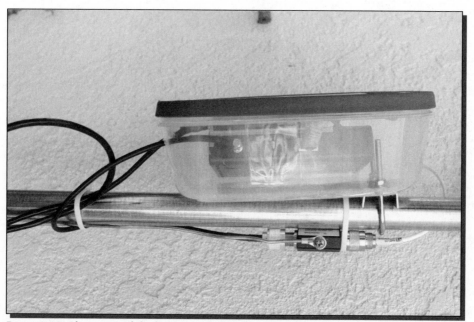

FIGURE 8-19: Placement of the lightning protector on the pole.

Screw the lightning protector into your antenna connector and then attach the pigtail to the other side of the lightning protector. Add the 8 gauge grounding wire to the lightning protector and run it down the pole with your other cables.

As you work with the cables, be sure to add so-called "drip loops." These are loops in the cable where rain will naturally drip off instead of running down the cable and inside connectors or cases. See Figure 8-20 for an example of a drip loop. This simple cabling trick keeps water from pouring down onto the connectors.

Anatomy of a drip loop:

- Leave a curve in the pigtail as it exits the bottom of your case before it goes back up to the antenna. Rain will run off the case and down your cable until it gets to the curve and drips off. If you have the cable so tight that it doesn't have a curve, then water may run down the cable from the antenna and into your case.

- If your antenna has a short length of cable on it before the connector (rather than a fitting right on the antenna), you may have enough room to put a loop in the antenna cable before it goes into the lightning protector. Again, this will allow rain to run down the antenna, down the antenna cable, and then drip from the bottom of the loop—instead of running down the antenna cable and right into the lightning protector.

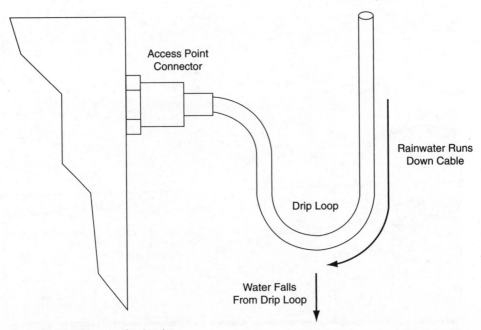

FIGURE 8-20: Diagram of a drip loop.

- Put a complete loop in the Ethernet cable where it exits at the bottom of the box and fasten it to the pole. This is the least critical cable as it has no outside fittings, but it's still good to get water off the cable

Use plastic fasteners, such as plastic zip ties, to hold things in place. However, don't tighten them too much on the antenna or Ethernet cables. This dents the cable, which reduces its effectiveness and decreases your signal.

**Tip**  If you have a choice, buy plastic fasteners labeled "UV resistant." Otherwise, they may become brittle and break due to sun exposure.

When all the cables are in the correct places, it is time to waterproof the connectors and install the final cable ties.

For most installations, standard electrical tape will work great for waterproofing (see Figure 8-21). Apply the tape liberally by wrapping from the bottom to the top with lots of overlap. You may need to remove and reinstall some of your cable ties to do this properly.

**Tip**  Applying the electrical tape from bottom to top helps stop rain from creeping under the edges and loosening the tape over time.

FIGURE 8-21: Wrapping the connectors in electrical tape.

For extreme weather conditions, there are lots of exotic waterproof solutions, including waxes, glue-like materials, and layers of different types of tape. Search online for waterproof connector tape to find a solution that meets your needs and budget.

When you're all done, stand back and admire the beauty of your creation. (See Figure 8-22.)

## Temperature and Water Testing

There are just two steps left before climbing on the roof. Temperature testing ensures that the access point electronics stay within tolerable limits. If things run too hot, frequent errors and lockups can occur, and the lifespan of your equipment will be diminished.

Test for water tightness in the optimal working conditions: while it's dry and sunny. Your nerves will be rattled enough worrying about the equipment in a rain storm, even if you know it passed water tests on the ground.

### Temperature Testing

Look carefully at your access point. Chances are, there are ventilation slots in its case. These are designed to encourage a convection flow of air to cool the electronics. Now that it is enclosed in your outdoor case, it won't be cooled as originally intended, so you need to see if the box needs ventilation holes.

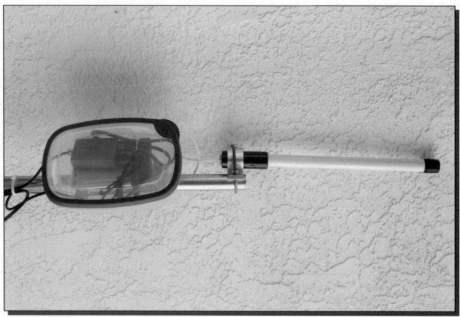

FIGURE 8-22: It's a beautiful thing!

Plastic cases tend to get hotter inside than metal cases. The metal walls drain heat from air inside the case, which keeps it closer to the outside air temperature. For the same reason, it's important for the metal case to be a light color. A black case can get very hot and makes it hot inside. For a great demonstration of this, touch a black car and a white car that have both been in the sun for a while.

Here's how to temperature-test your case:

1. Find a suitable thermometer and put it in your case. Use the manufacturer's stated operating temperature as a guide for selection. For example, the pictured D-Link has a range of 32 to 131 °F (0–55 °C), so you can use an oven or BBQ thermometer if it starts around 100 °F (37 °C).

2. Find a convenient shaded location, plug the Ethernet cable into the PoE adapter and your home network, and test that everything is working okay.

3. Close the case up as it will be when finally mounted.

4. Stress the access point by copying a large file via wireless from another computer on your network. This will ensure a high-speed transfer that will heat everything up more than running at idle.

5. Check the temperature frequently at first, to be sure you don't fry anything.

If you can read the temperature without removing the thermometer, you'll see when it reaches a steady state and you can stop. Otherwise, a few hours should be enough.

If the box gets too hot, then add cooling holes in a way that keeps the box dry inside. You could start by adding an open hole at the bottom. Then if water does find its way in, it will eventually drain out.

Another way to cool a plastic box is via the mounting bolts that go through to the mast. Screw a heat sink to those bolts on the inside of the case. This will transfer heat from inside air to the outside mast via the metal fittings. The heat sink can be as simple as a piece of scrap metal that fills the entire bottom of your case. See Figure 8-23 for an example.

When it's running at a good temperature in the shade, move it to an environment that matches your final location, such as in the sun. Then repeat the test steps and confirm that it's still okay.

If the box won't stay cool enough, some possibilities are:

- Add a matching hole near the top, on a side, and at the bottom to encourage convection cooling. Keeping water out might be hard though.

- Find a different mounting case (for example, switch from plastic to metal).

- Add a case fan (a simple solar powered fan would be easiest).

- Find a cooler location to install the box (such as under an overhang in perpetual shade).

- If the case is close to the maximum temperature, install it anyway and plan on replacing the access point after its run hot for a few days, weeks or months (this might be cheaper to try than messing around a lot with the case).

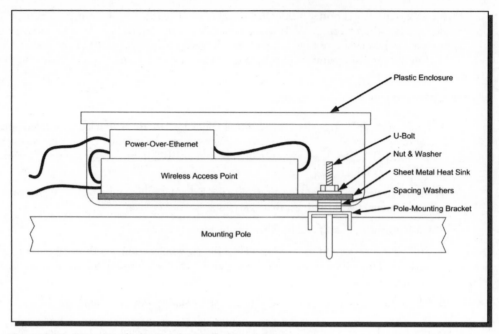

FIGURE 8-23: Diagram of a heat sink installed in a container.

## Water Testing

Now the final step, will the box stay dry inside? Grab a bucket of water, dunk it, and find out—no wait, just kidding!

Seriously, it is useful to see how watertight your box is, but you need to do it the right way. A garden hose on a gentle spray setting is a good way to start, or under a shower nozzle. Be sure to simulate rain by holding it above your case and then leave it there for several minutes before checking. Place toilet paper in your case before testing to provide a fast visual indication that all is still dry. Leave everything powered off while you're doing these tests.

Gradually increase the test length until you get to 20 or 30 minutes of gentle spray. Pat yourself on the back for a job well done when you retrieve your nice dry toilet paper afterwards. Congratulations!

If the case leaks, find a tube of outdoor sealant at your local hardware store and apply appropriately. Realize that when you seal, it blocks cooling, so it's prudent to retest your operating temperature if you need to add a lot of sealant. Repeat until dry.

Make sure that all electrical equipment is completely dry before you apply power. Expect 30 minutes or more (depending on the weather) for the slow effects of evaporation to dry out electrical equipment.

## Put it On the Roof Already!

After all the assembly and testing, everything is ready to go. Find a nice safe ladder and mount your new outdoor access point.

Run the Ethernet cable back inside the house, plug it into the PoE adapter and confirm that everything is working.

 Some areas receive frequent lightning strikes. Before mounting your access point outside in such an area, find some local person who understands grounding and follow his or her advice. Local amateur radio operators are a great source of information, as are TV or cable installers. Your local fire department can also provide information and resources.

Last, but not least, find a good ground for the lightning protector grounding cable. The 8 gauge copper wire should be run via the most direct route possible to a ground rod. Ground rods should be either solid copper, copper-clad steel, hot-dipped galvanized steel or stainless steel. They shouldn't be smaller than 8 feet in length and 1/2 inch in diameter.

You'll need fittings designed for grounding to connect everything together. Ground your case (using the same wire) if it is metal. You may be able to use a metal water pipe in place of a ground rod. Clean the pipe with a wire brush to expose bare metal and use a fitting designed for grounding to attach the ground wire to the pipe.

Complete grounding protection advice is beyond the scope of this book. Search online for "antenna grounding lightning guide" for more information. Some useful starting places are:

```
www.qsl.net/ccarc/light.html
www.polyphaser.com/ppc_pen_home.asp
```

With grounding completed and unit powered on, you're ready to e-mail the neighbors to start a nightly WLAN party gamefest.

# Taking It To The Next Level

Now you're sharing with the neighbors and surfing from the park, what's next? So glad you asked! How's this for starters:

- *Traffic plotting*—Track your network usage over time. Maybe it's time to upgrade your connection, or block that neighbor downloading movies 24 hours a day.

- *Do-it-yourself access point*—Why buy something off-the-shelf when you can pay twice as much to build it all yourself (but have a lot more fun doing it)?

There isn't enough space to cover these topics in detail, but here are some pointers to get you started.

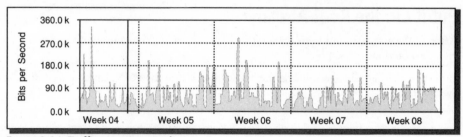

FIGURE 8-24: Traffic mapping graph.

## Traffic Graphing

Some access points support Simple Network Management Protocol (SNMP) and use it to provide basic traffic statistics. With the right software, you can retrieve these statistics and log them over time to produce graphs like the one shown in Figure 8-24. In this residential wireless LAN, traffic peaks each evening after work. Business hours are the best times for large downloads.

The classic free server software for producing graphs is Multi Router Traffic Grapher (MRTG) at http://people.ee.ethz.ch/~oetiker/webtools/mrtg/. It's still popular, though its more powerful successor RRDtool is gaining ground via add-ons such as Cacti (www.raxnet.net/products/cacti/).

To use this and similar software, you'll need a machine running Linux and either some reasonable Linux skills or a lot of patience to get it running.

Another option is to run the monitoring software directly on your desktop machine. The main disadvantage is that the machine needs to be on all the time to gather full statistics. Many free and shareware programs are available.

A good starting point for SNMP monitoring software is the Google directory at:

http://directory.google.com/Top/Computers/Software/Internet/Network_Management/

## Do-It-Yourself Access Point

A typical consumer access point consists of a custom-designed computer board running a low power (though high-speed) Million Instructions Per Second (MIPS) processor, a stripped-down radio card, and some fancy custom software.

With a little time and exploration, you can build something with much greater capabilities, including more power, more fine tuning possible, and extra features only limited by your skill and imagination.

One popular alternative to off-the-shelf access point hardware is the Soekris single board computer using a mini-PCI wireless card (see Figure 8-25). With some special software, a little configuration and a PoE adapter, this board becomes a professional-grade access point.

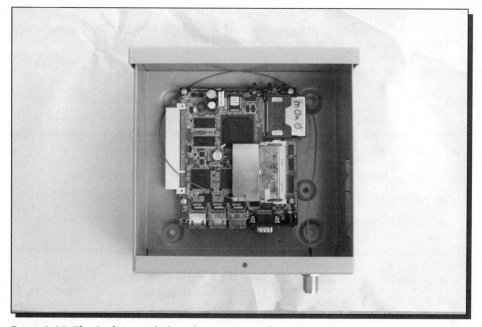

FIGURE 8-25: The Soekris single-board computer configured as a wireless access point.

## DIY Hardware

The logical hardware for a homebrew access point is a PC-based architecture. They're cheap, plentiful, and well supported with free software. An abandoned 486 computer with a tiny hard disk will be more than sufficient to make a powerful access point.

However, if you really want bragging rights at your next geek meeting, then take a look at custom "single-board computers" that strip out all the unnecessary PC parts like video and keyboard support, video display and hard disk drive controllers. Some manufacturers of these and similar hardware are:

- www.soekris.com
- www.pcengines.ch
- www.mikrotik.com
- www.openbrick.org

They use a compact flash card as a hard disk and thus have no moving parts, are very low power, and run silently.

You'll need to add a radio card for wireless support. Wireless radio cards previously come packaged as PC cards (also known as PCMCIA cards). But with the addition of wireless support to laptops, they're also readily available in a "mini-PCI" format, which is slightly cheaper and somewhat smaller.

When choosing a radio card, you can buy one with more power than a standard laptop wireless card supplies. Generally, laptop cards output 30–50mW of power, but you can buy cards up to 200 mW which can double your range. One popular brand amongst DIY builders is called Senao and is made by Engenius. Use a good search engine to find suppliers, or check with the supplier of your other specialized wireless gear (antenna, pigtails, and so on).

## DIY Software

Cool hardware is an expensive (and lousy) boat anchor without software to go with it. Many consumer access points use Linux underneath, and you can too. There are many free distributions tailored specifically for building wireless access points. They include:

- M0n0wall—www.m0n0.ch/wall
- Pebble—http://nycwireless.net/pebble
- WISP-Dist—http://leaf-project.org/

There are also some popular commercial suppliers of reasonably priced access point software:

- RouterOS—www.mikrotik.com
- StarOS—www.star-os.com

## More DIY Resources

Many Web sites discuss different aspects of building your own access point. Some starting points:

- www.socalfreenet.org/standardap—comprehensive design and description for a wireless access point used in a community network
- www.nycwireless/poe—how to build a PoE adapter from $10 worth of parts for your existing access point
- www.seattlewireless.net—a treasure trove of hardware comparisons, specs, and vendors
- www.socalwug.org—wireless projects, reviews, and vendor presentation videos

There are also many active mailing lists where DIY-related information appears regularly, including BAWUG and ptp-general from www.bawug.org and www.personaltelco.net/, respectively.

## Related DIY Projects

Consumer access point hardware is hard to beat on price, so some people prefer to improve them instead of starting from scratch. Some popular access points to hack are:

- Linksys wap-11 and wet-11—hacks include replacing the radio card with a more powerful version, as well as modifying the hardware to support more PoE options
- Apple Airport—the first true consumer access point

- Linksys WRT54G—this runs Linux, so enthusiasts are hard at work with new firmware that provides new functionality

Some creative searching online will reveal similarly fascinating projects and ideas. Have fun hacking!

# Summary

Building and installing an outdoor access point can extend your wireless coverage far beyond what's possible indoors. This creates exciting opportunities for sharing your coverage with other people or creating completely new uses.

This chapter provided a lot of information to get you started. You've learned how to think about location. There's a detailed list of what equipment to buy and the inherent trade-offs that are necessary. Clever innovations like Power-over-Ethernet simplify your installation.

Putting everything together isn't as simple as it appears. Planning for cooling, weatherproofing, and lightning are important to increase the reliability and safety of your installation.

This may just be the beginning of even more ambitious projects. Take some of the ideas from this chapter and build on them to see how far you can get.

Read on to create the ultimate outdoor wireless access point using solar power. The next chapter will show how to take a 75 W solar panel and create a completely stand-alone, totally wireless access point and repeater system. This system can be placed 10 miles or more from the nearest DSL line and doesn't require any power lines.

# Building a Solar-Powered Wireless Repeater

Imagine placing an access point high up on a hilltop. What a view that system would have! And now that you have an outdoor wireless system on your roof, the next question you will have is, "How do I extend the reach of my network?"

A wireless repeater can be used to reach out beyond the limits of your wired access point. By pulling energy directly from the Sun with a solar panel, the system can be located out as far as the eye can see.

Revolutionary advancements in harnessing the Sun's power to create energy have flourished over the last decade. Solar power is becoming an accepted and, in some cases, required component in structural designs of the 21st century.

While once only viewed as a novelty, solar power is quickly becoming an integral part of powering human requirements. A combination of improved efficiency coupled with the proliferation of the technology has reduced cost and opened entire new markets for this stable energy source.

It was only a matter of time before solar power was harnessed to drive remote networking components. That time has come and as you create the system described in this chapter (see Figure 9-1), you will be a part of the energy revolution and a friend to our fragile environment.

Implementing solar can be expensive. Yet, with some creative sourcing and some do-it-yourself construction, a solar repeater can be put together for less than you may think.

The items used in this chapter's project are:

- Solar Panel rated at 75 W, 12 V, 4.4 A
- Two wireless antennas, one each for downlink and end-user access
- Antenna cables and pigtails
- Two wireless access points operating in Bridge mode

- One wireless access point operating in Access Point mode
- Crossover network cable
    - Several feet of 10 AWG wire (black and red)
    - Two 35 ampere-hour (Ah) deep cycle lead-acid batteries
    - Solar system charge controller
    - DC-to-AC power inverter rated at 300 W or higher with a modified sine wave output
    - AC Power strip with no surge suppression circuitry

FIGURE 9-1: A solar-powered wireless repeater.

- Galvanized steel outdoor enclosure rated for outdoor operation (NEMA 3R)

- Water sealant tape

- Adhesive Velcro tape, 2-inch width

- Wiring tie downs (optional)

- Flexible rubber conduit and end connectors

- Galvanized steel angle-iron to construct the solar panel mount

- 2-inch diameter, 10-foot pole, and concrete

While solar power lends itself to limitless possibilities, this chapter will focus on integrating a wireless infrastructure. Once we've opened your eyes to the potential, we encourage you to harness the Sun's power to provide a reliable and free source of power for your networking and computing needs.

# Learning Solar Basics

*Photovoltaic* power generation systems (also known as solar or PV) are made up of interconnected components, each with a specific function. One of the most attractive features of a PV system is its modularity. As your requirements change, individual components can be added or upgraded to provide increased capacity and flexibility. Although your initial components will vary depending on your application, PV systems generally conform to these specific configurations (see Figure 9-2):

- *Solar Array*: The solar array consists of one or more PV modules that will convert sunlight into electric energy. The modules can be connected in a series or parallel configuration to provide the voltage and current requirements of your application. Typically the array will be mounted on a metal post or structure and tilted to face the sun for maximum exposure.

- *Charge Controller*: Although charge controllers can be purchased with many options, their main function is to maintain the batteries at the proper charge level, and to protect them from overcharging, which would damage or reduce life expectancy.

- *Battery Bank*: The battery bank contains one or more deep-cycle batteries, connected in series or parallel depending on the voltage and current requirements of the application. The batteries store the power produced by the solar array and discharge it when you need it.

- *Inverter*: An inverter is required when you want to power AC devices directly from the solar system. The inverter converts the DC power from the solar array/batteries into AC power.

- *AC and DC Loads*: These are the appliances or devices that consume the power that you are generating with your solar array.

■ *Balance of System*: These components provide the interconnections and standard safety features required for any electrical power system. Included in this group are:

- Switches
- Fuses
- Circuit Breakers
- Meters
- Cabling

Several new technologies are emerging, including fuel cells and microturbines that can generate electric power in a distributed fashion, that is, from locations close to the end-user. However, solar electric power offers many unique benefits apart from other distributed generation systems.

By crafting a successful solar application, you can reap the benefits that come with using a renewable energy source. As a direct result of improving technology and declining PV prices, practical applications for solar cells have steadily expanded from space missions to remote power and personal electronic devices. Since the mid-1990s, PV has become a practical source of solar electric generation in the $800 billion electric power industry.

Using solar power in your application creates a highly available wireless network without the electrical delivery costs. A system like the one you will build in this chapter can run for years with little more maintenance than the occasional "window cleaning" wipedown of the solar panel.

FIGURE 9-2: Components of a solar system.

# Setting Up a Wireless Repeater

Before getting in to powering a solar system, you will need to determine where this repeating network node will be located. Much of this information is covered in Chapters 8 and 13, so here we will briefly cover how to determine a repeater site.

The concept of a wireless repeater is simple: use a wireless backhaul to beam a signal to an access point that is accessible by the client. Figure 9-3 shows how this would work. The access point sits where client devices (i.e., a laptop computer) could connect while the backhaul links the signal down to the wired Internet.

**Note**  A *backhaul* is a point-to-point network link created to maintain a connection between a remote site and the network base station. The wireless backhaul is meant to carry network traffic from the repeater station down to the base station. Traffic on the backhaul is generally only between the two points. The wireless backhaul has an *uplink* (to the repeater) and a *downlink* (from the repeater).

The wireless repeater system consists of a total of three Wi-Fi radios. One is set up as an access point that your users will connect to via their laptop, PDA, or other wireless device. The second radio is set up in a dedicated bridge mode. The *bridge* is used to link directly to the network base station, which is the third radio.

**Tip**  When configuring multiple radios in a single location, as used in the repeater enclosure, it is a good idea to select channels as far apart as possible, for example, channels 1 and 11 in the United States. If both radios were on the same channel you would get far too much interference, even though the antennas are pointed in different directions. This separation helps prevent signal overlapping because the radios are physically so close together.

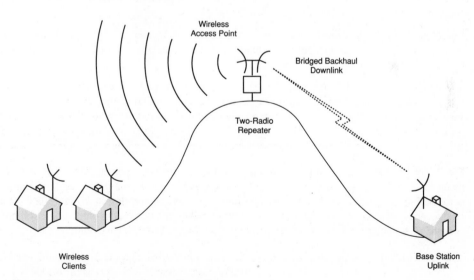

**FIGURE 9-3: Wireless repeater configuration.**

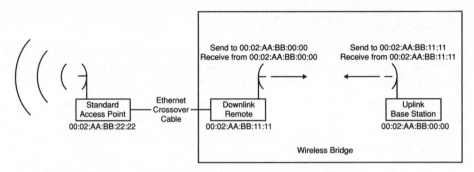

**FIGURE 9-4: Bridged access points and the MAC address relationship.**

The system will require two antennas on the repeater structure, one for the bridged backhaul, or downlink, and one to link to wireless clients. Depending on distance and interference issues, the bridge link would usually require a highly directional antenna. The access point would need an antenna suited to the coverage area.

This configuration requires three wireless devices (not including the clients). Two devices operate in bridge-mode, while one device acts as an access point. Of course, this is just one configuration of many. It's conceivable that a wireless signal could be repeated over and over. Although, in practice, a large number of repeaters cause processing time delays that could create synchronization problems with traditional Internet protocols.

A wireless bridge is where two wireless devices are configured to allow connections only to each other. This is usually done by entering the MAC address of each access point into the other access point. See Figure 9-4 for an example. Access points in bridge mode will only accept traffic from the other end of the bridge.

Before getting into the solar installation, configure the wireless equipment in a lab setting. You will need to configure the bridges individually, and the access point should also be configured at this point.

The wireless radios used in this chapter are basic off-the-shelf D-Link access points. These are not necessarily what you would want to run in this type of situation. Considering the money, time, and effort of integrating a solar system, extra cost on the wireless radio components can be justified. These radios can vary widely. Any wireless hardware can be used for the repeater section. Refer to Chapters 8 and 10 for examples of hardware used for providing wireless Internet access.

**Tip** The D-Link product is one of the few on the market with a built-in repeater mode. This repeater mode can function well in some environments. However, a single-radio repeater has less than 50 percent of its bandwidth available due to the simultaneous uplink and downlink. Also, the D-Link product does not work well with two antennas. Indeed, the recent version has only a single antenna connection. Optimally, two radios are needed for a 100 percent 802.11b bandwidth repeater.

The key to a wireless repeater is the bridge. Some products that support bridging are listed in Table 9-1. These products should have documentation available with details for bridge configuration. Please refer to the documentation of your specific equipment for details.

**Table 9-1    Products Supporting Bridge Mode**

| Vendor | Product Name | Access Point Mode | Bridge Mode |
| --- | --- | --- | --- |
| Cisco | Aironet 350 series | Only on AP model | Only on Bridge model |
| Linksys | WAP11 | Yes | Yes |
| Linksys | WET11 | No | Yes |
| D-Link | DCS-900+ | Yes | Yes |
| D-Link | DWL-810 | No | Yes |
| Proxim | Orinoco AP-2500 | Yes | Yes |
| Senao/Engenius | 2611-CB3 | No | Yes |
| Buffalo | WLA-L11G | Yes | Yes |
| Netgear | ME103 | Yes | Yes |

# Integrating Solar Power

Aside from the obvious free source of power, there are several other benefits to "solarizing" this leg of your network infrastructure. First and foremost, having an un-tethered wireless access point will enable great flexibility in how and where you get network services within the local region.

Hilltops are no longer out of the equation. By placing a node on a remote hilltop, line-of-sight and interference issues can be minimal. Additionally, a solar repeater mounted to a tower would have a commanding view over a low undulating landscape like farmlands, desert, or wilderness areas.

## Understanding Solar Modules

For this application, a 70-watt PV system will be sufficiently adequate. This system will be pre-configured to 12 V and produce 4.7 A. We recommend using a PV module with a glass surface that is impact-resistant and allows maximum light transmission.

**Tip** Choose a single crystalline solar cell, encapsulated and bonded to the glass in multiple layers of ethylene vinyl acetate (EVA) and laminated with a backing to insure long life in severe conditions. The Shell Solar model SP75, 75-watt solar module fits the bill nicely.

The model we are using (a Shell Solar SP75, see Figure 9-5), uses a proprietary technology (CIS Thin Film Technology) to efficiently create electricity from the sunlight. This module is designed for use in 12 V systems. This system's ability to deliver battery-charge power in

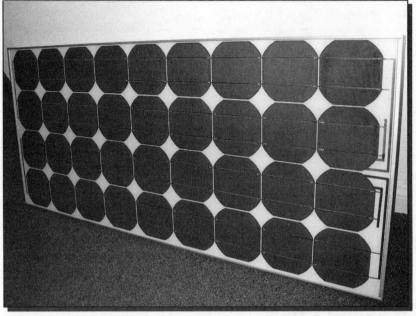

FIGURE 9-5: A Shell Solar SP75, 75-watt solar panel still carries the Siemens name.

low-light situations makes it particularly effective for specialized applications and in adverse or changeable environments.

**Note** Siemens solar division was acquired by Shell in early 2002. Shell (now Shell Solar) did not begin renaming the Siemens product line until mid-2003. You will still find products carrying the Siemens name. The Siemens branded products will eventually disappear from the marketplace as new products are developed.

These panels are engineered and manufactured for durability and ease-of-use. They are fully framed in anodized aluminum with pre-drilled, strategically positioned mounting holes to ensure secure and easy installations. A clamp-type mounting system can be used, so no drilling is required.

You will also want to use a weather-resistant junction box mounted to the solar module that will accommodate all wiring. It should include moisture-tight strain relief connectors, electrical conduit, and a bypass diode. Figure 9-6 shows the junction box on the SP75. Notice the jumpers and bypass diode. These components connect the panel junction in such a way as to provide 12 V. This particular solar module can also be configured for 6 V operation.

## Solar Power Specifications

Output values of various solar modules are shown in Table 9-2. This is an approximation based on several manufacturers' claims for power productivity. Your results may vary depending on

FIGURE 9-6: The junction box built in to the Shell SP75 solar module.

the physical location of your solar system and the availability of consistent sunlight exposure. The row in bold is an optimal choice for the project in this chapter. More power will charge batteries faster, keeping them topped up for cloudy days. Too little power may cause a power outage from drained batteries due to decreased charge capacity.

## Table 9-2    Solar Panel Power Output

| Rated Power (Watts) | Rated Voltage (Vmp) | Rated Current (Imp) | Open Circuit Voltage (VOC) | Short Circuit Current (Isc) | Dimensions (H × W × D in inches) | Panel Weight (lbs) |
|---|---|---|---|---|---|---|
| 20 W | 12 V | 1.29 A | 22.9 V | 1.54 A | 29.5 × 13.0 × 1.3 | 13.0 |
| 40 W | 12 V | 2.41 A | 22.2 V | 2.59 A | 50.9 × 13.0 × 1.4 | 22 |
| 50 W | 12 V | 3.15 A | 19.8 V | 3.35 A | 48.0 × 13.0 × 1.3 | 17 |
| **70 W** | **12 V** | **4.25 A** | **21.4 V** | **4.70 A** | **47.3 × 20.8 × 2.2** | **23** |
| 100 W | 16.7 V | 6.00 A | 21.0 V | 6.70 A | 56.93" × 20.8 × 2.2 | 26 |

**Note** Solar power ratings assume operation at a Maximum Power Point (MPP), which is generally considered impossible to achieve in real-world deployments. Panel output will vary based on factors such as temperature, panel tilt angle, atmospheric conditions, and even cleanliness. Expect output power somewhere in the 80 to 90 percent efficiency range during peak hours of sunlight.

### Finding PV sources

There are many high-quality products that are suitable for this application. Now that you have established your baseline requirements, we will recommend a couple of options that you can choose from.

Of course we have our favorite based on optimal output, quality of construction, and quality service from the vendors, but based on your geographic location; you may need to find options that will meet both your cost requirements as well as time constraints.

PV panels are a somewhat specialized product and generally cannot be picked up at the local retailer. However, some electronics stores can special order solar panels designed for RV battery backup power. Largely due to the demands of retail distribution and availability, systems available at local stores can costs hundreds more than a solar module from a distributor or local solar specialist.

Since your wireless repeater system is relatively small and specialized, you may be able to find a local solar specialist with spare 75-watt panels lying around. We found this one from a residential system installer that was using panels like this for decorations around the office. Buying a solar panel from extra inventory can reduce the price considerably.

Popular models include:

- Shell Solar SP75
- BP Solar BPSX-70U

Both of these products provided all the features and requirements outlined above. Either choice will result in a successful exercise and provide years of high-quality power to your system. This is not meant to preclude other quality products, but to use as a baseline for you to look at and compare with.

**Tip** Solar power is obviously based on sunshine. Solar providers will know a lot about your local sunlight coverage. That is, incoming solar radiation or "insolation" will vary from place to place on the globe. Talk to a local solar specialist about hours of sunlight for your area. Maps and figures are also available online. One such resource is provided by Solar4Power at www.solar4power.com/solar-power-global-maps.html. The global map they've posted online shows insolation values for every part of the globe.

# Configuring Your Solar System

To understand the various configurations for solar power, we will cover a few different applications.

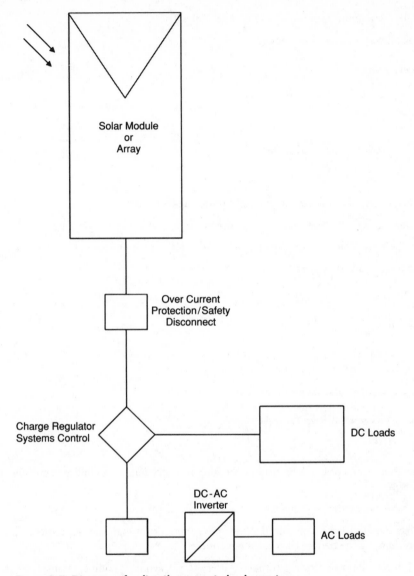

**FIGURE 9-7: Diagram of a directly connected solar system.**

A *directly connected system* is shown in Figure 9-7.

Characteristics:

- No battery storage
- Load operates in sync with sunlight

- Peak operation during summer and middle of the day
- Special inverter can add AC power

Typical applications:

- Ventilation fans
- Water pumping

A *stand-alone system* is shown in Figure 9-8.

Characteristics:

- Battery storage allows operation at night or during bad weather
- Charge regulator prevents battery from over-charging and over-discharging
- System controls can include circuit protection and remote monitoring
- Inverter can add AC power

Typical applications:

- Telecommunications telemetry
- Outdoor lighting
- RV or boat electric power source
- Remote homes or storage facilities

There are also a number of *hybrid systems*.

Characteristics:

- Generator plus rectifier allows battery charging for full energy availability in any climate or season
- Generator can be multifuel source (natural gas, diesel, propane)
- AC bus allows direct AC power to loads from generator through transfer switch, while also recharging the battery through the rectifier
- DC Bus has all power flowing through battery (DC), avoiding complex transfer switching and any anomalies in the power load

Typical applications:

- Large telecommunications stations
- RV with generator

The wireless repeater in this chapter will be designed using the stand-alone model.

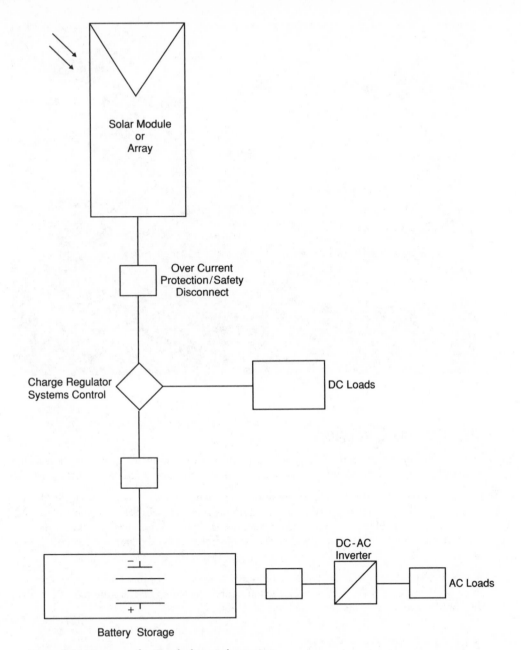

FIGURE 9-8: Diagram of a stand-alone solar system.

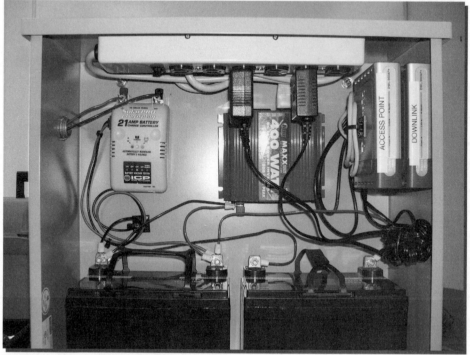

FIGURE 9-9: The enclosure cabinet.

## Installation Overview

The heart of the system is the solar panel, while the body is the enclosure cabinet. The enclosure will house all of the electronics and keep them safe from the weather and other predators.

The enclosure will be directly connected to the solar panel and wireless antennas. Flexible conduit is recommended for the solar panel junction box interface, while Times Microwave LMR-400 cabling is suitable for the antenna connections. If your enclosure has "knockouts" for conduit, so much the better; otherwise, drill out the holes for your pigtails and electrical conduit.

Figure 9-9 shows the enclosure layout. Components are spaced evenly for ease of maintenance. Electrical wiring exits the enclosure on the left. Antenna cabling exits on the right through bulkhead pigtail connectors connected to LMR-400 cable.

## Assembling Your System

Since this system is to be deployed in an outside remote location, it is recommended that you first unpack all of your items indoors to ensure that you have all the required pieces and that they are all in good condition prior to beginning.

In addition, you may want to build as much of the control cabinet as possible before deployment to test components and minimize the number of total items that will eventually be carried to your destination.

It is critical to closely inspect your PV panel, because it may be the most fragile and valuable part of this configuration. Specifically, look for any cracks or breaks in the glass or framing that may have occurred during the shipping process. If you notice any irregularities, contact your dealer for immediate replacement. Once you are satisfied that all the contents are present and in reasonable condition, you are ready to begin.

You should start by assembling the contents of the control cabinet first. This is due to its complexity, and it is the core of your system. Once all of the items are mounted and wired into the cabinet, the balance of the installation will require little more than erecting the pole, mounting the PV panel, control box, and antennas to the pole, and then testing. Figure 9-10 shows a diagram of the cabinet layout for this installation.

For ease of installation, and to simplify future maintenance requirements, various lengths of Velcro Strips are part of the list of materials. This Velcro will be used in place of drilling, nuts and bolts. Moreover, this approach will eliminate the need to punch holes into your control cabinet which could later result in problems from leakage.

**Tip** For that professional look and feel, use an enclosure with built-in standoffs and a mounting panel. The panel becomes a backboard for drilling and mounting equipment without piercing the rear of the cabinet.

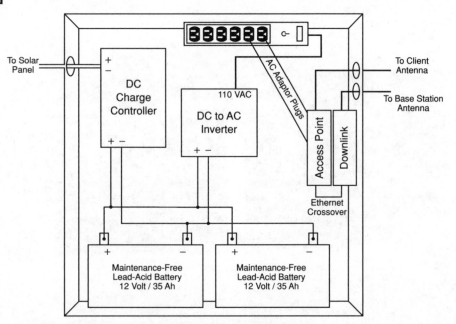

FIGURE 9-10: Diagram of the control cabinet enclosure layout.

The cabinet used in this chapter is an 18 inch × 18 inch × 6 inch enclosure (18 inches square and 6 inches deep). We drilled the holes necessary for the pigtails with bulkhead connectors and for the solar panel conduit. Angle iron was used to adapt the cabinet for U-bolt pole mounting.

Hundreds of cabinets are available from suppliers like Hammond and B-Line. Search the Internet for these companies, or visit the wireless supply companies like Tessco, Talley, and Electrocom.

### Step 1: Install the Battery Cell

Install the battery (or batteries in this case) into the cabinet, as shown in Figure 9-11. Apply 4-inch Velcro strips to the battery cell, one strip on each end, and apply corresponding Velcro strips to the bottom of the control cabinet. Finally, insert the battery cell into the control cabinet and test alignment of battery with respect to the cabinet. Be sure that the battery is not touching either side of the cabinet and the space is relatively equal from side-to-side.

 **Note**    Charge the batteries before installing them into the cabinet. A standard car charger set to trickle-charge the battery should work fine for topping them off before "the great on-turning."

FIGURE 9-11: Battery installation.

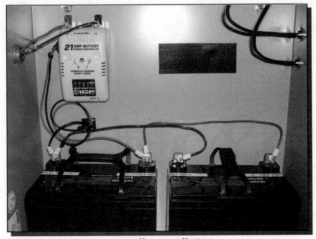

FIGURE 9-12: Charge controller installation.

## Step 2: Install the Charge Controller

Refer to your internal cabinet diagram for component orientation and organization. You may choose to design your cabinet differently, and that is fine, just ensure that you have a proper cable management plan before you get too far into the project. This is extremely important in future days and weeks when maintenance procedures may be required and taking parts in and out could be hampered by inefficient arrangements. Figure 9-12 shows the charge controller in place. Substantial Velcro adhesive holds the charge controller in place.

Wiring from the charge controller connects directly to the batteries as shown in Figure 9-13. When connecting multiple batteries, connect only the negative (−) terminals to each other, then connect only the positive (+) terminals to each other. Do not cross the streams! This is a parallel connection where voltage remains the same (12 V) but the current capacity increases (70 Ah).

**Caution** Only connect positive (+) to positive (+) and negative (−) to negative (−). Do not short-circuit the battery. Just like a car battery, these batteries need to be treated with care and connected properly.

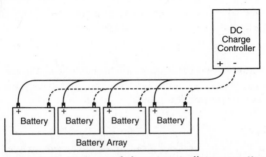

FIGURE 9-13: Diagram of charge controller connection to the battery array.

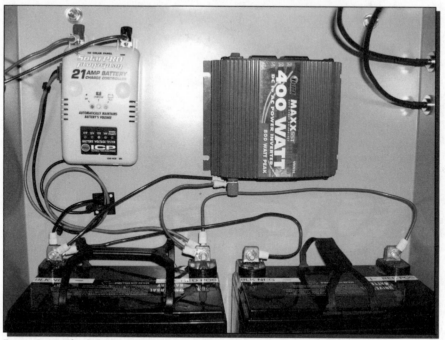

FIGURE 9-14: The DC-to-AC inverter installed and connected to the battery array.

### Step 3: Install the DC-to-AC inverter

The DC-to-AC inverter converts the DC battery power into AC power for the power strip and wireless components. The battery directly connects to the DC inputs on the inverter. Figure 9-14 shows the inverter installed and connected to the battery.

By choosing to use an inverter to provide universal AC power, you have the option of easily changing out radio equipment. Also, while on-site at the repeater system, extra AC power comes in handy.

**Tip**  When choosing a DC-to-AC inverter, a low-cost "modified sine wave" inverter works fine with this type of equipment. However, parasitic power is a factor. Try to find an inverter with low internal current consumption. Anything with less than 0.2 A (200 mA) is fine.

As you may have noticed, the charge controller and the inverter are both connected to the battery. Solar energy is used to charge the battery via the controller, while simultaneously, the inverter pulls electricity out of the battery for the wireless radios.

### Step 4: Install the Wireless Radios

The wireless equipment will be stacked with the access point on top of the bridge, so keep that in mind as you begin to install this component. Additionally, the radios will be AC-powered devices, and you will need to route the power cords so that they can cleanly access the power strip that will be mounted shortly.

**FIGURE 9-15: Wireless radios in place and connected via an Ethernet crossover cable.**

You will clearly need to modify this step if your product is a single-board computer with integrated radios, like a Soekris or open brick computer described in Chapter 8.

**Note** Products from the same manufacturer will often be designed with cases that make stacking a cinch. Consider this fact when selecting the access point and bridge devices.

Connect the radios via an Ethernet crossover cable. Remember the configuration is for the access point to connect back home via the wireless bridge. If the bridge is configured correctly, the access point should believe it is sitting on the wired network back at the bottom of the downlink. Figure 9-15 shows the radios mounted and connected.

## Step 5: Install the AC Power Strip

The installation of a power strip will add enormous convenience and flexibility in your system. Not only will it be responsible for supplying power to your critical communications devices, but it will also give you the ability to serve any other electronic device that meets the output requirements this system has been designed for.

For instance, you will be able to operate low power tools, temporary lighting, cell phone and laptop chargers and any other AC-powered convenience devices that may become useful during the installation.

Your AC Power Strip will be mounted to the top of the cabinet (see Figure 9-16). We recommend attaching it the way you did all the other devices, with Velcro as the primary fastener. Adding a third strip of Velcro to the middle of the AC Power Strip and to the corresponding place on the cabinet back wall will add stability since this device will be subject to more strain from plugs being inserted and removed. You are certainly welcome to use two-sided tape, but we don't recommend drilling holes through the exterior of the cabinet. Any water leakage in this area could be hazardous to the equipment.

At this point, your cabinet should be fully populated. Charge the batteries by using a 12-volt power source attached to the leads of the charge controller. Anything supporting a few amperes at 12 V is acceptable. A car battery charger set to low-current trickle-charge works fine.

When charging the battery, check the status lights on your charge controller. There should be a "power on" indicator along with a "battery charging" light. When the batteries are topped off, the "battery full" light will come on.

**Caution**

Do not apply more voltage or current than the charge controller is rated to handle. The controller used in this chapter (shown earlier in Figure 9-13) is rated for 12 V and 21 A. We charged the batteries with a 12 V, 4 A source to match the solar panel output.

FIGURE 9-16: The AC Power Strip in place and attached.

Once charged, you can remove the batteries and other components for ease of installation and travel. As you've already noticed, Most of the weight in this system comes from the batteries.

# Time to Go Outside

Before you head up to the installation site, one last item needs to be created, purchased, or built: the solar panel mounting system. A solar panel mount can vary greatly in price depending on options. A high-end mount costing hundreds of dollars can be automatically or manually tilted during different seasons to account for the angle the Sun's rays strike the panel. If you are in low sunlight areas, an adjustable mount like this may be the best option to maximize exposure. If you want to go crazy, robotic mounting systems can be found that track the sun as it moves across the sky during the day.

If you happen to be in an area where sunlight is plentiful, a fixed mount is less costly and easy to build.

## Building a Mounting Bracket

You need to determine the installation angle before building a fixed-angle mount. For most installations a tilt angle of 45 degrees is sufficient. For systems at latitudes higher than 45 degrees from the Earth's equator, a panel tilt of 60 degrees or more is necessary.

Building a mounting system out of angle iron is cheap and easy. The structure dimensions are shown in Figure 9-17. To accommodate the SP75 solar panel, the mount was cut into 21-inch long angles, with 15-inch horizontal and vertical braces. The side connectors were cut in two feet lengths.

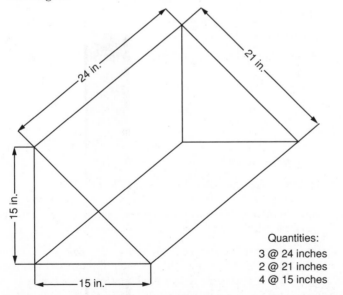

Quantities:
3 @ 24 inches
2 @ 21 inches
4 @ 15 inches

FIGURE 9-17: Mounting structure diagram and dimensions for a 45-degree tilt.

FIGURE 9-18: A solar panel mounting structure built using angle iron.

Fortunately, the SP75 panel came with custom mounting rails designed to hold the panel down by pressure, without the use of drilling or bolts.

The entire structure was bolted together and stands ready to accept the SP75, as shown in Figure 9-18.

## Sinking the Pole

A pole mount was chosen for this project because of high availability and low cost. Other in-the-field mounts include guyed tower and cinder-block secured frames. These alternatives are available from most wireless equipment distributors.

When using a basic 2-inch diameter pole, you should dig at least a 36-inch deep hole to securely mount the pole. It will be supporting upwards of 100 pounds and in order to ensure that it tolerates mid-range wind conditions, we strongly recommend that you cement this pole into the ground. This will make for a sturdy and professional installation.

Select a location on the site that will offer the widest coverage area in the spots you will most need it. For instance, you may be able to install this gear in the center of your coverage radius, but due to terrain features or landscaping that could reduce sun hours, other spots may be more suitable. Ensure that shade or shadows will not fall across the solar panel. Anticipate the Sun's angle during winter and summer months.

Once you have settled on the perfect spot, you will need to dig a hole at least 3 feet deep and 3 feet in diameter. Mix adequate amount of concrete as specified by your local hardware store specialist and fill the hole completely. Slip the pole into the hole filled with concrete and use a level or plumb bob to make sure that the pole is truly vertical. Wait overnight for concrete to set before proceeding to the next step.

After sufficient time has elapsed and you are comfortable with the hardness of the concrete, go ahead and cover up the concrete with dirt to hide the base and help restore the natural surroundings.

## Mounting the Equipment

The placement of all of the components on the pole is not critical, but needs to be planned for space. The diagram in Figure 9-19 shows the components of this system and how they are located on the pole. Place the solar panel at a height that makes it inconvenient for critters to climb on and low enough that birds will not feel comfortable roosting for an extended time. The goal is to minimize scratches and keep the panel as clean as possible.

At least two people should work together to mount this equipment to the pole. Safety is paramount when working on heavy equipment. One or two people should hold the equipment in place while another tightens down the hardware.

The equipment will be attached to the pole using U-bolts. Mount the mounting system to the pole, leaving the solar panel to the side for the time being. You will connect the solar panel last.

When attaching the panel mount structure, ensure the panel will point due South once attached. Use heavy-duty U-bolts to bolt the structure to the pole (see Figure 9-20).

The control cabinet is next. Remove extra components if necessary to reduce weight while mounting. Keeping the batteries aside is a good idea. Removing the other components is optional.

Once again, use heavy-duty U-bolts or other appropriate fasteners to secure the cabinet in place. Figure 9-21 shows the cabinet in place behind the panel mount structure.

Once you have completed the mounting of the Cabinet, open the door and slightly rock the Cabinet side-to-side to verify its sturdiness.

With the cabinet installed and secured, install the batteries and attach any wiring that was disconnected before the move.

## Mounting the Antennas

The antennas should be mounted as high as possible on the pole. Direction will be determined by the coverage area and uplink source. If possible, try to keep the antenna from casting shadows over the panel. This cannot always be avoided. Select low-profile or "shadow-friendly"

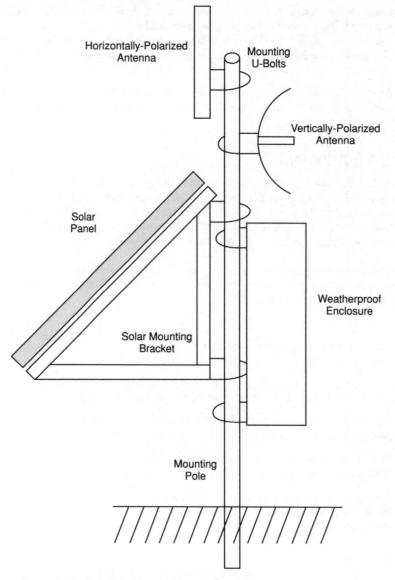

Horizontally-Polarized
Antenna

Mounting
U-Bolts

Vertically-Polarized
Antenna

Solar
Panel

Weatherproof
Enclosure

Solar Mounting
Bracket

Mounting
Pole

FIGURE 9-19: Component mounting configuration.

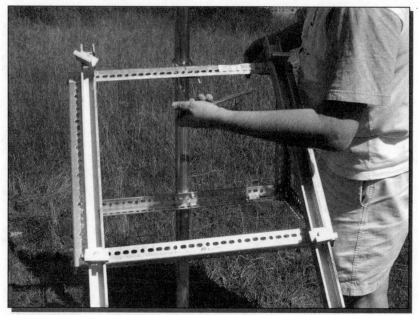

FIGURE 9-20: Bolting up the panel mount structure.

FIGURE 9-21: Cabinet installed and loaded.

FIGURE 9-22: Antennas mounted to the top of the pole.

antennas if possible. For example, a parabolic grid antenna or Yagi will cast less of a shadow as compared to a panel antenna.

U-bolts will be used to fasten the antennas to the pole. Some antennas use articulating mounts for angle adjustment. Other antennas may have built-in electrical down-tilt. Check the specifications for your antennas and mount them as needed.

When mounting antennas for different radios as you are doing here, interference becomes a major factor. One method of reducing radio interference is by adjusting the polarity of the signals to be 90 degrees apart. That is, set up one antenna in a vertical polarization, with the other using a horizontal polarization. The antenna documentation will denote polarization.

In Figure 9-22, the parabolic grid antenna is vertically polarized, while this particular sector antenna from SuperPass.com is electrically designed for horizontal polarization (even though it's vertically mounted).

**Tip**    To further reduce interference, you can use signal filters on the antenna lines. Filters made for specific channels of the 802.11b spectrum are available at a cost of a few hundred dollars each.

Remember to make the antenna connections water-tight. Electrical tape is a fair alternative, but since this is a remote site, and support calls would require a special trip, the best solution is

**Figure 9-23: Sealant tape protecting microwave connectors.**

sealant tape. At ten dollars a roll, it's not cheap, but it is the best product out there for this task. For comparison, Figure 9-23 shows the tape in place on the top antenna connector.

## Mounting the Solar Panel

The final step is to place the solar panel reverently onto the mounting structure and bolt it down (see Figure 9-24).

Keep the panel covered with an opaque material when you're attaching the electrical wiring. Use a large piece of cardboard, a beach towel, or anything that covers the surface entirely.

After the panel is securely in place, attach the conduit to the junction box on the underside of the solar panel. And connect the black wire to the negative (−) terminal and the red wire to the positive (+) terminal. Do the same on the charge controller attachment points.

Follow the precautions and directions included with the solar panel you are using. The electrical attachment points in the junction box may vary widely with each manufacturer and product.

Remember that the panel creates electricity when illuminated by sunlight. The voltage from a single 12-volt panel is not considered a shock hazard, but to avoid sparks and possible damage, do not short the leads while attaching the panel connections to the charge controller.

FIGURE 9-24: Solar panel installed!

# Applying Power and Testing

Apply power by removing the opaque covering from the solar panel (the cardboard or beach towel from the previous section). If it's sunny, there should immediately be a "power on" indicator and the "charging" or "full" lights will be lit. Switch on the power strip to apply AC power to the wireless radios. Check for the usual link and status lights on your wireless equipment.

**Note**  When you remove the opaque covering, the solar panel will immediately begin pumping out electricity as fast as the sun will allow. Also, since your batteries are already charged, the radios and inverter should be up and running even without sunshine.

With the pole securely sunk into the ground and the solar panel boldly facing the sun, it already looks very impressive. Anyone who sees it will be very impressed with your technical acumen and desire to improve the future of our planet.

The final stage is to move a short distance from the panel/repeater and break out your laptop for a wireless test. Ensure that your connection is to the solar-based access point and that your network settings match the wired network to which you are down-linking (DHCP, IP Address, and so on).

Congratulations! You should now be surfing through your repeater. Anytime day or night, the repeater will extend your network reach. Free and abundant daylight recharges the batteries that ran the system overnight. The system can work perpetually over many years.

Over the years to come, you may find opportunites to expand your repeater. You may wish to install new Wi-Fi radios or expand capabilities by installing a network camera. If your power needs increase, the system built in this chapter can be expanded simply by adding more batteries to the array. Or you may opt for a solar panel with a higher power output for quicker recharging. Either way, the basic components of your system will serve you well into the future.

 **Note**  An amateur radio satellite placed into Earth orbit in 1984 is still operating after thousands of cycles of charging and discharging on-board batteries. The satellite, named UoSat Oscar 11, celebrated its twentieth anniversary of solar-powered radio operation. May your new solar repeater see this much uptime!

# Summary

In this chapter, you learned how to set up a wireless repeater and power it with free solar energy. You learned the background and history of photovoltaic energy, and how solar can be used in wireless communications. With two radio repeater/bridges, you've extended your network to the furthest reaches possible, beyond network cables, beyond telephone lines, and even power lines. With the system you've installed in this chapter, you are now truly wireless.

In the next chapter, you will learn how to set up a free wireless hotspot. Read on to discover how to create a captive portal system where wireless Internet users are automatically presented an information screen when they open a Web browser.

# Creating a Free Wireless Hotspot

**T**here comes a time in the life of every wireless fanatic when he or she wants to share the thrill of wirelessness with every other human being on the planet, or at least those who come within range. Perhaps you have a high-speed Internet connection at home, which goes unused when you are at work. Why not let the neighbors use it? Why not let the whole neighborhood use it? And if your neighbors share with their neighbors...

There are, in fact, several sizable projects underway based on this vision. As of early 2004:

- NYCWireless (www.nycwireless.net), dedicated to providing free wireless Internet service to mobile users in public spaces throughout metropolitan New York City, had a database of over 180 nodes or *hotspots*.

- Houston Wireless (www.houston-wireless.net), a community wireless group promoting pervasive, high-speed wireless data in urban and suburban Houston, was at 93 nodes and growing.

- Seattle Wireless network (www.seattlewireless.net), which envisions a not-for-profit, community-owned wireless network covering metropolitan Seattle, had more than 30 nodes operating, and half a dozen more on the verge of operating.

- The So Cal Free Net (www.socalfreenet.org) is rolling out free hotspots and wireless backbone locations in the San Diego and Los Angeles areas of Southern California.

- The Personal Telco Project (www.personaltelco.net) consists of a volunteer group of Portlanders with over 100 active nodes aiming to cover the entire city of Portland, Oregon.

- The NoCat network (www.nocat.net), based in Sebastopol north of San Francisco, listed two-dozen active sites, almost as many in progress, and many more that were deemed "interested."

## chapter 10

## in this chapter

☑ Discovering NoCatAuth

☑ Setting up your network and server

☑ Installing NoCat

☑ Configuring and testing NoCat

☑ Troubleshooting your access point

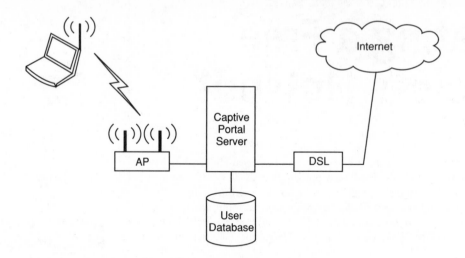

**FIGURE 10-1: Diagram of an open wireless "hotspot" network.**

There are many other free, public wireless networks all over the world, including Asia, the Middle East, Australia, New Zealand, the Pacific region, the Caribbean, and Europe. To get an idea of the magnitude of this phenomenon, check out the Personal Telco Web site, which lists hundreds of community wireless groups that are building free and open networks (www.personaltelco.net/index.cgi/WirelessCommunities). The most ambitious of these envision not just isolated nodes but an interlocking "network of networks" or *Metropolitan Area Network* (MAN) designed to allow roaming from site to site within the area served by the network. Hiccup-free roaming is a technical challenge that has not been entirely solved at this time, however.

Figure 10-1 shows a common configuration for an open wireless "hotspot" network. Users with a laptop computer log in, click "I agree" or authenticate in some manner. And then they are allowed to access the Internet.

This community-based approach to networking can allow you to bring high-speed data to your neighborhood, even if your local telephone companies or wireless ISPs are moving too slowly, not moving at all, or have tried and failed due to financial factors. Because noncommercial services can be much cheaper in the long run (basically, just the investment in equipment and expertise), they may garner a wider user base than commercial services could. If even a small percentage of those users set up their own free wireless hotspots, a "positive feedback" loop is created, in which the benefits of joining the "free" wireless community increase, bringing more users and still more hotspots. (The network effect says that the value of a network increases exponentially with the number of users.)

If you want to be part of this wireless revolution, this chapter is for you!

In this chapter, you'll build a wireless hotspot that can share your Internet connection with anyone who comes within range, while giving you the ability to implement a *splash screen* (the first screen the user sees when they access the hotspot), and control which sites users can access. The system is designed to support user IDs and passwords, as well, so you'll have the potential to expand to that in the future.

You'll need the following hardware:

- Wireless access point (AP).

- A PC (486 or better) with at least 10GB disk space, 256MB RAM and two Ethernet network interface cards (NICs). This computer serves as a gateway between your local wireless network and the Internet. It will run the Linux operating system.

- At least one client computer (usually Windows or Mac) for testing. Each client must have either a wireless NIC or a standard Ethernet card and cable to connect to the AP.

- A high-speed Internet connection such as DSL, with an appropriate wide area network (WAN) device such as a DSL modem and an Ethernet cable to connect this device to the Linux computer.

You'll also need the following software:

- Linux. Ideally, you should have Red Hat 9.x with kernel version 2.4.x, with IPtables and gpgv. NoCatAuth, the free software that will provide the management and control capabilities for your hotspot, uses IPtables to route traffic between the two NICs. We'll give instructions for Red Hat 9 in this chapter. You may have to adapt these instructions to other flavors of Linux. Another software-related requirement is root access to the Linux server. You should do everything in this chapter as the root user.

- The nightly build of NoCatAuth. Download it from the NoCat network site (www.nocat.net). It is standard procedure to warn you that a particular nightly build could be buggy. Peruse the mailing list a bit before downloading, to see if people seem to be having trouble with recent builds. If so, download the most recent stable build. That being said, when I downloaded NoCatAuth in early 2004, it looked like the code hadn't changed since mid-2002. (I guess they were on to working on NoCatSplash, a software package being groomed as the successor to NoCatAuth. Dates on NoCatSplash files were very recent.)

- DHCP (Dynamic Host Control Protocol) server somewhere on your network. This could be a DHCP daemon running on your Linux machine (this seems to work best in most situations), or it could be on your AP or another server. In general, implementing a DHCP server is not a huge stumbling block. For instance, the default configuration for many access points includes DHCP service. If your network clients are configured to obtain an IP address automatically, and they are able to access the network, then they already have access to a DHCP server.

- If you want to set per-user bandwidth limits using throttle.fw, you will need tc installed on your server. (This is a standard component of Red Hat 9.x.)

- Optionally, you can install a local caching DNS (domain name service) server. You get an option to install a DNS when you install Red Hat 9.x from scratch.

Be aware that you are undertaking a challenging project. There are a lot of things that have to go right for your hotspot to work, and each one of these things is capable of going wrong in many different ways. Basically, there are five areas where you may have to do some tinkering: the AP, the WAN hardware (such as a DSL "modem"), Ethernet and TCP/IP networking, the

Linux computer, and the client computer(s). If you're not a guru in all these areas, here's an opportunity to learn, and achieve something cool in the process.

The centerpiece of the solution described in this chapter is "captive portal" software, NoCatAuth, which you download free from the NoCat network site (www.nocat.net) and run on a Linux computer, which thus becomes a gateway. Just the potential complications associated with this one piece of software can drive you batty.

It is not unusual for questions on the NoCat mailing list—especially newbie questions—to go unanswered for days, or even forever, despite sometimes piteous pleas ("Nobody will help me?"). There is no official support for the NoCat software, and if you can find somebody to provide support for a price, the price could be fairly steep (say, $75 an hour).

NoCat isn't the only software available for setting up a free hotspot. If you're interested in checking out alternatives, a good starting point is www.personaltelco.net/ index.cgi/PortalSoftware. But NoCat seems to be the most popular of the free options.

# What Is NoCatAuth?

NoCatAuth is a "captive portal" software. A *portal* is a Web site or service that offers access to an array of other resources and services. A captive portal is the one in which users are initially "captured" and restricted in what they're able to do. They may be restricted to just a login screen, or a screen describing an acceptable use policy (AUP). In that case, they must log in or accept the policy before they can do anything else. Alternatively, the captive portal may allow users to access a restricted number of Web sites without logging in or agreeing to the AUP. It is also possible to include a Skip button on the login screen, allowing the user to skip the login process.

In this chapter, you'll set up two basic NoCatAuth configurations: One uses NoCatAuth's "Open" mode to create a portal that does not allow login using a user name and password, but does redirect users to a splash screen. Users have to click a button to continue.

The other configuration uses NoCatAuth's "Passive" mode to create a portal that allows, but does not require, a login. The user can press the Skip button, not provide a user name or password, and be automatically logged in as "unknown."

You can create a Passive mode NoCatAuth system in which the user has to log in—no Skip button allowed. However, this requires that you install not only the gateway component of NoCat, but also the authorization server ("auth server") component. The gateway component provides (or refuses to provide) access to the Internet. Every NoCat hotspot is based on a gateway, which manages local connections, enforces locally configurable firewall rules (and optionally bandwidth limitations), and times out idle logins. The auth server displays the login and logout screens in Passive mode (though not the splash screen in Open mode—that's served locally at the gateway) and handles the "backend" processing for the login. This chapter does not go into any detail about setting up your own auth server.

There is an auth server at nocat.net that everyone is free to use. This chapter assumes that you will use that. There are some very significant limitations for "outsiders" using this server. In particular, when it hands out permissions, the auth server assigns one of three classes of service: Owner (sometimes called "Priority"), Co-op, or Public. Outsiders always get Public class access. In other words, you have to create a one-size-fits-all security configuration. Setting up your own auth server gives you much more flexibility.

Even if you do plan to eventually set up your own auth server, you probably want to start by getting a gateway working with the auth server at nocat.net first. That way, you'll have a "known good" gateway for testing, and will not be trying to debug both the gateway and the auth server at the same time.

After getting past the splash or login screen (see Figure 10-2), the user can be redirected to the site originally requested. In the Open mode configuration, it is also possible to edit the splash screen to redirect all users to a site that you specify. (If you have your own auth server, you can edit the login screen, too.)

In either Open or Passive mode, you can configure a set of allowed domains, and the user will not be able to browse any domains other than those. Any attempt to access nonallowed domains will just bring up the splash screen or login screen. This can be a bit tricky to configure, depending on the particular allowed site. The basic configuration is easy, as explained in

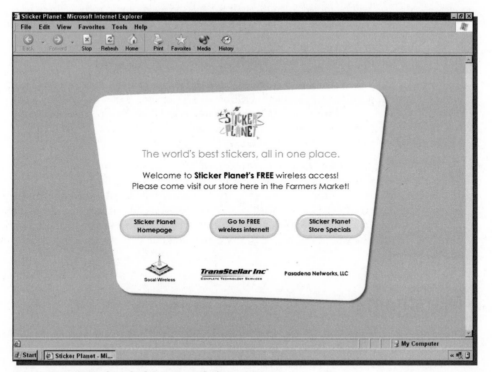

FIGURE 10-2: Typical "splash" page with three options.

the "Configuring NoCat" section later in this chapter. However, you may encounter situations where you put a site into the AllowedWebHosts list and still can't get through to it consistently. Instead, you encounter situations where you are eternally returned to the splash screen or login screen. It can take some troubleshooting to determine what is wrong and how to correct it, as you'll see in the section on "Troubleshooting NoCat." Unfortunately, you'll also see why it is not possible to guarantee a smooth experience for every user when only a limited number of domains is allowed.

The NoCat log (`/usr/local/nocat/nocat.log`) records the user's IP address, the hardware (MAC) address of the user's Ethernet card, the URL of the site that the user originally requested, and what level of access (class of service) is granted. In Passive mode, the log also shows the login name, if the user provides one. Otherwise, it shows "unknown." All log entries are time-stamped.

If you were ever required to demonstrate that it was someone else, not you, who did something on your network (something illegal, for instance), the MAC address could be particularly useful, since it is associated with a particular computer—or, more precisely, with a particular Ethernet card. This contrasts sharply with IP addresses, which you will probably be assigning dynamically (using a DHCP server, for example), so that any given IP address gets used over and over again for different clients.

Both Open and Passive configurations enforce idle time-outs. After a configurable period of inactivity, the user will be forced to go through the splash page or login page again in order to continue accessing the Internet.

Neither configuration requires any special client software—just an ordinary browser. This is a major strength of the captive portal approach.

Note that, in addition to the NoCat software described in this chapter, there is a NoCat community network operating in Sebastopol, California. This chapter assumes "outsider" status, as far as this network goes. That is, I assume that, in the security database maintained by the NoCat community network, users of your gateway will not be defined as members of the NoCat community or of any other group defined in that database.

There is a newer piece of software, NoCatSplash, which currently did not support authorization at the time I tested it. It simply displayed a splash screen, forcing the user to click a button in order to continue. NoCatSplash is billed as the successor to NoCatAuth. However, when I played with it in early 2004, NoCatSplash was alpha software, and not as stable as NoCatAuth. Therefore, I decided to stick with NoCatAuth for this chapter. However, once you are familiar with NoCatAuth, you will probably find it very easy to migrate to NoCatSplash, should you decide to do so.

# Risk Management

When you decide to provide wireless data services, you essentially become a wireless ISP. As such, you have a responsibility to try to prevent your hotspot from being used irresponsibly or for illegal purposes. That could mean anything from spam to child pornography. Although I don't know of any cases where a free hotspot operator has been prosecuted for traffic on his or her network (and I am not an attorney and do not mean to offer legal advice), it seems only prudent to take some basic precautions. Anyway, you're probably a basically good person and don't want your hotspot used for bad purposes.

There are three things you can do to control what happens on your hotspot, and perhaps cover yourself if violations of the law or of Internet etiquette occur:

1. Make users agree to an Acceptable Use Policy (AUP). Your "splash" page (the page that all users are initially redirected to) might say, for example, that the user will not use your network to send spam, or access or upload child pornography, and so on. This doesn't actually stop anybody from doing anything, but it demonstrates your good intentions, and lets "law-abiding" users know what is expected of them. Either NoCatSplash or NoCatAuth can ensure that users click a button before being allowed to do anything else.

   Check out the following Personal Telco sites for more ideas about what exactly you might want to put on your splash page:

   www.personaltelco.net/index.cgi/NodeSplashPages?action=
   highlight&value=splash

   www.personaltelco.net/splash/

2. Set up a system that limits what users can do. Either NoCatSplash or NoCatAuth can apply some blanket rules to all users. For instance:

   As an anti-spam measure, both are configured by default to prevent outgoing SMTP packets, which prevents most e-mail clients from sending mail. (Web mail services, such as Hotmail and Yahoo! Mail, are not affected.)

   Users can be restricted to particular Web sites.

   In addition, the auth server can place users in one of the three classes of service (Owner, Co-op, Public), based on user names and passwords. You can define different rights and permissions depending on which class they belong to. For instance, some users can be limited to browsing a few specific Web sites, while others may be free to browse the whole Internet. However, you can modify the auth server database in order to enable the different classes of service. This generally means setting up your own auth server.

   There is also a ("highly experimental") facility for throttling bandwidth based on membership in these same groups. (After you install the NoCatAuth gateway, check out the throttle.fw file for more information on throttling bandwidth.)

3. Monitor use. This could allow you to detect network abuse and take steps to end it. Most free wireless network operators seem to have done little, if any, monitoring in the past—a policy that has been likened to walking around with your eyes closed. However, both historical and real-time monitoring are possible.

   Historical monitoring involves analyzing the NoCat log file. Ongoing monitoring of the log file would have to be automated. Try a Google search on "nocat.log analyzer" to find out about work that has been done in this area, which you may be able to take advantage of.

   Real-time monitoring could be based on a tool like MRTG (Multi Router Traffic Grapher), which produces graphical images at regular intervals (every 5 minutes by default) representing traffic on network links. You could use this to detect a user flooding your network with traffic, for example, either maliciously or unintentionally. (MRTG may come free with your Linux system. To download it or just to find out more about it, go to www.mrtg.org.) To get more detailed information on who is causing the problem and what exactly they are doing, you could go to the NoCat log. You might also use a packet capture utility such as *Ethereal,* a free network protocol analyzer for Unix and Windows. (See www.ethereal.com.) This type of analyzer gives you the most detailed information, though not always the easiest to interpret.

You may have reasons other than security for wanting to monitor your network. For instance, perhaps you want to be able to limit each user's free access to a particular length of time, such as half an hour. Or perhaps you are starting with free access now, but want to position yourself to charge in the future. Time limitations (other than time-outs after a period of idleness) and billing are not standard parts of the current NoCat implementation. However, a number of approaches have been discussed and tried. One approach starts by analyzing the log file to determine usage. A more flexible and sophisticated approach is to record information in a MySQL database. Perhaps the most natural approach, however, is integrating with the RADIUS authorization and accounting server. To find information on this, try www.pogozone.net/projects/nocat/, or do a Google search on "nocat radius."

# Pre-Install Setup

You have to install and configure your network hardware before installing NoCat. There are three basic areas you need to work in: the AP, the Linux box (including configuring the two Ethernet cards), and the WAN connection (which I will assume to be DSL, for this discussion).

The basic hardware setup looks like that shown in Figures 10-3 and 10-4. It involves three boxes: the wireless AP, the Linux gateway and the DSL "modem." One Ethernet card connects to the DSL modem. The other Ethernet card connects to the AP. The names assigned to the Ethernet cards in Linux ("eth0" and "eth1") are typical. However, you can assign any names you want (using System Settings, Network in Red Hat).

If you don't already have your DSL working, it's probably best to make sure that things are at least minimally functional on the Linux side first. Then get the Linux box talking to the WAN. Finally, add the AP into the mix.

## The Linux Box

To set up your NICs on the Linux box, click on the red hat and go to System Settings ⇨ Network. A minimal requirement here is to have two active NICs. If one or both are either not on the list or inactive, things are not going to work. In addition, the status should be ok.

If one of the cards is inactive, try clicking Activate. It may activate, or you may get an error message giving you a clue about what is wrong.

FIGURE 10-3: A basic hardware setup, with a DSL modem, a Linux box with two Ethernet cards, and an AP.

If one of the cards is not on the list, click the New button and use the installation wizard to install it. If nothing else seems to get a card working, you may want to try deactivating, deleting, and reinstalling the card. It only takes a few minutes, and it's a low-risk operation, if you make sure to write down all the information necessary for reinstalling. So, before you delete a card, write down all the information in all the tabs on the Network Configuration screen (Devices, Hardware, IPsec, DNS, Hosts), as well as the information available by clicking the Edit button.

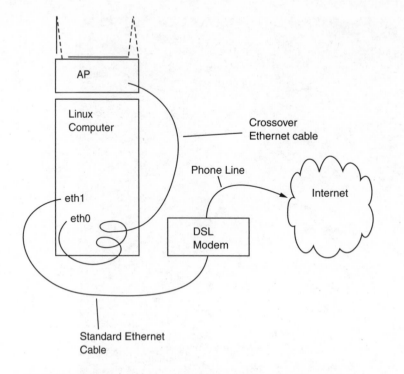

FIGURE 10-4: Diagram of a hardware setup as shown in Figure 10-3.

## Software Installation for a NIC

The procedure for installing a card is as follows. Click the New button. Select "Ethernet connection" from the "Device Type" list, and click the Forward button in the lower right.

Hopefully, on the "Select Ethernet Adapter" screen, both your cards will be there in the list, making it easy to select them. If not, click on "Other Ethernet Card" and choose from the drop-down menu based on your knowledge of the manufacturer and model of the card. Do not worry about the empty boxes in the "Resource" section, or the "Unknown IRQ." Although you can set these things manually, they usually auto-configure correctly. Click "Forward."

The information you enter on the "Configure Network Settings" screen will be crucial to making your NoCat server work correctly. One potentially easy way out is to accept the defaults, "Automatically obtain IP address settings with dhcp," and "Automatically obtain DNS information from provider." If this works, fine. If not, you can go to System Settings ⇨ Network ⇨ Edit and try something else.

If you end up having to set static IP addresses (because automatically obtaining them doesn't work, for whatever reason), there are many right ways, and probably more wrong ways, to configure your network.

Here are three general principles you should be aware of:

1. You can't successfully configure your NICs in isolation from the other components of your network. Thus, network setup may be an iterative process, in which you tinker with one part of the network (such as AP configuration), and then go back and change other parts of the network (such as NIC configuration) to make them compatible.

2. No two devices on your local network can have the same IP address.

3. Each NIC must be configured to talk directly to the network device to which it is connected. That generally means being in the same Class C network. In terms of IP addressing, that means that, of the four sections of the IP address, the first three are the same. For instance, if the IP address of your DSL modem is 192.168.1.1, the NIC that connects to your DSL modem will have an address like 192.168.1.XXX, where XXX is a number from 2 to 254. (It can't be 1 in this case, because that's already taken by the DSL modem.) Similarly, if your wireless AP is 192.168.2.1, the NIC that connects to your DSL modem will have an address like 192.168.2.XXX, where XXX is a number from 2 to 254.

You may find that it is easiest to set static IP addresses for both NICs. If you do this, I recommend assigning them to different Class C networks, which means having different numbers in the third section of the IP address (called the "network number"). For example, 192.168.1.254 and 192.168.2.254.

First, however, make sure that the DSL modem and the AP use those same Class C network numbers. Otherwise, you'll find that you are unable to talk to the DSL modem and AP. You'll get a "connection refused" message in your browser, because you violated rule number 3 above.

There are at least three other items that you may have to set: the subnet mask, the default gateway, and one or more DNS addresses.

The subnet mask basically says which portions of the IP address define the subnet. Assuming that you are using Class C networks, as we suggested, the subnet mask should be 255.255.255.0, indicating that the first three sections of the address define the subnet.

The default gateway is the address of the next device in line along the path to the Internet. Figure 10-5 shows one possible setup for IP addresses and default gateway addresses for the AP, two NICs, and the DSL modem.

DNS permits "resolving" domain names like www.google.com into IP addresses. Thus, getting the correct addresses for the DNS servers is crucial for making things work. If you use your provider's DNS servers, you should be able to ask your ISP what IP addresses are for the provider's DNS servers. Or you may get the DNS server addresses automatically using DHCP. Your DSL modem may also function as a DNS server, in which case one valid DNS address would be the address of your DSL modem, such as 192.168.1.1 from our examples above.

When you have finished filling in the "Configure Network Settings" screen, click "Forward." On the "Create Ethernet Device" screen, review the information displayed to make sure it is correct. If it isn't, click "Back" and correct the information. Otherwise, click "Apply."

You'll be taken back to the main "Network Configuration" screen, where you can activate the new card. Finally, go to the command prompt of the GNOME terminal, (click on the red

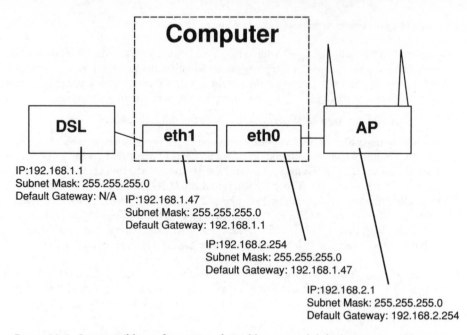

FIGURE **10-5: One possible configuration of IP addresses and default gateway addresses for an AP, two NICs and a DSL modem.**

hat ⇨ System Tools ⇨ Terminal) and type service network restart. Any time you want to check the settings of these cards, go to the command prompt of the GNOME terminal (click on the red hat ⇨ System Tools ⇨ Terminal) and type ifconfig.

### Testing, Testing

Once your NICs seem to be configured correctly, open the browser on the Linux box and make sure you can access both the DSL modem and the AP. You do this simply by typing the IP address of the device in the address bar at the top of the browser. You should either get instant access to the device, or else a login screen.

If you get an error such as "connection refused," the problem could be a bad cable, a loose cable, or a crossover cable used where a standard cable is required. Or you may have violated rule number 3, as discussed above. You could also have connected to a bad port on the device.

## The WAN

If your service provider has turned your service on, and it is properly configured on their side, you should be able to follow their instructions and get things working. One possible wrinkle is that you may prefer to run DHCP on your Linux box, whereas the provider's instructions may assume that the DSL modem will be the DHCP server. Remember that you should not have two DHCP servers accessible to any DHCP client. So, if you are using the Linux box for DHCP, you should turn off the DHCP capability on the DSL modem and the AP.

If the Linux box and the WAN device are configured correctly, you should be able to browse the Web from the Linux box. If you can't, see if the lights on the front of the DSL modem indicate a good WAN connection and a good Ethernet connection. Use the browser to access the DSL modem and check out its status screen. If everything seems OK on the DSL modem side, then you probably have a problem in the Linux box configuration.

## The AP

With many APs, the recommended setup is to put the AP in bridged mode and use a crossover cable to connect to the Linux box. However, what "bridged" means here is simply that the AP is transparent to the IP network, acting as a simple Ethernet bridge. For example, your clients would not use the address of the AP as their default gateway. Instead they use the address of the Ethernet card that is connected to the AP. Clients essentially do not see the AP. Instead, they see through it to the Ethernet card.

Unfortunately, terminology is not consistent among AP manufacturers or models. The Linksys WAP11, for instance, has a "bridged" mode in which it can only talk to other Linksys WAP11s. Do not use the bridged mode on the Linksys WAP11 for this project. The Linksys WAP11 is inherently a transparent Ethernet bridge and does not need to be put into any special mode to act that way.

When you're buying an AP for NoCat, the simpler, the better. If you have a more sophisticated AP, set it up in its simplest mode. For example, the AP may have a "gateway" mode, which would be preferable to a "router" mode.

Whether you should use a crossover cable depends on how the AP port you are using is wired. On the WAP11, you should always use a crossover cable when you are not connecting to a hub. Since you are connecting directly to a NIC in this case, you would use a crossover cable with the WAP11. Some APs have both crossover and "straight" wired ports, and you can generally use either one, as long as you use the right kind of cable with it. You can usually tell whether you are using the right kind of cable by looking at the lights on your AP, to determine whether it is seeing a good Ethernet connection on the port.

 Unfortunately, there are a thousand things that can go wrong with hardware, IP, DHCP and DNS setup. Make sure that the hardware and basic networking functions are working correctly before jumping into the NoCat install. You'll be glad you did.

# Installing NoCat

Here are the instructions for installing NoCatAuth on your Linux box:

1. Make sure you are logged on as the root user.

2. Go to the temporary directory where you downloaded the NoCatAuth software and decompress it using the File Roller or a similar utility. All the files for installing the gateway will be unpacked into a subdirectory named NoCatAuth-nightly.

**3.** Go to the NoCatAuth-nightly subdirectory and type: make gateway. This installs the unpacked program files in their operational folders. Although it's possible to edit the Makefile to specify your own paths for installing program files, I would recommend that most people install in the default configuration first, if possible. Using a custom configuration creates one more possible source of problems. You should try to simplify things as much as possible at this point.

That's it. NoCatAuth should be installed.

Do a very basic test by typing /usr/local/nocat/bin/gateway at the command prompt to start the gateway. You should see something like this:

```
[2004-02-12 08:39:23] Resetting firewall.

[2004-02-12 08:39:23] Detected InternalDevice 'eth0'

[2004-02-12 08:39:23] Detected ExternalDevice 'eth1'

[2004-02-12 08:39:23] Detected LocalNetwork '192.168.2.0/255.255.255.0'

[2004-02-12 08:39:24] Binding listener socket to  0.0.0.0
```

If you get error messages, read the INSTALL file for possible fixes. Some problems may also be fixable by modifying the configuration file as described in the next section.

However, it is common for installation to go smoothly up to this point. That doesn't mean that you are out of the woods. In fact, you just stepped into the woods.

# Configuring NoCat

Once NoCat is installed, the next step is to review and edit the configuration file, /usr/local/nocat/nocat.conf, to reflect your network and preferences. Note that most of the parameters can remain commented out in most cases. Many do not need to be manually configured. For instance, NoCat is usually smart enough to figure out which of your Ethernet cards is connected to the Internet, and which is connected to the local ("internal") wireless network. That is why, at the end of the previous section, you may have been able to fire up NoCatAuth, and, without changing anything in the configuration file, get start-up messages like Detected InternalDevice 'eth0'. NoCat also usually figures out the IP address of the internal subnet.

That being said, here are some of the more important parameters that you may need to or want to set:

- GatewayName— The gateway name displayed to users on the locally stored splash and status pages (/usr/local/nocat/htdocs/splash.html and /usr/local/nocat/htdocs/status.html). Note that this does not affect the login and logout screens displayed by the public NoCat auth server.

- GatewayMode— This parameter configures the gateway to operate in Open, Passive, or Captive mode. Open mode displays a local splash screen that you can edit, and does not support username/password login. The other two display a login screen served by the auth server, and do support username/password login. The difference between Passive and Captive is that Passive allows the gateway to operate even if there is a Network Address Translation (NAT) device between the gateway and the auth server. Captive mode is present for compatibility with past versions of NoCatAuth; you won't use it in this chapter. Use Passive instead of Captive for new installations.

- `InternalDevice`—Usually auto-configured. The NIC connected to the AP. In Red Hat 9, usually `eth0`.

- `ExternalDevice`—Usually auto-configured. The NIC connected to the WAN. In Red Hat 9, usually `eth1`.

- `LocalNetwork`—Usually auto-configured. The subnet address of the `InternalDevice`. Examples: 192.168.2.0/255.255.255.0 or 192.168.2.0/24 (two ways of expressing the same thing)

- `DNSAddr`—If you have a local caching DNS server on your Linux box, you should leave this option commented out. Otherwise, this parameter should specify the IP address of the external DNS server.

- `AuthServiceAddr` and `AuthServiceURL`—These specify the authentication server's IP address and URL. Just leave the defaults if you want to use the auth server at nocat.net.

- `AllowedWebHosts`—A list of allowed domains. All other Web sites are inaccessible.

- `MembersOnly`—Disables the Public access class of service when set to 1. (But hosts named in `AllowedWebHosts` remain accessible to everyone.) In Passive mode, users can prove that they belong to the Owners or Co-op class by submitting a username and password to the auth server. In Open mode, since there is no opportunity to submit a username and password, all users are treated the same: Uncommenting `MembersOnly 1` disables Internet access, except to hosts named in `AllowedWebHosts`. `MembersOnly` is commented out by default.

- `IncludePorts` and `ExcludePorts`—These allow you to restrict the use of certain ports for Public class users, either by allowing certain ports and no others (`IncludePorts`) or by disallowing certain ports and permitting all others (`ExcludePorts`). This is where, by default, outgoing mail is blocked by excluding port 25. If you set up a public portal, comment out the `Exclude Ports 25` line in `nocat.conf` if you want your users to be able to send mail using mail clients such as Microsoft Outlook. The alternative will probably be dealing with lots of questions and complaints. (It will not be clear to users why they can't send mail. It just won't work. Of course, you can explain it on the splash page, which everyone will read with meticulous attention.) If both these parameters are commented out, all ports are allowed.

## Testing and Using NoCat

This section describes some basic tests to make sure your hotspot is working properly. These tests are designed to be performed in order, without leaving any of them out. In other words, each test assumes the configuration changes of the previous test.

## Test #1 Accessing NoCat

This tests whether you can access the NoCat network site, which you should always be able to do in the default configuration, since NoCatAuth puts no restrictions on access to this site by default.

1. Start with the default NoCat configuration file (`/usr/local/nocat/nocat.conf`). If you have already edited this file, you can rename your edited file to a unique name, copy `gateway.conf` from the NoCatAuth install directory and rename it `nocat.conf`. In the default configuration file, everything below `LogoutURL` is commented out, with the exception of `ExcludePorts` *25*. Important settings include:

   ```
   GatewayMode: Passive
   ```

   ```
   AuthServicerAddr: auth.nocat.net
   ```

2. Reboot the gateway machine and start NoCatAuth by typing `/usr/local/nocat/bin/gateway` at the command prompt.

3. Assuming a smooth start-up, as described above in "NoCat Installation," go to a client machine and associate with the wireless AP by selecting its SSID. (For testing purposes, you could also access the gateway from a cabled workstation. From the gateway's point of view, there is no difference between wired and wireless clients coming in over the same interface, such as eth0.)

4. Start your browser and type `nocat.net` in the address bar. You should immediately be taken to `http://nocat.net`

If you get an error message indicating that the server cannot be found, the problem may be DNS-related. Try typing `216.218.203.211` in the address bar. This is the IP address of `nocat.net`. If this works, then apparently the problem was in resolving the name `nocat.net` to an IP address. Some things you might check:

- Make sure the DHCP server is handing out good DNS addresses. You should be able to determine this through the DHCP server management interface.

- Make sure the client machine is either configured to automatically obtain its DNS information or is configured with known-good DNS addresses.

- Try setting one or more known-good DNS addresses in the `DNSAddr` parameter in nocat.conf.

If you only make adjustments on the client, type `/usr/local/nocat/bin/gateway -R` at the Linux command prompt, to reset any firewall rules that have been changed.

**Tip**  Keep a terminal window open on the Linux box just for starting and restarting the gateway. Press Ctrl+P to repeat the previous command. (This works even after you have rebooted the machine.) Since you may be repeating the same command many times, this can save you a lot of keystrokes.

If you change things on the server side, reboot the server and restart the gateway. Then try navigating to nocat.net again.

## Test #2 Accessing Google

This tests whether you can access Google, which requires you to go through the login screen.

1. Type www.google.com in the browser address bar. You should get the NoCat login screen, as shown in Figure 10-6.

2. Click the Skip button.

3. After a small NoCat Logout Agent window opens (don't close it—it keeps your connection alive and allows you to log out), you will be taken to the Google site. From there, you should be able to go to any site on the Internet, without any further involvement with NoCat.

## Test #3 Registering and Logging In

This is pretty much like the last test, except that you will register and log in this time, instead of hitting the Skip button.

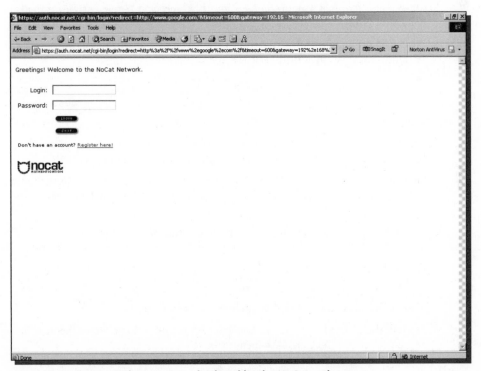

FIGURE 10-6: The NoCat login screen, displayed by the NoCat auth server.

1. Type `/usr/local/nocat/bin/gateway -R` at the Linux command prompt, to reset NoCatAuth firewall rules.

2. On the client, type `www.google.com` in the browser address bar. You should get the NoCat login screen, as shown in Figure 10-6 above.

3. Click "Register here."

4. Fill out the registration form and click "Register." A "thank you" screen will be displayed briefly. Then you will be returned to the login screen.

5. Log in with the name and password that you just created. As in the previous test, you should get the NoCat Logout Agent window and then be forwarded automatically to Google. From there, you should be able to go to any site on the Internet.

## Test #4 Checking IPtables

NoCatAuth uses IPtables to create firewall rules. Therefore, IPtables gives you a way to "look under the hood" and determine whether NoCatAuth is operating properly. This test describes one simple interaction with IPtables.

1. Open a new terminal window on the Linux box, and type `IPtables -L` at the Linux command prompt.

   Near the bottom of the displayed information, you should see the following, but with the IP address of your client instead of 192.168.2.100.

   ```
   Chain NoCat_Inbound (1 references)

   Target      prot      opt      source        destination
   ACCEPT      all       --       anywhere      192.168.2.100
   ```

   The line beginning ACCEPT is a firewall rule that says traffic using any protocol (`prot all`), from anywhere, and destined for your client will be accepted.

2. Go to the terminal window where you restarted the gateway. Use Ctrl+P to bring up the `/usr/local/nocat/bin/gateway -R` command, and hit the Enter key to reset NoCatAuth firewall rules.

3. Go back to the terminal window where you executed the previous `IPtables -L` command. Use Ctrl+P to bring up the command again, and hit the Enter key. You will see:

   ```
   Chain NoCat_Inbound (1 references)

   Target        prot      opt      source        destination
   ```

   The rule allowing traffic to get your client has been removed.

4. Try refreshing the Google screen. You will get the NoCat login screen, because in step 2 above you "erased" NoCatAuth's memory of you.

## Test #5 Open Mode

This test checks Open Mode operation.

1. Edit nocat.conf as follows:

   GatewayMode: Open

2. Optionally, change GatewayName to reflect the change. You might make it "My Open NoCat Portal," for instance.

3. Reboot the computer and then use /usr/local/nocat/bin/gateway or Ctrl+P to start NoCatAuth.

4. On the client, type www.google.com in the browser address bar.

   You should get the NoCat splash screen, as shown in Figure 10-6.

5. Click "Login." You will be taken to the Google site. From there, you should be able to go to any site on the Internet. (Note that there is no NoCat Logout Agent window in this case.)

## Test #6 Allowed Web Hosts

This test makes sure that the "Allowed Web Hosts" feature is working properly.

1. In nocat.conf, uncomment MembersOnly 1 and AllowedWebHosts. Edit as follows:

   AllowedWebHosts: rockisland.com

   MembersOnly 1

   (Leave GatewayMode: Open)

2. Reboot the computer. Use /usr/local/nocat/bin/gateway or Ctrl+P to start NoCatAuth

3. On the client, type www.google.com in the browser address bar, or attempt to refresh the Google screen, if it is already open. You get the NoCat splash screen, as shown in Figure 10-7. The first time the gateway is accessed, a "none" message will appear. It will be replaced by a date and time after the first login.

4. Click "Login." You are not taken to the Google site, because it is not an allowed site. Instead, you are returned to the splash screen.

5. Type www.rockisland.com in the browser address bar. You are taken to that site. If you attempt to go to any other site, you will be returned to the splash screen.

6. Change back to Passive mode, reboot, and restart the gateway. The behavior is essentially the same, except that you get the login screen instead of the splash screen.

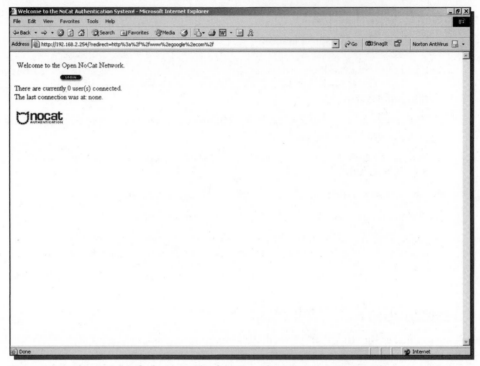

FIGURE 10-7: The NoCat splash screen the first time the gateway is accessed.

Note that a user whose initial request is for an allowed site will never see the splash screen at all. This is the intended behavior of AllowedWebHosts. However, if you want all users to view and accept an AUP, it is an unfortunate behavior. One possible workaround is editing the splash page to always redirect to a particular site (see instructions in the next section) and putting the AUP on that site instead of on the splash page.

## Test #7 All Roads Lead to Rome

This tests a configuration in which all users are redirected to one particular site, no matter which site they initially request.

1. Make a copy of the splash page (/usr/local/nocat/htdocs/splash.html) so that you can always go back to the original.

2. Open the splash page using your preferred text editor. (In Red Hat, you can get to the gedit editor by clicking on the red hat, then selecting Accessories ⇨ Text Editor.) Toward the bottom of the page, where you see value"$redirect", substitute a URL for $redirect. For example: value="http://www.rockisland.com" (be sure to include the http://.)

3. Make any other changes you wish, as well, in the splash file. This is your chance to insert an AUP, for instance. In addition, since users are not logging in, you may want to edit the splash page so that it has a Continue button rather than a Login button. Toward the middle of the page, where you see `src="images/login.gif,"` substitute `src="images/continue.gif."` If you want to see all the possible button images, look in `/usr/local/nocat/htdocs/images`. Or you can create a new image and use it, instead.

If you have multiple allowed sites, you can put links to all those sites on your splash page. Be sure to include the `http://`, like this:

```
<a href="http://www.rockisland.com".Rockisland,</a.>
```

4. Save the file.

5. Edit `nocat.conf`, to change back to Open mode. Leave the other settings as shown in the previous section.

6. Reboot the computer and restart the NoCatAuth gateway.

7. On the client, type www.google.com in the browser address bar, or attempt to refresh the Google screen, if it is already open. You get the NoCat splash screen, as shown in Figure 10-8.

FIGURE 10-8: At subsequent logins, the splash page displays the time and date of the most recent login.

**8.** Click "Login." You are immediately taken to www.rockisland.com. With splash.html edited in this fashion, all users will be forwarded to www.rockisland.com when they click "Login." If there are other allowed domains in the AllowedWebHosts parameter, users will be able to navigate to those domains from www.rockisland.com.

# Troubleshooting NoCat

If you run into problems configuring or using NoCat, three useful troubleshooting tools are the NoCat log file (/usr/local/nocat/nocat.log), the Ethereal protocol analyzer, and IPtables. Here are descriptions of a couple of troubleshooting sessions I was involved in. Hopefully, they will give you some hints about how you might cure your own troubles.

## Trouble #1: Allowing a Redirected Site

Basically, what you're doing here is following the directions for Test #6 and Test #7, but using greendept.org instead of rockisland.com. It doesn't work. Ethereal and IPtables reveal the problem, suggesting a solution.

**1.** Edit nocat.conf as follows:

```
GatewayName: My greendept-only NoCat Portal

AllowedWebHosts: greendept.org

MembersOnly 1

GatewayMode Open
```

**2.** Edit splash.html to redirect to www.greendept.org. (See the section *All Roads Lead to Rome* for instructions on editing splash.html.)

**3.** Reboot the server and start the gateway.

**4.** On the client, type www.google.com in the browser address bar, or attempt to refresh the Google screen, if it is already open. You get the NoCat splash screen, as shown in Figure 10-7 or 10-8 (depending on whether this is the first login or a subsequent login). So far, everything is going the same as in Test #6 and Test #7.

**5.** Click "Login." At this point, you would expect to be redirected to www.greendept.org. Instead, you get the splash screen again. What is wrong?

**6.** In a new terminal window, at the Linux command prompt, type IPtables -L. You should see something like the following:

```
Chain INPUT (policy ACCEPT)

target        prot opt source          destination

Chain FORWARD (policy ACCEPT)

target        prot opt source          destination
NoCat         all  --  anywhere        anywhere

Chain OUTPUT  (policy ACCEPT)

target        prot opt source          destination


Chain NoCat (1 references)

target        prot opt source          destination

NoCat_Ports   all  --  anywhere        anywhere

NoCat_Inbound all  --  anywhere        anywhere
ACCEPT    all  --  192.168.2.0/24       anywhere          MARK match 0x1
ACCEPT    all  --  192.168.2.0/24       anywhere          MARK match 0x2
ACCEPT    tcp  --  192.168.2.0/24       216.218.203.211   tcp dpt:http
ACCEPT    tcp  --  216.218.203.211      192.168.2.0/24    tcp spt:http
ACCEPT    tcp  --  192.168.2.0/24       216.218.203.211   tcp dpt:https
ACCEPT    tcp  --  216.218.203.211      192.168.2.0/24    tcp spt:https
ACCEPT  tcp -- 192.168.2.0/24 ip-64-202-167-129.secureserver.net tcp dpt:http
ACCEPT  tcp -- ip-64-202-167-129.secureserver.net 192.168.2.0/24 tcp spt:http
ACCEPT  tcp -- 192.168.2.0/24 ip-64-202-167-129.secureserver.net tcp dpt:https
ACCEPT  tcp -- ip-64-202-167-129.secureserver.net 192.168.2.0/24  tcp spt:https
ACCEPT    all  --  dslrouter            192.168.2.0/24
ACCEPT    tcp  --  192.168.2.0/24       dslrouter         tcp dpt:domain
ACCEPT    udp  --  192.168.2.0/24       dslrouter         udp dpt:domain
ACCEPT    all  --  apollo.rockisland.com 192.168.2.0/24
ACCEPT    tcp  --  192.168.2.0/24       apollo.rockisland.comtcp dpt:domain
ACCEPT    udp  --  192.168.2.0/24       apollo.rockisland.comudp dpt:domain
ACCEPT    all  --  mars.rockisland.com  192.168.2.0/24
ACCEPT    tcp  --  192.168.2.0/24       mars.rockisland.comtcp dpt:domain
ACCEPT    udp  --  192.168.2.0/24       mars.rockisland.comudp dpt:domain
DROP      tcp  --  !216.218.203.211     anywhere          tcp dpt:5280
DROP      all  --  anywhere             anywhere


Chain NoCat_Inbound (1 references)
target        prot opt source          destination
ACCEPT        all  --  anywhere         192.168.2.100
```

```
Chain NoCat_Ports (1 references)
target    prot opt source         destination
DROP      tcp  --  anywhere       anywhere      tcp dpt:smtp MARK match 0x3
DROP      udp  --  anywhere       anywhere      udp dpt:smtp MARK match 0x3
```

This printout shows six "chains"—six linkable sequences of firewall rules. (Each line is a rule.) When the firewall receives an IP packet, the packet has to "run the gauntlet" of six chains, in order, from top to bottom. Within each chain, rules are processed in order, unless control is passed to another chain. If control is passed, than the other chain is executed, after which control is passed back to the first chain. At any point, a rule may indicate that the packet should be accepted or dropped.

The INPUT and OUTPUT chains deal with packets originating or terminating in the Linux box itself. NoCatAuth is interested only in packets originating or terminating outside the Linux box. Therefore, the INPUT and OUTPUT chains are empty, and you can ignore them. The FOR-WARD chain deals with packets originating outside the Linux box, and the one rule in that chain simply says to pass all packets to the NoCat chain.

The NoCat chain does the following:

1. First rule: Passes the packet to the NoCat_Ports chain, where the packet is dropped if it is Public class traffic on a port that is disallowed in the ExcludePorts parameter in the nocat.conf file. (The MARK section on the far right indicates Public class with the hexadecimal number $0 \times 3$. Owner class is $0 \times 1$, and Co-op class is $0 \times 2$. See /usr/local/libexec/nocat/initialize.fw.)

**Note** The "mark match" extension is used to match packets based on "marks." A mark is a special field, maintained only within the operating system kernel, while the packets travel through the computer. This was previously done with the FWMARK target in ipchains, and many people still refer to FWMARK even when dealing with IPtables.

2. Second rule: Passes the packet to the NoCat_Inbound chain, where it is accepted if its destination is the client (192.168.2.100).

3. Third rule: Accepts all Owner class traffic from the internal network (192.168.2.0/24). (The /24 is the same as a subnet mask of 255.255.255.0. That is, it means that only the first three sections of the IP address are significant. The last section can be anything.)

4. Fourth rule: Accepts all Co-op class traffic from the internal network.

5. Next four rules: Accept everything, coming or going, between the internal network (192.168.2.0/24) and 216.218.203.211 (http://nocat.net).

6. Next four rules: Accept everything, coming or going, between the internal network (192.168.2.0/24) and ip-64-202-167-129.secureserver.net.

7. Thirteenth rule: Accept everything originating in the DSL router and going to the internal network. This would typically be DNS or DHCP traffic. (Other traffic passes through the DSL router, but does not originate in it.)

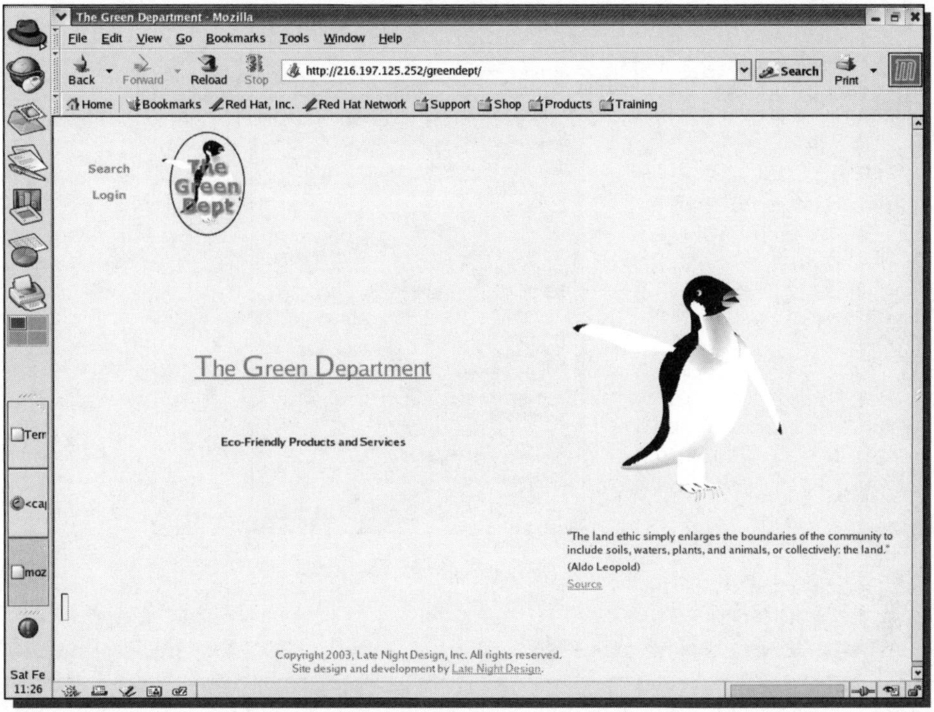

**FIGURE 10-9: Typing greendept.org in the address bar of the browser brought up this screen. Note the IP address in the address bar.**

**8.** The next eight rules all have to do with accepting DNS-related traffic. (`Rockisland.com`'s DNS servers were being used.)

**9.** The last two rules drop traffic that has made it this far without being accepted anywhere.

The key to the problem lies in the rules concerning `ip-64-202-167-129.secure-server.net` (step 6 above). One would expect to find rules concerning `greendept.org` here, since that is the site listed in `AllowedWebHosts`. However, when NoCatAuth sent out a DNS query to find out where to send traffic for `greendept.org`, it was told, in effect, that ip-64-202-167-129.secureserver.net was taking calls for `greendept.org`. NoCatAuth did not know that this address refers to a Web forwarding service that forwards traffic for `greendept.org` to still another domain.

Which other domain? Type `www.greendept.org` in the address bar of the browser on the Linux machine. (Use the Linux machine, because the client can't contact `greendept.org` at the moment.) You see that you are redirected to a page at IP address 216.197.125.252 (see Figure 10-9). This redirection is not set in stone, by the way, so it could have changed by the time you read this. However, the principles remain applicable.)

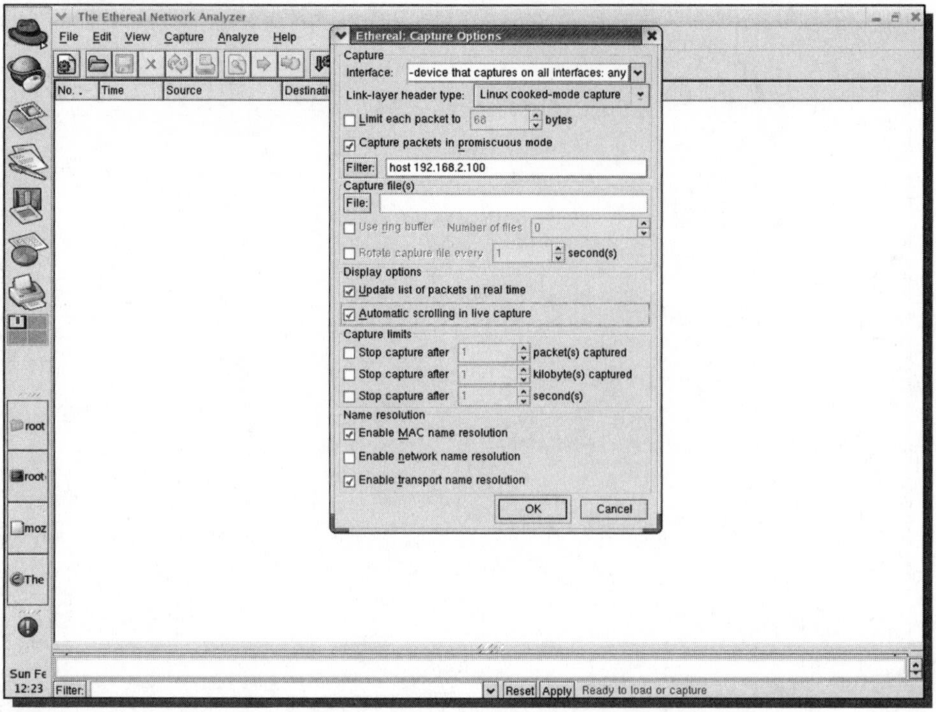

FIGURE 10-10: Ethereal, a free Ethernet protocol analyzer for UNIX and Windows.

What is happening is something like this: The browser on the client sends out a request for greendept.org. The Web forwarding service raises its hand and says, "That's mine." At this point, NoCatAuth creates the rules in the firewall, using the address of the Web forwarding service (ip-64-202-167-129.secureserver.net). However, when the browser actually requests a page, the Web forwarding service tells the browser that the page has been moved to 216.197.125.252. When the browser tries to access it there, the firewall won't let it, because there are no rules permitting traffic to or from 216.197.125.252.

You can confirm this scenario using Ethereal. Refer to Figure 10-10 for the following instructions.

1. Bring up Ethereal. (In Red Hat: Internet ⇨ More Internet Applications ⇨ Ethereal.)

2. Click the left-hand button, "Start New Capture."

3. In the "Ethereal: Capture Options" dialog, click the "Capture Interface" drop-down menu and select "Pseudo-device that captures on all interfaces."

4. In the "Filter" box, type something of the form host 192.168.2.100, but substituting the address of your client machine. This will limit the capture to packets to and from the client.

5. Select the check boxes for "Update list of packets in real time" and "Automatic scrolling in live capture."

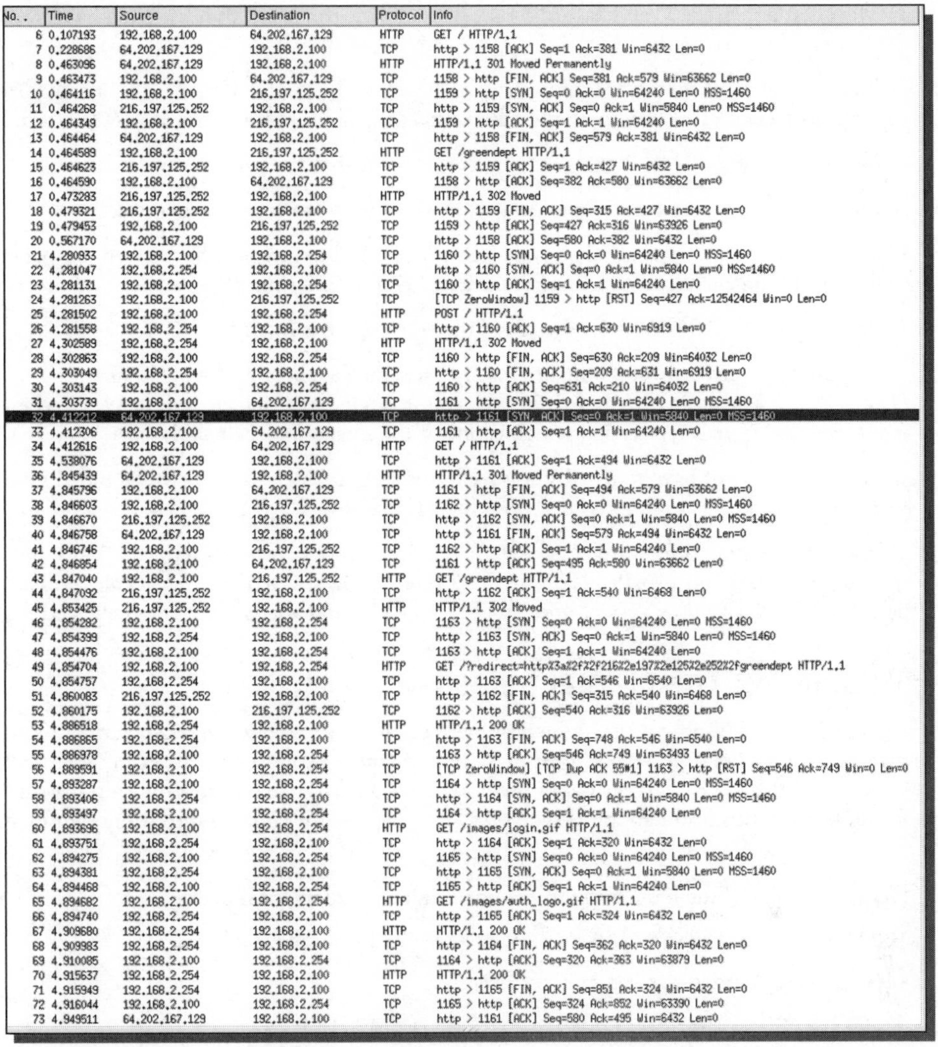

| No. | Time | Source | Destination | Protocol | Info |
|---|---|---|---|---|---|
| 6 | 0.107193 | 192.168.2.100 | 64.202.167.129 | HTTP | GET / HTTP/1.1 |
| 7 | 0.228686 | 64.202.167.129 | 192.168.2.100 | TCP | http > 1158 [ACK] Seq=1 Ack=381 Win=6432 Len=0 |
| 8 | 0.463096 | 64.202.167.129 | 192.168.2.100 | HTTP | HTTP/1.1 301 Moved Permanently |
| 9 | 0.463473 | 192.168.2.100 | 64.202.167.129 | TCP | 1158 > http [FIN, ACK] Seq=381 Ack=579 Win=63662 Len=0 |
| 10 | 0.464116 | 192.168.2.100 | 216.197.125.252 | TCP | 1159 > http [SYN] Seq=0 Ack=0 Win=64240 Len=0 MSS=1460 |
| 11 | 0.464268 | 216.197.125.252 | 192.168.2.100 | TCP | http > 1159 [SYN, ACK] Seq=0 Ack=1 Win=5840 Len=0 MSS=1460 |
| 12 | 0.464349 | 192.168.2.100 | 216.197.125.252 | TCP | 1159 > http [ACK] Seq=1 Ack=1 Win=64240 Len=0 |
| 13 | 0.464464 | 64.202.167.129 | 192.168.2.100 | TCP | http > 1158 [FIN, ACK] Seq=579 Ack=381 Win=6432 Len=0 |
| 14 | 0.464589 | 192.168.2.100 | 216.197.125.252 | HTTP | GET /greendept HTTP/1.1 |
| 15 | 0.464623 | 216.197.125.252 | 192.168.2.100 | TCP | http > 1159 [ACK] Seq=1 Ack=427 Win=6432 Len=0 |
| 16 | 0.464590 | 192.168.2.100 | 64.202.167.129 | TCP | 1158 > http [ACK] Seq=382 Ack=580 Win=63662 Len=0 |
| 17 | 0.473283 | 216.197.125.252 | 192.168.2.100 | HTTP | HTTP/1.1 302 Moved |
| 18 | 0.479321 | 216.197.125.252 | 192.168.2.100 | TCP | http > 1159 [FIN, ACK] Seq=315 Ack=427 Win=6432 Len=0 |
| 19 | 0.479453 | 192.168.2.100 | 216.197.125.252 | TCP | 1159 > http [ACK] Seq=427 Ack=316 Win=63926 Len=0 |
| 20 | 0.567170 | 64.202.167.129 | 192.168.2.100 | TCP | http > 1158 [ACK] Seq=580 Ack=382 Win=6432 Len=0 |
| 21 | 4.280933 | 192.168.2.100 | 192.168.2.254 | TCP | 1160 > http [SYN] Seq=0 Ack=0 Win=64240 Len=0 MSS=1460 |
| 22 | 4.281047 | 192.168.2.254 | 192.168.2.100 | TCP | http > 1160 [SYN, ACK] Seq=0 Ack=1 Win=5840 Len=0 MSS=1460 |
| 23 | 4.281131 | 192.168.2.100 | 192.168.2.254 | TCP | 1160 > http [ACK] Seq=1 Ack=1 Win=64240 Len=0 |
| 24 | 4.281263 | 192.168.2.100 | 216.197.125.252 | TCP | [TCP ZeroWindow] 1159 > http [RST] Seq=427 Ack=12542464 Win=0 Len=0 |
| 25 | 4.281502 | 192.168.2.100 | 192.168.2.254 | HTTP | POST / HTTP/1.1 |
| 26 | 4.281558 | 192.168.2.254 | 192.168.2.100 | TCP | http > 1160 [ACK] Seq=1 Ack=630 Win=6919 Len=0 |
| 27 | 4.302589 | 192.168.2.254 | 192.168.2.100 | HTTP | HTTP/1.1 302 Moved |
| 28 | 4.302863 | 192.168.2.100 | 192.168.2.254 | TCP | 1160 > http [FIN, ACK] Seq=630 Ack=209 Win=64032 Len=0 |
| 29 | 4.303049 | 192.168.2.254 | 192.168.2.100 | TCP | http > 1160 [FIN, ACK] Seq=209 Ack=631 Win=6919 Len=0 |
| 30 | 4.303143 | 192.168.2.100 | 192.168.2.254 | TCP | 1160 > http [ACK] Seq=631 Ack=210 Win=64032 Len=0 |
| 31 | 4.303739 | 192.168.2.100 | 64.202.167.129 | TCP | 1161 > http [SYN] Seq=0 Ack=0 Win=64240 Len=0 MSS=1460 |
| 32 | 4.412212 | 64.202.167.129 | 192.168.2.100 | TCP | http > 1161 [SYN, ACK] Seq=0 Ack=1 Win=5840 Len=0 MSS=1460 |
| 33 | 4.412306 | 192.168.2.100 | 64.202.167.129 | TCP | 1161 > http [ACK] Seq=1 Ack=1 Win=64240 Len=0 |
| 34 | 4.412616 | 192.168.2.100 | 64.202.167.129 | HTTP | GET / HTTP/1.1 |
| 35 | 4.538076 | 64.202.167.129 | 192.168.2.100 | TCP | http > 1161 [ACK] Seq=1 Ack=494 Win=6432 Len=0 |
| 36 | 4.845439 | 64.202.167.129 | 192.168.2.100 | HTTP | HTTP/1.1 301 Moved Permanently |
| 37 | 4.845796 | 192.168.2.100 | 64.202.167.129 | TCP | 1161 > http [FIN, ACK] Seq=494 Ack=579 Win=63662 Len=0 |
| 38 | 4.846603 | 192.168.2.100 | 216.197.125.252 | TCP | 1162 > http [SYN] Seq=0 Ack=0 Win=64240 Len=0 MSS=1460 |
| 39 | 4.846670 | 216.197.125.252 | 192.168.2.100 | TCP | http > 1162 [SYN, ACK] Seq=0 Ack=1 Win=5840 Len=0 MSS=1460 |
| 40 | 4.846758 | 64.202.167.129 | 192.168.2.100 | TCP | http > 1161 [FIN, ACK] Seq=579 Ack=494 Win=6432 Len=0 |
| 41 | 4.846746 | 192.168.2.100 | 216.197.125.252 | TCP | 1162 > http [ACK] Seq=1 Ack=1 Win=64240 Len=0 |
| 42 | 4.846854 | 192.168.2.100 | 64.202.167.129 | TCP | 1161 > http [ACK] Seq=495 Ack=580 Win=63662 Len=0 |
| 43 | 4.847040 | 192.168.2.100 | 216.197.125.252 | HTTP | GET /greendept HTTP/1.1 |
| 44 | 4.847032 | 216.197.125.252 | 192.168.2.100 | TCP | http > 1162 [ACK] Seq=1 Ack=540 Win=6468 Len=0 |
| 45 | 4.853425 | 216.197.125.252 | 192.168.2.100 | HTTP | HTTP/1.1 302 Moved |
| 46 | 4.854282 | 192.168.2.100 | 192.168.2.254 | TCP | 1163 > http [SYN] Seq=0 Ack=0 Win=64240 Len=0 MSS=1460 |
| 47 | 4.854399 | 192.168.2.254 | 192.168.2.100 | TCP | http > 1163 [SYN, ACK] Seq=0 Ack=1 Win=5840 Len=0 MSS=1460 |
| 48 | 4.854476 | 192.168.2.100 | 192.168.2.254 | TCP | 1163 > http [ACK] Seq=1 Ack=1 Win=64240 Len=0 |
| 49 | 4.854704 | 192.168.2.100 | 192.168.2.254 | HTTP | GET /?redirect=http%3a%2f%2f21%2e19732e12%2e2%2f2greendept HTTP/1.1 |
| 50 | 4.854757 | 192.168.2.254 | 192.168.2.100 | TCP | http > 1163 [ACK] Seq=1 Ack=546 Win=6540 Len=0 |
| 51 | 4.860083 | 216.197.125.252 | 192.168.2.100 | TCP | http > 1162 [FIN, ACK] Seq=315 Ack=540 Win=6468 Len=0 |
| 52 | 4.860175 | 192.168.2.100 | 216.197.125.252 | TCP | 1162 > http [ACK] Seq=540 Ack=316 Win=63926 Len=0 |
| 53 | 4.886518 | 192.168.2.254 | 192.168.2.100 | HTTP | HTTP/1.1 200 OK |
| 54 | 4.886865 | 192.168.2.254 | 192.168.2.100 | TCP | http > 1163 [FIN, ACK] Seq=748 Ack=546 Win=6540 Len=0 |
| 55 | 4.886978 | 192.168.2.100 | 192.168.2.254 | TCP | 1163 > http [ACK] Seq=546 Ack=749 Win=63493 Len=0 |
| 56 | 4.889591 | 192.168.2.100 | 192.168.2.254 | TCP | [TCP ZeroWindow] [TCP Dup ACK 55#1] 1163 > http [RST] Seq=546 Ack=749 Win=0 Len=0 |
| 57 | 4.893287 | 192.168.2.100 | 192.168.2.254 | TCP | 1164 > http [SYN] Seq=0 Ack=0 Win=64240 Len=0 MSS=1460 |
| 58 | 4.893406 | 192.168.2.254 | 192.168.2.100 | TCP | http > 1164 [SYN, ACK] Seq=0 Ack=1 Win=5840 Len=0 MSS=1460 |
| 59 | 4.893497 | 192.168.2.100 | 192.168.2.254 | TCP | 1164 > http [ACK] Seq=1 Ack=1 Win=64240 Len=0 |
| 60 | 4.893696 | 192.168.2.100 | 192.168.2.254 | HTTP | GET /images/login.gif HTTP/1.1 |
| 61 | 4.893751 | 192.168.2.254 | 192.168.2.100 | TCP | http > 1164 [ACK] Seq=1 Ack=320 Win=6432 Len=0 |
| 62 | 4.894275 | 192.168.2.100 | 192.168.2.254 | TCP | 1165 > http [SYN] Seq=0 Ack=0 Win=64240 Len=0 MSS=1460 |
| 63 | 4.894381 | 192.168.2.254 | 192.168.2.100 | TCP | http > 1165 [SYN, ACK] Seq=0 Ack=1 Win=5840 Len=0 MSS=1460 |
| 64 | 4.894468 | 192.168.2.100 | 192.168.2.254 | TCP | 1165 > http [ACK] Seq=1 Ack=1 Win=64240 Len=0 |
| 65 | 4.894682 | 192.168.2.100 | 192.168.2.254 | HTTP | GET /images/auth_logo.gif HTTP/1.1 |
| 66 | 4.894740 | 192.168.2.254 | 192.168.2.100 | TCP | http > 1165 [ACK] Seq=1 Ack=324 Win=6432 Len=0 |
| 67 | 4.909680 | 192.168.2.254 | 192.168.2.100 | HTTP | HTTP/1.1 200 OK |
| 68 | 4.909983 | 192.168.2.254 | 192.168.2.100 | TCP | http > 1164 [FIN, ACK] Seq=362 Ack=320 Win=6432 Len=0 |
| 69 | 4.910085 | 192.168.2.100 | 192.168.2.254 | TCP | 1164 > http [ACK] Seq=320 Ack=363 Win=63879 Len=0 |
| 70 | 4.915637 | 192.168.2.254 | 192.168.2.100 | HTTP | HTTP/1.1 200 OK |
| 71 | 4.915949 | 192.168.2.254 | 192.168.2.100 | TCP | http > 1165 [FIN, ACK] Seq=851 Ack=324 Win=6432 Len=0 |
| 72 | 4.916044 | 192.168.2.100 | 192.168.2.254 | TCP | 1165 > http [ACK] Seq=324 Ack=852 Win=63390 Len=0 |
| 73 | 4.949511 | 64.202.167.129 | 192.168.2.100 | TCP | http > 1161 [ACK] Seq=580 Ack=495 Win=6432 Len=0 |

FIGURE 10-11: Ethereal's capture window, showing a failed attempt to access greendept.org.

6. Click OK at the bottom of the dialog. Ethereal starts capturing packets.

7. Try to access greendept.org from the client. You see a burst of packets in the Ethereal capture window. When the burst of activity is over, click the Stop button in Ethereal. In Ethereal's capture window, you will see something resembling Figure 10-11.

In line 6 (the first line displayed in the figure), the client requests the page from the Web forwarding service (64.202.167.129). This traffic is allowed, because the firewall is set up to allow communication with the Web forwarding service.

However, in line 8, the Web forwarding service informs the client that the page has "Moved Permanently."

In line 10, the client starts communicating with 216.197.125.252. Clearly (though the packet capture display doesn't show this), the client has been told that the file is at 216.197.125.252.

In line 27, NoCatAuth (192.168.2.254) tells the client that the page has moved.

In line 34, the client once again tries to get the page from the forwarding service.

Once again, the Web forwarding service tells the client that the page has moved permanently (line 36) and the client turns once again to 216.197.125.252 (line 38).

In line 45, 216.197.125.252 tells the client that the page has moved.

After that, the conversation is almost entirely between the client and NoCatAuth (192.168.2.254), culminating in loading the splash page. For instance, in line 69, the client requests /images/login.gif, which is one of the images on the splash page.

Although you might have to be a bit guru-ish to follow the details, the general plot-line seems to confirm the surmise you formed by looking at IPtables.

The solution is straightforward: Add 216.197.125.252 to AllowedWebHosts. With both greendept.org and 216.197.125.252 in AllowedWebHosts, the firewall rules will allow both the Web forwarding service and 216.197.125.252, and you will get the requested page.

## Trouble #2: The Eternal Splash

The most serious problem that I encountered when trying to use the AllowedWebHosts parameter was clients getting caught in a cycle of endless splash screens, even when requesting a site that had been accessible in previous tests. I can't give you step-by step instructions for replicating this problem, but I won't be a bit surprised if you run into it on your own.

Here's a snippet of the NoCat log from the period of time in question:

```
[2004-02-12 17:53:54] Peer  12.40.110.242  requests
liveupdate.symantecliveupdate.com
[2004-02-12 17:53:54] Capturing peer 12.40.110.242
[2004-02-12 17:53:54] Spawning child process 30554.
[2004-02-12 17:53:54] Connection to 12.40.110.1 from 12.40.110.242
[2004-02-12 17:53:54] Peer  12.40.110.242  requests 12.40.110.1
[2004-02-12 17:53:54] Displaying splash page to peer 12.40.110.242
[2004-02-12 17:54:02] Spawning child process 30555.
[2004-02-12 17:54:02] Connection to 12.40.110.1 from 12.40.110.242
[2004-02-12 17:54:02] Peer  12.40.110.242  requests
liveupdate.symantecliveupdate.com
```

```
[2004-02-12 17:54:02] Capturing peer 12.40.110.242

[2004-02-12 17:54:03] Spawning child process 30556.

[2004-02-12 17:54:03] Connection to 12.40.110.1 from 12.40.110.242

[2004-02-12 17:54:03] Peer  12.40.110.242  requests 12.40.110.1

[2004-02-12 17:54:03] Displaying splash page to peer 12.40.110.242

[2004-02-12 17:54:16] Spawning child process 30558.

[2004-02-12 17:54:16] Connection to 12.40.110.1 from 12.40.111.238

[2004-02-12 17:54:16] Peer  12.40.111.238  requests www.livejournal.com

[2004-02-12 17:54:16] Capturing peer 12.40.111.238

[2004-02-12 17:54:16] Spawning child process 30559.

[2004-02-12 17:54:16] Connection to 12.40.110.1 from 12.40.111.238

[2004-02-12 17:54:16] Peer  12.40.111.238  requests 12.40.110.1

[2004-02-12 17:54:16] Displaying splash page to peer 12.40.111.238

[2004-02-12 17:54:16] Spawning child process 30560.

[2004-02-12 17:54:16] Connection to 12.40.110.1 from 12.40.111.238

[2004-02-12 17:54:16] Peer  12.40.111.238  requests 12.40.110.1

[2004-02-12 17:54:16] Displaying splash page to peer 12.40.111.238
```

The problem here appears to be a Symantec virus checker trying to check its home site for updates to its virus definitions. The requests are refused (because the virus checker's home site is not in AllowedWebHosts), causing the Windows client to return to the splash screen. The one "legal" request (for greendept.org, for instance—not shown above) is lost in a hail storm of "illegal" requests made by the virus checker.

Another culprit in a similar incident was an e-mail program that automatically tries to connect to a particular Web site, to display news headlines and so on.

Many programs now generate network traffic automatically, and sometimes repetitively and insistently. One solution to this problem is simply to allow such traffic. The log file will tell you which domains you need to put on the AllowedWebHosts list. However, it is likely that no matter how many domains you add, new ones will keep popping up. There are too many applications that access the network automatically to have any hope of offering a smooth experience for every user.

That said, you can offer a smoother and smoother experience over time, as you reconfigure your firewall rules to handle the vagaries of clients. If you need to add large numbers of rules, and Perl scripting is an option for you (either because you know Perl or are willing to learn it), considered modifying /usr/local/libexec/initialize.fw by adding rules at the end of the file.

## Trouble #3: More Eternal Splash

Do not be lulled into thinking that you now know "the cause" of the eternally returning splash screen. There is an endless variety of problems that can cause this same symptom. You have to use troubleshooting tools such as the log file, IPtables and Ethereal to determine what is happening.

For instance, at one point, I put Google in `AllowedWebHosts`. NoCatAuth created a set of firewall rules with 216.239.57.104. That address indeed accessed Google when entered in the browser address bar. Everything worked fine the first time I tested via the gateway from a client, too. It looked like I was set.

However, the next time I tried to access Google through the gateway, I encountered the eternal splash. The log file just showed that the client was trying to access Google; there were no unexpected or extraneous requests as in the previous example.

Ethereal, however, showed that the client was trying to access 216.239.57.99 (which the firewall didn't know about) instead of 216.239.57.104 (which the firewall did know about). So, instead of putting `google.com` in `AllowedWebHosts`, I put both IP addresses in. NoCatAuth created firewall rules for both addresses, and once again everything worked as expected in the first test.

It wasn't long, though, before I was again encountering the eternal splash when I attempted to access Google. Consulting Ethereal, I found that the client was now attempting to access 216.239.53.99, which turned out to be another valid Google address, but not one covered in the firewall rules.

A little investigation (via Google searches!) educated me to the fact that Google had, at that time, over a dozen data centers, each of which could use many IP addresses. And it was adding a data center every few months!

One easy way to make Google one of a small group of allowed hosts is to put a link on the splash page with the IP address of the Google site that is in the firewall rule. That way, users are always asking for the IP address that the firewall knows about. You could even put in several links with different IP addresses for Google, in case one of them doesn't work for some reason.

Another option, of course, is to comment out `MembersOnly 1`, which allows users to access any site on the Web after clicking the Login (or Continue) button. In other words, give your users Google by giving them the whole Web.

# Summary

In this chapter, you've learned the basics required to successfully install, configure, and troubleshoot the NoCatAuth "captive portal," which will help you secure, manage, and monitor your free wireless hotspot. If you have actually succeeded at this task, you probably have a gorgeous cathode ray tan by now, and have not seen daylight or your friends for days, possibly weeks. Time for some outdoor fun! Read on to Chapter 11, "Playing Access Point Games," for a fox hunt (you're the fox), driving games, chatting, and other ways to be sociable wirelessly.

# Playing Access Point Games

Traditionally, an *access point*, or AP, is thought of as a type of networking hardware that is used solely to provide wireless access to a network. Although this may be so for the average wireless user, a subset of dedicated wireless fanatics have found several ways to transform your typical access point into a source of entertainment and hours of delight. This chapter outlines several types of exciting access point games and details on how to play them.

These games come in many forms, such as a "fox and hounds" game, capture the flag, or a treasure hunt. However, they are all based on the nature of an access point to "give itself away"—that is, broadcast the configured SSID to all willing listeners.

In order to truly enjoy playing access point games, you must first remember a few key details about access points and their functionality. An access point is a radio transmitter and receiver. When a laptop client requests basic information from an access point, such as SSID, manufacturer, channel number, WEP status, and other networking information, the access point will respond with that information. This broadcast/request pattern is the key to playing AP games.

### in this chapter

☑ Detecting access points

☑ Hunting a fox

☑ Finding treasure

☑ Capturing the flag

☑ Taking a virtual tour

**Tip** Playing access point games implies that the access point should be "discoverable." That is, SSID broadcasting is enabled. When discoverable, regular wireless clients and war driving tools would be able to discover the access point. Of course, hard-core AP gamers could bump up the difficulty by turning off SSID broadcast so only passive war driving tools (such as Kismet Wireless) would discover the access point. The choice is yours!

To play most of the games covered in the chapter, you will need only standard wireless equipment properly configured, similar to that required for war driving.

Items you will need include:

➤ Laptop computer

➤ Wireless adapter

➤ Wireless access point

➤ GPS receiver

➤ Kismet, NetStumbler, or other war driving software

➤ External antenna (optional)

Although this is simply a "bare-bones" list of what you need to get started with the games outlined in this chapter, there are several optional items which could significantly increase the impact of your game.

Some optional equipment includes:

■ Mobile battery power

■ DC-to-AC inverter

■ A varied selection of external antennas

■ Mapping software or other in-car navigation

■ Access point enclosure

■ Paper map for offline reference

Some of the basic items are shown in Figure 11-1.

FIGURE 11-1: AP games hardware: laptop computer, wireless client adapter, wireless access point, and GPS receiver.

**Note** An external antenna can be attached to many different wireless adapters and will significantly increase range. Omnidirectional antennas are preferred for 360-degree sweeping coverage, while a unidirectional antenna, such as the famous cantenna you built in Chapter 3, can be used for focused, directional coverage.

# The Basics of AP Gaming

The idea of access point gaming is that you are out to find and log wireless access points. These access points can be placed beforehand as with a treasure hunt, placed to seed a playing field as with a traditional AP hunt, or set up in specific locales to create a real-world social networking environment.

The game coordinator will design the rules, layout, and boundaries of the game being played. Briefly, the games described in this chapter are:

- *Foxhunt*—Find the hidden access point
- *AP-Hunt*—Discover the most access points in a set amount of time
- *Treasure Hunt*—Step through a planned route where each new discovery gives you a clue to the next destination
- *Capture the Flag*—Find all the "enemy" access points and return to base with your booty, a log file showing their locations
- *Virtual Real-Space Tours*—Bridge the digital and the real with location-aware content fed to visitors within a matrix of access points. (Not quite a game, but very entertaining!)

In order to be successful while playing the games covered in this chapter, you will be constantly refining your skills in pinpointing the location of access points. Pinpointing access points can be achieved by using two standard methods:

- *Drive-by detection*
- *Triangulation*

Both methods are valuable in different circumstances, and you may even employ both methods during the same game.

## Detecting an Access Point on a Drive-By

This is the traditional war driving scenario. As you travel past an access point, the war driving software detects the access point and logs its position. As you drive around, the signal level will grow stronger or weaker—usually indicating that you are closer or further from the access point.

Figure 11-2 shows a diagram of this process. The access point is in a building and different signal levels help to betray its approximate location. As your detection computer comes within close proximity of the access point, the signal strength gets higher.

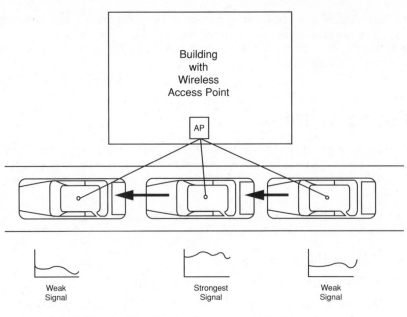

**FIGURE 11-2: A drive-by detection locates access points through proximity.**

Always play AP games with at least one passenger (the more the merrier). The task of driving safely while managing the computer in an AP game may well be impossible. As the driver, it's your job to assign the task of detection and navigation to the passenger(s) and stay safe.

## Finding an Access Point by Triangulation

Triangulation may well be the oldest radio-wave positioning method known. Triangulation is a method of taking a directional sample of a radio source, moving some distance and taking another directional sample. If all went well, the two directions you sampled should end up pointing to a single third location, making a triangle.

Figure 11-3 shows a triangulation pattern using a directional antenna. Directional antennas are the easiest way to detect an access point by triangulation. The cantenna, a panel antenna, or a Yagi antenna is usually sufficiently directional to aid in pinning down an access point.

When you're discovering access points by triangulation, you can get a misreading due to the nature of wireless reflections and the concept of multipath signals. It's possible to receive a stronger signal bouncing off of, say, a building than when you point directly at the access point. Keep this in mind and perhaps add more points to your "triangle."

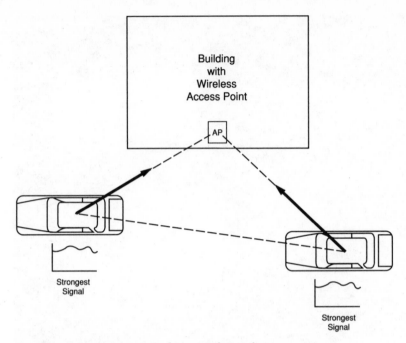

FIGURE 11-3: The three points of a triangulation discovery pattern.

# Crazy Like a Foxhunt

Foxhunt is a challenging and exciting access point game that requires the setup of a remote access point (The Fox) in a location unknown to the participants of the game. After general boundaries are set, the participants set out with the objective of pinpointing the exact location of the hidden access point. The first participant or group to pinpoint the access point wins.

This AP game is quite simple, and probably the easiest to coordinate and start playing.

1. Get a fox

2. Send the fox out running

3. Wait some amount of time

4. Chase the fox

## The Fox

The heart of this game is based around an access point, The Fox, and the components that enable its operation. Although the placement and setup of The Fox is ultimately your choice, a modular setup is preferable. Being able to place it in a variety of locations will enhance gaming immensely.

FIGURE **11-4: A look at the inside of The Fox.**

Figure 11-4 shows a simple "Fox" setup. Notice careful attention paid to the organization of the access point, battery pack, and power inverter, as well as the cleanly run wiring. This attention to detail helps prevent unforeseen outages during the game.

This game does not necessarily employ a special SSID. But a unique, pre-determined SSID will help the hunters easily identify the target.

**Tip**

An SSID of "Fox" is too simple and you may easily come across it in the wild. Try an SSID of "LA-FoxHunt-Aug2004" or some sort of named and date-stamped SSID. You may find it amusing to later discover The Fox listed on an online war driving database!

A standard modular access point setup includes (see Figure 11-5):

- Access Point—A standard 802.11b access point is the heart of The Fox.

- 12-volt Battery Pack—A 12-volt battery pack supplies the power to the unit. The battery is the key to the modularity of The Fox.

- Power Inverter—A power inverter is used to convert the voltage of the battery to that of the access point.

**FIGURE 11-5: The Fox ready for game play.**

■ Canvas Duffle Bag—A canvas duffle bag will serve as the platform to house all of the equipment required in one simple package and allow The Fox to be moved from one location to another quickly and easily.

**Note**  A tip about batteries: A 7.0 ampere-hour (Ah) battery will run for one hour at 7 A, or 7 hours at 1 A. In tests, a broadcasting access point connected to an inverter while running on battery power was pulling 900 mA or 0.9 A, and ran for over 9 hours on a single 7.0-Ah battery. This came out to about 8.1 Ah, somewhat better than the 7.0 Ah rating.

## Variations of a Foxhunt

Although the general game play and rules are the same throughout, there are a few variations of an AP games Foxhunt:

■ Standard Foxhunt

■ Mobile Foxhunt

■ Room Service Foxhunt

The standard variation of the game is usually played with two to six players. Standard Foxhunt requires that the participants of the game track The Fox solely on foot. A smaller set of boundaries is usually required, typically a few hundred yards square, as it would be no fun to have to search an overly large area on foot. A mid-sized park is optimal, as The Fox may be hidden in many places, such as small brush.

The Mobile Foxhunt is a variation of Foxhunt in which two to six teams comprised of two to four participants each track The Fox using automobiles. A larger set of boundaries is required for Mobile Foxhunt, as the use of automobiles permits a much greater relative scale. A good set of boundaries is 20 to 40 blocks square. The Fox is typically placed in a host automobile and parked in a remote location.

Room Service Foxhunt is a great variation of Foxhunt intended for fun on vacation, but can be played anytime and can host a number of participants ranging from 2 to 40. Room Service Foxhunt is best played in a hotel setting. It is a good general rule of thumb when playing this variation of Foxhunt to have a maximum of two to four times the number of participants as there are floors in the hotel. The boundaries can range from inside the hotel itself to the entire area of the hotel depending on the size of the group, courtesy to other hotel guests, and tolerance of hotel management. The Fox is typically hidden in a room or a common area.

 **Note** A GPS and mapping software may prove to be invaluable in quickly pinpointing The Fox while playing variations of Foxhunt with a larger set of boundaries such as Mobile Foxhunt.

## Foxhunt Tips

Set up rules ahead of time. Determine the boundaries and timeframe for success. As the game coordinator, stay in contact with The Fox either by cell phone or radio. Also, ensure you have all of the participants' contact information in case the game has a problem and must be aborted. As a player, there's nothing more annoying than looking for an access point that isn't there.

Determine the winner. Perhaps the winner is the person or team that finds The Fox in the least amount of time. Or perhaps the first team to return with a digital picture of The Fox is the winner. Are GPS coordinates enough or does the team need an address? Or perhaps a visual description is more suitable (for example, "Building 4 in the bushes near the South Entrance")?

There is probably an unlimited number of variations on this AP game. The foxhunt is an old tradition which has carried over into HAM radio, CB radio, and now wireless access points. Uphold the tradition and host a foxhunt this weekend!

# Finding Mass Quantities of Access Points

This game, AP-Hunt, is an access point game inspired by the famous pasttime of war driving. AP-Hunt simply requires basic wireless hardware and software and a means of transportation. The objective is to accumulate the most number of points. Generally, the more access points discovered, the more points awarded.

Points are awarded based on a specific scoring system weighted towards awarding unique and hard-to-discover access points. To help prevent cheating, only access points with associated GPS coordinates will score points.

To reduce the chance of cheating, the game coordinator may seed the area before the game. This entails setting up a number of access points with a unique SSID in the playing area beforehand, and switching them to another SSID during game play. If a team's results include the "before" SSID, they are submitting a log from before the contest timeframe. Also, a team must discover one of the seeds during game play to ensure the data is not from days or weeks prior to the contest.

The team with the highest number of points wins.

## Scoring System

The essence of a contest is in determining a winner. To make things interesting, an AP-Hunt game should have some sort of scoring system beyond simply finding "the most."

This scoring system here was inspired by the DefCon Wardriving Contest of 2003. The DefCon contest is a type of access point game with a set of rules created to distinguish hard-core participants from the casual wardriver and encourage unusual war driving techniques.

A basic AP-Hunt scoring would look like this:

- One point for each AP discovered
- One extra point for each AP with the default SSID
- Two extra points for each AP with WEP enabled
- Three extra points for each unique AP (your team is the only team that detected the AP). This score is optional and implementing it will make sense only with a high number of participants
- Variations: Add points for local wireless landmarks such as schools, stores, coffee shops, and so on. Add points for furthest AP from the contest starting line. Or possibly, add points for off-road APs.

Obviously, scoring is up to the game coordinator. Maybe in your first time out, just try to find the most access points in a given time, like 1 hour. Then return to base and have pizza while comparing results. The winner gets bragging rights.

## Hunting Equipment

There are some factors that can affect your game play and ultimately your overall success while AP-Hunting: hardware, antenna, software, and vehicle selection.

Hardware selection is a vital issue. It can mean the difference between detecting an access point or not, and thus winning or losing. There are two basic types of supplemental hardware involved with hunting: a wireless adapter and an external antenna. To be amongst the top ranks of competitors, a wireless adapter has two essential elements: power output (and, therefore, receiver sensitivity) and the ability to accept an external antenna.

A standard wireless adapter has a power output of about 30 mW, while an enterprise adapter will usually have 100 mW. And carrier-grade adapters boast an output of 200 mW. In general, the higher powered adapter will also have a more sensitive receiver, which directly relates to how well the adapter can "pull in" a weak signal and log the access point.

Once you've selected a suitable wireless adapter, the next step is to choose an external antenna. If at all possible it is best to have both an omnidirectional and a highly-directional antenna for all foreseeable scenarios. You should have at least an external, vehicle-mounted omnidirectional antenna.

Figure 11-6 shows an example of an AP-Hunt setup including wireless adapter, omnidirectional, and highly directional patch panel antenna.

**Tip**    While playing AP-Hunt, users of Kismet Wireless will have a considerable advantage because Kismet can detect access points that are not broadcasting their SSID or beacon signals. Oftentimes, sheer numbers may be the pivotal factor between winning and losing.

Transportation plays a great role in AP-Hunt. Traditionally, automobiles are used in conjunction with GPS mapping software to sweep the area as it approaches, detecting access points along the way. Although this is still the most widely accepted method of transportation, several

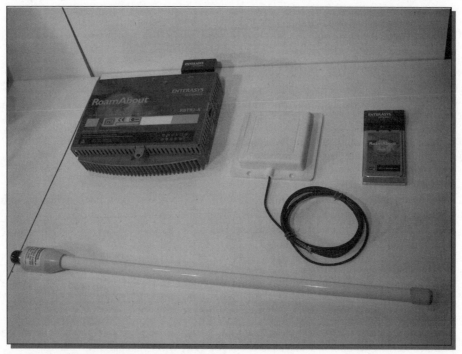

FIGURE 11-6: A typical AP-Hunt hardware setup.

nonconventional methods have proven to provide much broader coverage than an automobile could hope to achieve. Recently, helicopters and private airplanes have been used to scan large swaths of the landscape to pick up dozens more access points outside the range of ground-based vehicles.

**Note**   Using airborne vehicles while scanning for access points is known as "warflying." Perform a Web search for warflying, and among the usual combat aircraft Web sites will appear many sites on war driving with aircraft.

## AP-Hunt in action: The DefCon Wardriving Contest

For the past eleven years at the beginning of August, thousands of the world's most fervent hackers, security professionals, and even government officials have converged on the city of Las Vegas to participate in what has become one of the largest underground security and technology conferences in existence, fondly named "DefCon."

Although DefCon began simply as an underground hacking conference, it has evolved into something much greater. In the past few years emerging wireless technologies have made their way into the conference, spawning entirely new facets such as the DefCon Wardriving Contest. The DefCon Wardriving Contest has grown to become a cutthroat battle royale of wireless network detection, pushing war driving and access point gaming in an ever-improving direction.

In recent years, participants armed with laptops, wireless adapters, and external antennas have used everything from standing still on top of a building, to vans, cars, and motorcycles in order to claim the title of DefCon Wardriving Contest champions. DefCon Wardriving contest participants have even gone to the extent of renting a private helicopter, allowing them to detect access points typically unreachable through traditional AP-Hunting methods. Who knows what strategies and tactics will be used at the next contest?

# An Access Point Treasure Hunt

Treasure Hunt is an access point game in which teams search for access points based on clues discovered in the SSID. As the game unfolds, each access point discovered leads the team to the next access point, and so on until the trail ends. There are two main categories of play in the Treasure Hunt access point game.

- Best Time—The winner of the "Best Time" category will be the team that is able to complete the course in its entirety in the least amount of time possible.

- Best Signal—The winner of the "Best Signal" category will be the team that is able to record the highest Signal-to-Noise Ratio for each of the given access points.

## Playing Treasure Hunt

Treasure Hunt is one of the most rewarding access point games but it also requires much setup and planning. When organizing a treasure hunt, several access points are required to be spread out over a relatively large area. It is best to organize the field of play based on several maps sliced into grids. Often a local paper-based street map will have a grid coordinate and a well-known page numbering system.

**Tip**    If the game participants do not have a local map publication, create a simple map layout using mapping software to generate the map, and an image editing program to divide the map into squares covering about one-half mile each. Print these out for each participant.

Each access point should be spread apart by a significant distance and each access point SSID will contain the clue necessary to determine the location of the next access point. Each access point should contain a similarly formatted SSID in order to provide clues.

A sample SSID might be:

```
TH0504-P5-J-4-03
```

The first section, "TH0504" is a unique game name (TH) and date (May 2004). The second section, "P5" means page 5 in a pre-determined map handout, booklet, or publication. "J-4" represents the grid coordinates on that map (see Figure 11-7). And the final section "03" means this is clue number three (numbering is optional, but it's nice to have).

This SSID points to where the next access point can be found on the map. Each access point is a link pointing to the next site to discover and proceed from there. Figure 11-8 shows a diagram of how this contest works. Plan the path of travel to help avoid participants finding clues out of order.

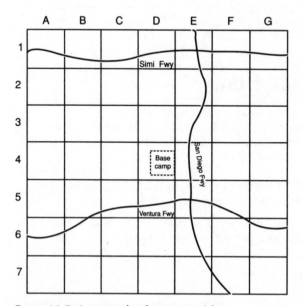

**FIGURE 11-7: An example of a map used for Treasure Hunt.**

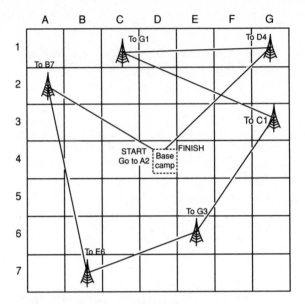

**Figure 11-8: Diagram of SSID linking.**

To begin with, each team is given the rough grid coordinates and a specific map in order to determine the location of the first access point and using the clues located in the SSID's of the access points, each team must then locate each additional access point until the course is completed.

## Variations for treasure hunting

A treasure hunt can be so many things. The SSID pointer is probably the most basic: pointing you to the next link in the chain. But with some imagination, you can develop a truly unique game.

Some ideas to consider are: Have the SSID provide a clue, instead of a directional pointer. For example, "boardwalk canals and musclemen" could mean Venice Beach. Or, make the SSID a phone number (that is, "TH0504-555-1212") with an answering machine message, "Get to the payphone by the stadium and find the access point to the East."

Another fun, though even more painstaking alternative, is to make each access point forward the user to a Web site holding the next clue. A team member would need to associate with the access point, obtain a dynamically assigned TCP/IP address, and surf to a Web site unique to that access point. Once at the Web site, any type of clue or challenge could be presented. Imagine a treasure hunt where participants had to solve a riddle, puzzle, or pass a quiz before being given the next clue.

With these few variations, the Treasure Hunt AP game can be a potentially challenging event for participants and game coordinators!

# Other AP Games

This section discusses two more fun ways to employ access point location sensitivity and content delivery: Capture the Flag and the difficult to name, real-world virtual tour.

## Capture the Flag

Capture the Flag is a merging of the AP-Hunt game into a sort of treasure hunt. Two teams are created (and of course there's a game coordinator). Each team has the object of finding all of the other team's access points and returning to base. The winner is the first team to return to base with the locations of all of the enemy "flags."

Capture the Flag takes little planning. Each team's access point (also known as a flag) should be assigned an SSID and the AP owners need to log the GPS location with the game coordinator before starting. An example SSID scheme could be:

```
CTF0604-blueteam-roxors-3
```

```
CTF0604-redteam-rulez-C
```

The SSID is broken down as follows: Game-name (CTF), date (June 2004), team, a motivating comment, and the access point identification. For the blue team, "3" represents flag three of five. For the red team, "C" represents flag three of five.

In setting up the game, draw a line across the game play area to separate the two teams. Access points should be on each side of the line like they would be in any good CTF map. Figure 11-9 shows a CTF map with red team and blue team access points strewn about the battle field.

Capture the Flag can be played with as few as two people (without a referee) or as many as feasible. One can envision a parking lot full of wardrivers ready to be unleashed into each other's enemy territory trolling for specially named access points. Time is your only ally. It's up to you to devise some defensive tactics.

## Virtual Touring in the Real World

The virtual tour is difficult to name accurately, but a simple concept: location-aware digital content is delivered to visitors to a space in the real world. This can be done with special equipment as is being done by experimenters in the Netherlands. Or you can set up a virtual tour yourself with a few access points and a Web site.

Employ the Web site to give guided tours of the local area. Foot traffic with a wireless PDA or laptop will discover a locally installed access point, obtain an IP address, and load a Web page with content about the local surroundings. The visitors can surf to the Web site manually, or use a captive portal system (like that shown in Chapter 10) to direct users to visit the appropriate Web page.

Figure 11-10 shows a diagram of a virtual tour. Access points are placed in strategic locations to deliver content about the surroundings.

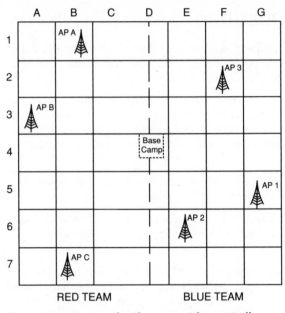

FIGURE 11-9: Capture the Flag map with a centrally located headquarter.

This can be done for parkland tours, historic neighborhood facts, walk-throughs of museum grounds, and any other form of locally-based content. Virtually any self-guided tour could be delivered over a wireless network access point. And location-aware content brings the tourist on-site in the real world and the digital world in a single moment.

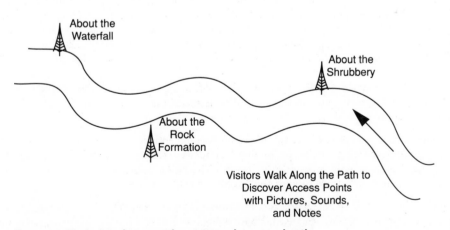

FIGURE 11-10: A virtual tour guides visitors along a real path.

# Finding an Edge in Competition

When you're getting started in AP gaming, just about any software will do the job. But what do you do when winning becomes your determined goal? Here we will discuss some of the finer points of software choice and how it relates to AP games.

The software choices available are often defined by the operating system used on your computer. When choosing the software and operating system for your platform, you want to choose an OS that fits within your current support network of technically savvy friends and associates. Being a lone-adopter can be trying when you're attempting to install a new network driver at 2:00 in the morning.

The two popular choices for access point detection are the same as for war driving: Linux running Kismet, and Windows running NetStumbler.

There are advantages to Linux in its low cost to implement and huge amount of free, open-source software available. Windows also boasts a long history of easy-to-use software that's easy to obtain and install.

Linux users can run the Kismet Wireless scanner, the gold standard of free war driving software. Kismet is quite powerful, but setting it up is not trivial. It requires obtaining, compiling, installing, and configuring several packages with little direct support. This is where your personal technical support network comes in handy.

Windows users can download and install NetStumbler. NetStumbler requires little effort to get working as compared to Kismet. Some users are able to download, install, and run NetStumbler in a few clicks. NetStumbler is the easy-entry war driving software. Although Kismet is more powerful, most wardrivers still choose to run NetStumbler. See Chapter 6 for more on NetStumbler.

**Note** Although Windows/NetStumbler users can use a GPS and mapping software in conjunction with NetStumbler, it is important to note that NetStumbler only pinpoints your GPS coordinates during scanning. Linux users may find themselves at an advantage, in this case, by using Kismet and GPSDrive/Gpsd, which allows a user to pinpoint the actual location of an access point in real-time based on multiple Signal-to-Noise Ratio readings along with GPS coordinates. The result of this on-the-fly logging is superior accuracy and speed when pinpointing access points.

NetStumbler is designed to identify access points within a given range. It detects them by transmitting and receiving beacon signals, which are then in turn used to synchronize communication along the network.

NetStumbler users can use a program called StumbVerter, available at www.sonar-security.com, which converts NetStumbler log files to create plotted maps based upon their coordinates. Unfortunately, it requires Microsoft's MapPoint, a fairly expensive mapping tool (see Chapter 7 for more on MapPoint and NetStumbler).

Kismet is not only able to detect access points through Signal-to-Noise Ratio graphs, but is also able to sniff packets. You can use GPS mapping plug-ins to automatically triangulate the actual GPS coordinates of an access point. You may also view Signal-to-Noise Ratio graphs in real time. A "hot/cold" system is able to automatically track optimum signal and the approximate location of the access point. Additional plug-in software is available to switch between location mapping and access point locating tasks.

Kismet has been designed with the intentions of seamless interaction with the GPSDrive software, thus creating powerful maps in real time, on-the-fly, from the data recorded during the session. Access points are plotted in their approximate location for easy identification, through the use of either custom or pre-made maps downloaded off the Internet.

**Note** In order to fully utilize the capabilities of Kismet, you should have the latest version of the software installed on your PC. The latest version can be found at www.kismetwireless.net/.

# Summary

This chapter has introduced you to several ways of using wireless access points, as more than just a way to get on the Internet. Playing Fox Hunt, Treasure Hunt, Capture the Flag, and creating Virtual Tours are pushing access point functionality to its limits in a way never intended by the manufacturer. Using an access point in the manner described here is on the cutting edge and can only become more interesting.

Access point gaming is continually increasing in popularity and, with wireless technology becoming more and more widespread, you can count on access point gaming being a vital part of recreation using wireless equipment.

Read on to Chapter 12 and discover how to add a wireless Internet connection to your TiVo digital video recorder. Download program updates without a telephone line. Subscribe to the TiVo Home Media Option and stream music to your entertainment center over the TiVo. Create a slideshow and transfer movies from one TiVo DVR to another in a different part of the house, all using your in-home wireless network and TiVo.

# Just for Fun

part

IV

# Wi-Fi Your TiVo

**T**iVo is a marvel of modern technology. At first glance, it is little more than an automatic VCR. But with all of the automation and additional broadband multimedia features now available, it could easily become the cornerstone of your home entertainment center.

TiVo is a product in the ever-increasing market of *digital video recorders* (DVRs), but TiVo is different from most other DVRs—very different. Primarily, this DVR excels above others in the unique TiVo service plan. For a modest fee, the TiVo box becomes a gateway to entertainment unlike anything you've seen. The service plan manages and controls TiVo recordings. There are so many ways to record shows, including by actor, keyword, title, team, or by searching the entire program guide. And, like other DVR machines, TiVo brings you the ability to pause and rewind live TV.

You can make your experience that much better by adding a wireless client adapter and break your TiVo from the wires that bind it.

By eliminating the slow telephone line and using a broadband network connection with the Home Media Option, you can stream MP3 music, create a digital photo slideshow, and schedule recordings over the Web. Also, you pave the way to more in-depth TiVo explorations with a high-speed wireless link to your TiVo.

Adding digital photo viewing is a feature a long time coming to home entertainment. Other products just coming to market have been designed to show digital pictures on TV screens. Now TiVo adds that capability for a fraction of the cost of those other systems. You no longer have to imagine the impact a digital photo makes when presented on a 40-inch screen. Make a slideshow for your next party!

In this chapter, you will learn how to get your TiVo on a wireless network. And you will also be introduced to some aspects of the Home Media Option which requires a high-speed connection. With a wireless connection, you open up high-speed network access to your TiVo. In addition, but not covered explicitly in this book, you can delve further into the hackability of TiVo. A wireless connection will make many TiVo hacks more accessible.

Here's what you will need:

1. Broadband-capable TiVo

2. Wireless client adapter

**3.** Wireless access point

**4.** PC computer on your home network (optional)

**5.** TiVo Home Media Option (optional)

## TiVo Models

The TiVo digital video recorder comes in many models. These can be grouped as Series 1, Series 2, and Integrated Series 1 or 2. The different series and models vary greatly in form and function. And there can be some limitations on what the manufacturer supports with Integrated TiVo. So it's important to determine if your TiVo can support broadband.

If using an Integrated TiVo, the easiest way to determine broadband support is to contact your TiVo manufacturer or TiVo service provider. For example, due to the specialized software used on the integrated platform; a DirecTV system with a built-in TiVo DVR may not support broadband. It will depend on their plans. Let them know that TiVo users want broadband support.

**Note** While adding features, the functional limitations are usually greater when using any integrated product. If you want the most functionality and "hackability" from TiVo, make sure to get a stand-alone unit.

The following sections cover the differences between the two major platforms, Series 1 and Series 2. Figure 12-1 shows the Series 1 and Series 2 stand-alone TiVo DVRs.

FIGURE 12-1: TiVo Series 1 (top) and TiVo Series 2 digital video recorders.

| Table 12-1 | TiVo Series 1 Models |
|---|---|
| **Manufacturer** | **Models** |
| Hughes | GXCEBOT |
| Philips | HDR112, HDR212, HDR312, HDR412, HDR612, DSR6000(R, R01) |
| Sony | SVR-2000, SVR-3000, SAT-T60 |
| TiVo | PTV100, PTV300 |

# Series 1: Wi-Fi for Early Adopters

The original Series 1 TiVo was noticeably lacking in one area: high-speed connectivity. Hardware hackers soon developed various methods to escape this limitation. Online retailers now have a variety of upgrade components available for Series 1 TiVo. Table 12-1 shows the Series 1 models. Series 1 TiVo are no longer being manufactured.

Installing a broadband adapter (wireless or Ethernet) in a Series 1 TiVo can be significant, and goes beyond the scope of this book. However, if you do have a Series 1, we'll cover some of the basics to point you in the right direction.

**Note** Series 1 TiVo upgrades require breaking the case and removing or installing hardware components. Opening the case may void the manufacturer's warranty.

Companies like 9th Tee Enterprises, www.9thtee.com, have made the process easier than it used to be for Series 1 owners. 9th Tee provides two distinct products made for Series 1 TiVo. 9th Tee provides detailed instructions for each adapter:

- TiVo TurboNet—Ethernet adapter
- TiVo AirNet—wireless PC-card adapter

TiVo software version 3.0 or higher directly supports the TiVo TurboNet Ethernet adapter without the additional software hacking needed to enable basic network connectivity. This method is more direct, but does not provide extra network features like Telnet and FTP service for the TiVo.

**Caution** High voltage is present inside TiVo DVRs. Even when unplugged, a TiVo unit can produce a hazardous electric shock. Before opening the case of the TiVo, remove all power (pull the plug) and do not touch any power supply components.

This step relies on a standard Ethernet-to-wireless bridge. The Linksys WET11 or the D-Link DWL-810 are good examples of this easy-to-find product. The bridge simply connects an Ethernet jack to a wireless access point as just another wireless client. It effectively places any wired device onto a wireless network.

FIGURE **12-2: Series 1 TiVo with installed TurboNet adapter and Ethernet-to-wireless bridge.**

In this case, the Ethernet-to-wireless bridge is configured to connect to the TiVo Ethernet jack to your existing wireless network. Follow the instructions that come with your particular bridge to configure it for your wireless network.

To install the TurboNet:

1. Unplug the TiVo.
2. Open the TiVo case.
3. Insert the TurboNet adapter onto the edge-connector plug.
4. Install an Ethernet-to-wireless bridge (see Figure 12-2).

5. From a PC, configure the Ethernet-to-wireless bridge.
6. Boot up the TiVo and configure the dialing parameters, as specified in the instructions.

The TiVo AirNet adapter is not supported by TiVo software version 3.0, but it may be supported in future versions. Here is a guideline for the AirNet adapter software install:

1. Download the AirNet install CD image and burn it onto a CDR.
2. Remove the hard disk drive(s) from TiVo.
3. Install the drive(s) in a desktop PC.

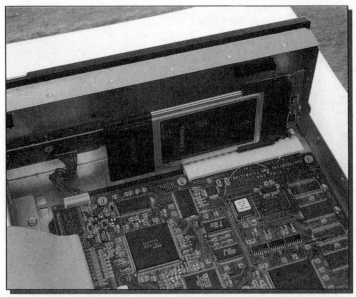

**FIGURE 12-3: TiVo Series 1 with the TiVo AirNet adapter and PC card.**

**4.** Boot the PC using the CDR (this loads a Linux kernel).

**5.** Follow the instructions to back up the TiVo drive.

**6.** Follow the instructions to add the AirNet driver.

**7.** Shut down the PC and reinsert the TiVo drive(s) back into the TiVo. (If you changed the hard drive jumper settings, make sure you return them to the original positions!)

**8.** Insert the AirNet adapter and a compatible PC-Card into the edge-connector plug inside the TiVo unit.

**9.** Boot up the TiVo unit and reset the dialing parameters as specified in the instructions.

Figure 12-3 shows a TiVo AirNet adapter with a compatible PC card installed.

The AirNet adapter software adds extra network features to the TiVo software. Telnet and FTP are now available to directly access the TiVo.

To really go further with a Series 1 TiVo, pick up one of the many books available on hacking TiVo.

## Series 2: Wi-Fi for Late Arrivals

Series 2 TiVo are more readily upgraded to wireless. There's no need to open the case. It may take some experimentation to get it working, though. Series 2 TiVo include two USB connectors on the back of the unit. Figure 12-4 shows these connectors. Either one can be used successfully.

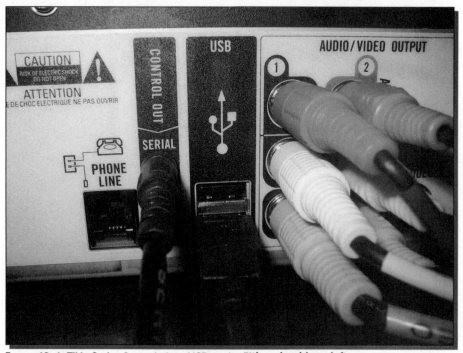

FIGURE 12-4: TiVo Series 2 sports two USB ports. Either should work fine.

Series 2 TiVo are far more numerous than Series 1 models. To see which Series you have, check the service number on the back of the TiVo unit. Series 2 TiVo begin with the following service number prefixes (with more to come):

110, 130, 140, 1F0, 230, 240, 264, 275, 2F0, 2F4, 2F5

For example, the service number "240-0000-3298-21EC" starts with 240, and is therefore a Series 2 TiVo DVR.

There are dozens of wireless USB adapters on the market. Unfortunately, TiVo only works with a small number of the most popular adapters. The TiVo software is patched periodically with driver updates for the most recent USB network adapters.

**Note**  When it was discovered that many wireless USB adapters available in stores did not work with the current TiVo software, the company offered no timely solution. "Wait a month or two" was the response from TiVo technical support. This frustrating but true comment indicates the software upgrade path used by TiVo central. As new wireless products are brought to market, TiVo is engaged in a game of continuous catch-up. If you happen to buy a USB adapter at the wrong time in the lifecycle, these words may be your only solace.

To set up your TiVo Series 2 with a wireless connection, you need to follow these steps:

1. Get a USB adapter from your local computer store.

2. Make sure your TiVo's software is up-to-date.

3. Plug in the adapter.

4. Configure the wireless network.

These are discussed in more detail in the following sections.

## Step 1: Raiding the Computer Store

The first thing you need to do to is get your TiVo connected to a wireless network, which means you'll need a USB adapter. This should be as simple as going to the store and buying one, but unfortunately, it's not that easy. TiVo doesn't support all the major USB adapters, and support varies by the TiVo software on your model as well.

You may be tempted to buy your favorite brand of wireless USB adapter and return home to set up your TiVo. Yet, the path of least resistance is not always an option. To ensure a successful installation, raid the store of every full-size USB adapter available from major manufacturers. Table 12-2 shows a list of some of the adapters we tried.

Note the subtle distinction between adapters that are supported and those that are not. The Linksys WUSB11 version 2.6 works, while version 2.8 did not. Also, TiVo states support of the D-Link DWL-120, but not the DWL-120+. The "+" makes all the difference. Chances are, the USB adapters listed in the table will be supported by TiVo eventually. However, as new adapters are released, TiVo will need to keep updating their software to work with them.

**Table 12-2    Not All USB Adapters Are Supported**

| Manufacturer | Model | Supported by TiVo model TCD240080 |
| --- | --- | --- |
| Linksys | WUSB11 ver. 2.6 | Yes |
| Linksys | WUSB11 ver. 2.8 | No |
| Microsoft | MN-510 | Yes |
| D-Link | DWL-120 | Yes |
| D-Link | DWL-120+ | No |
| D-Link | DWL-122 | No |
| Netgear | MA111 | No |
| Belkin | F5D6050 | No |

**Tip** TiVo maintains a list of recommended adapters at www.tivo.com/adapters. Some are directly supported, while others carry caveats like, "we have had positive reports on these makes," which is the same as telling you to try them. Who knows if it will work or not.

There is a simple solution:

1. Visit the computer store.

2. Verify their return policy (shoot for 30 days with no restocking fee).

3. Buy every USB adapter from every different manufacturer.

4. Try them one at a time until you are successful.

5. Return all of the ones that didn't work.

**Note** If none of the adapters work, there is one more option: Buy a new adapter, and return it as defective to the manufacturer. When asked what model is needed for replacement, specify the version number that is known to work. For example, with Linksys, request the WUSB11 version 2.6 while sending back version 2.8. This trick only works with products using the same model number. Linksys technical support recommended this procedure to overcome the TiVo compatibility problem since they discontinued version 2.6.

## Step 2: Ensuring TiVo Is Ready

If this is a new TiVo just out of the box, make sure it's connected to a phone line first. TiVo requires activation through a regular phone line. Also, it may need to download software updates to bring the version to a level that will support USB broadband (version 4.0 or higher).

Many TiVo units are shipped with older software. This is not a problem because TiVo sends updates directly over the phone. However, it may take several connections to the TiVo service and a few reboots to apply all of the updates. The process can take a couple of hours with manual intervention, and probably would take days if left untouched.

Figure 12-5 shows the system information screen. Make sure TiVo is running version 4.0 or higher before inserting a USB adapter.

Manually activate the TiVo update service to get caught up with updates. These menus vary from TiVo to TiVo. Use this as a guideline:

1. Press the TiVo button on the remote

2. Click TiVo Messages and Setup

3. Click Settings

4. Click Phone and Network Setup

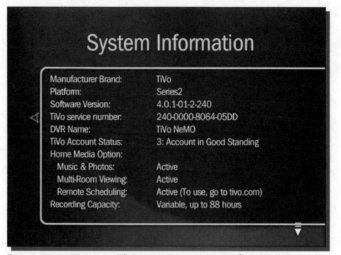

**System Information**

| | |
|---|---|
| Manufacturer Brand: | TiVo |
| Platform: | Series2 |
| Software Version: | 4.0.1-01-2-240 |
| TiVo service number: | 240-0000-8064-05DD |
| DVR Name: | TiVo NeMO |
| TiVo Account Status: | 3: Account in Good Standing |
| Home Media Option: | |
| Music & Photos: | Active |
| Multi-Room Viewing: | Active |
| Remote Scheduling: | Active (To use, go to tivo.com) |
| Recording Capacity: | Variable, up to 88 hours |

FIGURE 12-5: TiVo provides extensive system Information, including software version and connection status.

5. Click Connect to the TiVo service now

6. Press Select on the remote to start the update procedure

Now go to the System Information Screen, and follow these steps:

1. Press the TiVo button on the remote

2. Click TiVo Messages and Setup

3. Click System Information

Check the "Software Version" on the first page. Press Channel Down on the remote to monitor the "Service Connection: Current/Last Status."

Sometimes, the status will show that a reboot is required. Perform a restart by following these steps:

1. Press the TiVo button

2. Click TiVo Messages and Setup

3. Click Restart or Reset System

4. Click Restart the TiVo DVR

5. Follow the on-screen confirmation instructions and observe the warnings

Now check the System Information again. If the status is "Succeeded," try another update connection until the system is at the required software version: 4.0 or higher.

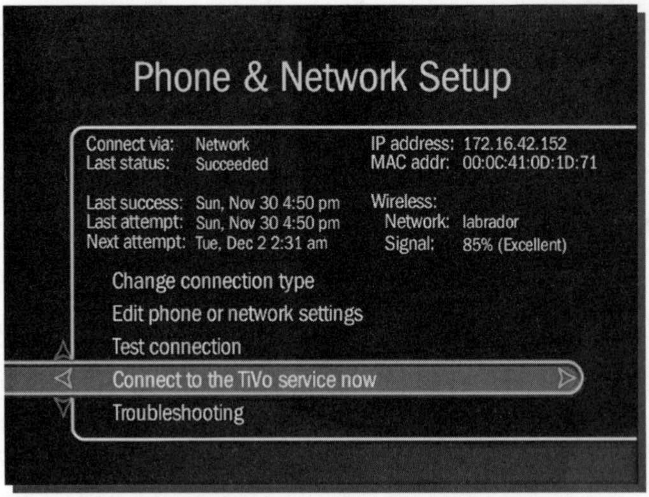

## Phone & Network Setup

| | | | |
|---|---|---|---|
| Connect via: | Network | IP address: | 172.16.42.152 |
| Last status: | Succeeded | MAC addr: | 00:0C:41:0D:1D:71 |
| | | | |
| Last success: | Sun, Nov 30 4:50 pm | Wireless: | |
| Last attempt: | Sun, Nov 30 4:50 pm | Network: | labrador |
| Next attempt: | Tue, Dec 2 2:31 am | Signal: | 85% (Excellent) |

Change connection type

Edit phone or network settings

Test connection

Connect to the TiVo service now

Troubleshooting

FIGURE 12-6: The TiVo Phone and Network Setup screen updates status in real-time.

# Step 3: Plugging In

Now that TiVo is running the latest software, it's time to start plugging in all of those USB adapters until one works. The tricky part here is knowing when it has worked. Figure 12-6 shows the best screen to see network adapter status: Phone and Network Setup. Follow these steps to get to this screen:

1. Press the TiVo button

2. Click TiVo Messages and Setup

3. Click Settings

4. Click Phone and Network Setup

When an adapter is present and detected by TiVo, the IP address and MAC address will appear in the top right corner of the screen. Also, wireless network information will be displayed just under the MAC address.

TiVo recommends a lot of troubleshooting steps, but you can circumvent all of the hassle by plugging and unplugging one adapter after the other. Wait about 30 seconds in between swapping adapters.

**Note** Before TiVo detects its first adapter, the Phone and Network Setup screen will show an entry like, "Click here to learn about networking." This will disappear when an adapter is detected and it will be replaced with network options.

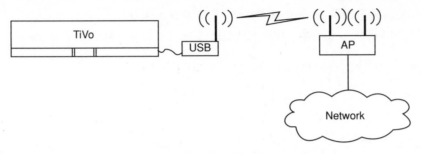

FIGURE 12-7: TiVo connects to the WLAN like any other client.

## Step 4: Configuring for Wireless

The TiVo connects to your home wireless network like any other client. The wireless and TCP/IP settings need to be configured to coincide with the wireless LAN settings. Figure 12-7 shows a standard wireless network and how TiVo will connect.

TiVo will walk you through the wireless network setup. Follow these guidelines:

1. Go to Phone and Network Setup

2. Click Change connection type

3. Select Network

4. Go back one screen

5. Click Edit phone or network settings

6. Select Wireless Settings

7. Follow the on-screen guide to configure the wireless adapter

8. Check the final status screen to ensure connectivity. The TiVo will let you know if it does not connect to the wireless network.

**Note** If you're using WEP on your network (which is highly recommended) try to use a hexadecimal password (also called a *WEP key*). This will ensure the same key is used on all devices. Some alphanumeric to hexadecimal converters follow different algorithms. Entering an alpha password like "wi-tivo-link" can be converted differently on different wireless devices.

Try making names out of regular hex characters (A-Z, 0-9), like "cafe2feed1decaf4fadedface1."

Next, set up the TCP/IP settings:

1. Go to Phone and Network Setup

2. Click Edit phone or network settings

3. Click TCP/IP Settings

**4.** Follow the on-screen guide to configure the TCP/IP settings

**5.** Check the final status screen. The TiVo will attempt to verify the TCP/IP settings

Now test the network settings by connecting to the TiVo service:

**1.** Go to Phone and Network Setup

**2.** Click Connect to the TiVo service now

**3.** Press Select to connect

**4.** Make sure the screen displays something like, "Connecting to the TiVo service via the network."

Congratulations! TiVo is now connected to your wireless network. Now there's so much you can do. The following sections will explore some of these options.

If you have problems connecting to the TiVo service at this point, the problem is probably one of two things: an incorrect WEP key or a TCP/IP configuration problem.

First, double check that the WEP key is entered correctly. Often, the network will respond well to a connection, but no traffic is passed because the keys don't match. You may wish to temporarily disable WEP on your access point to eliminate this possibility.

Second, ensure your TCP/IP settings match those of your network. Check another computer on your network to see if it uses DHCP (automatic IP address assignment) and make sure the TiVo matches that setting. If you are using static IP addresses, make sure you use an unused IP address for your network and that the Subnet Mask, DNS, and Gateway addresses all match one of your working computers.

**Tip**

In Windows 2000 and XP, use the command prompt and enter `ipconfig/all` to see TCP/IP settings. In Windows 98, use the winipcfg command from the Run menu.

# PC to TiVo to PC

TiVo Series 2 really shows its colors when piloted with the TiVo Home Media Option. This is a software add-on for the TiVo that enables broadband streaming music, digital picture slideshows, sharing recordings across multiple TiVo, and setting recording options through the TiVo Web site.

**Note**

TiVo Series 1 does not currently support the Home Media Option, but serious hackers can use the broadband readiness for getting under the hood of TiVo. Transferring files to and from the TiVo, adding software hacks, and playing MP3s are among the many Series 1 hacks available.

We'll cover the following scenarios:

- Playing music on TiVo
- Viewing a slideshow
- Watching on another TiVo
- Sharing with your neighbor

## Publishing with the Home Media Option

Purchase Home Media Option direct from TiVo to open the floodgates. Download the TiVo Desktop software from the `Tivo.com` Web site, and install it onto a Windows PC running Windows 98 or higher or a Macintosh running OS X 10.2 or higher.

**Note** For some reason, TiVo Desktop may also be called TiVo Publisher. On the `Tivo.com` Web site, the references are to TiVo Desktop software. When installed, the shortcut and software title is TiVo Publisher.

The TiVo Desktop software has two components that work together:

- The Publisher File Manager
- The TiVo Server

### Desktop Publisher and Server

The Publisher is a graphical user interface to browse files on your PC hard drive. TiVo Publisher has two categories: Music and Photos.

The music feature plays MP3 files directly. It recognizes MP3 playlists and extracts the MP3 files into the selector window. The photo feature recognizes many different file types, GIF, JPG, BMP, PNG, and DIB.

To publish a file, drag and drop the file from the file selector listing to the "Published" pane. Figure 12-8 shows the publisher with several MP3s published and ready to play on TiVo.

After selecting and publishing the files, click the Server menu item and Start the TiVo Server. A black TiVo icon should appear in the system tray indicating the server is running. If the server is "paused," a red "X" will be placed over the icon.

To play music or view photos, follow these steps:

**1.** Ensure the TiVo Server is running on your PC.

**2.** Press the TiVo button on the remote.

**3.** Select Music and Photos.

FIGURE 12-8: TiVo Desktop Publisher serves up music and pictures.

**4.** Wait up to 30 seconds for the TiVo to discover your PC files.

**5.** Select the appropriate media and press Play to start the slideshow or music.

Note

Press the Enter button on the TiVo remote to select options while playing a slideshow or music.

Note

You can also play media content from TiVo's central servers. This feature is called "TiVo Online." Select TiVo Online as you would a TiVo Publisher source.

## Remote Viewing

The Home Media Option also allows two separate TiVo units to work together. You can watch shows recorded on your family room TiVo from your bedroom TiVo. Not only does it allow this "Multi-room viewing," but now the show can actually be copied from one TiVo to the other.

This requires at least two TiVo DVRs under the same account. Both must have a network connection to each other. And both must have the Home Media Option upgrade.

A few steps are required at the `Tivo.com` Web site to get started:

1. Buy the TiVo Home Media Option for both TiVo DVRs.
2. Surf to the "Manage My Account" section on www.`Tivo.com`.
3. Select "DVR Preferences."
4. Enable "Permit Multi-Room Viewing" for all TiVo that will trade content.
5. Click Save Preferences on the Web site.
6. Now on the TiVo DVR screen, go to Phone and Network Setup and select "Connect to the TiVo service now" to download the latest settings.

Once the Home Media Option is enabled on both TiVo units, an update to the TiVo service has taken place, and 5 minutes have elapsed, the TiVo units will now be able to view content on each other through the "Now Playing on TiVo" screen.

Scroll to the bottom of the "Now Playing on TiVo" screen to see other TiVos in your home network. Click the TiVo icon to view its contents.

Make sure the TiVo units are all on the same TCP/IP subnet due to possible limitations with Home Media Option discovery and routing. Theoretically, two TiVo units can share content even though they are miles apart. Try it out!

# TiVo Hacks

To really dig in to the possibilities of using TiVo to the extreme, open up the world of hardware and software hacks. There are myriad sites available with endless helpful hints on hacking TiVo.

There are also books available that spell out step-by-step instructions for performing a number of tweaks and upgrades. If you have a TiVo, it is money well spent to pick up one or two of these TiVo hacking books.

Table 12-3 shows a list of TiVo hacking destinations.

And for a wealth of information, search `Google.com` for "TiVo Hacks" or "TiVo Hacking."

**Table 12-3    Some TiVo Hacking Resources**

| Name | Description | From |
|------|-------------|------|
| Hacking TiVo | Book by Jeff Keegan | John Wiley & Sons |
| TiVo Community | Online discussion forums | www.tivocommunity.com |
| DealDatabase | Online discussion forums | www.dealdatabase.com/forum |

*Continued*

**Table 12-3**   *(continued)*

| Name | Description | From |
|------|-------------|------|
| PTVupgrade | Online discussion forums | forum.ptvupgrade.com |
| TiVo Hack FAQ | Web site devoted to TiVo hacks | www.tivofaq.com/hack |
| TiVo Steve-o | Web site by Steve Jenkins | tivo.stevejenkins.com |
| 9th Tee | Online TiVo Upgrade Retailer | www.9thtee.com |

# Summary

TiVo has some great features. If you own one, you already use it to time-shift your viewing like crazy. Adding wireless makes it even better. Now program updates occur in a flash. All of the media options break the barrier between TV and PC. Listening to MP3s on an entertainment center surround sound system is tremendous!

TiVo has changed the way we watch TV. With a wireless connection, you have unlocked additional features that may change the way you share digital media.

Next, get into a long-distance relationship by creating a wireless network capable of communicating over 15 miles or more. Learn what you need to know to set up a link and keep it running. Beam a signal from your house to a friend in the next county with a couple of add-on antennas and a little planning.

# Create a Long-Distance Wi-Fi Link

There will come a time when you are ready to span a great divide using wireless. It's obvious that free space radio signals can travel great distances. Previous chapters spoke at length about high-gain antennas, picking up signals while wardriving, and even broadcasting a signal to the neighbors.

But what about beaming a signal 5, 10, 20 miles, or more? Wireless is a natural replacement for land lines, T1s, DSL, and other high-speed data when needed in a remote location. Or even a location that's not so remote, but where DSL or cable Internet may not be available. Figure 13-1 shows a prime example. A long-distance Wi-Fi link creates a high-bandwidth connection to the mountain operating at the speed of light.

Creating a long-distance link gathers many of the essentials of wireless and adds a healthy dose of physics to overcome the obstacles of a long-distance, free space link.

This chapter is a compilation of practical guidelines designed to enable you to establish a long-distance Wi-Fi link of your own . For your convenience, we've condensed the most essential aspects of strategy, design, and experimental deployment for you here. We'll start with site selection, then take on design considerations including antenna location considerations, and work our way through important hindrances—such as Fresnel zones, path loss, and the Earth's curvature—many of which can be mathematically determined. We'll move on with a discussion on link planning and actual deployment strategies, and conclude the chapter with tips and recommendations for creating a successful link.

A typical long-distance Wi-Fi link will require:

➤ Two wireless access points or wireless bridges

➤ Two high-gain, directional antennas

➤ Two people

➤ Spotting scope or binoculars (optional)

➤ Topographic software (optional)

➤ Handheld radio system/cellular phone

➤ GPS

FIGURE **13-1: Experimental link to a mountaintop eight miles away.**

# Selecting a Site

One of the most important fundamental aspects of setting up a long-distance wireless link lies in the matter of site selection. Choosing the proper location of your links can mean the difference between a quick and easy setup and a long day of problems when it finally comes time to establish the link.

The time you spend on initial site selection can be drastically reduced by using topographical mapping software. This easy-to-use software can show the terrain profile of a line drawn between two or more points (see Figure 13-2). From that line, you can quickly gauge whether or not line-of-sight is possible given the terrain.

In the case of large obstructions blocking your path, you'll need to seek an alternative. One alternative is to employ a repeater, as was described in Chapter 9 (see Figure 13-3). Other solutions are to shift the site requirements slightly. You can run Ethernet cabling up to 100 meters from network equipment, and fiber cable can be run for several kilometers. The possibility of stretching the wired portion of the link horizontally or vertically to a suitable transmission point is apparent.

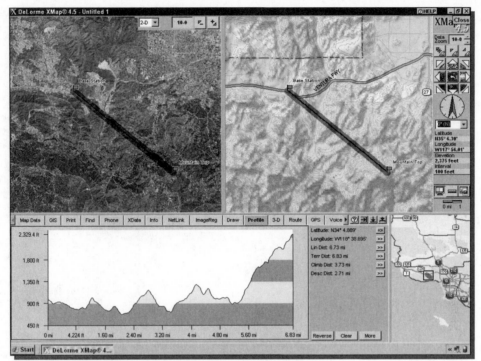

FIGURE 13-2: Forgiving terrain for a mountain-to-valley link.

Software is only the first step. You'll need to make an actual site visit to determine if foliage, buildings, or other obstructions will interfere with the link path. One of the best tools for this is a spotting scope (see Figure 13-4). Binoculars will also help, but the magnification level is not as high as a spotting scope.

**Tip**

As magnification increases, things like field of view, image brightness, image steadiness, and even sharpness decrease. Also, higher magnifications are much more sensitive to atmospheric turbulence and pollution. Be sure to use the magnification to just cover the distance between your antennas.

# Design Considerations

When you set up your long-distance Wi-Fi link, there are several factors to consider, including background research and testing. Through the course of this section, we'll work our way through the most commonly used types of antennas, followed by antenna location, and finally review potential obstacles and impedance problems and how to deal with them accordingly.

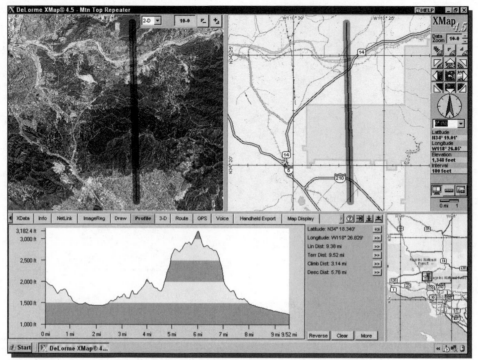

FIGURE **13-3: A mountaintop repeater may be necessary to establish this link.**

FIGURE **13-4: Spotting scope used to determine direction and angle.**

# Antenna Types

There are several types of antennas and characteristics to consider for deployment in a distanced WLAN. This section is a synopsis of the most common types you should be aware of. First, let's review some important general definitions.

- Isotropic antenna. A hypothetical, loss-less antenna that has an equal radiation intensity in all directions. Used as a zero dB gain reference in directivity calculation (gain).

- Antenna gain. Basically a measure of directivity, it is defined as the ratio of the radiation intensity in a given direction that would be obtained if the power accepted by the antenna was radiated equally in all directions. (Antenna gain is expressed in dBi.)

- Radiation pattern. A graphical representation in either polar or rectangular coordinates of the spatial energy distribution of an antenna.

- Side lobes. The radiation lobes in any direction other than the main lobe.

- Omnidirectional antenna. Radiates and receives equally in all directions in azimuth.

- Directional antenna. Radiates and receives most of the signal power in one direction.

- Antenna bandwidth. The directiveness of a directional antenna is defined as the angle between two half-power ($-3$ dB) points on either side of the main lobe of radiation.

We'll only focus on three types of antennas you could deploy in your outdoor WLAN as a link between two points or point-to-multipoint: the dipole antenna, coaxial antenna, and the dish antenna. Albeit interrelated, each type has its own design strengths.

A *dipole antenna* is a straight electrical conductor measuring half a wavelength from end-to-end and connected at the center to a radio frequency. This antenna, also called a doublet, is one of the simplest types of antennas, and constitutes the main RF radiating and receiving element in various sophisticated types of antennas. The dipole is inherently a balanced antenna, because it is bilaterally symmetrical. For best performance, a dipole antenna should be more than half a wavelength above the ground, the surface of a body of water, or other horizontal, conducting medium such as sheet metal roofing. The element should also be at least several wavelengths away from electrically conducting obstructions such as supporting towers, utility wires, guy wires, and other antennas.

A *coaxial antenna* is a variant of the dipole antenna, designed for use with an unbalanced feed line. One side of the antenna element consists of a hollow conducting tube through which a coaxial cable passes. The shield of the cable is connected to the end of the tube at the center of the radiating element. The center conductor of the cable is connected to the other half of the radiating element. The element can be oriented in any fashion, although it is usually vertical.

A *dish antenna* (also known simply as a dish, see Figure 13-5) is common in microwave systems. This type of antenna consists of an active, or driven, element and a passive parabolic or spherical reflector. The driven element can be a dipole antenna or a horn antenna. The reflector has a diameter of at least several wavelengths. As the wavelength increases (and the frequency decreases), the minimum required dish diameter becomes larger. When the dipole or horn is properly positioned and aimed, incoming electromagnetic fields bounce off the reflector, and

FIGURE 13-5: A parabolic dish antenna.

the energy converges on the driven element. If the horn or dipole is connected to a transmitter, the element emits electromagnetic waves that bounce off the reflector and propagate outward in a narrow beam.

## Antenna Location

A long-distance Wi-Fi link is not an easy accomplishment. There are many factors working against successful communications such as distance, open space, interference, obstructions, and inherent equipment limitations. To start building a strategy, you should consider location very carefully. Your radio signal path must have a clear, line-of-sight path—end-to-end—and a clear Fresnel zone (covered in more detail later on). Be sure to use GPS and a spotting scope to visually map and sight your path over long distances. Incidentally, Fresnel zone losses of up to 6 dB can be avoided by ensuring that there are no objects large enough to act as diffracting edges within the first 0.6 Fresnel zone. If a large, rounded object is in your path, losses may exceed 20 dB through several Fresnel zones. This will force you to mount your antennas on towers or buildings at a significant height. Unfortunately, microwave frequencies can also be affected by too much antenna height, and the signal can be degraded due to ground reflections canceling out the signal. Signals will propagate through a few obstructions such as trees or small buildings, and the radio signal will slightly extend over the line-of-sight horizon, but you shouldn't always count on it.

**Table 13-1    Microwave Attenuation**

| Frequency (MHz) | Approximate Attenuation (dB/meter) |
|---|---|
| 432 | 0.10–0.30 |
| 1296 | 0.15–0.40 |
| 2304 | 0.25–0.50 |
| 3300 | 0.40–0.60 |
| 5600 | 0.50–1.50 |
| 10000 | 1.00–2.00 |

For all practical purposes, it's safe to assume that if light can't penetrate a stand of trees, microwave losses will be unacceptable. Consider Table 13-1.

## Potential Obstacles and Impedance

Although typically microwaves are not affected by the ionized layers in our atmosphere because these layers are higher than the normal line-of-sight transmission of the signals, temperature inversions can still prove to be a problem. This is because as the hot air rises, moisture rising within the air causes attenuation of the signal. One might assume that lower microwave frequencies are affected by water vapor and oxygen, but this is not the case.

Also consider the temperature effects on paths such as: reflections, refractions, diffractions, transmission "ducts" and even tropospheric reflections and scattering. These atmospheric conditions can cause a link to fail even though you have visual line-of-sight. A basic understanding of these conditions may help you when troubleshooting a long-distance link.

Other sources of performance degradation in frequency hopping systems are spectrum background noise, received signal fading, interference from other services in that frequency range, random FM components in the signal, "click" noise resulting from the phase discontinuities between frequency hops, errors in receiver synchronization, or even the wind moving your antennas.

### Polarization

The antennas will also have to have the same RF signal polarization. The polarization of the signal will depend on the direction the actual antenna is positioned. If it's up/down, the polarization is vertical; if the antenna is left/right, the polarization is horizontal. If the antenna is diagonal (45 degrees usually), you'll have diagonal polarization. By not having the same polarization on your network's antennas, you can receive a 20 dB loss of signal strength. This is an enormous loss, but can also be very useful. By changing antenna polarization, you can help eliminate certain types of radio interference, or allow many antennas in one location. Horizontal antenna polarization at microwave frequencies will generally provide less multipath and may also provide lower path loss in non line-of-sight situations, but you should always experiment with different polarizations.

Try to avoid installing your antenna in areas that are located near *multipoint microwave distribution system* (MMDS) or *instructional television fixed service* (ITFS) transmitter sites. You can query FCC or PerCon frequency databases for the coordinates to transmitter locations in your area. You can then look up the sites via these coordinates at the Tiger map server here: `http://tiger.census.gov/cgi-bin/mapbrowse-tbl`. You should also note that MMDS uses horizontal antenna polarization, so if you need to locate your antenna site near one, use vertical polarization. Other things to look out for at your antenna site are high-power PCS wireless cell phone transmissions in the 1.8–1.9 GHz band, broadband noise from high-power colocated transmitters, harmonics from mobile radio and paging transmitters, and other nearby microwave links.

## Grounding

The proper Earth grounding of your antenna tower is essential for lightning protection and static discharge. Many towers are inadequately grounded by using only a few grounding rounds and large gauge round copper cables. This is not correct. The small number of grounding rods are inadequate, and round copper cable has a relatively high impedance to an instantaneous rise in electric current (lightning hit). Extremely high voltages will develop across these cables and instead of going to ground, these charges will go directly into your building equipment. A minimum of four ground rods per tower leg with some sort of chemical grounding material should be used. The chemical grounding material will help to lower the ground rod resistance. Copper straps should be used to connect the ground rods to the tower due to their low inductance. In areas with sandy soil or excessive wind-generated static, it's advisable to use a more elaborate grounding method. Most likely a radial grounding system like that found in AM radio.

You should also try to have all your transmission line runs inside the tower column. This will help shield them from lightning if it hits the tower. You should also securely bond the lines to the tower every 15 meters or so. Use the recommended bonding kits that your tower manufacture approves of.

## Beam Tilt

Antennas mounted on very high towers may need to take into account beam tilt. Beam tilt is needed when a radiating signal's vertical beam width is narrowed (by using high-gain antennas), and the areas near the tower location lose service because most of the signal is wasted by broadcasting into open air. The beam must be tilted either mechanically or electrically to steer the signal back into its proper location.

Mechanical beam tilting is relatively easy. The antenna can be mounted slightly less than 90 degrees from the horizontal plane so the tilted beam illuminates the desired service area. However, in the opposite direction, the signal will be pointed toward the sky, reducing the effective service area in that direction of the antenna.

If the signal needs to be "bent" downward in all directions around the antenna site, an electrical tilting method must be used. This is commonly referred to as "null fill". Electrical tilting is produced by controlling the current phase in the antenna itself. Thus, it must be done during the antenna's design stages by an engineer with expensive equipment.

## Weather

Finally, consider potential weather problems. Ice buildup on antenna elements will result in an increased SWR (impedance mismatch, standing wave ratio) that will de-tune a transmitter system, significantly reducing its output power. Ice can also cause severe transmission line damage, and falling icicles can kill. The easiest way to prevent ice buildup is with special antenna heaters or by covering the antenna system with a fiberglass radome. Radomes will increase the wind load on the tower and antenna heaters can be expensive. For more information, visit the Web at: www.teletronics.com/tii/documents/Antennas/2.4%20GHz/Antennas_Omni.pdf.

**Note** There's a great guidebook to building your own custom WLAN antenna on the Web at www.saunalahti.fi/elepal/antennie.html.

# Determining the Fresnel Zone

In radio communications—especially given a point-to-point signal between two antennas—the Fresnel zone is part of the concentric ellipsoids of revolution of a circular aperture. In other words Fresnel zones are caused by diffraction by a circular aperture; it's an elliptical region surrounding the line-of-sight path between the transmitting and receiving antennas. To further explain, imagine line-of-sight between two antennas with a signal that spreads out in an elliptical path between the ends (shown in Figure 13-6). The path is divided into different zones that accommodate radio waves that are traveling at different velocities. The Fresnel zone's radius at the point where the ends of the ellipse peak out (known as the midpoint) should be free and clear to provide adequate signal strength. In a good long-distance Wi-Fi design, you should calculate the elliptical shape to determine height and placement of your antennas. In this section we will examine Fresnel zone calculations in detail, but first we'll review some of the obstacles to take into consideration.

## Path Loss and Earth Curvature

Path loss between two antennas in a long-distance Wi-Fi link can be caused by a number of objects, including buildings, trees, and landscape features such as protruding hills (see Figure 13-7), and even open air (which we'll talk more about later). However, although many times it is insignificant, one entity to also consider is the curvature of the Earth given by the distance between the two endpoints. Typically this can be an issue when the distance between endpoints is over 10 miles.

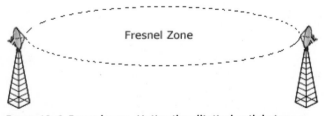

FIGURE 13-6: Fresnel zone. Notice the elliptical path between endpoints.

FIGURE 13-7: Path loss. The elliptical path between endpoints should be clear from obstruction.

For all practical purposes, let's assume that the earth is a sphere with a radius of 3,958 miles. If you are at some point on the Earth and move tangent to the surface for a distance of 1 mile, then you can form a right-angled triangle as shown in the diagram in Figure 13-8. Next, using the theorem of Pythagoras, $a^2 = 3958^2 + 1^2 = 15665765$. Therefore, $a = 3958.000126$ miles.

As a result of this calculation, your position is $3958.000126 - 3958 = 0.000126$ miles above the Earth's surface. Furthermore, $0.000126$ miles $= 12 \times 5280 \times 0.000126 = 7.98$ inches. For this reason, we can speculate that the Earth's surface curves approximately 8 inches given the particulars in the scenario. Eight inches isn't very much, and a mile isn't all that far either. But this "dropoff" of the horizon adds up over distance. If your long-distance link goes much farther than a few miles, you will need to raise antenna elevation to compensate for the curvature of the Earth.

As shown in Figure 13-8, we're assuming the Earth has a radius of 3,958 miles and you are at some point on the surface moving in tangent for 1 mile.

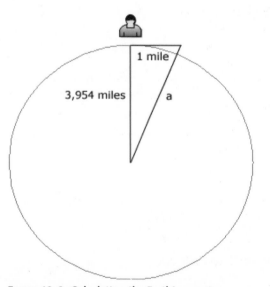

FIGURE 13-8: Calculating the Earth's curvature.

**Note** The Theorem of Pythagoras states that if a triangle has sides of length *a,b,c*, with sides *a,b* enclosing an angle of 90 degrees ("right angle"), then $a^2 + b^2 = c^2$. By the way, a right angle can be defined here as the angle formed when two straight lines cross each other in such a way that all four angles produced are equal.

## Fresnel Zone Calculations

As mentioned earlier in this chapter, the Fresnel zone's radius at the point where the ends of the ellipse peak out, or the midpoint, should be free and clear to provide adequate signal strength. A rule of thumb is to keep blockage under 40 percent, but transmission loss is imminent if there's any obstruction of the Fresnel zone.

In your long distance Wi-Fi design you should calculate the Fresnel zone to determine height and placement of your antennas to ensure there will be no hindrance. It's also important to consider physical obstacles and their relation to the time of year. For example, during the warm seasons leaves will sprout again and over time young trees could grow into the zone as well.

For purposes of performing Fresnel zone calculations let's look at a real world example and factor in the potential obstacles. The formula we will use to calculate the Fresnel zone radius is shown in Figure 13-9, where *f* is frequency in GHz, *d*1 (distance from transmitting antenna to mid-point) and *d*2 (distance from receiving antenna to mid-point) represent the statute miles, and *h* is the radius in feet.

**Caution** For best transmission results you should keep the link path of the Fresnel zone at least 60 percent free from obstruction.

For an example scenario, we surveyed the following specifications:

- The distance between endpoint antennas is 9.5 miles.
- The curvature of Earth is $y = L^2 / 8R$ or $y = 9.5^2 / 8(3958)$ or $y = 90.25 / 31664$ miles; therefore $y = 15$ feet.
- The highest mid-point obstacle is a one-story building at 22 feet.
- The frequency in GHz is 2.4.

$$h = 72.1 \sqrt{\frac{d_1 d_2}{f(d_1 + d_2)}}$$

**FIGURE 13-9: Fresnel zone formula, where f is the frequency in GHz, d1 and d2 represent the statute miles, and h is the radius in feet.**

Using the Fresnel zone formula, we simply follow these steps to calculate the radius of the mid-point ellipse:

1. Divide 9.5 by 2 to get the $d1$ and $d2$ values: 9.2 / 2 = 4.6.

2. Multiply $d1 \times d2 = 4.6(4.6) = 21.16$.

3. Multiply the total distance by frequency or $f(d1 + d2) = 2.4(9.5) = 22.8$.

4. Divide the value from Step 2 by the value from Step 3 or $(d1 \times d2)$ / $f(d1 + d2) = 21.16 / 22.8 = 0.928$.

5. Take the square root of the value in Step 4 (as 0.928) = 0.963.

6. Multiply the value from Step 5 by 72.1 to get $h = 72.1(.963) = 69.4$ feet, which is the radius of the mid-point Fresnel zone ellipse.

That's it! Simply factor in the height of the obstacles and you have the antenna height for this long-distance Wi-Fi link in feet: 69.4 + (15 + 22) = 106.4. However, remember the 40 percent blockage rule from earlier in this section? If necessary, you could reduce the height of the antennas by further multiplying by 0.6, which accommodates 60 percent signal transmission strength (with 40 percent blockage). By doing so, the final antenna height would decrease to 106.4(0.6) = 63.8 feet.

Following are some popular ways you can improve the line-of-sight between end point antennas:

■ Raise the antenna mounting point on the existing structure.

■ Build a new structure, that is, a radio tower, that is tall enough to mount the antenna.

■ Increase the height of an existing tower.

■ Locate a different mounting point, such as another building or tower, for the antenna.

■ Cut down problem trees.

# Budgeting Your Wireless Link

Now that you've made calculations to work around obstacles and accommodate Fresnel zone radius requirements, it's time to calculate whether or not the signal strength for your equipment will meet the receiver's signal threshold. This process is called *link planning* or *link budgeting* and involves several variables, all of which we'll cover in this section.

We'll break a WLAN link into the following elements:

■ *Effective transmitting power*: transmitter power (dBm) − cable and connector loss (dB) + antenna gain (dBi)

■ *Propagation loss [dB]*: free space loss (dB)

■ *Effective receiving sensibility*: antenna gain (dBi)—cable loss (dB)—receiver sensitivity (dBm)

With regard to the specific equipment you plan on or are considering using, check the specification sheets or contact the manufacturers' technicians for the values mentionedearlier. Also, for more accurate results taking into account the different transmitting and receiving properties at both ends of the link, link budgeting should be performed in both directions. Moving forward let's break down each element and detail its individual components.

**Caution**

The link budget formula is actually not too difficult. Basically, to pre-suppose a positive connection, the transmitting power + propagation loss + receiving sensibility must be greater than zero. A strong link, on the other hand, should have a 20 dB margin.

## Effective Transmitting Power

The effective transmitting power consists of the transmitter power, cable, and connector loss, and antenna gain. For simplicity, let's look at each individual component:

The transmitter power (in watts or milliwatts) can be expressed on a logarithmic scale relative to 1 milliwatt in dBm (deci-Bell relative to one milliwatt). Therefore, the output is compared to one milliwatt: $(1 \text{ dBm} = 10 \times \log10(P / 0.001))$; ($P$ in watts).

- To convert watts to dBm: 10 log (watts $\times$ 1000) = dBm
- To convert dBm to watts: $10^{(dBm / 10)} / 1000$ = watts. (Note: 10 to the (dBm / 10) power is the inverse log of (dBm / 10))

For cable and connector loss, be sure to account for the cable length when calculating cable loss and don't forget to add the (negative) value for the connector. Cable manufacturers will supply the cable and connector loss you can expect for a given frequency. A very nice cable loss calculator is available at the Times Microwave Web site: www.timesmicrowave.com/cgi-bin/calculate.pl.

Antenna gain is important as it defines the antenna pattern with regard to where the far field is strongest and weakest and in the middle, and by how much. Antenna gain is normally given in decibels over an isotropic antenna (dBi). It's the power gain in comparison to a hypothetical isotropic (all directions equal) antenna. If your antenna specifications express gain in dBd, you should add 2.14 to obtain the corresponding gain in dBi, since it's compared to a dipole antenna. We specify maximum antenna gain in terms of dBi.

**Note**

There's an excellent discussion about antenna gain on the Web at this address: www.marcspages.co.uk/tech/antgain.htm.

## Propagation Loss

Propagation loss (PL) can be simply defined as loss of a wave in free space. Technically it is defined as the signal attenuation between transmit (TX) and receive (RX) antennas due to the

$$PL_{FS}(d) = 10n \log_{10}\left(\frac{4\pi l}{\lambda}\right)\Bigg|_{n=2}$$

**Figure 13-10: Path loss in an ideal free-space path.**

TX to RX separation and multipath (scattering). Basic transmission loss is given by the following formula: $PL(dB) = P_t(dB) - P_r(dB) + G_t(dB) + G_r(dB)$, where $P_t$ is the transmitted power, $P_r$ is the received power, $G_t$ is the transmit antenna gain, and $G_r$ is the receive antenna gain. An ideal free space (FS) path (no ground reflection, no multipath) has a path loss which is proportional to the square ($n = 2$) of the separation $d$, where $l$ is the wavelength, as shown in Figure 13-10.

This typically represents the minimum path loss and serves as a lower limit. Values of n on the order of 4 are more representative of realistic, cluttered environments.

**Note** For more information on path loss, visit the following Web page: `www.wireless. per.nl:202/multimed/cdrom97/pathloss.htm`.

## Effective Receiving Sensibility

The first two components of effective receiving sensibility, antenna gain (in dBi) and cable loss (in dB), were covered previously. Therefore, we'll only touch upon the third component, namely receiver sensitivity (in dBm).

Receiver sensitivity is one of the vital specifications of any receiver. Whether measured as a signal to noise ratio, SINAD, or noise figure it is essential that any receiver has a sufficient level of sensitivity. In other words to achieve a required bit rate, the receiver power threshold on the card connector must be up to par. Otherwise, there will be a noticeable decrease in performance. This specification is provided by the manufacturer; however, some of the most common values are indicated in Table 13-2.

**Table 13-2   Common Client Adapter Receive Sensitivity**

| Client Adapter | dBm at 11 Mbps | dBm at 5.5 Mbps | dBm at 2 Mbps | dBm at 1 Mbps |
|---|---|---|---|---|
| Orinoco PC-Card | −82 | −87 | −91 | −94 |
| Cisco Aironet 350 PC-Card | −85 | −89 | −91 | −94 |
| Edimax USB Client | −81 | n/a | n/a | n/a |
| Belkin Router/ Access Point | −78 | n/a | n/a | n/a |

You will notice that the lower bandwidth commitment (towards the right of Table 13-2) increases receive sensitivity. For an ultra-reliable, but slightly slower link, try setting your hardware to a maximum of 1 Mbps.

# Putting It All Together

Don't be overwhelmed by the formulas and calculations required for link budgeting. If you're not comfortable with the mathematics, there's an automated online calculator at www.olotwireless.net/castella/radio.htm. More importantly, link planning can save your time and money when you make equipment purchasing decisions. Calculating a link budget beforehand will allow you to change components (based on their component values) to better score in a positive margin.

To recapitulate, you can assume a positive signal connection by taking the combined values from the transmitting power, propagation loss, and receiving sensibility with a final value greater than zero. A strong link, on the other hand, should have a margin of 20 dB. Therefore, referring back to our example scenario, we surveyed the following specifications:

- The distance between endpoint antennas is 9.5 miles.
- The curvature of Earth is $y-L^2/8R$ or $y-9.5^2 / 8(3958)$ or $y-90.25 / 31664$ miles; therefore $y-15$ feet.
- The highest midpoint obstacle is a one-story building at 22 feet.
- The frequency in GHz is 2.4.
- Using the Fresnel zone formula, we calculated 69.4 feet; which is the radius of the midpoint Fresnel zone ellipse between antennas over our line-of-sight.
- After factoring in the height of surveyed obstacles, we found the antenna height for this long-distance Wi-Fi link should be 106.4 feet.

So based on the link budgeting factors, considering obstacles, and accommodating the Fresnel zone radius following (also depicted in Figure 13-11) is a synopsis of a realistic long-distance link experimental design:

- Antenna height on each end: 106.4 feet
- Antenna type on each end: 21 dBi Parabolic Dish Directional Antenna
- Cabling on each end: Just enough low loss cabling to ensure the greatest distance

**Tip**  You might assume that in order to double the distance of your long-distance Wi-Fi link, you would simply double the signal power, yet this is not the case. When dealing with long-distance Wi-Fi links you must first understand that wireless signal strength degrades as the square of the distance covered. Doubling the distance of your long-distance Wi-Fi link will require $2^2$, or four times the power, which is represented by a +6 dB gain.

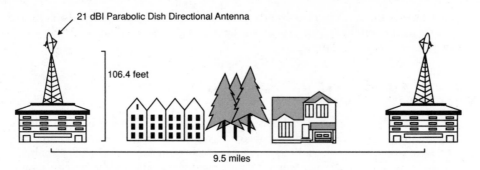

21 dBI Parabolic Dish Directional Antenna

106.4 feet

9.5 miles

FIGURE **13-11: An experimental long-distance Wi-Fi bridge design based on our example survey results.**

## Cabling the Antenna

Begin by measuring the distance from your computer to your outside antenna location. Be sure to choose a route that will protect your coax run and allow easy upgrading. Use a long extension cord to simulate your coax and help make the measurement more realistic. Try to keep the coax cable run as short as possible to minimize the RF power loss, and avoid sharp bends, which can damage the coax, or in some cases, change the coax's impedance. Next, choose a high quality brand of coax and cut it to that distance, plus about one meter extra, for slack. Avoid the low-quality, high-loss cable such as RG-58, CB or TV/satellite coax. The LMR series from Times Microwave is highly recommended. The coax you choose must have a 50 ohms impedance. Any other impedance, such as 75 ohms, may cause too much loss for this application.

**Note** Use of the 75 ohms hard-line used in cable TV service might be possible, though some experimentation will be required. You may also be able to pick up very high-quality, hard-line coax from cellular phone or broadcast installations. They usually give the spool end runs (the last 15 meters or so) away for free or even throw it away because it's of no use to them. The connectors for commercial hard-line are very expensive and hard to make, so remember that.

Prepare the coax for installation of the two N plugs on each end. You'll need a suitable brand of N-type connectors due to the large center conductor if you use LMR-400. The RF Industries RFN-1006-PL N-Connector is a good brand. You may also need to route your coax before terminating the N-Connectors if it has to run through small diameter holes. Take your time installing the connectors. See Chapter 1 for more instructions on building your cable.

After attaching the connectors, wrap some 3 M Scotch Super 33+ electrical tape, or equivalent stretchy tape, around the bottom of the connector and a few centimeters of coax. Pull the tape as tight as possible to help make the connector waterproof. If your antenna is going to be exposed directly to heavy rain or high humidity, you may want to consider wrapping the connection with some self-fusing silicone tape (Radio Shack part number 64-2336).

Next, route your coax to your outside antenna. Secure the cable to keep it from flopping around in the wind or from people pulling on it. Leave a small loop of coax where it enters the building.

This will act as a drip loop and will keep rain from seeping into your building. You may also at this time want to install a quality brand of inline coax lightning protection. PolyPhaser is one such protector. Refer to the documentation on the proper grounding techniques that will be required for lightning protectors to work properly.

Connect the cable up to your antenna's connector jack. Wrap some Coax Seal, Mastic tape, or any other pliable waterproof tape around the connector and then also wrap all that with Super 33+ electrical tape. Secure the wrapped connector against the antenna mast.

 **Tip** When using rubberized Coax Seal or Mastic tape, don't apply the tape to the connector directly, you'll just end up with a mess. Instead, wrap the connection with electrical tape and then wrap the Coax Seal around the tape, sealing any small holes. This will save you a lot of hassle when you have to remove the connection.

For onsite testing, you may wish to obtain a proper pigtail to connect your computer to the N-type connector on the cable. You may also want to make some type of stress relief holder to support the weight of the coax and adapter. For more information on connectors and cabling see Chapters 1 and 2 or visit the Web at: `http://home.deds.nl/~pa0hoo/connectortypes/index.html`.

# Testing and Troubleshooting

Now that your link is installed, you should give it a nice going over with some common testing tools. Also, use the network as you actually would on a regular basis. That is, download e-mails, surf the Web, transfer files, and so on.

In setting up your actual link, proper planning needs to take place beforehand because you and the person who will be helping you will be quite some ways apart and it may be difficult to communicate, not to mention exchange extra parts.

On the day of your test, you should create a "pre-link checklist" before leaving for the site. Forgetting equipment or other necessities can mean the difference between spending the day surfing the net or sitting in traffic.

A typical pre-link checklist includes the following.(Note: there should be two of everything on this list because there are two nodes required.)

- Laptop computer
- Extra laptop battery or power inverter with 12-volt adapter
- Wireless adapter
- Access point or bridge
- Directional antenna—panel, grid, Yagi, dish
- Pigtails
- Temporary mounting solution—tripod, lightstand, or something similar

- Cellular phone or handheld radio
- Spotting scope or binoculars
- GPS or a good map

**Tip**

Keep yourself organized and stick to the checklist, and you can leave the aspirin at home. Always remember to bring more than one pigtail per node, as their fragile end connectors are prone to breaking, and you may be many, many miles from a replacement. Extra batteries for your laptop, in addition to a power inverter, also will ensure success because a laptop on a single charge will clearly not be sufficient for a full day of testing.

## Making the Link

After you reach the site, survey the initial area to find a spot with good line-of-sight to the intended direction of the link. Setting up the antenna, tripod, access point/bridge, and laptop should be a very simple and standard procedure. Connect all of the subsequent hardware and run a program that measures signal-to-noise ratio (SNR) such as NetStumbler. (See Chapter 6 for more on NetStumbler.) You will be able to detect the reception of a beacon frame, and then use the SNR measurment for link tuning. You will need to adjust and fine tune the direction of the antenna to achieve optimum signal strength. Make sure you do this in coordination with the person in control of the other end of the link to ensure precision and accuracy. Make adjustments on one side at a time.

Once you feel that you have optimized the wireless link quality to your satisfaction, confirm the success of your project by testing the network transport over the wireless link.

Set up a continuous connection to the far-side computer. Adjust the settings on both computers to enable communication between them. It will depend on your network topology, but you can often insert a laptop on either end and configure them for direct communication to each other. If your wireless radios are also routers, you will need to configure the computers to participate on each side of the network.

Once your network settings are configured as needed, a good first test is to ping the remote computer over the wireless link. (Your pal on the other end should also do this and other steps with your computer.) Run the Command Prompt and enter `ping -t ip_address`. The -t option tells ping to keep going forever. If the link doesn't work at this point, jump to the Troubleshooting section below. Ping should resolve the address and start replying once a second. This will help show you the link quality but it won't measure throughput or continuous connectivity.

**Tip**

Sometimes a stray DHCP server may give you the wrong address and send your traffic over an Internet connection away from the wireless link. If this happens, you will be able to surf the Web, but you will not be able to connect to the computer on the other end of the wireless link. Perform a `tracert ip_address` command to the far-side computer. Tracert will report on which devices are routing your network traffic.

Next, use the link as it will actually be used on a daily basis. If you will be surfing the Web and checking e-mail, do that. If it will be used for videoconfereincing or voice-over-IP (VoIP), try that, too. Watch streaming videos, copy files back and forth to each other, and so on. You could also try using Microsoft NetMeeting to send video or transfer files acrosss the link. Basically, you want to exercise the link in any way you can.

While doing these link excercises, insert some attentuation into the system to simulate a low signal condition. The "Go/NoGo Tester" from Wireless Info Net (www.ask-wi.com) is a neat, simple way to test how your link will perform on a bad day. Just plug this loss-inducing barrel connector into your cabling and see if the link stays up. If the link dies, you need to carefully reconsider the components comprising the network. Check antenna selection, cable lengths, connector quality, radio sensitivity, and of course antenna direction and physical aim.

Once you have accomplished these tasks and kept the link up and running, you have successfully designed and deployed your own long-distance Wi-Fi link.

## Troubleshooting

Even when you've planned carefully, there can still be troubleshooting issues that may arise when establishing a wireless connection of this type. The most common troubleshooting problems are something that most wireless users will experience at some time or another.

Broadly, problems arise in one of two areas: the wireless connection and network settings.

If you don't have any experience setting up a TCP/IP network, try to have a good friend that knows the stuff onsite, or at least on the other end of a cell phone. Dozens of things can go wrong in configuring a basic network connection on a regular wired Ethernet link. By adding wireless to the mix, you could be in for a long day without proper support.

We are here to help. Try some of these basic solutions to common link problems:

- *Antenna alignment*: Often, if the antenna mount is not secure, the alignment may skew from its original position, causing a link disruption. Make sure that everything is mounted securely, and that the antennas have been properly aligned. Double-check the link after tightening down mounting bolts. Contents may have shifted during tightening.

- *Bad cables*: Any pigtail cables in use as the connection between your laptop and the antenna will likely have very fragile end connectors and often will break easily if not handled properly. Ensure these cable ends are not damaged and are seated properly.

- *Network configuration*: TCP/IP settings must be properly configured or you will not be able to establish your network link. If you can detect the presence of the network from the laptop, the link is probably fine. Ensure that all network settings are configured for access across the wireless link, and make sure that both computers are fully configured to receive traffic. Disable any firewalls.

- *Ping problems*: Immediately check your wireless components and TCP/IP settings. These settings can vary wildly based on your actual deployment. On a basic level, ensure that the two computers are on the same IP subnet or can route to each other, and make sure your gateway is set to the correct router device, if applicable.

- *Fresnel zone obstructions*: Trees, buildings, and other obstructions in the Fresnel zone will degrade your link quality severely, and appropriate actions must be taken to ensure a clear Fresnel path. You may need to move the link, or raise the antennas above the obstruction.

- *Intermittent signal*: This toughest of all problems to troubleshoot can be caused by a number of things. Check for some of these: bad wireless devices or poor configuration, damaged antennas or connectors, bent or cut cables, too many connectors, RF design errors, RF interference, other Wi-Fi radios, and possibly vehicular traffic, birds, or other intermittent antenna obstruction. Also, check for water damage or any sign of seepage into your electronics or antenna components. And finally, make sure you removed the Go/NoGo tester.

With all of these tips, you should have little trouble in making your link a success. Enjoy your new-found freedom!

# Summary

A long-distance wireless link bridges two remote locations and allows data to travel where it has never traveled before. A high-speed Wi-Fi link can bring another building online, light up a remote outpost, or establish a temporary uplink to the Internet. Beaming wireless signals across long distances makes just about any personal, research, or business task much easier. The technology has enabled researchers to keep in constant contact with each other and their test subjects, businesses to save money by connecting multiple offices, and sharing of Internet access to friends or relatives. Entirely new business models and research methods are being revealed through long-distance wireless connectivity.

Creating a successful long-distance Wi-Fi link is certainly not unproblematic. Yet, as this chapter has shown, a good design begins with an accurate survey, Fresnel zone and path loss calculations, followed by level-headed link planning. If you're not up to the task mathematically, use the online link budget calculator at `www.olotwireless.net/castella/radio.htm`. Also, remember that most, if not all, of the specifications required for the calculations in this chapter are available in your hardware manuals, on the manufacturer Web sites, or through quick customer support phone calls. The task is not without challenges. The reward is limitless.

Now we'll lighten the subject a bit. Read on to Chapter 14, where we employ some unusual wireless link tactics to create a car-to-car videoconferencing session. Prepare for a road trip with a 1970s-style convoy, this time with Wi-Fi video instead of CB radio! 10-4 good buddy. I mean, "lights, camera, action!"

# Deploy a Car-to-Car Wireless Video Link

You've got high mobility wireless, a car with computer power on the passenger seat, and your pals are following you down an obscure back road. Their view is perpetually of your back bumper. The conversation is limited to cell phones, two-way radio, or shouting out the window. Ditch old-school analog communication and set up a Wi-Fi video session!

Use a simple webcam or another video source and the folks in the trailing car feel as if they are riding shotgun on point. With two cars on a road trip sporting wireless and videoconferencing, you will have a virtual party on the highway.

In this chapter's project, you're going to create a wireless *videoconferencing* system between two cars. The passengers in each car will be able to see and talk to the people in the other car up to a distance of 300 feet or more.

Before we get started, there's a small amount of preparation and testing you'll need to do. You will need the following:

➤ Video source compatible with Microsoft "video for Windows" (VFW), such as a USB webcam

➤ Two Windows laptop computers (Windows 98 or higher)

➤ Wi-Fi card with external connector on each laptop

➤ Car-mounted Wi-Fi antenna on each car

➤ DC-to-AC inverter (optional)

➤ Mounting system (can be as simple as Velcro)

➤ Videoconferencing software (such as Microsoft NetMeeting)

Once the components are assembled and tested, install them in the car and go for a road trip! (See Figure 14-1.)

in this chapter

☑ Understanding videoconferencing

☑ Selecting a camera

☑ Setting up the software

☑ Establishing a wireless link

☑ Setting up the cars

**Caution** The very idea of a video screen operating in the car means that there should be a driver and a passenger at a minimum. The passenger will act as an electronics operator (EO) handling all of the equipment and computer management.

FIGURE 14-1: Videoconferencing road trip!

Driver safety is paramount. A video system like the one you build here could be a distraction to the driver. Ensure that all precautions are taken against driver distraction. When planning a trip like this, extra care is essential.

# Introduction to Videoconferencing

Videoconferencing is more than just video. It also includes audio and data sharing. In its highest form, videoconferencing enables multiple participants across the globe to share documents and presentation materials, and perform instantaneous collaboration in a nearly transparent "window" to another part of the world.

There are systems that cost over $50,000 and use multiple flat-panel video displays for corporate boardroom meetings, like the incredible system by Tandberg shown in Figure 14-2. There are also near-zero-cost person-to-person systems like Microsoft NetMeeting.

This chapter barely scrapes the surface of videoconferencing. To learn more, visit www.packetizer.com and head to the "VoIP Information" section.

FIGURE 14-2: Tandberg 8000 boardroom videoconferencing system.

Whether the system being used is the free program like NetMeeting, a medium cost package like the Polycom ViaVideo desktop system, or the high-end system like Tandberg's, they all interoperate based on videoconferencing standards. These standards (developed by the International Telecommunications Union, or ITU) define every aspect of the videoconferencing experience. The ITU standards make it possible to use programs by different vendors on different platforms.

Some of the relevant videoconferencing standards:

- H.320—Videoconferencing standard using Integrated Services Digital Network, ISDN (a digital telephone service)

- H.323—Videoconferencing standard used over packet-switched networks (LANs, WANs, and Internet)

- T.120—Real-time data conferencing protocol

- VoIP—Voice-over-Internet Protocol

- CIF—Video format standard, 352–288 pixels

- QCIF—Video format standard, 176–144 pixels

- Multipoint—Three or more participants connect through a central server or *multipoint control unit* (MCU).

- Point-to-point—Two participants connecting directly.

This is just a snapshot. There are hundreds of protocols involved in a single videoconferencing session. You can find more about these standards at www.packetizer.com by searching for "h323."

As the computer entrenches itself more firmly into every facet of entertainment and communications, you can bet that things will change rapidly. This chapter will introduce a single facet of the video/computer integration and add a wireless link to make things interesting.

Microsoft NetMeeting will be used in a point-to-point videoconference over a point-to-point wireless connection. That is, we will set up a NetMeeting session over a peer-to-peer wireless link.

**Tip** The worlds of videoconferencing and wireless communications each use the terms "point-to-point" and "multipoint." The definitions are as you'd expect, one-to-one versus many-to-many. But it can be a little confusing when not paying attention.

The steps for accomplishing a videoconferencing session over Wi-Fi are as follows:

1. Set up a camera

2. Obtain and configure the videoconference program

3. Develop a data transmission path

4. Mount into the cars

**Note** Although in-car data conferencing is quite possible, it won't be explored in this chapter. Possibilities include war drive program sharing, editing documents while driving to a meeting, text chatting about the guys in the front seat, transferring files, and so on.

First things first: get a video source working on the laptop. There are several methods for doing, this depending on what's available to you.

# Step 1: Choosing a Camera

A video source (more commonly called a camera) is obviously the first step in getting a video-conference going. Here, a few of the most popular cameras are listed and the interaction with your computer is explained. Most computer-capable cameras are digital and communicate directly with the computer. The more ubiquitous analog camera needs a capture device to convert the analog into a digital format. And the Ethernet camera bypasses all of this by including its own computer and serving Web pages with embedded video.

## USB Cameras

By far, the easiest cameras to get working on a modern Windows laptop are the USB cameras, popularly marketed as *webcams*. These cameras bring in a video signal to the Windows *video for windows* architecture. The VFW architecture is used by most video-capable Windows applications.

The downside to USB cameras is their relatively poor quality as compared to consumer video products, like camcorders. USB webcams are designed for use over the Web at low bandwidth. The largest USB camera picture size is 640 × 480 pixels. Figure 14-3 shows a Logitech webcam.

## Camcorder Using IEEE1394

Some camcorders can display DVD-like video on the computer. With many newer camcorders supporting the IEEE1394 standard (Apple FireWire and Sony i.LINK) the incoming video is pure digital with no degradation of quality. Unfortunately, few videoconferencing programs

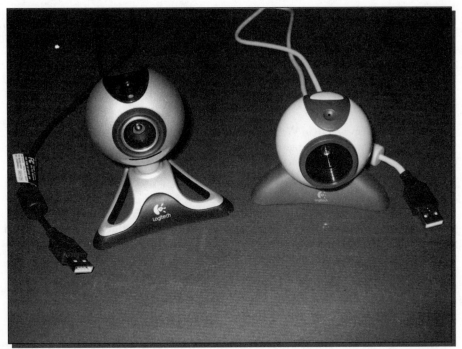

FIGURE 14-3: Logitech USB webcam.

directly support the IEEE1394 interface. The workaround is to use third-party software as an IEEE1394 to VFW converter. One product that does this is WebCamDV by OrangeWare, available at www.orangeware.com.

Gnomemeeting is an open source NetMeeting-like program for Linux systems. It is one of the few programs that directly support IEEE1394 video. Find it at www.gnomemeeting.org.

## Analog Video Cameras

Most cameras have outputs for composite video in the form of RCA connectors or analog video using an S-Video connector. The computer will need a video capture device to work with video in these popular analog formats. The Dazzle division of Pinnacle Systems makes several products that capture video via USB. Find them at www.dazzle.com. There are also a few PCMCIA cards that capture video, although they are harder to find.

The upside to analog video is the huge availability of cameras that support it. Composite video is a format available for almost all televisions these days, so virtually all camcorders have composite video at a minimum. Also, there are thousands of dedicated camera products that output composite video. Security cameras, for example, tend to support output composite video. The downside is the poor quality of composite RCA video.

Composite video generally uses the ubiquitous "RCA jack" connector while S-Video uses a special 4-pin mini-DIN connector. When capturing, use S-Video if possible. It's the highest quality analog video format.

## Ethernet Cameras

Ethernet cameras have built-in Web servers and do not generally include direct computer connections. The method of use for an Ethernet camera is to attach the camera to an Internet connection, then browse to the camera using a standard Web browser.

In effect, an Ethernet camera creates a video feed automatically. If you want a plug-and-play car-to-car video feed try this: place a wireless Ethernet camera in each car, and connect to each other's camera via its Web browser. Figure 14-4 shows a diagram of how this more expensive solution would work. By definition, this is not videoconferencing. But you can still see and hear each other. Ethernet cameras usually cost from a couple hundred to several thousand dollars depending on features and quality.

Ethernet cameras are often used in remote surveillance situations. Due to the stand-alone design of Ethernet cameras, they are not generally suitable for videoconferencing.

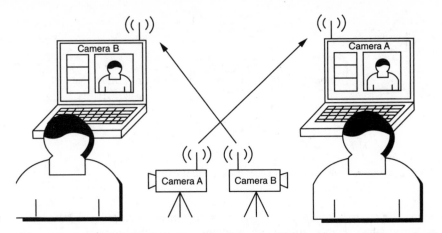

**FIGURE 14-4: Wireless Ethernet cameras and wireless Web browsers watching each other.**

## Video Capturing in Windows

As we stated before, the computer needs to bring in a video signal. This is either done through the USB port, or an analog capture device (which can also be USB). In any case, the camera or capture device manufacturer must include Windows software to allow Windows to work with the webcam. This is in the form of an "imaging device" driver.

**Note** A "device driver" is a small program that translates information from the software world of the operating system to the hardware world of the camera, printer, network adapter, or whatever. Windows has hundreds of built-in device drivers. New hardware products need to install updated device drivers, usually from a CD-ROM packaged with the hardware.

Most video applications on Windows use yet another software layer called Video for Windows (VFW). High-end applications like Adobe Premiere do not require VFW. But less expensive or free programs like NetMeeting usually need it. Figure 14-5 shows the basic configuration of a video and audio capture.

Up until the later versions of Windows, there was no way to see if your video source was working properly. Windows 98, for example, only included a "test camera" button in the Device Manager. So, the easiest way to see if video is working in Windows is to use a video-capable program and attempt to capture or display live video from the camera.

Most camera manufacturers include video capture programs. Follow the instructions with your camera to get the program up and running. Then test the camera with that program. If it works okay with the vendor's choice program, chances are good that it will work with Windows and other programs.

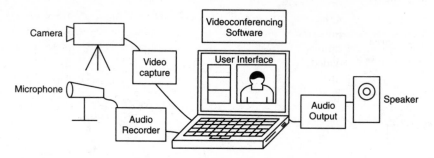

FIGURE 14-5: Diagram of how video capture works, including audio.

NetMeeting keeps getting mentioned because it's automatically installed with Windows. But there are dozens of good videoconferencing programs available that go beyond NetMeeting's very basic capabilities.

## Two-Party Videoconferencing

Two-party, or point-to-point, videoconferencing is the most common form of videoconferencing. This method only requires that each participant's computer have the software installed. Calls are placed directly from one person directly to the other over a common medium (like the Internet). Figure 14-6 shows a directly connected point-to-point videoconferencing session.

Videoconferencing products are merging (as with all technology) into video phones, instant messaging plug-ins, and even cellular multimedia messaging services. Tracking this field is becoming very difficult as definitions are changing.

That said, let's point out a few popular videoconferencing products:

- Microsoft NetMeeting—unsupported, easy to find, full-featured, free
- CU-SeeMe—unsupported, hard to find, features vary, free
- Polycom—full-featured fully supported hardware/software package, approximately $600

There are many more applications, but most of them cost more than $1000, and they certainly fall outside the scope of this book. Many low-cost or free video chatting programs are entering

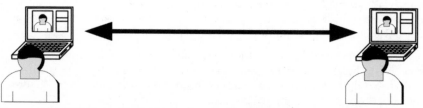

FIGURE 14-6: A point-to-point videoconference directly connects two callers.

the market in the form of instant messaging clients (AOL IM and Microsoft MSN are the biggest). These are not really videoconferencing products as they do not interoperate. Also, many of the newer applications need full-time access to the Internet, so they are not a viable option for high mobility video.

**Note**   Videoconferencing software tends to disappear from the market after a time. This is, in part, due to the expensive software technology licensing needed to employ the various interoperability standards. By removing a product from "supported" status, a vendor can discontinue paying for the technology but savvy users will keep using it.

**Tip**   The extremely popular CU-SeeMe software from Cornell University has changed ownership over the years. The original software has evolved into more of an online chat service. The older software is no longer supported but there is still a significant user base. Information and downloads of the old CU-SeeMe can be found on the Internet using popular search engines.

## Multi-Party Videoconferencing

Multi-party, or multipoint, videoconferencing is where multiple participants connect to each other. The key element in multipoint videoconferencing is the central server, or multipoint control unit (MCU). Calls are placed from each user to the MCU server. The MCU receives calls from each participant and relays the video to every other participant. See Figure 14-7 for an example of multipoint videoconferencing.

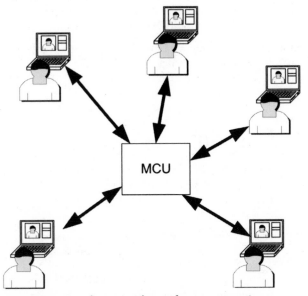

FIGURE **14-7: A multipoint videoconference connects many callers.**

**Note** MCU servers are usually hosted by an MCU service provider. Companies that frequently hold multipoint videoconferencing sessions can set up their own MCU in-house, often at great cost. A good alternative is emerging from the open source community (surprise!) known as the "OpenH323 Project." More on this and free software is at www.openh323.org.

Multipoint Control Unit servers act as call handlers. Software that is meant to only handle a single videoconferencing session can interact with many participants through an MCU.

## Understanding Internet Video Chatting

As mentioned previously, many newer products are entering the scene as video "chatting" clients. The most popular of these are Microsoft Messenger and AOL Instant Messenger. Some others include Apple iChat, iVisit, iSpQ, CUWorld (descendant of CU-SeeMe), CamFrog, ICUII, and TrackerCam.

**Note** For another list of video products, visit: http://myhome.hanafos.com/~soonjp/.

The problem with Internet video chatting is the reliance on a single, central, authentication system. Users must register with the service provider first, then sign-on to the service over the Internet. After that a managed list of "buddies" or "rooms" is made available.

This works fine when you're "tethered" to the Internet, but it will not do for a highly mobile peer-to-peer video session. This project requires a completely stand-alone system, without reliance on a central server. NetMeeting fits the bill perfectly.

# Step 2: Configuring NetMeeting

Since 1996, Microsoft has been working on videoconferencing in the form of its NetMeeting program (see Figure 14-8). Until recently, this has been downloadable from the Microsoft Web site. In 2002 Microsoft decided to change direction away from this stand-alone application to its centralized MSN Messenger video system.

However, Microsoft continues to include NetMeeting in its current operating systems. Windows 2000 and Windows XP have NetMeeting installed as part of the system. Earlier versions of Windows (Win 95, 98, ME, and NT) will need to download and install NetMeeting if it's not already installed. Since Microsoft has removed the download from their Web site, finding the NetMeeting setup program will require an Internet search.

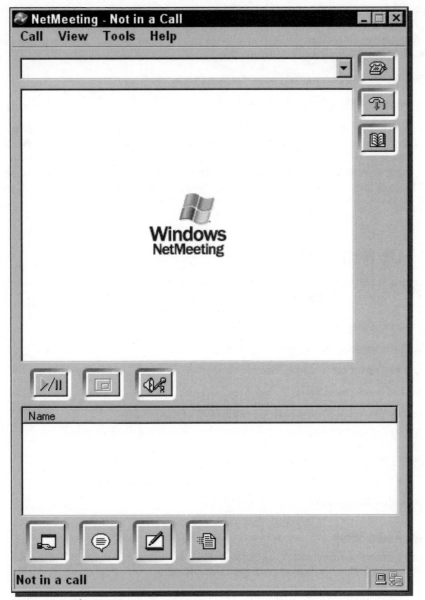

FIGURE 14-8: The NetMeeting program.

## Finding NetMeeting on Your System

NetMeeting, although installed on Windows 2000 and XP, does not have a shortcut anywhere on the Start Menu. There is a simple fix for this:

1. Click on the Start button and open the Run dialog.

2. In the Open text box, type conf.exe.

If this is the first time NetMeeting has been run on this computer, it will launch the Setup Wizard. See the next section, "Configuring NetMeeting," for details on filling in the Wizard.

 **Note**  If you are using an early Windows version and installed NetMeeting from the downloaded version (nm301.exe) there will be a shortcut in the Start ⇨ Programs menu.

## Setting Up NetMeeting

When starting NetMeeting for the first time on a system, the startup wizard will automatically launch. The following will step through the screens of the startup wizard:

1. NetMeeting introduction screen: Click Next

2. User Information: Fill in your name and e-mail

3. Directory server information: Disable "Log on to directory" and enable "Do not list"

4. Speed of connection: Select "Local Area Network"

5. Desktop shortcuts: Ensure both are selected to add shortcuts

6. Audio setup: Click Next

7. Speaker test: Click Test to check speaker volume

8. Microphone test: Speak into the computer microphone and adjust level

9. That's all: Click Finish

### Windows Audio Setup

A common problem discovered during the wizard is the microphone setup. If there are problems, just click Next and read on. If the microphone worked, skip ahead to the next section.

To adjust microphone settings, perform these steps:

1. Go to Start ⇨ Control Panel ⇨ Sounds.

2. Under "Device volume," click the Advanced button.

3. The Master Volume Control window should open.

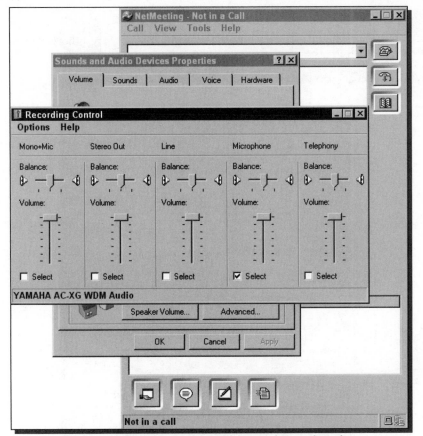

FIGURE 14-9: Recording Controls window with Microphone selected.

**4.** On the Options menu, click Properties.

**5.** On the Properties panel, under "Adjust Volume for," click Recording.

**6.** Under "Show the following volume controls," ensure that Microphone is enabled.

**7.** Click OK on the properties panel. The window displayed should now look something like Figure 14-9, the Recording Control window with several slider bars, including the Microphone control.

**8.** Ensure that Microphone shows a checkmark in the Select box (see Figure 14-9).

**9.** Ensure that the slider bar is at or near the top of the Volume control (see Figure 14-9).

**10.** Close the Recording Control window.

The microphone recording level should now be set and ready to use in NetMeeting. To make fine tuning adjustments within NetMeeting, use the Audio Tuning Wizard under the Tools menu.

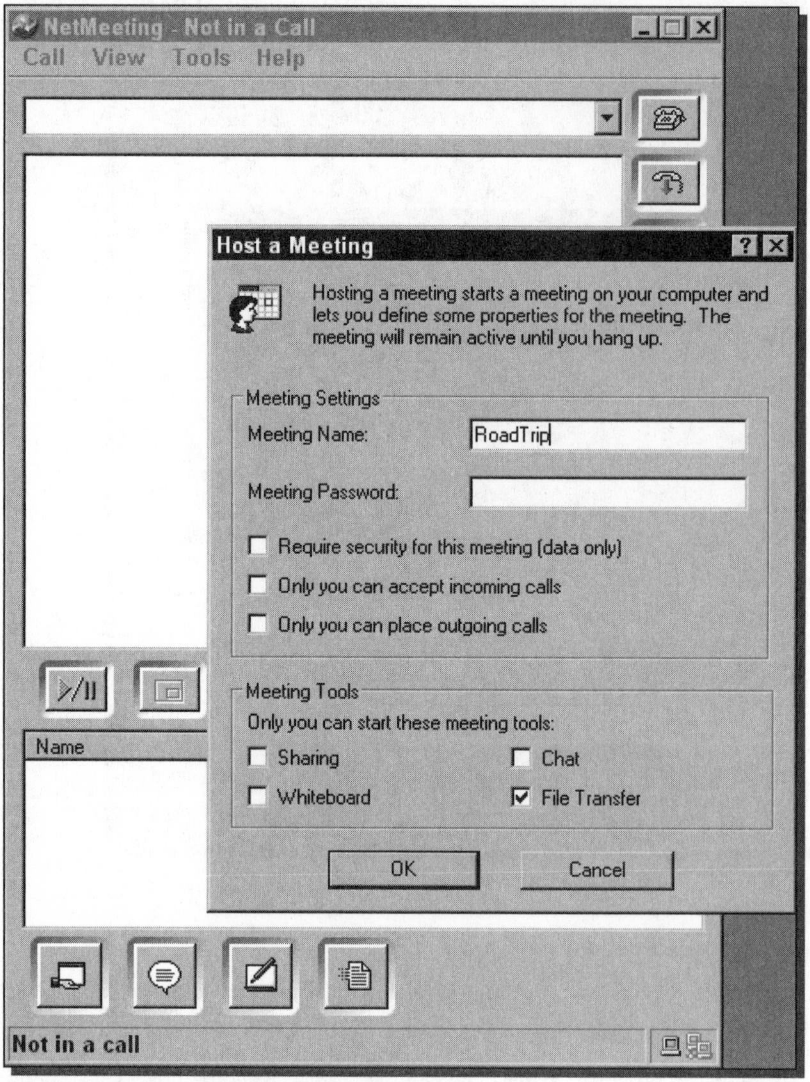

FIGURE 14-10: Host a Meeting settings window.

## NetMeeting Video Setup

NetMeeting will automatically detect if a camera is installed and select it. If there is more than one camera, NetMeeting will prompt you for which to use as the video source.

When NetMeeting is running, it does not show your video by default. To enable video, go to the Tools ➪ Video menu and select Send. If video is not displayed at this point, further troubleshooting is required. Make sure the camera is attached and is powered on. If the camera is still not detected, further troubleshooting is required. Contact the camera manufacturer for support.

**Tip** If the Video menu item is disabled in NetMeeting, that means a compatible camera was not detected. Follow the same troubleshooting procedures as if there were no video. Additionally, check with the manufacturer if there is support for Video for Windows.

### Making a NetMeeting Call

To connect to other computers with NetMeeting, one computer acts as a host, and the other "calls" the host. Determine which computer will act as a host and select the Call, or Host Meeting menu item. A new options window will open like that shown in Figure 14-10. Assign any values that are relevant and click OK.

To make a call to the host, all you need is the host computer's TCP/IP address. To get the IP address in NetMeeting, have the host open the Help ⇨ About dialog. It lists all the IP addresses on the system.

To place a call, open the Call menu and select New Call. In the "To:" field, enter the IP address of the host computer and click OK. That's it.

## Step 3: Setting Up a Wi-Fi Link

The concept is to have two cars communicate while being fairly close to each other, but not too close. Figure 14-11 shows two cars in a videoconference session.

To create a link between the two cars, set up a peer-to-peer (ad-hoc) wireless network between the two laptops. Alternatively, use a wireless access point in one car, and have both computers connect to the AP.

**Tip** If you decide to use a wireless access point as the central network device, ensure that the AP allows wireless clients to connect to each other over the wireless link. Certain APs may inhibit wireless clients from connecting to each other for enhanced client security.

First, set up the two laptops within range of each other, perhaps a few feet, and establish a peer-to-peer connection between the computers. The precise method for doing this will vary greatly for each computer and wireless card, but make sure these settings match:

- SSID—same on both
- Channel—same on both (if available)
- WEP key—same on both
- Network Mode—ad-hoc (not infrastructure)

Figure 14-12 shows the Wireless Network Configuration screen on Windows XP. This example shows the configuration for an ad-hoc network. Notice the option is enabled for "This is a computer-to-computer (ad hoc) network."

FIGURE 14-11: Car-to-car videoconference in progress.

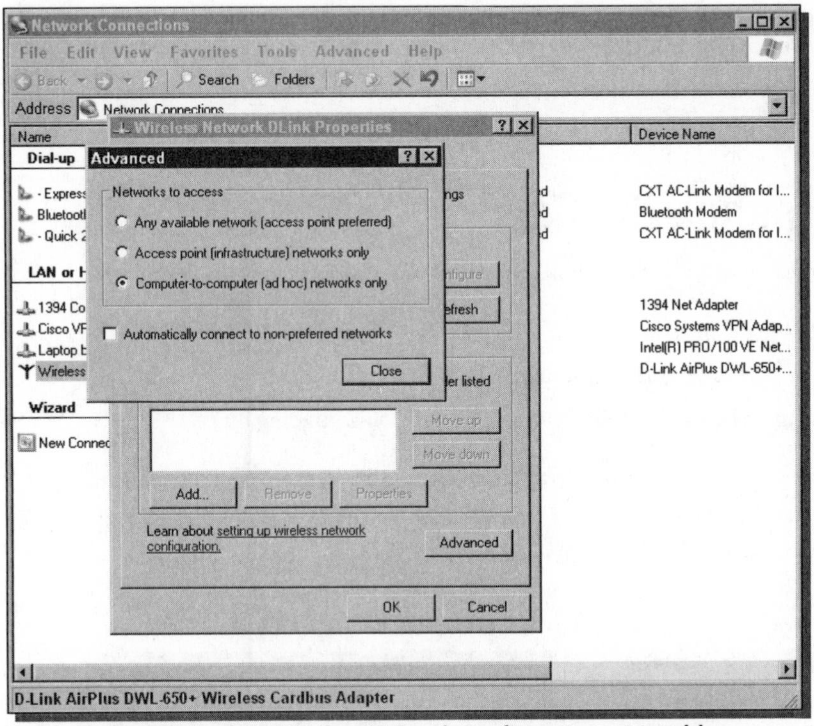

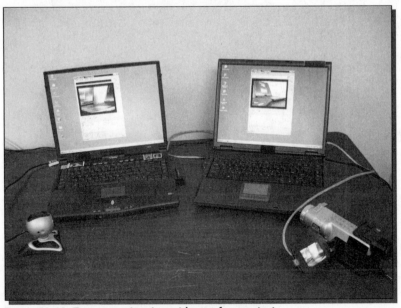

FIGURE 14-12: Windows XP Wireless Network Configuration set to ad-hoc.

FIGURE 14-13: Two computers in a videoconference test.

When your ad-hoc network is active, start a NetMeeting conference as a test. Figure 14-13 shows this ridiculous yet necessary test.

Now that the computers are able to engage in a conference, it's time to mount them in the cars.

## Step 4: Preparing the Cars

In getting ready for a car-to-car link, some important options must be considered.

- How long is the trip?
- What type of terrain are you traveling?
- Will there be a leader and follower? Or will you be trading off?

Trip length will determine if battery power or laptop-charging AC power is needed.

It's best to have a plan before launch. For example, if using one car as the lead, directional antennas may be possible. If the cars will trade off, then an omni antenna is necessary.

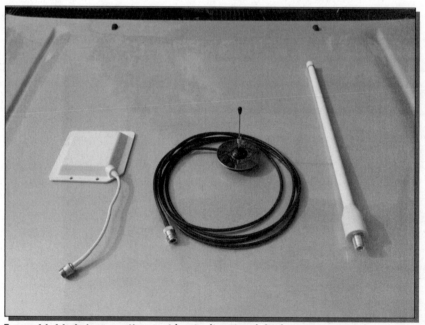

FIGURE 14-14: Antenna options: mid-gain directional, high-gain omni, and mid-gain omni.

## Selecting the Antenna

By the time you read this chapter, antenna selection should be straightforward. A highly directional antenna would make continuous connection difficult but possible in serious, cross-country straightaways. Figure 14-14 shows some antennas that could be used. An omni would probably be the best overall in any situation. Opt for a high-gain omni, like 11 dBi, for very flat roads. Use a lower-gain omni, like 5 dBi, for variable elevations.

Also, remember line-of-sight. Mountain roads are probably going to kill the signal no matter what antenna or power is being used.

Be careful where and how the antenna is mounted. Do not have someone try to hold the antenna inside the car. Too many variables can cause brief video-session-stopping outages. It's best to mount the antenna on the roof of the car. A magnet mount antenna is ideal. Otherwise, clamping the antenna to a roof-rack is possible. If you're using an antenna not made for vehicle mounting (like, perhaps, a panel antenna as in Figure 14-15) take into account the high wind velocity at vehicle speed.

FIGURE 14-15: Directional panel antennas mounted on the cars.

## Powering Your Rig

If everything will run on battery, skip to Equipment Management. Check the AC adapter on your laptop and video camera (unless using a USB-powered camera). Multiply the voltage times the amperage to determine the necessary wattage for the DC-to-AC inverter.

- Laptop: $20\ V \times 3.5\ A = 70\ W$
- Camcorder: $8.4\ V \times 1.5\ A = 12.6\ W$
- Total: $70\ W + 12.6\ W = 82.6\ W$

An inverter of higher than 83 W would be sufficient to power this system. It's a good idea to use an inverter of at least double the wattage requirement. In this case, an inverter rated at 175 W (priced at around $40) would be ideal.

### Equipment Management

Cables should be run well out of the way of driver controls, including foot pedals and the transmission shifter. When placing cables, consider the possibility that something might fall during a sudden stop or evasive turn. The laptop and camera should also be safely out of the way.

### Placing the Camera

Determine the view that you want to send to the other car. Will it be the camera facing forward? Or do you want everyone to see the boisterous crew in the passenger cabin? Find a position for the camera and mount it using a suitable mounting system.

Adhesive Velcro strips work great with small USB cameras, as shown in Figure 14-16. For bulkier cameras, a tripod strapped down to the seat may be required, as shown in Figure 14-17.

To go in style, check out the offerings by Jotto Desk (www.jottodesk.com). The company offers top-notch laptop mounting systems.

**Tip**

When on a road trip with two cars, switch lead positions repeatedly when passing slower traffic. Pulling into the left-lane, the back car pulls out first, acting as a shield for the front car to stay in front. When moving back to the right-lane, the front car moves over first and the back car passes to become the new front car. This method of trade-off will prevent others from getting between your cars, keeping distance down and wireless signal strength high.

Now plan the trip by saying something like, "Let's go to Vegas!" Mount up the cars and go!

# Extra Credit: Multipoint Car Conference

This would be a challenge, but it's conceivable that a videoconferencing MCU running on a laptop could be installed in one of the cars. That server car would sport a wireless access point. A number of other cars could connect to the AP and call the MCU to establish a video session. This sort of arrangement could support at least a dozen videoconference participants, assuming they could all stay in range of the wireless AP. Figure 14-18 shows a diagram of this scenario.

FIGURE 14-17: Camcorder tripod strapped to the passenger seat.

FIGURE 14-16: USB camera stuck to the dashboard.

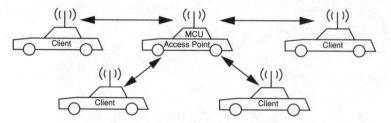

FIGURE 14-18: Multiple cars videoconferencing each other.

## Summary

Video is one of the most natural forms of human communications. This chapter introduced videoconferencing and added the new concept of highly mobile wireless videoconferencing. With a couple of laptops, video software, and a wireless connection, we overcame the isolation of driving in a caravan. This may open up a new era in vehicular transportation. Or it may not. At any rate, it's fun!

Now read on to enter another realm of visual communication. Break out your digital camera and give your pictures a new release. Create a wireless digital picture frame that's suitable for display in any home.

# Making a Dynamic Wireless Digital Picture Frame

**Y**ou probably have a digital camera or will get one soon. More people are buying digital cameras now than film cameras. Because it's essentially free to take a digital picture, more pictures are being taken than ever before.

But there's a problem. You have a hard disk full of pictures—what do you do with all of them? Printing is okay for the special ones. For the rest, though, watching a slideshow sitting at the computer just isn't convenient.

Hence, the digital picture frame. There are several on the market and many more will follow, but only recently have they become wireless. Often it's only the high-price models that sport a Wi-Fi interface.

This chapter will introduce the digital picture frame and show you how to make one for the cost of an old laptop computer and a few extra parts.

Figure 15-1 shows a digital picture frame that is updated over Wi-Fi. With a simple screen saver program, the digital picture frame, or *digiframe*, can cycle every 3 seconds or display a single photo for as long as you want. Changing pictures is as simple as drag-and-drop from your desktop computer to a network drive. The software automatically rescans the folder and updates the slideshow without any manual intervention. You have to love low-maintenance artistic expression.

Here's what you will need for this chapter's project:

➤ An old laptop computer with a PCMCIA slot (about $300 on eBay)

➤ PCMCIA Wi-Fi adapter

➤ Picture frame

➤ Picture frame matting

➤ Screwdrivers to take apart the laptop

➤ Wire cutters (some laptops may not need this)

➤ Soldering iron (again, some laptops may not need this)

FIGURE 15-1: Suitable for hanging.

➤ Electrical insulation tape
➤ Adhesive Velcro strips
➤ Coping Saw

# What is a Digital Picture Frame?

A digiframe merely stores pictures to display on a video screen. To make this happen, a few things must take place:

1. An image file is created, downloaded, scanned, or digitally photographed.

2. The file is moved to the digiframe.

3. The file is stored on the frame.

4. The frame displays the file on an LCD screen.

The frame needs to have enough storage to hold some number of pictures. The amount of storage on retail digital frame products in the sub-$500 price range varies from 10 pictures to

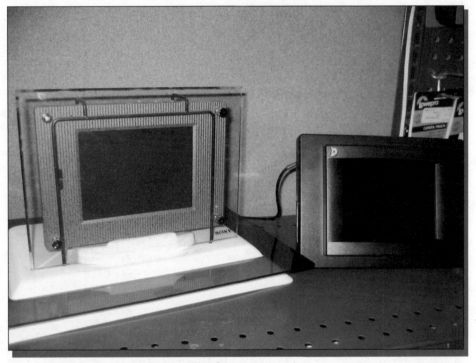

FIGURE 15-2: Digital picture frames for sale.

1,500. The frame you'll build here will hold thousands and costs about $300 for the computer and Wi-Fi card, and $50 for the frame and matting. Quite a bargain for an afternoon's work!

The problem with most digital frames on the market is they lack a convenient way to transfer pictures from the camera to the frame. The cheapest uses a dial-up network connection and a monthly service. Others use built-in memory card reader to read cards directly from the camera. A few have a wired Ethernet connection. Even fewer have a wireless connection, the ultimate in convenience. Figure 15-2 shows some of these products.

This market is rapidly changing, but you can jump ahead with a dismembered, fully functional laptop acting as a digital frame. And with Wi-Fi, your frame will be simple to use and manage.

# Choosing a Digiframe Computer

Three features will come forth in your quest for a suitable laptop:

- Price
- Size
- Hackability

Obviously, a sweet new $1000 laptop would be more cost-effective as a war driving computer than as cannibalized picture frame. And a tablet computer, while perfectly capable of filling this position, would cost more than the best manufactured frames on the market.

The size factor is more flexible. A modest, Windows-capable laptop with a 12-inch LCD screen goes for less than $300 on eBay. Twelve inches on an LCD screen is very close to a traditional 8 × 10 photograph. And it will fit well in a smallish 12 × 15 box frame.

Hackability will determine how easy or complicated it will be to convert the laptop to its new purpose. Ideally, the laptop will be easily disassembled and will require a minimum of wire management and re-routing.

Figure 15-3 shows the basic configuration used in this project. The laptop is split in two and the screen is unscrewed from the hinge and rotated all the way back until it is flat against the bottom of the laptop. The essential cables are re-routed or extended to keep the screen working.

The laptop is still fully functional, and can be used while still mounted in the frame, although it can be really hard to see the screen and the keyboard at the same time.

Unfortunately, you may not be able to tell how hackable a computer is until you take it apart, and internal pictures are often hard to come by. On the other hand, computers were made to be worked on when they are broken.

FIGURE 15-3: Laptop screen bending all the way back.

With this simple screen-folding method of creating a digiframe, most laptops should be pretty easy to convert.

**Tip** Carefully disassemble the laptop as a computer technician would to change a broken part. You should be able to get inside without doing anything destructive. Once inside, search for a way to remove the LCD panel and run the cables the slightly longer distance to the bottom of the laptop.

# Preparing the Computer

Before you make any irreversible decisions like cutting, twisting, or pulling, install the software your laptop will be running. It's a lot easier to get the laptop ready before mounting it in the frame, than afterwards.

Perform the following on the laptop before any physical modifications:

1. Install the Wi-Fi card and device drivers.

2. Configure the laptop for your wireless network.

3. Set up a shared folder on the laptop (for example, C:\digipix).

4. Install picture display software (like a slideshow screen saver)

5. Optionally install a remote control program (like PC Anywhere or RealVNC).

6. Set up Windows to enable the digiframe.

These procedures are covered in the following sections.

## Step 1: Installing Your Wireless Card

Chances are, the laptop you are using does not have a built-in Wi-Fi adapter, so you'll need to give it a wireless card. Figure 15-4 shows the laptop installed in a picture frame. There is clearly limited space in the frame. Choose a wireless card that allows enough clearance for the style of frame.

**Tip** USB dongle adapters can extend up to 2.5 inches from the USB port on the laptop. Use a USB extension cable to drop that distance down by an inch or so to about 1.5 inches (the length of the USB plug) and reposition the dongle. Or, use a PCMCIA card. PC cards with external antennas, like the DLink DWL-650 in Figure 15-4, extend out about 1 inch.

## Step 2: Configuring the Network Adapter

By this time, you probably have an access point and a wireless network set up at home. The digiframe computer will need to become a member of the network to be able to transfer files from a desktop computer in the same network.

FIGURE 15-4: Laptop mounted in the frame with a PCMCIA Wi-Fi card.

Set up the digiframe laptop as you would set up any other computer on the same wireless LAN. Use the correct SSID, channel, WEP key, and so on. Make sure the laptop will be able to get on the network automatically when booted and logged in. For example, if the card management software needs to be running, make sure it's set to start automatically.

Regardless of the wireless network mode (infrastructure or ad-hoc) the goal is to have the computer boot up to the desktop with fully operational wireless without any mouse-clicks or keyboard entries.

## Step 3: Setting Up a Shared Digipix Folder

You will copy files from your desktop to the laptop by dropping them into a shared folder. The exact mechanics of setting up a network share will differ for each operating system. But most versions of Windows have this feature.

Ensure that File sharing is enabled for the wireless adapter (see Figure 15-5). In Windows 2000, the steps are as follows (other Windows platforms will use very similar steps):

1. Click Start ⇨ Control Panel ⇨ Network Connections ⇨ Wireless Adapter.

2. Click Properties.

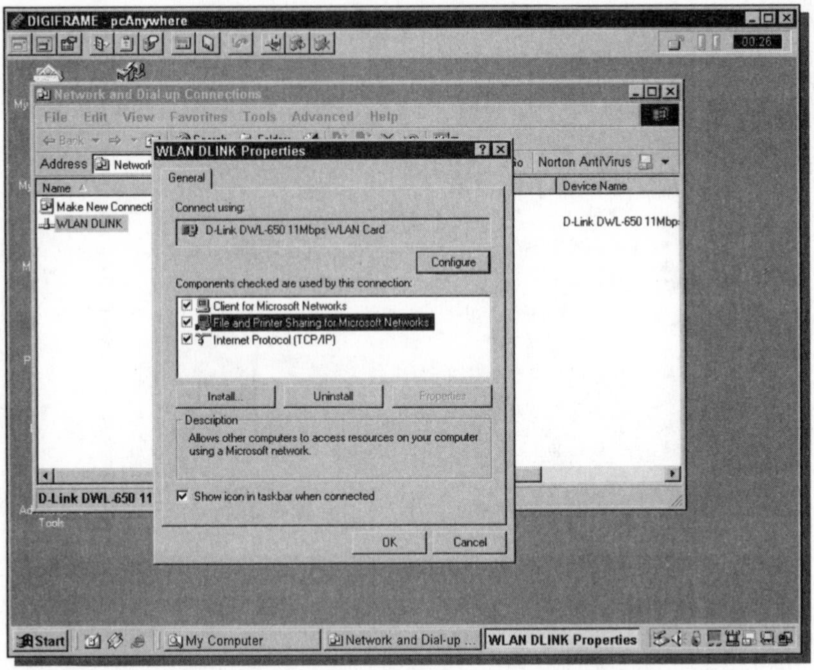

**FIGURE 15-5: The file sharing service is installed and enabled for the Wi-Fi adapter.**

3. On the wireless adapter properties "This connection uses the following items:", ensure that "File and Printer Sharing for Microsoft Networks" is installed and enabled (the checkbox should be checked).

4. If the entry isn't there, click the Install button and add the service, "File and Printer sharing."

5. Click OK to close the window and save changes.

Now share the folder by following these steps:

1. Create the picture storage folder (such as `C:\digipix`).

2. Right-click the folder in Windows Explorer and select Sharing in the context-menu that pops up.

3. Enable sharing and give proper permissions for the users that will connect. In this case, only the Administrator account is configured for access to the folder (see Figure 15-6).

Finally, test the link by transferring some pictures over to the laptop. From the desktop computer, use Network Neighborhood to find the digiframe computer and open the shared folder. For a recently shared folder, you may need to repopulate the list of neighbor computers. The easiest way to do that is to reboot. Drag and drop some JPEG files from the desktop computer over to the laptop.

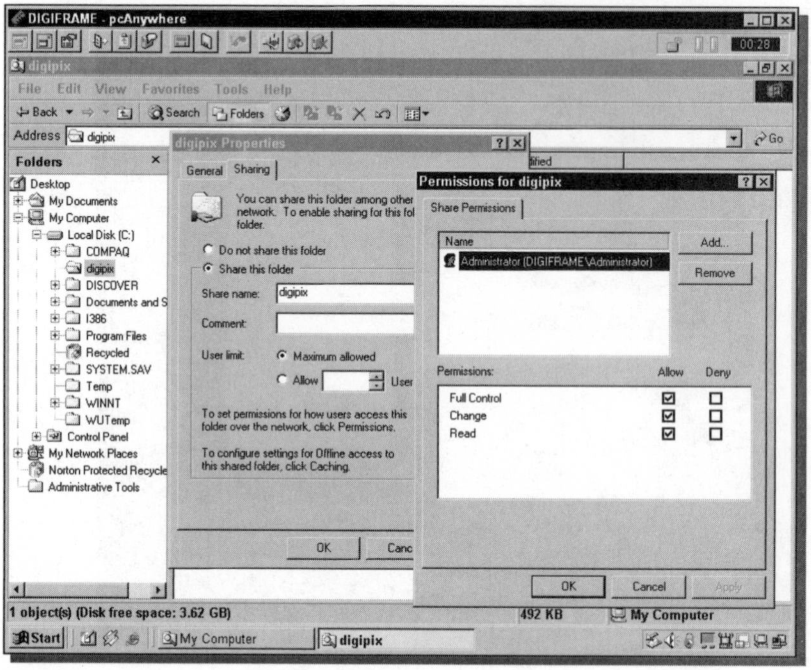

FIGURE **15-6:** Sharing the digipix folder to the administrator account.

## Step 4: Installing the Screen Saver Slideshow

The easiest way to handle picture rotation is to use screen saver software. That way, the laptop can be configured to boot up to the desktop without logging on. The screen saver would be configured to run a slideshow when activated.

Search the word "screen saver slideshow" in any search engine and you'll find hundreds of results. Although we didn't test every program out there, we found one that seems to fit the bill nicely. If you have a preference, by all means, try it out. It's called "gPhotoShow," available from www.gphotoshow.com. It's a free download. There is an upgraded shareware version, too.

The coolest feature of gPhotoShow that many other programs seemed to lack was dynamic updating of the file list. That is, even while the screen saver is running, the file list is recreated and displayed, so you don't need to stop and start the screen saver when changing digital pictures.

Figure 15-7 shows the main setup screen for gPhotoShow. This simple interface allows selection of the digital picture folder and, optionally, sub-folders from which to pull images. The Recursive Search option tells the program to check subdirectories.

The Advanced Options tab holds the selection for updating the directories on a continuous basis. Place a check in the Slide Show option for "At the end of the show rebuilds the full file list." When the Digital picture directory is updated, the screen saver will begin showing those new files immediately in the rotation.

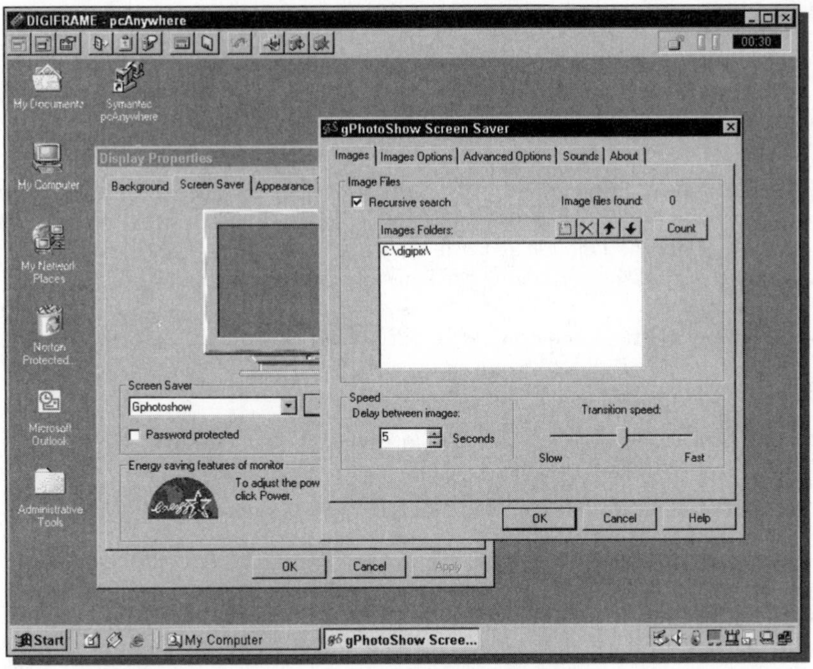

FIGURE 15-7: gPhotoShow screen saver settings dialog.

## Step 5: The Case for a Remote Controller

While the computer is happily cycling through images, Windows is doing its thing in the background. This invariably causes any number of popup windows, questioning dialogs, or other nagging queries for your attention.

Using the computer while it's mounted in the frame is quite difficult. So, for regular interaction with Windows, your digital picture frame requires a remote control program.

PC Anywhere is a useful program to help manage the computer as if you are there using the keyboard and mouse. There are several other remote control programs. If you don't have access to PC Anywhere, RealVNC (formerly WinVNC) is a free open source remote control program that works with Windows.

## Step 6: Configuring the Computer for the Role of Digiframe

Now that all of the network and picture settings are working, it's time to automate the computer. Remember that you are shooting for a hands-off boot-up to the desktop.

Exact details for a hands-off boot-up will vary by operating system. These are the requirements for Windows 2000 and XP:

- Disable "Users must enter a password to use this computer"

- Disable "Require users to press Ctrl+Alt+Delete before logging on"

For Windows 98 and ME, select the "Windows family logon."

**Tip**

If you are going to use the picture frame in an insecure environment, keep security in mind and use a local computer account, such as administrator. Do not use a domain or server account. Even though the keyboard and mouse are inside the frame and are more difficult for snoops, it's good practice not to use a server account when logging on automatically.

Check the power saver settings and ensure the LCD stays on:

1. Right-click the Desktop and choose Properties.

2. Select the Screen Saver tab and click the energy-saver Power button.

3. Switch the Power Scheme to "Always On."

4. In "Turn off monitor," select "Never."

5. In "System standby," select "Never."

6. Click OK to save the Power settings, and OK again to save the screen saver properties.

To have a sure way of turning on the frame without flipping the switch in the laptop, adjust the power settings in the *basic input/output system* (BIOS). The method to enter the BIOS varies widely by manufacturer. Look up the information for your computer, or try these keys during the boot-up sequence (before Windows starts to load): Esc, Del, F1, F2, F3, F10, and sometimes Ctrl+Alt+Esc.

If there is an option for your laptop, the BIOS setting would look something like "Power state when AC is applied: On, Off, Last-state." Set this to "On" to make sure the computer turns on when the AC is plugged in. In addition, if you're controlling power through the AC, remove the battery before installing in the picture frame.

**Note**

There is a Windows registry hack that will activate the screen saver of your choice. The hack details are different for each version of Windows. If you feel comfortable modifying the Windows registry, give it a try. More details can be found at support.microsoft.com; search for "logon screen saver."

# Hacking the Laptop

Now that everything is installed and ready, it's time to disassemble the laptop. Start by removing power and the main battery. (The complementary metal-oxide semiconductor [CMOS] battery is safe to keep installed.)

To keep the electronics safe from bumping or jarring while working on the laptop, remove any modular components, especially the hard drive. If the hard drive is not removable, you will want to be just that extra bit more careful against bounces.

**FIGURE 15-8: Laptop internals.**

Figure 15-8 shows a laptop striped down to the bare minimum. So far everything has been removed by using a screwdriver or pull-tabs. With this vantage point, scoping out cable runs is a lot easier.

Let's look at the Compaq Armada M300 in detail, step-by-step. Use this as a guide for modifying the lucky laptop in your project.

 Be very gentle with all connectors. For example, the LCD panel is controlled by a complex matrix of transistors which, in turn, are controlled by the tiny, flexible, and fragile cable attached to the motherboard. Damaged cables or connectors are hard to replace. Remove all cables and connectors with the utmost care.

## Step 1: Removing the Necessary Coverings of the Laptop Case

Since you won't always know what you need to remove, go ahead and remove everything. Just remember where it went so you can put it back. The plastic parts of the laptop case are usually snapped together, then screwed in place. After removing the screws, you may need to pry apart the two case halves. Do this carefully, always checking for any skipped screws or attached cables. (For example, the mouse trackpad on this laptop has a very short-circuit cable attached to the motherboard, as shown Figure 15-9.)

FIGURE 15-9: Cables attached underneath the keyboard and mouse trackpad.

## Step 2: Removing the LCD Panel From the Laptop

The LCD is attached with screws mounted to metal hinges. This can be as simple as unscrewing the machine screws and lifting off the screen (see Figure 15-10).

## Step 3: Checking for Cable Runs

Position the LCD panel on the back side of the keyboard and examine where the cables should run. In this case, we decided to extend the power cable for the LCD panel, while keeping the important LCD matrix control cable intact (see Figure 15-11).

Timing is often very important in the workings of an LCD panel. If you modify the matrix control cable, it's possible that the display will be adversely affected. It may stop working altogether.

## Step 4: Removing Obstructions

By removing the metal back panel surrounding the VGA, parallel, and serial connectors, a large enough gap was created to re-route the LCD matrix cable, as shown in Figure 15-12.

FIGURE 15-10: LCD panel removed.

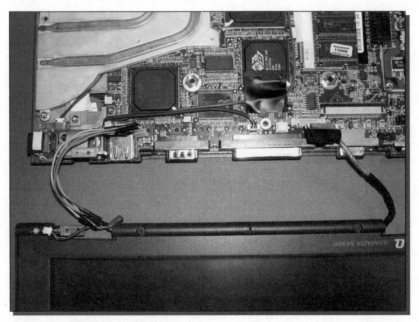

FIGURE 15-11: Examine cable runs.

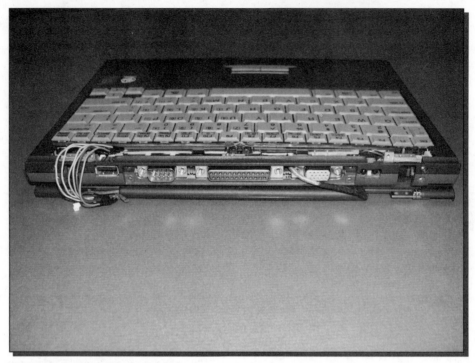

FIGURE 15-12: Creative cable routes.

## Step 5: Modifying Cables

Different laptops will have unique circumstances for routing and extending the LCD control and power cables. In our case, the LCD power cable was extremely short and needed to be extended by about two inches.

1. Cut the cable in half.

2. Strip the cable ends.

3. Solder the extension wires, noting the following (see Figure 15-13):

   ▪ Use the same or larger diameter wires than the original. The copper wire used inside of a CAT-5 UTP cable is often a suitable replacement. When you cut up a CAT-5 cable, eight individually insulated and color-coded wires are available for you to use.

   ▪ Make the extension no longer than necessary. Three inches is probably the limit, but some experimenting could reveal longer connections for your laptop.

   ▪ Keep the original connectors intact. The parts used inside of a laptop are often proprietary and hard to replace. Be careful with the original parts while working on them.

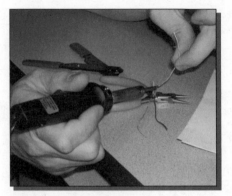

FIGURE **15-13:** LCD power and backlight cable reconstruction.

**4.** Cover the bare solder connections with electrical insulation tape. The cable modification should look similar to the apparatus in shown in Figure 15-14. Notice the original connector is used and electrical tape insulation prevents wires from short-circuiting. The microphone cable was left unattached because it will not be needed anymore.

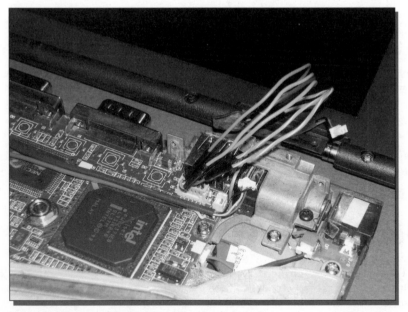

FIGURE **15-14:** A modified cable with extended reach.

FIGURE 15-15: Final configuration ready for mounting.

## Step 6: Trimming Off the Lid Latch

The laptop will not be closing up anytime soon, so cut the latch to make the screen completely flat for later mounting in the frame.

## Step 7: Attaching the Bodies Together

Mighty Velcro adhesive strips are used to attach the back of the LCD panel to the "bottom" of the laptop, as shown in Figure 15-15.

# Mounting the Picture Frame

When you know the system works in its new form, it's time to mount it in a suitable picture frame. The art industry has provided us with the perfect laptop-ready enclosure, called a box frame. It can also be called a keepsake frame. Measure the laptop dimensions and add any additional clearance for the power plug and wireless adapter. A 12 × 15 box frame works well with the laptop we've used in this chapter. Bring the laptop to a local art supply store and they

FIGURE 15-16: Box frame ready for installation.

can help find the correct box for your project. (However, they will be very surprised to see what you are working on!)

Once you've picked out the frame, you'll need to cut matting to match the frame size and leave an opening for the laptop screen. Make sure to cut the matting materials using the proper tools. You can purchase these tools at the art store, or have the store cut the matting to the size needed. Figure 15-16 shows the frame components with the matting already cut.

Again, you can use Velcro to mount the laptop to the matting inside the box frame. Velcro may not be a permanent mounting solution, but for this purpose it works well. You could custom-develop a more sophisticated hardware mounting solution for the specific laptop you're using.

As shown in Figure 15-17, the back panel is cut to allow the cord to pass through. Box frames tend to have stronger back panels than standard picture frames. Use a saw to cut a clean opening.

You can also consider future frame upgrades. You could cut cooling vents into the top and bottom of the frame to allow fresh air to flow up through the frame using the chimney effect (hot air rises). An external power switch would be a great addition, too.

Figure 15-17 shows the final product. Remember to plug it in so it boots up to the desktop. Wait a minute for the screen saver to activate. And then watch the show!

FIGURE **15-17: The digital picture frame.**

## Shutting Down the Frame

Shutting down the picture frame can be a tricky issue. If the laptop is unplugged, there's a risk of file damage. A better alternative is to initiate a shutdown remotely via PC Anywhere or the Windows shutdown command.

The shutdown command is run from a command prompt. The format varies per operating system, of course. On Windows XP, the syntax is

```
Shutdown -s -m \\computername
```

where *computername* is the network name of the digiframe laptop. It also works by entering a TCP/IP address instead of a computer name.

**Note** The shutdown command is available for Windows NT, 2000, and XP. Windows 98 and ME do not support remote shutdown.

## Updating Pictures

At this point, everything should be working, and the frame is sitting on a desk across the room, or hanging on the wall. The next thing to do is to add and remove pictures to keep this thing interesting.

Browse the computer in the Network Neighborhood. Open the folder you created earlier (C:\digipix in this chapter). Add, remove, or change the files in this folder. The screen saver should automatically pick up the changes.

## Extra Credit: Motion Video

Who says your picture frame needs to be frozen in time? Here are some ideas to liven things up:

- Play videos using Windows Media Player. Set the player to loop continuously and set it for full screen.

- Play Macromedia Flash animations using Internet Explorer. Press F11 in to expand the IE window to full screen mode.

- Play back a previously recorded gaming session.

- Install an information screen saver to feed headline news, stock quotes, and weather. If the frame has an Internet connection, the information will automatically update. Stay up to date with a wall-mounted digital dashboard!

 **Tip**  Symantec PC Anywhere can help to manage motion video. Screen functions like full-screen video work through PC Anywhere, but the frame rate will be very low, and color depth is reduced. Use PC Anywhere to transfer and start the video or animation.

Everything on the digital frame is, well, digital. Added functionality is accomplished by means of new components or devices. For example, you could add a USB video capture device and watch videos on the frame. Or add an external DVD-ROM drive, and watch DVD movies. This is getting a bit overboard, but the potential is there.

There is a lot of potential in having a computer display mounted on a wall at home or work. With Wi-Fi, there is no limit to the possibilities.

## Summary

This chapter showed you how to make a digital picture frame that can be so much more. By taking apart a laptop computer and reassembling it inside-out, a hands-off display is created. Digital pictures are just one way to use this wireless dynamic digital display.

With a digital display on the wall, so many other possibilities are opened up. It's just a matter of choosing software that suits the environment. And with such low costs for these types of older laptops, more than one per household is possible.

We covered a lot of projects in this book. With your new skill at pulling together parts and systems, many more projects are just around the corner. Here are some ideas to keep you going:

- Banish the phone company with wireless voice-over-IP.
- Install an MP3 player in your car and upload songs via Wi-Fi.
- Share ideas by starting a wireless user group in your community!

Visit the Wi-Fi Toys section of the Extreme Tech Web site at www.wiley.com/comp-books/extremetech and let us know what you come up with. Who knows? Maybe the next edition will feature your project.

Now go make some Toys!

# Index